Cinderella Goes
to Market

First published by Verso 1993
© Verso 1993
All rights reserved

Verso
UK: 6 Meard Street, London W1V 3HR
USA: 29 West 35th Street, New York, NY 10001-2291

Verso is the imprint of New Left Books

ISBN 0–86091–410–0
ISBN 0–86091–615–4 (pbk)

British Library Cataloguing in Publication Data
A catalogue record for this book is available from the British Library

Library of Congress Cataloging-in-Publication Data
A catalogue record for this book is available from the Library of Congress

Typeset by Keyboard Services, Luton
Printed and bound in Great Britain
by Biddles Ltd, Guildford and King's Lynn

Cinderella Goes to Market

Citizenship, Gender and Women's Movements in East Central Europe

BARBARA EINHORN

VERSO

London · New York

Contents

In memory of my father Helmut,
and of my aunt Ruth,
who didn't live to see the after-effects

Acknowledgements

I wish first of all to acknowledge the support of the John D. and Catherine T. MacArthur Foundation in Chicago, whose research grant facilitated the extension of my earlier work on the economic, political and social situation of women in the former GDR to a comparative study encompassing the former Czechoslovakia, the former GDR, Hungary and Poland.

In the course of research trips to these countries over three years, many of the women scholars, politicians, media people and activists whom I interviewed have become good friends. It is impossible to express my indebtedness to all those women who gave so generously of their time and information and afforded me such valuable insights into the quality of their lives. For their friendship, their practical and research help, and for all that I have learned from them, I would like in particular to thank Mária Adamik, Milica Antić, Zsuzsa Béres, Marina Beyer, Bärbel Bohley, Szilvia Borbély, Antonia Burrows, Zofia Dobrska, Irene Dölling, Ewa Gontarczyk-Wesoła, Brigitte Hussein, Hanna Jankowska, Eva Kaufmann, Mária Ladó, Hana Navarová, Christiane Schindler, Renata Siemieńska, Jiřina Šiklová, Júlia Szalai, Małgorzata Tarasiewicz, Olga Tóth, Bożena Umińska, and Natalia Zakharova.

Cinderella would not have reached the printed page without the warm support of friends and colleagues who variously encouraged me to write it, sustained me in the process, supplied contacts and information, read drafts and discussed concepts with me. My special thanks go to Sheila Rowbotham, also to Mary Kaldor, Zdeněk Kavan, Jenny Shaw, Judit Kiss, Gavin Williams, Tony Barta, Maxine Molyneux, Lynne Segal, Jacqueline Heinen, Crescy Cannan, Cynthia Cockburn, Míťa Castle-Kaněrová, Chris Corrin, Swasti Mitter, the *Feminist Review* collective, Esther Ronay, Curt Stauss, Valentine

Moghadam, William Outhwaite, Mary Barnett, Cathy Kaplinsky, Eileen Yeo, Viga Nicholson.

My family provided the loving spice without which this book could not have been written. I want to thank them: David for reading, for listening, for caring, and for keeping things going at home while I made my research trips; my mother Ester and sister Jule for believing in me and my fairy tales; Ben and Simon for being gently supportive and inimitably themselves.

Last but not least, I would like to thank Malcolm Imrie and Lucy Morton at Verso for remaining unflapped and for making it so easy and such a pleasure to work with them on the production process.

Introduction:
Why Cinderella?

I wish for a children- and woman-friendly civil society, in which people
have the deepest respect for one another and are mutually supportive.

                                                                Petra Kelly.[1]

A first reading of the title 'Cinderella Goes to Market' might suggest that
women in East Central Europe were disadvantaged both before and after
1989, or that a magic wand liberated them from their oppression under
state socialism in autumn 1989, transforming them into active agents who
enjoy full democratic citizenship rights in the new market conditions. I
shall, however, argue a third case, which highlights the ambiguities in the
situation of women both 'before' and 'after': namely, that, despite clear
improvements in the civil and political rights associated with democratic
citizenship, in the short run at least women in East Central Europe stand
to lose economic, social welfare, and reproductive rights. Moreover, a
newly dominant discourse threatens to subordinate women's citizenship
rights in many cases to the goals of nationalist projects.

   This book is motivated by, but does not claim to hold the answers to,
the big questions about the conditions for gender equity and for
women's empowerment. Did state socialism in East Central Europe
'emancipate' women? If not, then are democracy and the market likely to
do so? What *are* the prerequisites for improving women's personal
autonomy and social status? And can they be implemented from above,
or must they emanate from grassroots feminist struggle? This study
hopes to illuminate some of the complexities in order both to
understand the legacy of state socialism and to sketch the potential
future shape of gender relations in East Central Europe. Beyond that,
this book is informed by the deep conviction that sharing understandings across what was the Cold War divide – a divide which still remains,

as the Germans put it, as the 'Wall in our heads' – will help us to mould a new set of mutual hopes and desires, aspirations and demands, whose implementation may create societies characterized by social justice and gender equality.

My involvement with women in East Central Europe goes back a long way. In it, personal, professional and peace-movement engagements are intertwined. After I had completed a doctoral dissertation analysing the changing relationship of individual and society under state socialism through the perspective of postwar East German novels, my attention was caught in the mid-1970s by a wealth of vivid short stories by, and first-person interviews with, women in the GDR. These exploded, with acute observation and often trenchant wit, the pompous claim of official discourse that women's 'emancipation' had been achieved under state socialism, and exposed to a searching gaze the contradictions and problems with which women were confronted in their daily lives.

I then began to examine what this lived reality looked like, and it was out of this work that the current study grew. The research on which this book is based was due to begin in the autumn of 1989, but had to be postponed until the beginning of 1990. This, of course, was the period in which the 'revolutions' of autumn 1989 occurred. These fundamental shifts in the socio-political configuration of East Central Europe have been variously titled 'the velvet revolution' (in Czechoslovakia), or the 'turning point' ('*Die Wende*', in East Germany); they have been interpreted as the 'end of history' (Francis Fukuyama) or, conversely, as 'the rebirth of history' (Misha Glenny).

Whatever the viewpoint, it is clear that the events of autumn 1989 ushered in a period of substantive social, economic and political change involving the democratization and marketization of the formerly centrally planned and heavily bureaucratized state socialist societies of East Central Europe. These upheavals prompted me to go beyond the question of the contradictions between the rhetoric and reality of women's 'emancipation' in the declining years of state socialism, to ask: was the Cinderella of East Central Europe really transformed by the political, social and economic transformations that followed?

Gender and Citizenship

The central focus of this study is on gender, citizenship and the role of women's movements. My contention is that gender is a prism through which the process of social change itself can be both illuminated and evaluated. The concept of citizenship sharpens this focus. Women's status in society is not static: it is both influenced by and has an effect upon the process of social transformation itself. What is meant by citizenship here is not simply formal voting rights, nor even the right to call upon the state for certain forms of social provision, as in the social-democratic welfare model of society. Rather it implies active agency, the assertion of full individual autonomy within a community dedicated to the wellbeing of its members, who are bound by broader ties than those of family or kinship. This expands the concept of citizenship beyond the French Revolution's idea of political sovereignty vested in the individual, to encompass the notion of 'civil society' as it was projected by former dissidents in East Central Europe.[2]

Their dream was of a society in which individuals were endowed with both the right and the capacity to participate actively in society. They would transcend the status of recipient or beneficiary of economic, social and political change and become the agents of social transformation. As active agents, women too would make use of their newly granted democratic freedoms to exercise choice in shaping their lives. Their voices would be heard, their aspirations endorsed, their needs incorporated into the wider social project promoted by a democratically elected parliament in which women would be visible in significant numbers.

This notion of active citizenship had been propounded during the 1980s by dissident intellectuals in East Central Europe who felt that state socialism's suppression of informal associations and autonomous grassroots organizations negated any claims it made to democracy. They aspired to a form of 'politics from below', of thriving citizens' initiatives. For them, 'civil society' did not just mean the rule of law as opposed to the state of nature, or society composed by the existence of a state. Rather, it meant active 'social self-organization', as Adam Michnik put it. Václav Havel spoke about the primacy of moral or ethical imperatives over political pressures, based on his concept of 'living in truth'. He counterposed this moral right to 'living a lie', in a dichotomy between public (mendacious, ideological) and private (dignified, truthful) discourses. Together with George Konrád, he developed the concept of 'antipolitics', an arena of autonomous political space. The dissidents also emphasized the importance of non-violence and of internal peace based on the implementation of human rights.

This dissident discourse paralleled a similar line of thought that was being developed in particular by the peace, environmental and women's movements in Western Europe. A dialogue across the Cold War divide between Charter 77 in Czechoslovakia and KOR (the Workers' Defence Committee – Komitet Obrony Robotników) in Poland in the 'East' and END (the Campaign for European Nuclear Disarmament) in the 'West' revealed some differences of emphasis, but many underlying similarities, particularly in their equation of peace with the need for structural as well as attitudinal and political changes. Both saw active citizenship and a vibrant 'civil society' as prerequisites of peace and democracy. Indeed it was the Central Europeans who emphasized internal democracy as crucial to international peace. In his essay 'Anatomy of a Reticence', Václav Havel wrote:

> The cause of the danger of war is not weapons as such but political realities (including the policies of political establishments) in a divided Europe and a divided world, realities which make possible or simply require the production and installation of these weapons and which in the end could lead to their utilization as well. ... Thus the sole meaningful way to genuine European peace – and not simply to some armistice or 'non-war' – ... would require both sides to abandon in a radical manner their defensive policy of maintaining the status quo (that is, the division of Europe into blocs) ... subordinating all their efforts to ... the ideal of a democratic Europe as a friendly community of free and independent nations. ... Without free, self-respecting and autonomous citizens there can be no free and independent nations. Without internal peace, that is, peace among citizens and between the citizens and the state, there can be no guarantee of external peace: a state that ignores the will and the rights of its citizens can offer no guarantee that it will respect the rights of other peoples, nations and states. A state that refuses its citizens the right of public supervision of the exercise of power cannot be susceptible to international supervision. A state that denies its citizens their basic rights becomes dangerous for its neighbours as well.[3]

One thing Havel failed to appreciate in this essay was the key role played in the development of alternative political discourses and modes of action by the Western feminist and women's peace movements.[4] The Greenham Women's Peace Camp had a profound influence on Women for Peace in the former GDR.[5] And the spontaneous tactics and non-hierarchical structures which made the Greenham women and Women for Peace so effective were to have a transforming influence on all manner of grassroots and autonomous political groupings in both East and West.

A sense of individual responsibility for the collective welfare does not just happen. In the aftermath of state socialist bureaucracy, the feeling that no one could be held responsible led to a sense of anonymity and apathy, and to the withering away of individual responsibility. The Hungarian philosopher Éva Ancsel spoke in 1990 of the need to rehabilitate the individual in order to resuscitate the sense of responsibility for one's own fate and for that of one's fellow beings. It is simple, but not good enough, she maintained, to blame everything on 'the system', or on the Soviet Union – in reality everyone played their part in maintaining this system. There is no such thing as collective guilt, just as there is no such thing as collective responsibility.[6] So today, the hope is that out of the informal networks of political dissidence or the type of 'second' economy that developed in, say, Hungary might emerge a new feminist movement in the current transition period.

In order to understand the potential for and the constraints affecting such a development, the first chapter of this book begins by examining the past. What were the achievements and failures of state socialist policies for the 'emancipation' of women? Taking their cue from the paradigm developed by early Marxist theoreticians such as Friedrich Engels and August Bebel, the socialist states of East Central Europe and the Soviet Union attempted to resolve what they termed the 'woman question' by economic means. Their view was that, after the abolition of private ownership of the means of production, women's participation in the labour force was not only the necessary but also the sufficient condition for their 'emancipation' from the tyranny of patriarchy and the confines of the family.

This approach was anchored in a double contradiction. On the one hand women were defined as workers *and* mothers, without any equivalent definition of men as workers *and* fathers. On the other, the 'woman question' was from an early stage treated as a singular and discrete issue rather than as integral to the project of building an egalitarian society. This theoretical framework constituted a practice which was in effect gender-blind. In an effort to paper over these flaws, the state committed itself to socializing childcare, laundries and canteens in order that women could 'more successfully reconcile the demands of their job with their duties towards child and family'.[7] A third problem with the state socialist approach was that it presumed to confer citizenship rights upon women, but precluded the articulation of rights from below through grassroots political involvement.

Since 1989, the demands of economic transformation in East Central Europe are serving to retrench women, displacing them from participation in the labour force and planting them squarely back in the family, their 'primary sphere of responsibility'.

Chapter 2 explores the contrary meanings ascribed to the public/private divide in East and West. State socialism exhorted women to participate in the public sphere of work, and praised 'heroine workers' (who were also defined by law as heroine mothers). By contrast, women who were full-time housewives earned official disapproval and a low status both economically and socially. The private sphere was under-valued, though exceptions did occur: for instance, when the need for reproduction of the future labour force seemed endangered by the stresses emanating from women's dual role, that prevailed over the need for women's labour power in the workforce.

At the unofficial level, however, the private sphere was invested with a value in inverse proportion to state strictures. Family and friends filled the space where civil society could not exist; the private sphere was the only space for the development of individual initiative and autonomy. It was also seen as both haven from and site of resistance to the long arm of the state. Informally convened study courses, poetry readings or clandestine political gatherings in private apartments became the locus of anti-politics, in opposition to the over-politicized and didactic, exhortatory nature of the public sphere.

This stood in contrast to feminist interpretations of the public/private dichotomy as developed in the West. There, the private sphere was pilloried for its disadvantaging of women in under-valued, un-remunerated, isolated and largely invisible spheres of work. Western feminists emphasized the need to free women from the confines of the private and to facilitate their entry into the public spheres of work and politics. They pointed out that the state had always intervened to regulate the welfare of the family, negating the myth of the garden gate as the limit of state authority. And institutions of the public sphere, such as the police and the judiciary, *should*, they insisted, adjudicate in cases of violence perpetrated against women in private.

Far from exposing gender divisions within the family, the value attributed to the private in the state socialist countries both strengthened the public/private divide, and induced solidarity within the private sphere, against the impersonal and oppressive forces to which people felt subjected in the public sphere. What this constellation did not do was highlight women's rights or gender inequalities. Rather, it pitted the collectivity of family and friendship groups against the unitary interfering state, *and* discredited any public commitment to the equality of women. While Western feminism sought both to validate women's subjective experience and to have it accepted as a matter of public concern, Eastern European women subordinated their privations in

6

the family to an idealized notion of what the private sphere stood for.

Official and unofficial discourse in state socialism therefore attributed to the private sphere very different meanings. The official focus on women's labour force participation devalued reproductive labour in the family and rendered gender inequalities within it invisible, while the 'us versus them' dichotomy constructed a gender-neutral solidarity within the family as opposed to the state. In the post-state socialist period, this opposition of values attached to the private sphere has been quite simply reversed. Public discourse dominated by nationalist ideologies and often sanctified by the church defines the family as the basis of the ethnic or wider national group, and gives it, and women as mothers within it, a mission in the name of that community. The overburdened worker-mothers of state socialism have become the revered mothers of newly nationalist democracies. This enhanced familial role for women has, however, been more than offset by the shift away from the private, domestic sphere and into the public institutions of mainstream politics – themselves largely a forum for men. It is scarcely surprising that many women in East Central Europe today are not resisting their confinement to the private sphere. Indeed some embrace it as welcome respite from the rigours of the double or triple burden to which they were subjected by state socialism. Nor, given their experiences of the past forty years, and their relative lack of access to Western feminist literature or information about women's lives in Western societies, is it strange that they should have idealized the private sphere. They see women in the West as being able to 'choose' full-time motherhood, little knowing that the majority of Western women can no more afford this choice than they themselves can, little suspecting that temporarily relinquishing the right to work may mean long-term inability to enjoy the fruits of the market as a consumer. On the other side, however, Western feminists have tended to underplay the costs of entry into the public sphere: the stresses of the double burden, the inadequacies of childcare facilities and the impact on all members of the family of long hours of daily separation.

While the current ideological climate in East Central Europe posits the notion of women as lynchpin of the family, harsh economic reality imposes different constraints. Both engender a diminution of women's citizenship rights. Market realities of inflation and unemployment circumscribe women's choices both as consumers and as providers of welfare. Nor is the conferral of formal democratic rights necessarily synonymous with women gaining a political voice, since with democratic freedoms the locus has shifted from the diverse realms of anti-politics to the male-dominated arenas of formal politics.

Hungarian historian István Rév feels that there is a personal and a collective identity crisis in the face of state socialism's collapse. He describes the urge to rewrite history, to erase the memory of most people's failure to oppose the former régime, of their daily accommodation and collaboration in the struggle for survival. Nationalism is the convenient legitimizing factor in this: it defines the former Soviet Union as the quintessential 'Other', and state socialism as a 'foreign' system imposed from outside. This enables East Central Europeans to define themselves 'by right of birth' as 'insiders', who can thus assert, simply on the basis of their national identity, that they 'had always been against it'. In this way, self-definition in terms of nationalism provides a convenient mode of collective forgetting. What Rév calls 'post-Communist national identity' has a constant need for the 'Other', the 'enemy' who can be held responsible for past and present hardships. Thus he views the present intolerant and exclusionary forms of nationalism in East Central Europe as the inevitable legacy of the state socialist past, as a distorted attempt to come to terms with it.[8]

Such organic ethnic or national communities, bound together by a common heritage of values and traditions, echo the concept of *Gemeinschaft*, the community, which the nineteenth-century German sociologist Ferdinand Tönnies counterposed to *Gesellschaft*, or modern, market-based society. In the *Gemeinschaft*, commonly held and internalized values provide for concord as the basis of social relations. In the *Gesellschaft*, formal contract is the means whereby exchange and trade between atomized individuals are regulated.

Charles Loomis, who translated Tönnies's *Gemeinschaft und Gesell-schaft*, cites Tönnies as believing that 'society' evolved historically out of the earlier 'community'. 'With the development of trade, the modern state and science, the natural will and *Gemeinschaft*-like characteristics of social entities, norms and values gave way to rational will and *Gesellschaft*-like characteristics.'

Interestingly, in his last work, *Geist der Neuzeit* (1935), Tönnies (according to Loomis) 'hinted that the process of change from *Gemeinschaft* to *Gesellschaft* might be reversed by real causes if such existed; but not by speeches and sentimental romanticizing about the past'.[9] In the search for identity and new values to fill the vacuum left by the demise of state socialism, just this sort of romanticized reversal is occurring. Nascent concepts of the wider social group appear to reject not only what was perceived as the false collectivism of state socialism, but modern society (*Gesellschaft*) itself in the name of an ethnically-based national community (*Gemeinschaft*). It is ironic that such a panegyric to the supposedly organic community of an idealized earlier era should occur just at the point when the market is validating the values of individual enterprise and initiative.

According to Tönnies, the *Gemeinschaft* may become enlarged in that 'such a people (*Volk*) which feels itself bound together by a common language, when held together within a national association or even when only striving to become a nation, will desire to be represented in a unity or *Volksgemeinschaft*, which may become intensified by national consciousness and pride'.[10] Definition of the national language as the passport to citizenship rights in the nationalist fervour of many former state socialist countries sounds very like this 'organic' model of the *Volksgemeinschaft* in its aspiration for nationhood.

It is significant that Tönnies's view of the dominant and subordinate roles of men and women within the *Gemeinschaft* appears to coincide with the gender roles implied in the arguments of a variety of current thinkers, whether they derive their inspiration from an idealization of the market, from orthodox religion, or from nationalism.

Common to such ideological positions is an attack on women's reproductive rights. Gender issues are designated as a political luxury which the new democracies can ill afford to address. Yet one of the first pieces of state socialist legislation to come under attack, second only to that which had abolished private property rights, has been the right to abortion. Chapter 3 investigates the state socialist record on this issue and documents in detail the situation in Poland and the former GDR.

Chapter 4 looks at the transition to the market against the background of the contradictions within the state socialist paradigm of paid work as the path to emancipation. Policies for women's 'emancipation' focused exclusively on paid work and on education for employment, and resulted in an unprecedentedly high level of female labour force participation, and a highly educated female workforce. Today, however, market-induced pressures to shed labour are combining with ideologically determined constructions of women's role to hit women disproportionately. Indeed, the very array of economic rights and measures of positive discrimination that women enjoyed under state socialism are currently construed as making women more expensive to employ and therefore operate against their interests in the process of marketization.

Citizenship has historically been associated with suffrage and the exercise of democratic rights. The social and political transformations following the demise of the state socialist régimes have indisputably conferred these rights on the populations of East Central Europe. They have brought freedom of speech and the freedom to organize politically. Yet, as Chapter 5 points out, the impact of Western-style democracy could be regarded as privileging male autonomy and citizenship in much the same way as state socialism favoured the male working class. It raises the question of what women in East Central Europe have gained from the transformation in terms of political representation and asks, what was the true extent of meaningful political participation for women under state socialism.

State socialism was committed to the representation of women. However, the undemocratic way in which delegates were elected and the allocation of quotas to women's organizations, trades unions and political parties resulted in the election of token 'yes' women. Both Eastern and Western analysts writing since 1989 have claimed that although there are far fewer women representatives in the first democratic parliaments of East Central Europe, at least they are individuals in their own right and committed to political activity. The level of female political representation in the parliaments of East Central Europe has dropped from around a third to one tenth or less. This presents real drawbacks in terms of defending existing rights, not to speak of promoting new citizenship rights for women.

Most of the plethora of women's groups that have emerged in East Central Europe since 1989 are tiny minority organizations, many explicitly non-feminist or single-issue campaigns. There were civil rights, peace and environmental groups in East Central Europe during the 1980s, but why was there no women's movement to speak of at that time? Does this imply that as the sphere of grassroots 'anti-politics' revives, organizing around gender issues will remain a minority activity? Indeed, with abortion rights under attack, the closure of childcare facilities and high rates of female unemployment, why are broadly based new women's organizations not being born? More still, what lies behind the oft-encountered antipathy to feminism in these countries?

As Chapter 6 elaborates, the answers are complex and inconclusive. On the one hand they have to do with East Central European women's understandings of the rights they enjoyed in the past as obligations that encumbered them with heavy labour *and* a constant bad conscience. On the other, there is the factor of trauma, most fully documented in the case of the former GDR, where citizens lost a country as well as a political and economic system, leading to a deep crisis of national and individual identity.[11]

As Dr Dieter Angst, a West German working as State Secretary for Planning and the Environment in Saxony in the eastern part of Germany, put it: 'insecurity is the price of freedom'. For all its repressive nature, its contradictions and inadequacies, state socialism did provide a measure of certainty, with lifelong employment, affordable housing, free health care and social welfare. 'The old GDR social security meant that nobody starved. Nobody fell through the net. Now it is possible to slide down the social scale very quickly,' observed Rolf Scheibe, deputy mayor of Bautzen, a medieval town close to the border with Poland and Czechoslovakia. And if insecurity is the price of freedom, it takes some adapting to. It has been described as a level of trauma which it might take a generation to work through.[12] And, as one might expect, the brunt of traumas that affect individual family members is often borne by women.

Will a fairy godmother appear and make it come right, make sure that Cinderella is seen and heard, and her interests represented? Or will women themselves see the need for concerted action? The loss of political, economic and social rights outlined above underscores the need for women to engage in political activity on their own behalf.

Chapter 7 reconsiders some of the key issues raised in the book, as they are refracted through the looking glass of literature. The search for new role models in the dominant (largely male-authored) literary tradition implies relinquishing the notion of woman as citizen in favour of a self-sacrificing role as wife and mother. This image is also linked with the icons of religion (the Virgin Mary) and nationalism (woman as symbol of the nation), thus subordinating women to private patriarchy, to religion and to nationalist politics.

The introduction of market forces seems to foreclose choices for women: newly privatized women's magazines construe their idealized woman as consumer, mother and homemaker, or pander to escapism and the politics of envy. The surge of pornography on the market recasts state socialism's attempt to unite mother and worker into the old dualism of virgin and whore. And the experiences of new, small women's organizations seeking access to the media, or of the East German women's magazine *Für Dich* (*For You*), closed down ostensibly by ideology-free market constraints, seem to suggest that there is no place in the market for independent women's voices striving to articulate women's citizenship rights, to protest their loss of economic and social welfare rights.

11

Similarity and Difference

Generalizations linking four different countries are bound to be problematic, yet they are simultaneously difficult to avoid. In the particular case of East Central Europe, this problem is magnified. Past studies have often been marred by a tendency to treat 'Eastern Europe' as if it were monolithic and uniform, homogenized by its strategic incorporation into the Soviet sphere of influence, or by its political organization within the system of state socialism. However, the undeniable element of homogenization through the shared system of government in these countries did not eliminate their cultural and historical differences.

It is necessary to distinguish economically and culturally between the individual countries of East Central Europe, both in the state socialist era and in the present. The state socialist experiment was begun in very different conditions in each of them. Economically, Eastern Germany and Czechoslovakia were perhaps the two industrially most advanced of these countries prior to the Second World War, although it must be remembered that East Germany, when it became the GDR in 1949, was far more heavily agricultural than Western Germany with its remaining heavy industrial infrastructure. Nor did it have access to the same raw materials – while West German industry was built on the coalmines of the Ruhr area, East Germany possessed only inferior quality brown coal. Furthermore, the reparations exacted by the Soviet Union were punishing, while West German reconstruction thrived with the help of the Marshall Plan. Nevertheless, the GDR and Czechoslovakia had a head start in terms of industrial development compared with Poland and Hungary, both, until the end of the Second World War, largely agrarian countries, in which the majority of the population still lived in the countryside.[13]

There were also significant cultural differences. The GDR and the Czech lands were Protestant but largely urban and secular societies, while the Catholic Church and strong folk traditions were more influential in the predominantly rural peasant cultures of Poland, Hungary and Slovakia.

It was not only the starting points that differed; the extent to which state socialist policies on women's 'emancipation' were implemented, differed between countries. In the GDR, for example, childcare facilities were widely available and, together with free contraception and abortion rights, made for a certain degree of choice about whether and when to have children, and when to return to work after having a child;

12

in Poland policy wavered from pro-natalist to pro-workerist measures, with the result that there was never sufficient public childcare provision to meet more than a fraction of demand.

Likewise, the economies of each of the four countries under examination were at different stages in 1989. While the GDR was relatively more geared to satisfying consumer demand, Czechoslovakia was slowed by the giant heavy industrial conglomerates of a war economy, with arms its most important export. In Hungary, by contrast, the liberalization of the Kádar era had produced a buoyant and semi-legal 'second' economy based on small family business ventures. This meant that the process of marketization could build on considerable experience and expertise in entrepreneurial skills. Meanwhile Poland had staggered from one economic crisis to another since the attempt to remove food subsidies in 1971, which triggered the first mass demonstrations and ultimately led to the creation of Solidarity.

Poland was also the only one of the four in which intellectual dissent was linked with a mass working-class movement. This link was first established in the mid-1970s through KOR and later embodied in the trade union Solidarity. The Kádar régime left limited space for intellectual alternatives, so long as they were not too publicly aired, while in Czechoslovakia, post-1968 'normalization' turned intellectuals into janitors, boiler stokers, or prisoners, in an attempt to deprive them of their voice. In the GDR during the 1980s, peace, environmental and women's groups found shelter and the physical space to operate only under the umbrella of the Protestant Church. Perhaps because of their proximity to West Germany and consequent greater familiarity with Western feminist literature, the women's movement which emerged in the GDR during the 1980s was also explicitly feminist.

Nevertheless, it would be wrong to overlook the fact that women in these societies have much in common. Over-riding their diversities is, arguably, their shared state socialist past. Even while women in East Central Europe and the former Soviet Union consign this recent past to the dust heap of history, their lives are marked by common experiences. For two or more generations it was the norm for women to go out to work. Obviously this had positive consequences for their self-image, just as the worker–mother duality weighed on their daily lives. The present search for identity emphasizes national difference and individuality. Yet solidarity can be found in pooling shared experiences. Current attempts to set up East–East networking links between women, as well as East–West dialogue, bear witness to this insight and to the search for new understandings of women's situation.

Continuity and Change

Under state socialism, women were confronted on a daily basis with contradictions within the state socialist paradigm. Their dual role as worker and mother was predicated upon the delivery of socialized services which, in many of the countries of East Central Europe, remained sorely inadequate. The rejection of this double burden in favour of an ideal which constructs women as mothers dependent on a male breadwinner signals a fundamental change, especially in a situation where the state looks set to withdraw from public provision.

In the sphere of political participation, the high levels of female representation associated with tokenism in the past have been replaced by the notion of politics as a vocation to be chosen by a handful of particularly gifted women. But is this such a change as at first appears? In the past, in both official and dissident organizations, women played supporting rather than leading roles. Their continued marginalization together with their antipathy to feminism could lead East Central European women to revitalize the notion of politics itself. By validating their experience in the private domain, and building on their role within the family, women may succeed in transcending the opposition of state vs. people, mainstream vs. grassroots anti-politics, creating instead a people-friendly politics characterized by gender equity. This would realize the dream expressed by Petra Kelly in the first of three wishes – last wishes as it turned out – shortly before her tragic death in October 1992.

This study stresses a notion of active citizenship which parallels the concern of Western feminist movements and feminist scholarship to discover ways of maximizing opportunities for women to become active agents of their own fate. Not only does it offer an analysis of gender issues in the societies of East Central Europe, it is also intended as part of a two-way dialogue and mutual transformation between East and West. My attempt to understand the processes of transformation and women's participation in them also seeks to interrogate our understanding of feminism in the West. Does the widespread current East Central European 'allergy' to feminism imply the need for a revision or at least a rethink of Western feminist concepts?

The notion of active citizenship stands in direct contrast to the experience of disempowerment, of passivity and the inability to effect change which characteristically resulted from the patriarchal nature of state socialism. As with the concerns of feminism, this concept of the citizen active in civil society ultimately involves not only the conferral of rights, and the ability to utilize them, but, at its core, it also presupposes choice. It is this which distinguishes it from ideologies which instrumentalize women, whether these be state socialist, market-oriented or nationalist.

An optimistic vista might be that women's consciousness *was* affected by their experience of the identity of working woman as the norm: that they have a greater self-esteem as a result, and are more forthright and outspoken. Such a view implies that it will be only a matter of time before they defend or attempt to regain the right to work, the right to reproductive choice, the right to political representation, the right to be heard.

This study does not seek to prescribe solutions to the big questions. Rather, it is premissed on a belief that consideration of the experiences of women in East Central Europe during both the state socialist and the current transition periods will help to identify the issues at stake, and suggest productive ways of looking at them.

Notes

1. Petra Kelly's three last wishes [my translation, BE], appeared shortly after her tragic death in: Gabriele Presber, ed., *Frauenleben, Frauenpolitik* (Women's Lives, Women's Politics), Konkursbuch Verlag, Tübingen, November 1992, and was quoted in an appreciation of her life by Antje Vollmer in: *Der Spiegel*, no. 44, 1992. Antje Vollmer and Alice Schwarzer also wrote appreciations in the German feminist magazine *Emma*, no. 12, December 1992, pp. 20–24.

2. For an elaboration of the key concepts behind the notion of 'civil society' developed by Václav Havel in Czechoslovakia, Adam Michnik in Poland and George Konrád in Hungary, see Timothy Garton Ash, 'Does Central Europe Exist?' in: George Schöpflin and Nancy Wood, eds, *In Search of Central Europe*, Polity Press, Cambridge, 1989, pp. 191–215. Garton Ash refers in particular to the following works: Václav Havel et al., *The Power of the Powerless: Citizens against the State in Central-Eastern Europe*, ed. John Keane, Hutchinson, London, 1985; Adam Michnik, *Letters from Prison and Other Essays*, translated by Maya Latyńska, University of California Press, Palo Alto, 1986; George Konrád, *Antipolitics: An Essay*, translated by Richard E. Allen, Harcourt Brace Jovanovich, New York, 1984 (also Quartet, London, 1984). Also important are Václav Havel's 'Anti-Political Politics', in *Civil Society and the State: New European Perspectives*, ed. John Keane, Verso, London, 1988, pp. 381–99; and Havel's 'Politics of Hope' in his *Disturbing the Peace*, Faber, London, 1990.

3. The differences were relative. The dissidents' emphasis on the political realities underlying the arms race was shared by END, but they rightly perceived much of the Western peace movement as focusing too exclusively on weaponry. However, the understandable concern with their own situation within the Soviet constellation of power led some East Central European intellectuals to welcome the 1983 escalation of the arms race in which NATO stationed Cruise and Pershing II missiles in West Germany, on the grounds that it protected them from Soviet expansionism. This was the mirror image of Soviet arguments put forward, for example, by the GDR government's 'peace politics', which held the US responsible for escalations of the arms race and defined Soviet weaponry as 'good', since its purpose was to defend socialism from US imperialism.

Many of the East Central European dissidents later modified their attitude as a result of the dialogue with the Western peace movement. A significant manifestation of this was the 1985 Prague Appeal, and the rise of independent peace groups in Poland, Hungary and Czechoslovakia in the late 1980s. And in 1982/83, it was their stance in opposing the weapons of both sides in the Cold War confrontation which had driven the GDR 'Women for Peace' into the dissident corner. Another 'difference' in the East-West dialogue of the 1980s concerned precisely Havel's misapprehension of the contribution of the women's peace movement. For this East-West dialogue, see *END Journal*; excerpts from Havel's essay 'Anatomy of a Reticence', originally written as a submission to the Western peace movements at the 1985 END Convention, were first published in *END Journal*, no. 16/17, summer 1985, pp. 16–18. The full text was translated by E. Kohák and published as 'An Anatomy of Reticence', in: *Václav Havel or Living in Truth*, ed. Jan Vladislav, Faber, London and Boston, 1986, pp. 164–97. This quotation is taken from pp. 186–87.

4. In 'An Anatomy of Reticence' (pp. 179–83), Havel is patronizingly scathing about the courageous efforts of Italian women peace activists. They had travelled to Czechoslovakia and the former GDR to collect signatures for the first and only anti-nuclear petition which protested against the 1983 stationing of Cruise and Pershing and SS-22s and -23s with signatories from all five deployment countries on both sides of the Cold War divide.

5. Another seed from which this study germinated was the link in the early 1980s between END's Women's Committee and the GDR Women for Peace. My involvement in this exciting dialogue across the Cold War divide culminated rather unfortunately in my imprisonment by the GDR's Stasi (Staatssicherheitsdienst – State Security) in December of 1983, accused of 'treason' against the GDR. But my undiminished admiration for the courageous, resourceful and imaginative actions of the Women for Peace and other embryonic 'civil society' groups was central to the focus of this study. For a fuller account of the activities of the Women for Peace, see Chapter 6 below.

6. Éva Ancsel, interview with Barbara Einhorn, Budapest, 26.5.90. Ancsel's study *De l'homme en 194 paragraphes* was translated from Hungarian by Mireille T. Tóth and published in France in 1987.

7. Quotation from the Programme of the Socialist Unity Party (SED) of the former GDR, cited in: Barbara Einhorn, 'Socialist Emancipation: The Women's Movement in the German Democratic Republic', in: Sonia Kruks, Rayna Rapp, Marilyn B. Young, eds, *Promissory Notes: Women in the Transition to Socialism*, Monthly Review Press, New York, 1989, p. 292.

8. István Rév, 'Post-Communist Identity', lecture to the School of European Studies, Sussex University, Brighton, England, 18.1.93.

9. Charles P. Loomis, transl., Introduction to Ferdinand Tönnies, *Community and Association* (*Gemeinschaft und Gesellschaft*), Routledge and Kegan Paul, London, 1955/1974, p. xii.

10. Ibid., p. 26.

11. See for example Hans-Joachim Maaz, *Das gestürzte Volk oder die unglückliche Einheit* (*A Nation Dethroned, or Unhappy Unity*), Argon Verlag, Berlin, 1991.

12. Dr Dieter Angst and Rolf Scheibe were quoted by Quentin Peel, in 'Symbols of Hope and Hardship', *Financial Times*, 11.8.92.

13. Poland did have some major industrial centres for example in Łódź (textiles), and coalmining areas in Silesia, but could not compete with Czechoslovakia's or East Germany's pre-Second World War level of industrial development.

1

The 'Woman Question': The Legacy of State Socialism

You are right that this commitment to equality has always existed [in state socialism]. But it was absolutely formal and absolutely instrumental, it was not a commitment on behalf of women as such but was pursued only to achieve other goals, economic or demographic. ... There were certainly some prominent Soviet women and some 'heroines' who through their wonderful achievements showed that our women could attain everything they wished for. But behind these heroines stood the majority of women with very narrow life perspectives, and hard lives.

Anastasia Posadskaya, Director of the first Centre for Gender Studies in the former Soviet Union[1]

Opposition to the autonomous organization of women and the dismissal of feminism contributed to the imperviousness of the orthodox Communist régime even after the fall of Stalin to any social space for groups to organize outside Party control. There was consequently no means of challenging the body of ideas on the 'Woman Question' which fossilized over time.

Sheila Rowbotham[2]

In the present fundamental social, economic and political transformations of East Central European societies, the shift from command to market economy, and from state socialist to democratic forms of government, the study of gender relations can be viewed as a microcosm of the process and impact of social change itself. More than a century ago, Marx, following the French utopian socialist Fourier, declared that the status of women provided a barometer for the level of humanity attained by a society. August Bebel too wrote in his classic *Woman and Socialism*: 'There can be no emancipation of humanity without the social independence and equality of the sexes.'[3]

The role of women in the Soviet Union and the other Central and

17

East European state socialist countries has had an enduring fascination for Western feminists. Unlike the West, where any gains in equality of opportunity or the elimination of discrimination on grounds of sex have been the outcome of prolonged political struggle from below, governments in state socialist countries were officially committed to a policy of women's 'emancipation', to be achieved through legislation and social policy.

Until at least the mid-1970s, Western (mainly socialist) feminist theoreticians such as Simone de Beauvoir who attempted to follow events in state socialist countries tended to idealize what they saw, or perhaps hoped to see, unfolding in the Soviet Union and East Central Europe. In 1949, de Beauvoir wrote in *The Second Sex*: 'the Russian woman ... gets equal wages and participates on a large scale in production; and on account of this she has assumed a considerable social and political importance ... strictly subordinated to the State like all workers, strictly bound to the home, but having access to political life and to the dignity conferred by productive labour, the Russian woman is in a singular condition which would repay ... close study.'[4]

Closer scrutiny from the late 1970s onwards, however, revealed a situation fraught with contradiction, in which women could scarcely be regarded as truly 'emancipated'. In the wake of the new feminist analysis of the 1970s, Simone de Beauvoir was herself one of the first Western feminists to contest the state socialist record. In a 1978 interview with *Le Monde*, she observed wryly that 'socialism is a dream. It doesn't exist anywhere. And what is more, in the so-called socialist countries, the situation of women is no better than it is in the capitalist countries.'[5]

What *was* the socialist paradigm? And how was it implemented by state socialist societies? Before examining in detail women's life under state socialism and the way this is being affected by the current transformation process, it is worth looking at the theoretical framework and the legislation through which women's 'emancipation' state socialist-style was to be achieved. Socialist theories about one central focus of daily life, namely the family, will serve as an example of the contradictions inherent in both theory and practice.

The 'Woman Question' in Marxist Theory and State Socialist Practice

'The persistence of sexual inequality in socialist countries,' wrote Maxine Molyneux in 1981, 'appears to challenge the theoretical linkage upon which the unity of socialism and women's emancipation has supposedly rested.'[6] Such a unity was drawn from the classical Marxist texts upon which the authorized discourse of state socialism was premissed. Molyneux went on to point out that the writings of Marx, Engels and Lenin – and, one might add, August Bebel's *Woman and Socialism*, first published in 1879 – were both inconclusive and internally inconsistent. 'What has been created is a selective canonization of some of their observations to produce an apparently coherent theory ... an orthodox position on women ... based on an instrumental reading of the classical texts and on the official codifications of the early period of the Third International ... [which] has remained dominant and relatively unchallenged to this day.' Sheila Rowbotham has suggested that early Marxist theory on the 'Woman Question' became fossilized over time.[7]

The unity between socialism and women's emancipation, or rather the notion that women could become emancipated only through socialism, arose from this 'instrumental reading' of the early Marxist texts. Engels's essay *On the Origin of the Family, Private Property and the State*, published in 1884, claimed that the roots of women's oppression lay not in men's power over them, but in the institution of private property, thus in capitalist social relations. It was therefore logical to assume, as Bebel did, revising his *Woman and Socialism* to incorporate Engels's theories, that only the overthrow of private property through socialism could liberate women. While he conceded that women were doubly oppressed, by 'dependence on man' and 'economic dependence', Bebel contended, as did Lenin after him, that 'only the removal of the second will allow the removal of the first'.[8] This assertion not only highlights the emphasis on labour force participation as a necessary condition of women's emancipation. It also prefigures the subsequent relegation of the 'Woman Question' to secondary status.

If patriarchal family relations of individual male supremacy over women are the outcome of capitalist property relations, indeed if, in a mechanistic reading of Marxist theory, all individual social behaviour is conditioned by economic factors, then by the same token, to ask of men that they modify their behaviour, in other words to look to alleviating gender inequalities within marriage, was to grasp the wrong end of the stick. The origin of patriarchal relations of domination and subordination was capitalism, therefore – so went the reasoning – the elimination of this root cause would automatically preclude gender inequalities in personal relations. The dawn of the socialist era would usher in a new phase in relations between the sexes characterized by freely chosen and equal partnerships.

According to Engels, it was the accumulation of surplus value through capitalist production which allowed men to become dominant. Women remained in the household in which they had reigned supreme during what he saw as the matriarchal era of primitive communism. Now, however, they became chattels of the man on whom they were economically dependent. As several socialist feminist scholars have aptly remarked, neither Engels nor subsequent Soviet theorists appear to have noticed that the majority of working class and peasant women remained subordinate to their menfolk despite the fact that they too worked outside the home. Indeed, especially in Third World societies, women were and often are the main agrarian producers.[9] Nevertheless, the only solution, as posited by Engels, lay in women's mobilization into the workforce: 'The emancipation of women becomes possible only when women are enabled to take part in production on a large social scale, and when domestic duties require their attention only to a minor degree.'[10]

The privileging of production is therefore inherent in the classical theoretical canon. It remained only for reality to reinforce this in the difficult early years of the Soviet Union. Such was the unreconstructed theoretical framework inherited by the East Central European countries which became state socialist after the Second World War. From the linkage between socialist revolution and women's emancipation emerged the conceptually reductive notion that labour force participation was not only a necessary, but also *the sufficient* condition for women's emancipation. Later chapters will illustrate the way in which this narrowed state policies to a focus on women's paid work, to the exclusion of broader gender issues such as the domestic division of labour or discrimination on grounds of sex.

Legislating for Equality

'In socialist states the existence of progressive legislation and egalitarian policies can be understood as the effect of both principle and necessity,' maintains Maxine Molyneux.[11] Many analysts have conceded that there was, at least initially, genuine commitment to women's emancipation on the part of the socialist states. On the other hand, some studies have asserted that women's interests were always subordinated to and even instrumentalized by 'economic, demographic and patriarchal imperatives'.[12] There is fairly wide agreement, however, on the progressive nature of some of the early socialist legislation on behalf of gender equity, much of which predated the relevant UN Conventions.[13]

In proclaiming women's equality with men in all spheres of life, the early Constitutions of state socialist societies granted women the legal majority and personal autonomy denied them in the largely agrarian, semi-feudal peasant societies of East Central Europe. In the Soviet Union, Poland and Czechoslovakia women had gained the right to vote in 1918. By contrast, women in the other East Central European countries had to wait for the advent of state socialism after the Second World War.[14]

Constitutionally guaranteed juridical equality established the right of free choice in marriage, plus women's property rights and freedom of movement within marriage, thus eroding the influence of the patriarchal family of the past. The 1918 Soviet Family Code was far ahead of its time in establishing the idea of marriage as a union of equal partners, which could be dissolved at the request of either spouse. The Code's abolition of the property- and inheritance-based domination of women by men in marriage was epitomized by the clause giving all children equal rights, including those born outside wedlock.[15] In other East Central European countries, Constitutions, Labour Codes, and Family Codes established women's right to work, to education, and to social provisions guaranteeing that they could fulfil their role as worker in addition to their role as mother.

Maxine Molyneux documents the profound impact of such legislation in Third World socialist states and the Asian Soviet republics, where formerly not just the patriarchal family, but also the practices of orthodox religion placed additional fetters on the autonomy and freedom of movement of women. Social institutions such as polygyny, the brideprice and kin group control of marriage alliances, child marriages and female seclusion were integral to the subordination of women. Initial moves to overturn such long-entrenched traditions cost the lives of thousands of women.[16] It is a bitter irony for women that the current democratization process in many such countries is associated with attempts to reimpose some of the practices of Christian or Islamic orthodoxy which restrain women. Sharofat Rassulova, a woman born in Samarkand in 1907, reminisces about the liberating moment in 1927 when women tore off the veil. Speaking at a time in 1992 when voices were calling anew for women to hide their faces, she says:

When I was ten years old, I heard there was revolution in Petrograd. For us, nothing changed. It was not until ten years later that something happened. On the 8th March 1927 there was an announcement in the city: This

21

evening, we will tear off our veils. Many women went, many neighbours, many relatives from all over town. We marched to the Registan, the central square in Samarkand. It is a beautiful square, with high towers and bright colours. They say it is the most beautiful square in the world.

First my mother took off her veil and threw it in the fire, and then she lifted mine from my head.

It became light, even though the sun had already set. The horsehairs in front of my eyes were gone. The veil was heavy and uncomfortable and dark. I had never been able to imagine not wearing it. But on that day, everything was easy.

I wasn't afraid. I thought of nothing. There was just a feeling of relief. Everything became easier. I wasn't ashamed. ...

What if, now, they call for women to wear the veil again? Tell the young women: the *parandsha* is uncomfortable. They should refuse to obey...[17]

A comparative example bears out the claim that state socialist legislation was path-breaking. The original Constitution of the German Democratic Republic (East Germany – GDR) and the Basic Law of the Federal Republic of Germany (West Germany – FRG) in 1949 both stipulated that men and women should be equal before the law. However, the West German Basic Law provided for existing laws contravening the equal rights provision to remain in force for an interim period. As a result, the new civil law on equality of the sexes did not become effective until 1958. And while Article 3 of the Federal German Basic Law had envisaged full equality in political, economic and social matters, the 1958 civil code allowed restrictions on married women's rights to be perpetuated until the 1970s.

In contrast, the GDR's 1950 Act for the Protection of Mother and Child and the Rights of Women laid the basis for all subsequent GDR laws. The Act provided for the creation of state childcare facilities, maternity grants and paid maternity leave, for revisions in marriage and family law, and for measures designed to help women improve their level of qualification and gain access to previously male-dominated occupations. It followed the 1946 decree of the Soviet military administration, which, in giving women equal rights in all spheres and granting equal pay for equal work, had predated by five years the relevant UN Convention (no. 100). In the 1968 revised version of the GDR's Constitution a phrase concerning positive discrimination was inserted. Henceforth Article 20 not only stipulated that 'men and women shall have equal rights and the same legal status in all spheres of social, political and personal life' but added: 'The promotion of women,

22

particularly with regard to vocational qualification, shall be a task of society and the state.' While East German women had had the right to equal pay as of 1946, it was 1955 before an Equal Pay Act was passed in the Federal Republic. Even then, 'the legislation allowed the loophole that separate wage groups might be allocated to jobs normally done by women.'[18]

Despite the East-West juridical comparison undeniably favouring state socialism, the seeds of the later gulf between rhetoric and reality are already evident in state socialist laws. Most legislation explicitly enshrined woman's dual role as worker and mother without any equivalent definition of men. Thus Section 3 of the GDR's 1977 revised Labour Code declared that:

> The socialist state shall ensure that conditions are created everywhere which enable women increasingly to live up to their equal status at work and in vocational education and *to reconcile even more successfully their occupational activities with the duties they have to fulfil as mothers and within the family* [italics added – BE].

What this juridical emphasis on the dual role reveals is an ambivalence on the part of the state towards women's emancipation. As Sheila Rowbotham puts it, 'the rhetorical assertion that socialism allowed a woman to be liberated accompanied a state policy which oscillated between emphasizing women as producers and reproducers'.[19] Prioritizing women's role as producers, state socialist policy makers were alarmed to discover, had engendered a substantial decrease in the birthrate. In a move to stimulate women's reproductive function, therefore, revised versions of legislation pledged a commitment to positive discrimination. When Czechoslovakia's 1948 Constitution was updated in 1960, it contained a new article stating: 'The equal status of women in the family, at work, and in public life shall be secured by special adjustment of working conditions and special health care during pregnancy and maternity, as well as by the development of facilities and services which will enable women fully to participate in the life of society'.[20]

It is possible to interpret this revised Constitution (and the Labour Code of the GDR) in two diametrically opposed ways. A positive reading would see them as recognizing that the declaration of equality by itself, and even legislating for equality, is not enough; given women's unequal starting position, positive social measures are needed to ensure that legislation does not remain an empty letter. A negative reading might be that such explicit tagging of women's double role in practice serves to perpetuate existing gender inequalities.

How to legislate effectively for equality, and the role of positive discrimination in promoting women's emancipation, have been the subject of debate since the early days of the feminist movement in the nineteenth century. A prime example of this ambivalence was the debate between bourgeois feminists and socialist women around protective legislation, or laws barring women workers from jobs thought to endanger their reproductive function.

Clara Zetkin, born in Germany in 1857, championed women's right to work. She was one of the first socialist thinkers to assert that labour force participation was liberating in more than the merely material sense of economic independence from men. She exhorted working women to organize politically in order to improve their conditions, believing that involvement in public life was the route to greater confidence and political as well as economic liberation. She also argued successfully at the 1889 conference of the Second International for the need for specific organizational structures to promote political work among women workers. Zetkin took over *Die Gleichheit* (*Equality*), the women's journal of the Social Democratic Party, and in 1907 organized the first International Conference of Socialist Women.

Initially opposed to any form of special treatment for women workers in the joint struggle of the proletariat against capitalism, Zetkin was persuaded by Engels to change her views in the early 1890s. From then on, the issue of protective legislation became one of the main weapons in her campaign to separate socialist women from bourgeois feminists. Many English feminists of the time felt such legislation was discriminatory in that it weakened the bargaining position of women workers. Zetkin argued that bourgeois feminist insistence on the vote and access to education overlooked working women's need for jobs. She also accused them of merely arguing for concessions within the existing order, rather than uniting with working people in a class war to overthrow capitalism.[21]

The discussion in Chapter 4 below illustrates the manner in which legislating for positive discrimination in East Central Europe often did and still does operate to disadvantage women in the labour market, serving to entrench patterns of occupational segregation, barring women from promotion tracks, and currently making them the first to be dismissed. The case of protective legislation is controversial even now. All state socialist countries had quite far-reaching forms of protective legislation, excluding women and especially pregnant women from a wide range of occupations which would expose them to unacceptably high levels of noise, dirt, chemicals, radiation, or heavy lifting.

In Poland, a 1979 decree, amended in normd still in force today, stipulates in Article 1, part 1 that: 'It is prohibited to employ women in jobs particularly arduous and detrimental to their health,' and lists a staggering 90 occupations in 18 fields of employment. An additional number of occupations were prohibited for pregnant women.[22] In the Soviet Union women were not allowed to work nights, hence were barred from shift work. This prohibition was often disregarded. Simple semantics provide the route to lack of observance in the tale of one woman worker:

> I work at the train station in the mail transport department. . . . What is surprising and disturbing is that only women work this unbelievably labour-intensive job. Among four teams working in the package division, there was only one man – the team leader. . . . Even if the proletariat in our country is no longer an exploited class, women are now exploited twice as much. This abuse is not reflected in the laws, but it exists in reality. By law, women are not supposed to lift weights over twenty kilograms . . . But if the . . . packages do[es] not exceed this weight, it is assumed that a woman can lift this same weight over and over again, countless numbers of times. Here in our post office, the norm or quota is three hundred packages per person per day (during a holiday season the quota is as high as five hundred per day). Each package weighs from seven to ten kilograms. Thus, altogether, a woman must lift more than two thousand kilograms in one shift and during 'holidays' four to five tons.[23]

Reflecting official ambivalence on equality, not just on protective legislation, Dr Herta Kuhrig, director during the 1970s of research on women at the GDR's Academy of Sciences, stated: 'Such legislation must be used with discretion, but there are some kinds of work women simply cannot do. Protection and respect for motherhood are of utmost importance.' Dr Anneliese Klenner, economist and teacher of political economy at the former GDR's Party School of Economics and Market Research, went further: 'If they are allowed to decide for themselves, many [women] would choose the harder jobs because of better pay. And there simply is no generally accepted socialist position that women have the right to ruin their health. That is an anarchist, not a socialist position. Women are the weaker sex and they must be protected for their own sake and for the sake of their children'.[24]

Several possible objections to such a line of argument suggest themselves. Why *were* heavy manual jobs prioritized in terms of wages?

25

And as Maxine Molyneux points out, inconsistencies abounded in the application of this dictum, since protective legislation excluded women from heavy work in highly paid industrial sectors, but not in practice from more menial heavy tasks such as road-sweeping, nor from heavy labour in agriculture.[25] And why should men be thus 'allowed' to ruin their health? The paternalistic stance of 'knowing what is best' for women hardly suggests an acceptance of equality. In fact such tutelary attitudes comprised one of the main grounds for opposition on the part of both men and women to the socialist state.

Differences in protective legislation between the two Germanies provide an illustration of its contradictory effects. Whilst women did work shifts and hence nights in the former GDR, night work was prohibited for women in the Federal Republic. On the question of night work, Beate Hesse, Assistant Expert on Women at the Federal German Ministry for Youth, Family and Health, commented as early as the mid-1970s: 'It is not a matter of discrimination but rather a goal all employees should strive for.'[26] Yet at present, the closures of East German firms operating shifts are combining with the inadmissibility of working night shifts in the united Germany to bump up un- employment levels for women industrial workers in the new Federal states.[27] In their 1991 report on women in Poland, Helsinki Watch take the view that protective legislation must be seen as a form of discrimination and should be outlawed on those grounds, declaring that 'gender-specific laws have no place in a modern society ... even when meant as a protection, in effect they provide an opportunity for discrimination'.[28]

To summarize, positive discriminatory measures such as protective legislation in the economy, or the application of quotas in the sphere of political representation, are still hotly disputed as means to achieve equal status for women. The problem, under state socialism, seemed to be located in an internal contradiction. On the one hand, an argument can be made for positive discrimination where a social group is beginning from an unequal position. In a text on socialist definitions of human rights, Imre Szabó declared that 'equality before the law as a legal and formal principle does not cover the entire socialist equality principle. Such positive measures and such enactments are adopted which aim at accomplishing real equality among citizens.' He classified 'the additional rights of women' as examples of such measures.[29]

Where this approach becomes legislatively problematic (theoretically too, as already exemplified by Engels's *Origin of the Family* cited above) is in the assumption that the unequal starting point of women is naturally rather than socially determined. This in turn suggests that the domestic division of labour and woman's double burden resulting from it are also somehow natural and immutable. The notion of legal compensation for 'natural' disadvantaging is expressed by József Halász in the same text on socialist notions of human rights when he writes: 'The equal rights of men and women find expression in differentiated rules of law relying on the respective natural endowments of the sexes. Equality of rights is not uniform, but actually so by the guarantee of rights of equal value.'[30]

The 'Socialist' Family

Engels's book *The Origin of the Family, Private Property and the State* was published in 1884. On the basis of historical ethnographical studies of the time, he described a kind of primitive communism which he saw as matriarchal. This pre-capitalist society was displaced, in Engels's view, by the emergence of private forms of ownership and with it, monogamous marriage as a way of ensuring inheritance. The institution of private property and the growth of market-based capitalism were also responsible, he felt, for class antagonism, so that private property, class antagonism and the emergence of the modern form of the state are co-terminous with the patriarchal monogamous family.

Referring to slave society, Engels wrote: 'The first class antagonism which appears in history coincides with the development of the antagonism between man and woman in monogamous marriage, and the first class oppression with that of the female sex by the male.'[31] As this formulation illustrates, Engels did concede that gender-based inequalities were not synonymous with class-based inequalities, so that women suffered a double oppression. However, that did not prevent later theorists from conflating the two, such that they asserted eradication of the one – class society – would automatically eliminate the other – women's oppression. Nor did Engels suggest that the abolition of private property would result in the death of monogamous marriage. Rather, he 'speculated that the elimination of the economic justification for marriage opened the way to true monogamy based on an historically new element – individual sexual love'.[32]

Engels's vision of the family of the future built on that of nineteenth-century utopian socialists. He dreamed of a situation where: 'the individual family ceases to be the economic unit of society. Private housekeeping is transformed into a social industry. The care and education of the children becomes a public matter.'[33] The idea that industrialization would alleviate the burden of housework was reflected in August Bebel's *Woman and Socialism* by a eulogy on electricity as the means 'to render cooking scientific, peel vegetables, wash dishes and finally abolish the kitchen, the slave-pen of women'. Socialist construction was later cited by Lenin as the means to liberate women from the status of a 'domestic slave', by socializing the 'barbarously unproductive, petty, nerve-racking, stultifying and crushing drudgery' of housework.[34]

In the same essay, Lenin had criticized men for not sharing the burden of domestic labour, observing that: 'Very few husbands, not even the proletarians, think of how much they could lighten the burden and worries of their wives or relieve them entirely, if they lent a hand in this "woman's work" [which means] the domestic life of the woman is a daily sacrifice of self to a thousand insignificant trifles.'[35] It is worth noting that Lenin saw husbands as 'helping' women with *their* work. In a contradictory passage of his *Origin of the Family*, Engels too had seen this division of labour as a 'natural' one. Joan Landes has pointed out that 'the splits between private and public, inside and outside, domestic work and wage labour, are, in a surprisingly ahistorical fashion, transposed back onto early human social organization by Engels'. She quotes Engels as writing of the partners in his matriarchal household: 'The man fights in the wars, going hunting and fishing, procures the raw materials and the tools necessary for doing so. The woman looks after the house and the preparation of food and clothing, cooks, weaves, and sews. They are each master in their own sphere: The man in the forest, the woman in the house.'[36] In *The German Ideology*, Marx too had seen the division of labour as originating in sexual difference.

This is not to assert that gendered divisions of labour within the family were never questioned. Legislatively, the Family Codes in several state socialist countries provided for the equal rights and responsibilities of both marriage partners with regard to housework and childcare. The GDR's progressive 1965 Family Law, while continuing to define women in terms of their dual role, nevertheless provided for an equal responsibility of the marriage partners. Article 7 stated that:

> Both spouses do their share in the education and care of the children and the conduct of the household. The relations of the spouses to each other are to be so shaped that the wife can combine her professional and social activities with those of motherhood.

A subsequently published commentary on the GDR Family Law

specifically countered Lenin's admonition to husbands to 'help' with rather than sharing the housework, stating that:

> The husband may not content himself with 'assisting'. He must rather do his share, appropriate to the concrete family situation, in the education and care of the children and the conduct of the household.[37]

The GDR Family Law even specified that each partner had the right to develop her/his individual potential and as a result should expect the other to stand back in order to facilitate their career enhancement.[38] In practice, life lagged behind legislative prescription. And the legislation itself remained exhortatory and vague. In a 1978 letter to the magazine *Für Dich* (*For You*), one young GDR woman justified putting her own career into cold storage for ten to fifteen years on the grounds that both partners studying as well as working full-time would create unacceptable stress levels in the family. She therefore saw it as her role to protect her husband from the children's noise and from family problems so that he could study in peace. 'Where is it written,' asked an angry reply letter, 'that when compromises are necessary in the interests of the family, it is only the woman who has to make them, who has to postpone her life?' Ten years later, however, a 1988 survey in the then GDR revealed a hardening of traditional attitudes in which 37 per cent of women and 43 per cent of men believed that while the children are young, women should be the ones to make career compromises. Only 3 per cent of women and a paltry 1 per cent of men believed that men should at some time put their career on hold when there were children in the family.[39]

One could argue that gender inequity in the family was legally cemented from the start in the state socialist countries. Far from facilitating a more equitable division of domestic responsibilities, the juridical determination of women's dual role as workers and mothers reinforced the traditional allocation of gender roles within the family. Women's responsibilities as housewife and mother were to be eased by the socialization of domestic labour in the form of workplace and school canteens, communal laundries, and improved shopping and service facilities. This approach is evident in the report by the Central Committee of the GDR's ruling Socialist Unity Party (SED) to its Eleventh Party Congress in 1986, which lauded the successful achievement of the necessary 'preconditions to enable women better to harmonize employment, social commitment, and maternal duties, which generally benefits family life'.

In the early post-revolutionary period, Alexandra Kollontai and others had denounced the hypocrisy and moral double standards of the bourgeois family, and the fetters it placed upon women's opportunities for developing their potential as autonomous individuals. She envisaged fundamentally altering its patriarchal relations of domination and subordination. In her 1918 speech 'The Family and the Communist State', according to Richard Stites, Kollontai described the 'old type of family' as 'a microscopic state where husband ruled wife and children; and as the incubator of future citizens ... [which] was to be abolished: public upbringing of children would replace its traditional function; equality of sexes would dethrone its traditional ruler'. She went on to say:

> In place of the indissoluble marriage based on the servitude of woman, we shall see rise the free union, fortified by the love and the mutual respect of the two members of the Workers' State, equal in their rights and in their obligations. In place of the individual and egotistical family, there will arise a great universal family of workers, in which all the workers, men and women, will be above all, workers, comrades.[40]

Inessa Armand shared the view that the socialization of domestic labour and childcare were fundamental to the transformation of the family. On this in turn was predicated women's emancipation. Armand, unlike other theoreticians, felt that participation in social production alone was insufficient to guarantee this.[41]

In her writings, Kollontai had put the case for sexual relations as emotionally serious affairs, but not necessarily life-long unions. Sheila Rowbotham writes that 'her interest in sexuality and her dream of individual love merging with new forms of communalism increasingly diverged from the ethos of Soviet society. Production as a means of emancipating women became the orthodox approach, human beings' potential for loving as the basis for Communism appeared heretical.' The result was that 'Kollontai's attempt to acknowledge the complex intertwining of personal relations with social transformation was suppressed'.[42] The view gained pre-eminence that sexual relations were of secondary importance, and were confined within the family which itself was dedicated to the collective good in terms of the construction of socialism.

Among the early theorists, a rather conventional notion of sexuality also seemed to prevail. Bebel had written that 'marriage represents one side of sex life in bourgeois society and prostitution the other'. And although Bebel and Lenin supported the right to divorce, they appeared to favour the transformation rather than the eradication of the institution of marriage. Lenin in a famous letter to Inessa Armand expressly disapproved of adultery. Andrei Isaev, a Marxist economist of that time, wrote in his book *What Can Women Expect from Marxism?* that although the future socialist woman would enjoy the companionship of a variety of male companions, only one of them would enjoy her sexual favours. 'Sex, in any case, would not play an excessively large role in the life of the socialist couple,' he declared, 'since much of their energy would be deflected into public activity – an early adumbration of the theory of "revolutionary sublimation".'[43]

These analyses of sexuality and the family reveal that from very early in the history of state socialism, the public sphere was privileged over the private. This meant that there was a failure to address the fundamental contradictions, not only between women's productive and reproductive roles, but also in gender relations within the family.

By 1930, the early Bolshevik vision of a transformed family had foundered, not however, argues Wendy Zeva Goldman, through lack of ideological commitment, but rather through totally unfavourable material conditions in the form of crushing poverty and severe social dislocation caused by the First World War and the Civil War, compounded by the forced pace of industrialization and the drive to collectivize agriculture launched by Stalin in 1928.[44] Thus the material difficulties of the early Soviet years led to a watering down of the original Family Code. In addition, the *zhenotdel*, the women's department of the Party, was abolished in 1930, and new laws stressing family responsibility were introduced. In 1936, a new law made divorce more difficult to obtain, and abortion was abolished.[45]

The nuclear family was reborn as the 'socialist' family, in which worker-mothers were committed to bearing and rearing future socialist citizens in addition to their labour force participation. Visions of freeing women from the burdens of domestic labour and childcare were subsumed under a reliance on the family as the 'basic cell' of society guaranteeing some degree of social stability. Fundamental questions about the links between the family and women's oppression were brushed under the carpet.

The only explicit change in the family's perceived function was not to do with the gendered nature of relations within it, but rather with the family's responsibilities towards the wider society. Legislation had attempted to substitute a partnership with equal rights and responsibilities for the previously predominant patriarchal power relations of the family. But in general the family functioned not as a social unit embodying individual rights in a partnership of equals, but as one with specific duties towards society and the state. To women's productive and reproductive duties, Lenin had in 1919 added the exhortation that they should become involved in 'the management of public enterprise' and 'the administration of the state'.[46] Thus the triple rather than double burden which drained women's energies in the state socialist countries of East Central Europe was established early.

The subordination of social to economic goals in the 1930s meant that theoretical discussions of the family and its role in advancing or hindering women's emancipation ceased. From the 1930s until the mid-1960s, silence reigned on the subject of the 'woman question'. 'It had been answered, so the argument went, because women had been emancipated. This was already an "achievement" of Soviet socialism, so there was no need to work towards it. ... In the 1930s, many of the earlier gains for women were watered down by a renewed stress on the nuclear family. ... The liberation of women in practical ideology meant no more than participation in economic production.'[47]

Kollontai and Armand were out, as were other proponents of utopian socialist vision. Grim reality prioritized the sphere of production over that of reproduction in the drive towards industrialization. Through a selective reading of earlier texts and an abandonment of the theoretical debates of the 1920s, women's emancipation was once again seen as the inevitable outcome of the wider revolutionary transformation, to which it was subordinated.

This was the legacy the East Central European socialist states inherited after the Second World War. Its ordering of priorities remained virtually unchanged during the forty plus years of their existence. By virtue of this, women's emancipation was relegated from being a process integral and essential to the emancipatory project of society as a whole, to a separate and secondary status. The nature of gender relations as relations of power disappeared from the agenda. The dominant discourse dictated, in the words of Hilda Scott, that 'men set the goals, define the "socialist norms", and order the priorities by standards according to which men and women are equal but it is women who are different'. Most fundamentally of all, perhaps, in terms of the failure to address gender inequalities in social relations, 'they see equality as something that can be given to women without affecting the position of men'.[48]

Nor did the dreams about socializing housework come true. Whilst it is true that the record of individual state socialist countries in providing such services as workplace canteens and laundries differed, it must be conceded that the availability of goods and services was in general inadequate. Hilda Scott has also pinpointed the difficulty of changing prevailing attitudes which assign primary responsibility for domestic tasks to women, such that efforts to socialize and to modernize housework were in Czechoslovakia inevitably presented as 'the debt we owe our women'.[49]

Another factor in the failure of attempts to socialize domestic labour was popular rejection of the collective ideal. Early attempts in the GDR to instal shared washing machines in the basement of each block of flats were unsuccessful. Every family hankered after its own washing machine, competing not with 'the Joneses', but with the capitalist West as represented by their relatives in West Germany. The situation was similar in Czechoslovakia. The sociologist Vlasta Brablcová commented at the end of the 1960s that both 'the difficulties of automating services' and 'changing consumer preferences' would probably lead to a shift in state policy towards 'mechanizing domestic work through home appliances' as opposed to removing domestic labour from the home and relocating it in the social sphere. As a result, as early as 1973, 70 per cent of Czechoslovak households had refrigerators and 85 per cent had washing machines.[50]

The ironic heritage of the old devotion to collective ideals persists today in that relatively recently built apartment blocks in East Germany include a bathroom neither large enough comfortably to house a washing machine nor with washing machine connections plumbed in. As a result, plumbers together with other tradespeople formed the affluent 'ruling class' in East German society according to popular wisdom, and going to the toilet in such bathrooms requires the skill of a Houdini to negotiate the confined spaces constricted yet further by the inclusion of an unplanned washing machine.

By 1988, 67 per cent of young married East German workers in their twenties owned automatic washing machines, while all households owned some form of washing machine and a refrigerator. Approximately 54 per cent of households of employed people also owned a freezer, 60 per cent possessed colour TV and 59 per cent owned a car. These and the above figures make clear the GDR's and Czechoslovakia's relative affluence as expressed in terms of consumer durables, especially in relation to the former Soviet Union and some other countries of Eastern Europe. Despite their washing machines, however, most GDR households gave their sheets and towels to the communal laundry for washing once a month, evidencing a level of delivery of services to alleviate domestic burdens which was not necessarily available in all state socialist countries.

The element of consumer choice cannot be overlooked therefore, when considering issues of the dual role. Despite the fact that most children and adults in the former GDR enjoyed a hot meal at midday at their work or school canteen, most women chose to cook again in the evening, not believing somehow that the institutional meal would be sufficiently nutritious for their family. And the time spent cooking at home in all the state socialist countries was lengthened by the lack of pre-prepared or frozen foods. Not available in sufficient quantity or choice under state socialism, such foods had by 1990 already become prohibitively expensive in Hungary.

The record in relation to childcare provision was also patchy, reflecting ambivalence even within the orthodoxy of state socialism's attitude to women as producers *and* reproducers. For if the prime emphasis of the official canon was on women's labour force participation as the route to their emancipation, the resulting fall in the birthrate and predominant one-child family pattern raised qualms in governing circles. In the 1960s and 1970s, several governments restricted the right to abortion and introduced pro-natalist policies. These included material incentives to encourage women to stay home with their babies until the child's first (in the GDR) or third (in Poland and Hungary) birthday, thus simultaneously alleviating pressure on overcrowded childcare facilities and increasing the chances that women might overcome their reluctance to have more than one child.

Relocating responsibility for the care of young children in the home was also cheaper than providing public childcare facilities, even taking into account the cost of losing a worker, especially as with the years the economy had less urgent need of women's labour. The Hungarian sociologist Júlia Szalai has calculated that the annual cost per child of the extended childcare grant was only 'about one third of the additional costs of constructing and equipping public nurseries'. And since Hungarian women spent 30–40 per cent of their worktime on sick leave for children's illnesses, it was possible to argue that the investment in them as workers with the back-up of childcare facilities didn't pay.[51]

Levels of childcare provision varied between individual state socialist countries, but were high in comparison with most of Western Europe.[52] The former GDR remained an exception in that the pro-natalist policies of the late 1970s were not accompanied by restricted access to abortion, and did not alter the steady increase in the provision of childcare places, at either the infant or pre-school level. Although the Independent Women's Association (UFV) formed in East Berlin in December 1989 was scathing in retrospect about the 'Mummy policies' of the 1970s, it could be argued that the GDR went furthest of the state socialist countries in balancing its policies towards women as producers and reproducers, hence to a degree facilitating choice about whether and when to have children, and if and when to return to one's job afterwards.

The first generation of young mothers who had themselves spent long days in state nurseries often resisted imposing such a régime on their own children. Memories of being woken and taken, half asleep, by the hand in the dark of early morning, abound in fictional and documentary accounts. The impact of long days away from parents for very young children, the unfavourable child-carer ratios which resulted in a régimented day and a lack of individual attention, the frequent illnesses caught from other children – all these factors outweighed in the popular memory the advantages of early socialization so eulogized by early socialist theoreticians.

It must be said that the theoretical canon adopted from the classical Marxist writers was flawed in that it was sometimes contradictory and ultimately gender-blind. The nature of this flaw is expressed by the dominant focus on labour force participation as the sufficient rather than one of a number of necessary conditions for women's emancipation on the one hand, and becomes cemented by legislative definition of women's dual role, on the other. Chapter 4 will show that contradictions arose not only through the exclusion from the official canon of the power relations embedded in traditional gender divisions. They also appeared within the area of production prioritized by the dominant discourse, in the form of gender-based occupational segregation at the workplace.

It is significant that the early Marxist theorists focused on the family as the site of women's oppression, but that subsequent reductionist interpretations eclipsed its role in perpetuating gender inequalities by their privileging of the economy. The assertion of the need for positive discrimination, and the attempts to socialize domestic labour, were signs of unease at this eclipse. Yet state socialist attempts to legislate away women's disadvantaging foundered on the fundamental definitional contradiction. Labour force participation might give women economic independence from men; it might also give them satisfaction and an enhanced self-image. But it had no automatic or necessary impact on the domestic division of labour. And so long as women were defined as 'naturally' having two roles, compared with men who had one, no amount of positive discrimination or protective legislation could substitute for a social commitment to re-examining the nature of gendered role divisions.

Hilda Scott has pointed to the crux of the problem for state socialism, which lay in the fact that women's theoretically assigned and legislatively enshrined dual role construed women's 'difference' as 'natural'. A necessary condition for real gender equality would be that governments abandon measures aimed at women alone. This would entail recognition that the notion of a 'Woman Question' is anachronistic, and that what is needed are policies aimed at altering the balance of gender relations in society as a whole.

Notes

1. Anastasia Posadskaya, in conversation with Maxine Molyneux, 25 September 1990, published in: *Shifting Territories: Feminism and Europe*, Special Issue no. 39 of *Feminist Review*, winter 1991, p. 135.

2. Sheila Rowbotham, *Women in Movement: Feminism and Social Action*, Routledge, London, 1993.

3. August Bebel, *Woman and Socialism*, cited in Hilda Scott, *Women and Socialism: Experiences from Eastern Europe*, Allison and Busby, London, 1976, p. 58.

4. Simone de Beauvoir, *The Second Sex* (1949), Penguin, Harmondsworth, 1972, pp. 158–59.

5. Simone de Beauvoir, interview with Pierre Viansson-Ponté, *Le Monde*, 10.1.78, cited in: Mira Janova and Mariette Sineau, 'Women's Participation in Political Power in Europe', in: *Women's Studies International Forum*, vol. 15, no. 1, 1992, pp. 115–16.

6. Maxine Molyneux, 'Women in Socialist Societies: Problems in Theory and Practice', in: Kate Young, Carol Wolkowitz, and Roslyn McCullagh, eds, *Of Marriage and the Market: Women's Subordination in International Perspective*, CSE Books, 1981, p. 167.

7. Molyneux, ibid., p. 176; Sheila Rowbotham, *Women in Movement: Feminism and Social Action*, Routledge, London, 1993.

8. This discussion of Bebel's interpretation of Engels is taken from Richard Stites, *The Women's Liberation Movement in Russia: Feminism, Nihilism, and Bolshevism 1860–1930*, Princeton University Press, New Jersey, 1978, p. 235.

9. Molyneux, 'Women in Socialist Societies', 1981, p. 178; Christine White, 'Women and Socialist Development: Reflections on the Case of Vietnam', 1980, mimeo, p. 4.

10. Friedrich Engels, *The Origin of the Family, Private Property and the State* (1884), cited by Scott, *Women and Socialism*, 1976, p. 35.

11. Molyneux, 'Women in Socialist Societies', 1981, p. 167.

12. Mary Buckley, 'Soviet Interpretations of the Woman Question' in: Barbara Holland, ed., *Soviet Sisterhood: British Feminists on Women in the USSR*, Fourth Estate, London, 1985, p. 50.

13. For analyses of the progressive nature of early state socialist legislation for 'emancipation', cf. Molyneux, 'Women in Socialist Societies', 1981; Barbara Einhorn, 'Socialist Emancipation: The Women's Movement in the German Democratic Republic', in: Sonia Kruks, Rayna Rapp, Marilyn B. Young, eds, *Promissory Notes: Women in the Transition to Socialism*, Monthly Review Press, New York, 1989, pp. 282–305; Wendy Zeva Goldman, 'Women, the Family, and the New Revolutionary Order in the Soviet Union', in ibid., pp. 59–81; Alena Heitlinger, *Women and State Socialism: Sex Inequality in the Soviet Union and Czechoslovakia*, Macmillan, London, 1979. Jacqueline Heinen, 'The Impact of Social Policy on the Behaviour of Women Workers in Poland and East Germany', in: *Critical Social Policy*, Issue 29, vol. 10, no. 2, autumn 1990, p. 80, speaks of 'the wish to abolish the inequalities of status between men and women – a desire that one finds in the

Constitutions adopted in the early 1950s', which she characterizes as 'very progressive taking into account the legislation existing at the time in Western countries'.

14. For the year in which women in individual East and West European countries gained the right to vote, see Table A10 in the Appendix.

15. For a more detailed account of the first Soviet Family Code, and of its paradoxical effects, see Goldman, 'Women, the Family', 1989.

16. Molyneux, 'Women in Socialist Societies', 1981.

17. 'I, Sharofat Rassulova', in: *Der Spiegel*, no. 21, 1992, pp. 170, 180 [translation mine, BE].

18. For these comparisons of women's juridical status, past and present, in East and West Germany, see Harry G. Shaffer, *Women in the Two Germanies: A Comparative Study of a Socialist and a Non-Socialist Society*, Pergamon Press, Oxford and New York, 1981, pp. 12–13; Eva Kolinsky, 'Women in the New Germany', in: *Women in the German-Speaking Countries*, special issue of *Politics and Society in Germany, Austria and Switzerland*, vol. 3, no. 3, 1991, pp. 1–22.

19. Rowbotham, *Women in Movement*, 1993.

20. Cited by Scott, *Women and Socialism*, 1976, p. 105

21. For further discussion of Zetkin's political career and these issues, see Scott, *Women and Socialism*, 1976; Rowbotham, *Women in Movement*, 1993; Stites, *The Women's Liberation Movement in Russia*, 1978; Richard J. Evans, *Comrades and Sisters: Feminism, Socialism and Pacifism in Europe 1870–1945*, Wheatsheaf Books, Hassocks, 1987. Of significance in relation to the current outbreak of nationalist violence in East Central Europe and the former Soviet Union is also Clara Zetkin's passionate opposition to the First World War. The second conference of the Socialist Women's International, held in Copenhagen in 1910, named 8 March as International Women's Day and resolved that women's greatest task was to oppose the slide towards war. The World War caused a split in Social Democracy, and Zetkin later observed bitterly that 'the majority of organized Social-Democratic women sank under the leadership of the Second International to the position of defenders of the national "fatherlands" of imperialist bourgeoisie' (cited in Scott, *Women and Socialism*, 1976, p. 62).

22. The provisions of this law are cited in a 1991 study of Poland by Helsinki Watch and the US-based Women's Rights Project, 'Hidden Victims: Women in Post-Communist Poland', *News from Helsinki Watch*, vol. IV, issue no. 5, March 12, 1992.

23. Valentina Dobrokhotova, 'Woman Worker', Petrozavodsk, Karelia, speaking in: Tatyana Mamonova, ed., *Women and Russia: Feminist Writings from the Soviet Union*, Blackwell, Oxford, 1984, pp. 5–6.

24. Herta Kuhrig and Anneliese Klenner are cited by Shaffer, *Women in the Two Germanies*, 1981, p. 27.

25. Molyneux, 'Women in Socialist Societies', 1981, p. 184.

26. Shaffer, ibid.

27. Overall in East German industry before unification, 40.1% of production workers worked shifts in 1989, of which 9.3% were women. In female-dominated industries, the proportion was much higher. In chemicals, women constituted 15.1% of the 49.4% workers doing shifts; in light industry, women formed 11.1% of the 28.8% shift-workers, and in textiles, 22.1% of the 39% working shifts (Source: Gunnar Winkler, ed., *Frauenreport 90*, Verlag Die Wirtschaft, Berlin, 1990, p. 82, table 3.26).

28. Helsinki Watch, 'Hidden Victims: Women in Post-Communist Poland', 1992, p. 4.

29. Imre Szabó in: József Halász, ed., *The Socialist Concept of Human Rights*, Akademiai Kiado, Budapest, 1966, p. 75.

30. József Halász, in: ibid., p. 187.

31. Engels, *Origin*, cited by Scott, *Women and Socialism*, 1976, p. 34.

32. Scott, ibid., p. 44.

33. Engels cited by Stites, *The Women's Liberation Movement in Russia*, 1978, p. 265.

34. Bebel, *Woman and Socialism*, and Lenin, 'On the Emancipation of Women' (1919), cited by Stites, ibid., and p. 378.

35. Lenin, 'On the Emancipation of Women', cited by Buckley, 'Soviet Interpretations of the Woman Question', 1985, p. 35.

36. Joan B. Landes, 'Marxism and the "Woman Question"', in: Kruks, Rapp, Young, eds, *Promissory Notes*, 1989, p. 21.

37. Commentary to GDR Family Law cited by Shaffer, *Women in the Two Germanies*, 1981, p. 31.

38. Article 7, para 1 of the Family Law specified that 'if the spouse who hitherto had not been gainfully employed takes a job, or if a spouse decides to continue his (or her) education or engage in socially useful work, the other supports with comradely consideration and assistance the intentions of the spouse'.

39. Gunnar Winkler, ed., *Sozialreport 90*, Verlag Die Wirtschaft, Berlin, 1990, p. 274.

40. Stites and Kollontai cited from Stites, *The Women's Liberation Movement in Russia*, 1978, p. 351.

41. For Inessa Armand's views, see Buckley, 'Soviet Interpretations of the Woman Question', 1985, pp. 34–35.

42. Rowbotham, *Women in Movement*, 1993.

43. Stites, *The Women's Liberation Movement in Russia*, 1981, p. 262.

44. Wendy Zeva Goldman, 'Women, the Family, and the New Revolutionary Order in the Soviet Union', 1989, pp. 59–81.

45. On these retrogressive legislative measures, see Goldman, ibid., p. 61, and Rowbotham, *Women in Movement*, 1993.

46. Lenin, 'On the Emancipation of Women' (1919), is cited in relation to the triple burden by White, 'Women and Socialist Development', 1980.

47. Buckley, 'Soviet Interpretations of the Woman Question', 1985, p. 39.

48. Scott, *Women and Socialism*, 1976, p. 198.

49. Scott, ibid., pp. 194–97. Scott also cites evidence of non-delivery in socializing domestic labour in Czechoslovakia: she documents a decline in communal dining facilities, so that by the mid-1970s only about 20% of workers ate their main meal in factory canteens, compared with 47% in France (1964) and 45% in West Germany (1966). Similarly, she states that public laundries by the mid-1970s were taking care of only about 5% of the family wash, planned to increase to 10% by 1980, and that the worst aspects of the laundry service were the waiting time of 2–3 weeks and the lack of deliveries.

50. Vlasta Brablcová cited in Scott, ibid., p. 196.

51. Júlia Szalai, 'Some Aspects of the Changing Situation of Women in Hungary', in: *Signs*, vol. 17, no. 1, autumn 1991, p. 165.

52. For levels of childcare provision, see Table A1 in the Appendix.

2

New for Old? Ideology, the Family and the Nation

'A Questionnaire for Women': ... Oh – they really want to know everything about me. They're interested in my life hour by hour. ... How many hours do I spend (a) on housework; (b) with the children; (c) on spare-time cultural activities? ...

But the next question inhibits any desire to be witty: 'Days off due to illness: your own or your children's (number of days in the last year)'. ... My Achilles heel. ... Of course, the directors know that I have two children. But nobody's worked out how many days I've had to spend at home with them. If this statistic is unearthed it might frighten them. It might frighten me as well. ... Who thought up this questionnaire? ... 'and what exactly are *they* after anyway?'

'God knows,' she answers. ... 'Questionnaires are fashionable at the moment. What they really want to know is why women don't want to have babies.'. ...

We don't know how to work out what goes on what. The 'mums' get together. We decide that we must indicate the time spent on travelling: we all live on new housing estates and spend about three hours a day travelling. Nobody can apportion 'time spent with the children' either. We 'spend time with them' while doing everything else. ... Who really knows how much time family life needs? And what is it, anyway?

Olga, the narrator in Natalya Baranskaya's *A Week Like Any Other*.[1]

The state socialists renamed the nuclear family as 'socialist' while continuing to regard it as the basic cell of society and failing to interrogate the gendered division of labour within it. Now a more traditional family model is being envisioned by East Central European societies in transition, as the focal point in the search for identity and new values. This vision casts the family as the smallest unit in the wider ethnic community, invoking its central and salutary role in the process of establishing new mores. The family is thus seen as a crucial element in the claim to national identity and self-determination.

The role of women-as-mothers is central to the ideology of both models. State socialism 'emancipated' women not as equal citizens, but as worker-mothers. The dual role was legislatively enshrined as well as reinforced daily in practice. The maternal role ascribed to women in the dominant discourse was constructed as a social duty to bear and rear the 'socialist citizens of the future'. Now, the figure of the mother has eclipsed any expanded notion of alternative female role models such as woman-as-citizen. The unitary role of motherhood is being elevated to an ideal in the current transformation. Czech writer Eva Hauserová speaks of 'the "cult of motherhood": the glorification of the traditional female role of wife, mother, and proud homemaker'.[2]

Women's reproductive and 'feminine' nurturing roles are seen as crucial to the survival, not of a particular social system – as they were under state socialism – but of the national or ethnic community. All social ills are laid at the door of state socialism which it is argued undermined the family and women's role within it. In the former Soviet Union, for example, feminist Olga Lipovskaya speaks of 'a patriarchal tradition' and of powerful 'propaganda to send women home. ... From conservative writers, the Church and the media comes the familiar charge that the high divorce rate, juvenile delinquency and alcoholism can be directly attributed to women's absence from the family'.[3] Now, all this is to be rectified by a simple semantic shift. Women are to have babies 'for the nation', to teach them the national language and to inculcate in them a love of their ethnic or national heritage.

In the first model, women were exhorted to subordinate their aspirations, and socialist theory's promise of the full development of individual potential, to the needs of the wider society, by contributing to the idealized communist society of the future. In the second, women's self-sacrifice is glorified in the name of individual autonomy (male) in the marketplace and the reconstruction of an imputed past sense of community. The idea appears to be that in some mythologized past, personal and social relations were part of an organic and harmonious community ethic as opposed to what has frequently been described as the atomization of individuals within state socialism.[4]

Inherent in this opposition is a curious ambivalence. The collectivist and would-be egalitarian state socialist past is rejected in the name of an individualist, self-reliant present based on survival in the marketplace. Yet the individually attributed political rights of the democratization process and the notion of competition as the route to collective gain, sit somewhat uneasily with appeals to a bygone sense of identity and mutuality based on the 'natural' bonds of family and community.

The model of marketization espoused in the former state socialist societies hypothesizes individual entrepreneurs operating from within a family-based 'community', rather than equal citizens invested with rights to claim from 'society' the provision of some collective goods. The nod in the direction of social justice in many Western market economies such as the German (which calls itself a 'social market economy' – 'soziale Marktgesellschaft') appears to be, for the moment, missing from the equation. Revulsion at the all-pervasive socialist state has produced a violent swing of the pendulum to an extreme form of anti-statism.[5] The rejection of 'society' in favour of traditional 'community' harks back to the nineteenth century, echoing German sociologist Ferdinand Tönnies's ideal types which distinguish between the organic *Gemeinschaft* (community) based on the household, a unit of production and consumption characterized by mutuality in the fulfilment of needs, and the modern *Gesellschaft* (society) marked by rationality and based on exchange in the marketplace regulated by legal contract rather than by family ties.

Whatever the parameters of enquiry into the sources of women's continuing oppression in capitalist, state socialist or transitional societies, there is considerable agreement that gender inequalities within the family play a large part in disadvantaging women. The family was seen as the locus of women's subordinate status by nineteenth-century liberal political theorists like John Stuart Mill as well as by Marxists such as August Bebel or Friedrich Engels. Recent Western feminist enquiry of both radical and socialist variety has focused on the psychosocial or social reproductive aspects of gender relations within the private realm as a powerful nexus of unequal and indeed inequitable power relations which help to define women as second-class citizens in the public domain.

While in state socialist societies it was women's dual role which helped to perpetuate gender-based inequalities in the family, feminist analyses in Western democracies have identified the family as a key source of women's social isolation and subordination. State socialism sought to overcome the contradiction by socializing some parts of domestic labour and childcare. By contrast, Western feminism sought to free women from the bonds of the private, not only through their greater participation and visibility in the public sphere, but also through subjecting to scrutiny and attempting to alter the gendered power relations within the private sphere.

In both types of society, the concept of citizenship has expanded to include the right to expect or demand of the state the provision of certain levels of social equity and welfare. This broader view of citizenship rights has direct implications for the quality of life of families, and the rights and duties of women within them. In socialist states, such rights were given from above, as opposed to being won, and were employment-linked, rather than based on the family.[6] In the social democratic welfare model espoused by, say, the Scandinavian countries, there was a similar large-scale involvement of women in the workforce and generous welfare benefits linked with this participation. Some feminist analyses read this situation as perhaps not so liberating or empowering for women as may at first appear. They fear that for women it embodies simply a shift from economic dependence on an individual man to dependence on the state, in other words from private to public patriarchy.[7] Given the similar levels of female labour force participation and social welfare provision in both societies, this observation could be considered to hold true also for the state socialist case.

However, Western capitalism has operated different models of welfare state, each with different implications for women. Crescy Cannan points out that in the current transition period, East Central European societies may favour the Conservative-Corporatist model of social policy – a model epitomized by Germany – together with the 'Anglo-American' liberal model, but as opposed to the Scandinavian social democratic welfare-based model. She refers to the way Stephan Leibfried and Ilona Ostner have adapted Stephan Leibfried's and Gösta Esping-Andersen's 1990 models to draw out the gender issues: the Conservative-Corporatist model is 'predicated on male citizenship in conditions of full male employment and high industrial productivity. Its financial benefits are highly related to work performance and occupational status.' Leibfried and Ostner stress that what they call the 'Bismarckian' model favoured by Germany and Austria on the one hand 'emphasizes capitalist economic development and productivity, on the other the family is seen as a "one-voice one-heart venture"'.

Cannan extrapolates from this model that 'women who are not wives of economically secure men are particularly at risk: single or separated women with interrupted work cycles, women married to men in unstable work, are extremely vulnerable to poverty (cf. the feminization of poverty), as women are assumed to be dependent upon husbands and to be cared for by them. Within the family there is an assumption of privacy, and few services to socialize care and share women's caring burden with the state. Women's employment is assumed to be low and there is no assumption that this should be changed.'[8]

The way this model operates in the German case, according to Prue Chamberlayne, is that 'the subsidiarity principle, enshrined in the German Constitution, places responsibility for any particular function in society on the lowest organ capable of bearing it. In welfare, responsibility falls first on the family.' For East German women, as well as women in other East Central European countries, this means enormous change, 'for whereas social policy in West Germany privileges housewife roles, the East German system promoted a female employment rate of 90 per cent.'[9]

Cannan points out that in this Bismarckian model, 'perhaps due to the role of the church, identity and personal meaning are assumed to lie in the privacy of the family rather than in the public sphere as in the liberal or social democratic models'. The withdrawal of the state from welfare provision with responsibility devolved onto families clearly implies reliance on the unremunerated, (state-) unsupported and invisible labour of women to fill the gap.

The Hungarian sociologist Mária Adamik points to the current links between economic instrumentality, state withdrawal from public provision, the new Christian-based conservative ideology, and traditional family models:

> There are now powerful interests calling for full-time motherhood to be an officially recognized occupation. This well-known reaction to unemployment, i.e. political and economic problems, may soon join forces with a revived Christian morality to compel women back into their traditional roles. There will no doubt also be a wish to replace the disintegrating social services and health system, and the minimal levels of social benefits, with the unpaid work of women. With these new – but actually only too familiar – regulations, women will be left anywhere but in the Europe towards which the government and the rest of the country is allegedly striving.[10]

In practice, this means that women become the providers as well as the consumers of welfare. It also implies a return from public to private patriarchy. This is as true for some West European countries within the EC as for the emerging market economies of East Central Europe. The adoption of the Conservative-Corporatist model with its devolution of care from the public sector to the private sphere, and the economic dependence of women within that sphere, together imply this reverse shift from that observed in social democratic and state socialist régimes. Women's dependent position will become exacerbated in future as a result both of past policies linking social welfare entitlement to obligatory employment, and currently high levels of female unemployment. The Hungarian sociologist Júlia Szalai argues the case for welfare entitlement to be unhitched from labour force participation and based instead on some more fundamental notion of civil or citizenship rights.[11]

The notion that making women workers would mean liberation from oppression within the family failed, in part because it did not eliminate the assumption of 'natural' inequalities. Faced with the stresses of the double burden, women are therefore going along, for the present, with the shift back to the unitary role of mother. Women's maternal role in the state socialist and the current transitional societies of East Central Europe reveals both continuity and change. Continuity is evident in the centrality of the family for both state socialism and the newly emerging democracies, as well as in the nature of women's responsibilities within that unit. Change is implied by the contrary movement, the past shift from private to public, and current reversion from public to private patriarchy. This change simultaneously enhances and diminishes women's role within the family.

Ideologically there is affirmation of women's role in that maternal virtues are extolled; in practical terms, too, there is a welcome lessening of stress in the emphasis on a unitary rather than a double or triple role for women. In terms of citizenship rights, there are gains and losses. On the one hand, civil and political rights can be deemed to be augmented, some people in Eastern and Central Europe would argue, by the right to non-interference in the private sphere, or by the right to choose, in relation for example to schooling. However, it would appear that both ideological and practical emphases on the maternal role imply a devolution of state responsibilities which could result in a diminution of women's citizenship rights. Substituting 'care in the community' (for which read individual female carers within the family) for public welfare provision in the name of 'individual responsibility' in effect makes women, as those in Britain have learned over the past decade or so, silent pillars of society's responsibilities, to the detriment of their right to work outside the home or to political participation.

We have seen that the withdrawal of public provision seriously detracts specifically from women's citizenship rights. The way the public/private divide is constructed ideologically also has implications for women's rights. Here the role which nationalism plays is integral to current trends. In the state socialist era, official foregrounding of the public sphere was accompanied by an unofficial elevation of the private sphere. Its importance as the locus of individuality and independence was often given added meaning as a site of resistance against what was seen as the oppressively interfering state. While women's role within the family and friendship groups was depended upon but denigrated by the state, women gained extra kudos for maintaining the informal networks that formed the basis of a clandestine and embryonic civil society. Conversely, in the current transformation, the private sphere of the family is ideologically esteemed and imbued with spiritual significance. Yet in practice it is downgraded alongside the marketplace or parliament, both currently male-dominated.

The family form being reinvoked in reaction to what was perceived as the false egalitarianism of state socialism is traditional. It evokes strictly gender-demarcated roles and responsibilities in a hierarchy of male authority and female dependence. The search for untarnished values and identities has leapfrogged the often unpleasant realities of both state socialist and Second World War history, turning instead to the spirit of nineteenth-century or inter-war nationalism. For the family, this means in effect reinventing the doctrine of gender-segregated spheres. East Central European nationalist ideology divides the world 'into the public sphere of men's work and political life; and the private – women's – sphere of family and domesticity'.[12]

Again, this echoes Ferdinand Tönnies's ideal type community (*Gemeinschaft*), composed of households based on what he sees as a 'natural' division of labour:

> In defending their common property the task of the woman consists in the protection of valued possessions; the man has to keep off the enemy. To obtain and provide the necessities of living is the field of the man, to conserve and prepare them that of the woman, as far as food is concerned. And when other work and the instruction of the younger therein is needed, we find that the masculine energy is directed towards the outside, fighting, and leading the sons. The woman, on the other hand, remains confined to the inner circle of home life and is attached to the female children. . . . But such a division of labour may also be regarded as a relation between guidance and leadership, on the one hand, and compliance and obedience, on the other. It must be recognized that all these differentiations follow a pattern of nature . . .[13]

This model justifies gender divisions by the fact that 'women are usually led by feelings' and what Tönnies calls the natural will. They lack 'the requirements of rational will' which the male of the species, led more 'by intellect', requires in order to cultivate 'farsightedness', 'because to him falls the guidance and leadership, at least in all activities concerned with the outside world'. It follows that 'for women, the home and not the market, their own or a friend's dwelling and not the street, is the natural seat of their activity'.[14]

In their different ways, then, both state socialism and the current transitional societies have redefined and reinforced the gendered public/private divide. But if women's role within the private sphere had an enhanced significance under state socialism in terms of an embryonic civil society, current nationalist idealization of the maternal role by contrast prioritizes women's reproductive responsibilities within the family at the expense of their citizenship rights within the wider society.

Shifts in the significance attributed to their role in the family make women complicit in material and psychological limitations on their autonomy. For those women who have known the confidence as well as the relative economic independence conferred by labour force participation as the norm,[15] it would be surprising if the next few years did not witness a modification of their initial apparent collusion with relegation to motherhood as their primary sphere of responsibility. In the short term, however, the Hungarian journalist Zsuzsa Béres feels that 'sheer physical exhaustion and a deeply ingrained sense of guilt' explain Hungarian women's lack of resistance to 'awesome challenges to their human rights, dignity and self-respect'.[16] Whatever the shape of things to come, it is crucial to our understanding of how these processes affect women's citizenship status to analyse the role and significance of the family in the past and the present societies of East Central Europe.

Gender Divisions within the 'Socialist' Family

The family in the official canon of state socialism was seen not so much as the source of citizenship rights nor as a social unit embodying individual rights, but as the locus of duties towards society and the state. Women were not only productive workers, but were exhorted by the state to fulfil their reproductive duties. Chapter 1 described how early theoretical formulations were cemented in legislation enunciating women's dual or even triple role. It made clear how gestures in the direction of alleviating the impossible demands this placed on women by socializing housework and childcare were both conceptually contradictory and practically inadequate.

The dual role both contributed to and was reinforced by the failure to address traditional gender divisions within the family. Occupational segregation and wage differentials played their part in undermining notions of an equitable sharing of parental or housework responsibilities. Thus paid leave enabling parents to tend sick children was

46

taken overwhelmingly by women, even in those countries where it was available to either parent, since men often occupied positions higher up career pyramids and hence were regarded as less dispensable at work. In Poland, such leave was available only to mothers, fathers' eligibility for it having been rescinded in 1975.[17]

This 'natural' practice led to the extraordinary situation in Hungary, where it is calculated, mothers with young children spent up to 50 per cent of their total annual work time away due to legal entitlements such as maternity or sick leave. In Hungary, such sick leave was unlimited up to the child's first birthday, comprised 84 days annually up to the child's third birthday, 40 days until the age of 6, and 14 days annually from 6–10 years.[18]

Similarly, another form of positive discrimination, the 'household day – one day's leave a month on full pay enabling women in the former GDR 'to catch up on household tasks'[19] – was introduced as a short-term measure to alleviate women's double burden. Instead, it perpetuated the existing gendered division of domestic labour. Women only were eligible for the 'household day', unless men could show that they were lone parents or that their wives were certified ill by a doctor! If the state paid women to do household tasks, men argued, then why should they share them? The result was a self-perpetuating vicious circle.

Paid sick leave to look after children, extended maternity and childcare leave, and measures such as the 'household day' mitigated against women being considered suitable candidates for management positions, since they were too often absent from their jobs. And the fact that their jobs were consequently usually lower status and less well paid than that of their partners was not conducive to changes in gendered role allocation within the family. Conversely, the exigencies of their heavy domestic duties made women less willing to take on positions of responsibility at work or in politics. Thus it is clear that under state socialism, gender-specific elements of official social policy, instigated to alleviate women's double or triple burden, in effect reinforced both traditional gender-divided roles within the family and women's disadvantaged position in the public sphere.

The gender blindness of state socialist conceptions of the family not only reinforced the gender-based division of domestic labour, but also tended to reproduce gendered role expectations in the practices of upbringing and early childhood education. A GDR decree on pre-school education assumed equality of educational opportunity. It enjoined pre-school childcare facilities to 'ensure a harmonious physical, mental and linguistic training of children and the formation of socialist qualities and modes of behaviour'. Nowhere was there mention of gender differences or of any need to break down gender-based inequalities in the treatment of boys and girls. By contrast, the preamble to the GDR's Education Law stipulated equal opportunities for girls and women in education, to be achieved in part by positive discrimination such as the 'measures for the promotion of women' ('*Frauenförderungsmaßnahmen*') which enabled working women to attend vocational courses on a day-release basis. School curricula were uniform throughout primary and secondary education, so that the problem of gender-biased subject choices identified by Western feminist educational sociologists did not apply.

That preconceptions about gender roles nevertheless persisted in the GDR was obliquely acknowledged in official discourse by a passing reference to the need for overcoming 'obsolete traditions and habits' in the next generation.[20] This need was demonstrable in research into gender-specific attitudes among GDR school and pre-school children conducted in the late 1960s. The results revealed deeply entrenched gender stereotypes in children of both sexes, about whether boys or girls are cheekier, have more fun, and so on.[21]

Some studies suggest that great efforts were made at crèche and kindergarten level to institute non sexist behaviour.[22] Yet perusal of the illustrations in a standard pre-school text and the first reader used in GDR schools in the late 1970s reveals traditional gender-divided behaviour in the family and gender-segregated workplace occupations. The only time Daddy is portrayed as actively involved in family tasks is when he helps the children prepare a gift for Mummy on International Women's Day. Mothers and grandmothers are shown carrying shopping bags, serving the dinner, supervising play and picking up children from school. In a picture of children doing chores, it is of course the daughter who washes up, and tells her little brother to dry the dishes. Road awareness is inculcated with stories about Stefan who falls off his bike while learning to ride (read: boys are too wild, daredevils, not careful enough), Jutta who teaches her little sister how to cross the road safely (read: girls are cautious, prudent, little mothers), and Sabine who is crying because she is lost, but impresses the policeman with her knowledge of her address (girls are cry-babies, but sensible underneath it).[23]

In the sections of both books that describe the kinds of jobs done by adults, women or mothers appear as dairymaids, doctors, primary school teachers, textile workers, draughtsmen[24] and supermarket cashiers. Men and fathers appear in a far greater diversity of roles, as architects, engineers, construction workers, brigade leaders, steelworkers, machine tool operators, bus drivers, performing artists, and soldiers of the National People's Army (NVA).[25] There is no encouragement of alternative role models; and certainly men are not depicted in any of the caring or childrearing professions. In reality too, nursery and kindergarten teachers in the GDR were 100 per cent female, as were 77 per cent of all school teachers.

With such gendered patterns of socialization, it is hardly surprising that despite some suggestions of change among the younger generation, women in East Central Europe remained responsible for the overwhelming majority of domestic labour. While 66 per cent of women and 60 per cent of men in the former GDR asserted in 1988 that domestic labour was shared fairly equally between them, a 1985 survey had shown that in practice women were still shouldering at least 60 per cent of the work. This was less than the 75–80 per cent of household tasks and childcare performed by women in Poland and Hungary. And in the former GDR it represented a significant change from the 80 per cent female share recorded in a UNESCO study in 1970.[26]

Recent surveys reveal a high degree of congruence in family time budgets between individual state socialist countries. In most cases women spent on average more than four hours per day on household chores and childcare compared with just over an hour for men. Studies conducted in 1984 in Hungary and Poland suggested that women spent a staggering total of over six hours daily on household chores and childcare.[27] (Interestingly, a very small proportion of the total was spent on childcare.)

A breakdown of household tasks shows that where men did participate, they performed more attractive, occasional or traditionally male-designated tasks rather than the daily drudgery of mundane or repetitive jobs. Interviews with women in Bulgaria in 1980 revealed that 78 per cent of men took responsibility for winter heating and 81.3 per cent for household repairs, but that only 1 per cent helped with cooking, washing and cleaning. Increases in men's 'help' over time were registered in the area of childcare, at least in Bulgaria and the former GDR. Men tended to play with the children for a limited period in the evening, or help with homework, but not to feed, bathe or put them to bed. Some fathers took their children to crèche or kindergarten. One area where tasks were perhaps most equitably shared in Bulgaria and Hungary was cultivating the private plot or allotment so crucial to the family's material welfare.[28]

Where children were expected to help at home, their tasks tended to be gender-segregated. More girls than boys had fixed chores for which they were responsible; boys were granted more time to themselves. Boys were usually asked to help with repair jobs or work in the garden, whilst girls participated in cleaning the house or looking after younger brothers and sisters. In other words, boys learned neutral or technical skills, but girls were initiated into social and caring roles.[29]

Women's overwhelming share of domestic labour was amplified by the context in which they worked full-time, as opposed to the majority of women involved in labour market participation in Western Europe, who work part-time. For the duration of most of the former GDR's history, for example, this meant a 43¾ hour working week. Moreover, providing for the family did not mean a one-stop shop at the local supermarket. To varying degrees in the shortage economies of the different state socialist countries it involved repeated queueing and disappointment. Irregular supply of foodstuffs was augmented by the lack in many cases of a family car, necessitating daily shopping.

Alena Kroupová cites a 1983 survey of leisure time showing that women in Czechoslovakia were away from home for around ten hours per day with work, shopping and commuting. The quotation from Baranskaya's novella which opens this chapter makes it clear that in Russia the figure was nearer twelve hours a day, not including shopping. Adding four to six extra hours of domestic labour to this long stint goes a long way toward illuminating the chronic fatigue described by East Central European women. The resulting fourteen to eighteen hour working day combined with the gendered domestic division of labour to give men between one and three hours more leisure time per day than their wives, for rest and recuperation, or for personal and career development.[30]

As if the heavy demands of the dual role were not sufficient, official rhetoric urged women to become involved in socially responsible or political roles. Examples were voluntary activity in the trades union, or on school and neighbourhood committees. The stresses of this additional burden were resisted by some women, but shouldered by many.[31] Analyses by both sociologists and activists have revealed that one reason for the dearth of feminist consciousness in the former GDR was that women were made to feel any frustration or difficulty they might experience in trying to fulfil their multiple roles as a personal failure. And women themselves usually failed to recognize the structural causes of their inequality and oppression.[32]

Zsuzsa Béres decries the constant sense of inadequacy this engendered. Pressure to perform in two or even three roles left women

feeling 'constantly tormented by a guilty conscience over not performing up to the mark – in any capacity', labelled as '"unreliable"
worker, "bad" mother, and inattentive wife'. As a result, 'Hungary's
women don't want to be liberated'. Instead they dream of deliv-
erance from the multiple afflictions with which state socialism beset
them. This made them susceptible, asserts Béres, to the 'God,
Homeland, Family' slogans of the conservative political parties
currently in power, during the 1990 election campaign: 'Home and
hearth, glorious motherhood, Husband the Provider – the foolproof
answer to the woes of the tottering nuclear family. And we shall all live
happily ever after.'[33]

Irreconcilable Demands: The Worker–Mother's Story

Literature in state socialist countries by the late 1970s often gave voice
to the contradictions between rhetoric and reality for which there was no
alternative public forum. Political constraints held the media in a
straitjacket, so that novels were widely read for what they said 'between
the lines' about the social or political situation. It was this as much as
cultural policy urging writers to make their works accessible to ordinary
people which vouchsafed for literature a far wider reading public than
that enjoyed by most Western authors. Moreover, the fact that literature
was closely scrutinized by the state security forces enhanced its appeal to
some readers and brought writers (a sometimes unwelcome) political
prominence. 'For nearly two centuries, the literature of countries like
Poland, Czechoslovakia and Hungary ... has been the object of this
dubious style of official attention. In these circumstances, it ceases to be
a marginal leisure-time activity and becomes crypto-politics.'[34]

Literature's role as sociological evidence as well as political platform
makes it apt for us to look to fictional representations for portrayals of
the objective reality of women's overburdening as well as the subjective
experience of ambiguity and ambivalence. The rhetoric of official
discourse as well as early socialist realist literature tended to be
wholehearted and simplistic in its affirmation of socialist goals, 'black
and white' in its rendition of socially approved values and role models.
By the 1970s, however, there was a noticeable shift towards more
nuanced and problematic versions of the relationship between the
individual and society. Natalia Baranskaya's famous novella *A Week Like
Any Other* and short stories written by a new generation of women
writers in the former GDR began to voice the problematic nature of
women's dual or triple role, their constant sense of guilt and inadequacy.

Natalia Baranskaya writes of the simultaneous guilt and resentment felt by the harassed worker-mother as she tears from work to home and back again, always late, perpetually anxious, constantly having to apologize, to her boss who interprets her lateness as a sign of 'an attitude to work [which] does not seem to us sufficiently rigorous', to her family when they have to wait for dinner:

> I'm running again, to get home to them quickly. I run and my bag full of shopping bangs against my knees as I go. On the bus I see by my watch that it's already seven – they're home by now. I hope that Dima isn't letting them fill up on bread and has remembered to put on the potatoes. I run along the paths, cut through the waste-land, and run up the stairs. Just as I'd thought: the children are munching bread; Dima has forgotten everything and is absorbed in a technical journal. I light all the gas rings and put on the potatoes, the kettle and the milk. I fling some cutlets into the frying-pan and, twenty minutes later, our supper is ready.[35]

An oral history account of the same harried daily round stresses the psychologically as well as professionally damaging effects on women in the former Soviet Union:

> Tired after their workday, they hurry home to childcare centres. Bowed with the weight of grocery bags, they drag their children behind them. In a terrible crush of people, they wedge themselves into overcrowded public buses elbowing people aside and pushing their way through to an empty seat, if there is one. At last, they reach home. Here new cares await them: dinner must be prepared and the husband and children must be fed. The laundry and housecleaning still await because, for a working woman, there is no other time for these chores. She cannot depend on her husband for anything.
>
> The next morning, these women, with glum, blank expressions, take their children to school or childcare centres and hurry to work. They perform their jobs mechanically, without inspiration, without enthusiasm . . .[36]

A bitterly ironic testament to the impossibility of reconciling successfully the roles of career woman and mother, especially for lone mothers, is contained in Irmtraud Morgner's short story 'Das Seil' ('The Tightrope').[37] The title prefigures the story's message that being a worker-mother involved a constant balancing act which could easily fail, indeed could cost you your life. Dr Vera Hill is a research physicist and solo mother of a three-year-old son. One fine evening she is accused of witchcraft by the superstitious locals in the small town where she lives and works. At pub closing time, a delegation delivers a petition to the director of the atomic physics research institute where she works.

Grounds for the accusation are that the locals claim to have seen her traversing the town on foot, suspended high up in the air above them, twice a day, morning and evening. Not only has she knocked yellow plums and cherry branches off a local farmer's trees with her briefcase, thus threatening the orchard's economic survival, but worse still, they maintain, the sight of black nylon lace and garters from people's balconies is endangering the morals of the community.

Faced with the petition, the director is initially incredulous. He judges 'walking on air to be a ridiculous form of slander'. On reflection, however, he realizes the potentially serious implications of the case for the work of the institute. 'He was afraid of not getting the allocation of hard currency needed for the purchase of an English computer.' He confronts Vera, who readily acknowledges that it's true, she does use a tightrope.

Since she lives on the opposite side of town from the institute, travel time is a major factor in the juggling feat required to reconcile her various roles and responsibilities. Deprived of the short-cut by tightrope, she points out, she would not be able to complete her post-doctoral research by the due date. 'In contrast to him, she added, she did not have the services of a housewife or live-in maid at her disposal.' So after shopping, picking up her son from kindergarten, feeding and bathing him, reading stories and putting him to bed, washing and mending and preparing clothes for the next day, she can only sit down at her desk by 9 p.m., and has to get up again in the morning at 5 a.m.

Without the tightrope trick, she would get to her post-doctoral research an hour later each evening, and have to get up an hour earlier each morning. And with less than six hours' sleep at night, she says, she has no head for nuclear physics. The director, mesmerized by Vera's lips and his recent affair with her, nevertheless accuses her of putting her own interests before the fate of the institute. He implores her to desist forthwith. Unnerved by the force of his argument, Vera loses her footing next day. Her body is found by the lamplighter in front of the local library.

It is obvious that the kind of stress levels described by Baranskaya would find expression in tensions within the family. By the end of the week, the tension bursts for Olga, the first-person narrator of *A Week Like Any Other*:

> I carry Kotka off to bed myself (normally Dima does it) and see that ...
> Dima is sitting in an armchair reading a journal – he really is sitting and reading.

As I pass by I say loudly: 'Incidentally, I've got a degree as well, you know, I'm just as highly trained as you are.'

'Congratulations,' Dima replies.

This seems to me extremely nasty and hurtful. . . .

'You should be ashamed of yourself,' I shout, 'I'm tired, do you understand, tired.'[38]

Extremely high divorce statistics in most of these countries provided powerful indicators that all was not well with the 'socialist' family. Moreover, it was women who petitioned for more than two thirds of all divorces. In Czechoslovakia, Hungary, the former Soviet Union and the former GDR divorce rates were amongst the highest in the world, with a staggering 33–44 per cent of marriages failing.[39] The high divorce rate which characterized these four countries was not true of Poland (even though there too two thirds of divorce applications were filed by women). Presumably this reflects both the influence of Catholic morality and the persistence of traditional norms in relation to conceptions of the family.[40]

The incidence of divorce increased sharply throughout the state socialist period.[41] This suggests a causality directly linked with the irreconcilable stresses of women's dual role. Yet the fact that women initiated two out of three divorces also intimates a more positive interpretation. It suggests an increased autonomy on the part of women which itself may derive from their sense of identity as workers, partial though their economic independence may have been.

The high divorce rate also meant that the 'socialist' family itself, consisting of two parents and one or two children, had by the 1980s become an ideological construct which bore less and less resemblance to reality. In the former GDR, one third of all children – and over half of all first children – were born to unmarried mothers, even though some of these would have been living in stable relationships. Of all families with children, 18 per cent were single-parent households. By the end of 1989, the one-child family constituted half of all GDR families. In the former Soviet Union too, a 1983 survey in the city of Perm revealed that 41 per cent of children were conceived outside marriage.[42]

Despite the high failure rate and the considerable gender-based imbalances in the allocation of family responsibilities, in 1988 a majority of both women (55 per cent) and men (64 per cent) in the former GDR expressed themselves 'satisfied' with the domestic division of labour. And it seems that the institution of marriage itself was not questioned. Marriage remained an important life goal and aspiration, at least for young people in the GDR and Czechoslovakia.[43] Not only did people in the state socialist countries of East Central Europe continue to marry; they also married young, about five years earlier than their West European counterparts, only to divorce three to five years later.[44]

Yet as sociologist Hana Navarová has pointed out in her study of young families in Czechoslovakia, whilst marriage remained an aspiration, in practice it proved not so easy. She maintains that marriage was 'very often an idealized relationship, expected to secure intimacy, stability and the chance for self-expression' in compensation for the alienation experienced elsewhere in everyday life under state socialism. In conversation with feminist journalist Slavenka Drakulić from the former Yugoslavia, a Hungarian woman links this idealization of interpersonal relationships, derived from the lack of a public sphere, with the failure of marriages:

> When there is no space in society to express your individuality, the family becomes the only territory in which you can form it ... [and] express it. But a family is too limiting, there is not space enough in it for self-expression either, and negative feelings accumulate very soon. We started to hate each other, but we stayed together because of the bigger enemy, waiting for each of us, out there – the solidarity of victims, I guess.[45]

Reality was clearly not half so romantic as the ideal. Most couples lived in tiny apartments, often still with their parents due to acute housing shortages. Consumer satisfaction was limited due to the relative shortages of consumer durables and foodstuffs. Getting repairs done was a nightmare due to the severe shortage of tradespeople and an under-developed service sector.[46]

The stresses of daily life were not helped by the fact that all members of the family were out of the house and away from each other for long hours each day, so that family life was often limited to the weekend. Until spring 1989 in the GDR, children attended school on Saturday mornings, so escape from the pollution of the city to the family 'dacha' or allotment could not occur until lunchtime on Saturday. Inevitably, children suffered. Childcare facilities in many countries were considered to be impersonal, overcrowded and, as a result of poor staff-child ratios, overly régimented. Parents often tried to make up for the time they were unable to spend with their children by showering them with material goods. Children's toys and clothes were both subsidized and among the most highly developed consumer goods in terms of attractiveness and availability. Popular sentiment in many of these countries held that children (if not self-employed plumbers or electricians!) constituted the true 'ruling class' of state socialism.

55

The relative deprivations of family life, especially in its repercussions for children, found expression in several short stories by GDR women writers in the mid- to late 1970s. 'Hänsel und Gretel: Kein Märchen' ('Hansel and Gretel: Not a Fairy Tale')[47] by Charlotte Worgitzky describes the Holtzhauers, who 'could be used as an exemplary model for a publication on GDR families: two children, modern flat with central heating . . . the long since ordered Trabant (car) due for delivery in two years'. Elvira Holtzhauer is completing her economics degree, broken off when she had the children, in a course of study which is especially intended for young mothers but makes no concessions to their need for childcare coverage. Her exams are looming, so in the absence of available grandmothers, the Holtzhauers decide to put the children, three and five years old, into a weekly children's home. The children run away and find their way from the outskirts of the city back home. The scene repeats itself a year later. This time the police return the fugitive children to the children's home without the preoccupied parents even becoming aware of the drama.

In 'Und der steinerne Elefant' ('And the Stone Elephant')[48] by Angela Stachowa, a small boy whispers in the ear of the playground elephant, telling him how lonely he is. One or other of his parents is invariably away on work-associated trips. Or if not, then they are so exhausted from their working day that they require peace and quiet. Either way, he gets sent out to play by himself until 7 p.m. precisely, by which time it is already dark. In the night, the elephant gathers the other stone animals from the playground and ascends to the little boy's flat, trampling the parents in their sleep. Awoken from a 'terrible night' in which she also dreamed of Hendrik, his mother seriously considers consulting the child-rearing manual to see how many hours per day one should optimally spend with children. Henceforth she packs Hendrik into the car and takes him with her whenever she travels for her job. 'But mother has to work. And in the places she takes him to there are not even stone animals.'

Given the difficulties of family life, why should young people in these societies wish to marry at all? In her oral history account of 'Why Soviet Women Want to Get Married' Ekaterina Alexandrova speaks of an element of continuity in patriarchal patterns which construe marriage as 'perhaps the most important achievement in a woman's life, no matter how educated or independent she is and no matter how successful she has been in her profession'. In this, she adds:

> There really is something to be surprised about and something hard to understand. Here is a society that has proclaimed as its goal the

extrication of women from the narrow confines of the family and the inclusion of these women in all forms of public activity. And it would appear that this society had achieved its goal – Soviet women work at the most varied jobs, and many of them are well educated, have a profession, and are financially independent of men. And yet, in this very society, among these very women, a patriarchal social order and its psychology thrive.[49]

This paradoxical hankering for the married state persists in the former Soviet Union despite considerable evidence that young women's aspirations centre on a fulfilling job and a child, rather than on marriage. Tatyana, a young woman studying at the Moscow Lenin State Pedagogical Institute, suggested in 1988: 'My first priority is to love my work. . . . Once that's established, I can support a child.' She and her friends laughingly dismissed the idea of marriage, asserting that 'I, personally, wish to bring up a child by myself, without a man' and adding scornfully: 'A man! Who needs a *second* child?' Underlining this trend (which sets the former Soviet Union apart from Czechoslovakia, for instance) a survey in Azerbaijan in the early 1980s indicated that only 23 per cent of urban and 40 per cent of rural young people saw marriage as a valuable social institution.[50] Opinions such as Tatyana's and survey results such as these would seem to signal generational, urban/rural and possibly social group differences in attitudes to marriage.

The main reason behind the relative haste in marrying was the shortage of housing stock. In Budapest in 1990, there were 70,000 people on the council waiting list for approximately 7,000 flats. People in Warsaw expected to wait twenty to thirty years for a flat.[51] Young people moved up the priority list for access to a flat if they were married, and further increased their chances of a place of their own with each child born into the marriage. The units in new apartment blocks had a restricted ground plan designed with a nuclear family in mind. Hence, in a directly material sense, housing scarcity under state socialism can be seen to have favoured a traditional form of partnership and discriminated against alternative living arrangements.

Traditional (and orthodox religious) notions of sexuality and marriage were thus reinforced in these societies by a potent combination of state socialist puritanism and practicality. Since young people frequently lived with their parents (and sometimes grandparents) in cramped accommodation, gaining the privacy for sexual relations was problematic. Having sex was often possible only through the legitimation of marriage. Conversely, getting pregnant was sometimes seen as the only way to 'catch your man' or get a flat. Despite legally available abortion in Czechoslovakia, pregnancy was cited as a prime motive for marriage. In 1988, some 60–70 per cent of couples in the younger age bracket married because the bride was pregnant. And in Hungary, newspaper reports accused women of 'accepting the role of mother to gain an apartment'.[52]

Another explanation for the survival of marriage as the norm was located in traditional attitudes which labelled remaining single as aberrant or strange behaviour. In Poland, there was still a sense that to be an 'old maid' carried a stigma. In the former Soviet Union too 'it is just splendid, and utterly normal, to be a single, divorced mother ... [but] it is still a considerable stigma to be a spinster'. And in Hungary and Czechoslovakia, while it was acceptable for women to be divorced, never to have been married was seen as deviant: 'unmarried women are seen as being in some ways "deficient"'. And failing to take one's husband's surname leads to the assumption that one is not married, 'which is viewed in a very negative light'. Similarly, in the former Soviet Union, it was thought that in filling out the endless forms of state socialist bureaucracy, 'writing *not married* in the appropriate blank is shameful and degrading ... the word *divorced* looks better than *not married* in the eyes of Soviets, women included'.[53]

Further, the continuing attraction of marriage derived from the conflicting values attached to the family under state socialism. In official discourse the family was the basic unit of society, yet at the same time the private realm was demeaned beside the prioritized public domains of industry and politics. Writing of the early state socialist period in Hungary, sociologist Zsuzsa Ferge stated that ' "work" was a politically loaded concept from the start. The most "socialist" type of work was employment in the state sector. ... Work in other sectors, be it self-employment or the household, was strongly depreciated.'[54] Hence full-time wives and mothers were denigrated as 'bourgeois relics' and discriminated against in the sense that most social welfare entitlement came via labour force participation.

At the unofficial level, however, the private sphere enjoyed an enhanced aura both as haven from the long arm of the socialist state, and site of resistance to oppressive state power. Indeed 'a partial "rehabilitation" of the right for privacy' was explicitly granted to Hungarians by Kádar from the early 1970s in return for compliance in the public sphere.[55] Slavenka Drakulić gives voice to the ambivalent feelings about, but fierce defence of, private spaces universally felt by the women she visited across East Central Europe during early 1990:

Apartments were for us mythical cult objects ... they were life prizes, and we still regard them as such. ... An apartment, however small, however crowded with people and things, kids and animals, is 'ours'. To survive, we had to divide the territory, to set a border between private and public. The state wants it all public – it can't see into our apartment, but it can tap our telephone, read our mail. We didn't give up: everything beyond the door was considered 'theirs'. They wanted to turn our apartments into public spaces, but we didn't buy that trick. What is public is of the enemy. So we hid in our pigeonholes, leaned on each other in spite of everything, and licked our wounds.[56]

Perpetuating this defence of the private, a traditional view of the family and the division of labour within it began to resurface in Hungary already during the early to mid-1980s. This arose in part due to the impact of the 'second' economy, in which approximately 60–75 per cent of Hungarian families (mostly through the men) were involved by the late 1980s. Zsuzsa Ferge commented in 1989:

The attractiveness of the duality of the 'hardworking man' and the woman staying at home and taking care of her family has increased over the last few years. ... Because of the growing difficulties in providing a livelihood, more and more men spend more and more hours on extra work on the basis of the new possibilities.[57]

The Public/Private Divide: Paradoxes and Inversions

The role of the family is ambivalent and has carried diametrically opposed values. Contradictory meanings have been attributed to it by official discourse and unofficial practice in East Central Europe both in the state socialist past and in the nationalist present. These in turn differ from Western feminist ways of regarding the family's function as pivotal in oppressing women and in mediating their relations with the wider society.

Under state socialism, many people invested the family with meaning as the source of dignity and creativity in a society characterized by alienated labour processes. There was a tendency to idealize it, construing it as a harmonious collectivity pitted against the difficulties and strife of coping with the shortcomings of daily life, in a unity of interests against the intrusive state and over-politicized public domain. Benefits dispensed by this same state in the form of affordable housing, subsidized transport, food and children's clothing, public childcare facilities, and extended maternity and childcare leave, were so utterly taken for granted that they did not figure in the calculation.

The family was also regarded as fostering solidarity in an atomized society. It united the 'us' of non-existent or embryonic civil society against 'them' in state power. This explains, maintains Polish sociologist Renata Siemieńska, why 'subjectively, women [in Poland] were not so dissatisfied' with their unequal position within the family. Sociologist Mira Marody goes one step further, asserting that despite being 'objectively disadvantaged' in both their private and their public roles, women did and do not perceive their situation as involving *socially* determined gender inequalities'. Rather, they accept their inferior status as biologically rather than socially determined, so that it is 'natural that women spend more time at home and men – for public activity'. This perception of 'natural' roles is in turn reinforced by what Marody calls the ' "authorities vs. society" dichotomy'.[58]

In Poland, Elżbieta Tarkowska and Jacek Tarkowski maintain that 'distrust of the state and other official institutions can be traced back to when Poland was partitioned by foreign powers' (for 150 years from 1795). Bożena Umińska points out that 'with the disappearance of Poland as a state, there vanished a vast sphere of life where men played a dominant role (institutions of government, administration, education etc.), and family and home became a place where all national values could – and had to – be hidden and preserved for future revival. Thus the role of women was considerably enhanced.' Indeed 'woman ruled the nineteenth-century Polish family ... the only institution of national life on the territory once belonging to Poland'.[59]

Again, the link is drawn between withdrawal into the private sphere and nationalist aspirations thwarted by foreign domination. This link also provides a continuity of antagonism to the state between the 150-year period of partition of Poland, the period of Nazi occupation, and what were perceived as Soviet-dominated state socialist institutions. After a brief interlude when politics seemed possible in the Solidarity era of 1980-81, the imposition of martial law in 1981 fostered the continuity of the 1970s 'private society'. These analyses make plain that in the Polish case at least, there is an intimate connection between the private realm as bastion against state interference, gendered role divisions defined as 'natural', and nationalism. Marody writes in 1991 that 'the general division into "Us vs. Them" swallowed all other forms of social identity and promoted a negative social solidarity. Poles found it easier to integrate and unite *against* rather than *for* something. The fundamental category around which yearning for positive unity can be satisfied will most likely be the nation.'[60]

The solidarity of 'the people' versus state institutions and 'the system' obscured gender difference while making family and friendship groups not just subjectively but indeed objectively extremely important. Informal networks functioned as sources of information, as conduits for scarce goods, and as bases for the operation, in Hungary and Poland, of the 'second' economy. Although the 'second' economy mostly fulfilled material rather than spiritual needs, its networks also offered intimacy and intense loyalty as well as the human resources needed for the grassroots educational, social and political activities so sorely lacking because forbidden in the public sphere. According to Tarkowska and Tarkowski, these 'microstructures ... constituted an alternative public sphere' which 'generated social integration'.

On the darker side of this development however, 'internal ties frequently degenerated because of the rivalry of consumers caused by economic shortages ... and competition between microstructures leads to a world divided between "family members" and "strangers"'. This description sounds almost like a prophecy of the intense xenophobia associated with current ethnic and nationalist striving in East Central Europe. Tarkowska and Tarkowski use Banfield's term 'amoral familism' to describe it. They see it as caused by the shortage economy:

> ... compounded by residues of Poland's peasant tradition and mentality which stress the limited world of friends and family. Furthermore, there is the gentry tradition based on exuberant individualism and egoism as well as Catholic traditionalism. ... The Catholic ethic is tied to a value dualism. The Catholic worldview separates the private from the public and the values appropriate to both spheres.[61]

Although Tarkowska and Tarkowski do not consider the gender aspects of this phenomenon, these microstructures were clearly mediated by the women at the centre of the family. Polish sociologist Anna Titkow makes explicit the impact of Catholic ideology even before the current transformation on perpetuating the public/private divide and ascribing women responsibility for the latter sphere:

> The Church's influence on defining women's position in Polish society, where 75 per cent of women are faithful and practising Catholics, hardly has to be proven – especially when we constantly hear how woman's domain is home and family while man's world is his job, politics, and all activities outside the family circle.[62]

In the former GDR too, women were situated, through their role as wives, mothers, sisters, friends, at the focal point of the highly valued 'niche' society, as the privatized world of family and friends was known there. The centrality of this role, together with the gender-transcending solidarity of the private sphere, seems to have over-ridden any oppression suffered by women within it. Women were prepared to maintain privacy and non-intrusion by the state in the name of individual autonomy, even if that autonomy were exclusively male.

Idealization of the private sphere as the locus of freedom and individuality echoes nineteenth-century liberal notions of privacy. John Stuart Mill postulated a sphere of action in which the state has only an indirect interest as the 'appropriate region of human liberty'. Drawing out this liberal concept of privacy as a precondition for human freedom, Steven Lukes infers that:

> in general, the idea of privacy refers to a sphere that is not of proper concern to others. It implies a negative relation between the individual and some wider 'public', including the state – a relation of non-interference with, or non-intrusion into, some range of his thoughts and/or action. This condition may be achieved either by his withdrawal or by the 'public's' forbearance. Preserving this sphere is characteristically held by liberals to be desirable, either for its own sake as an ultimate value ... or else as a means to the realization of other values, such as that of (self-development).

Lukes cites as 'essential elements in the ideas of equality and liberty' the 'four unit-ideas of individualism – respect for human dignity, autonomy, privacy and self-development'.[63]

Feminist critics of Mill have pointed out, however, that while he espoused formal equality of rights for men and women in the public sphere, Mill failed to address the unequal power relations within the family which directly resulted from the continued confinement of women to the private sphere. As Jean Bethke Elshtain writes: 'He embraces a traditional division of labour *within* the family based on males being actively employed *outside* the home.' Hence it is clear already in Mill's proposed solution that formal citizenship rights alone are meaningless. Without a fundamental restructuring of gender relations within the private sphere, women are rendered powerless to exert their citizenship rights in the public domain.[64]

Hence gender relationships are power relations deriving from the nineteenth-century signification as 'natural', of a divide which attributes to men and women respectively, activity in the public domain and the private realm. The public/private split, and women's economically dependent status, located women's oppression squarely in the private sphere. This led nineteenth-century liberal feminists to emphasize the importance of women gaining access to the public sphere of work and politics, an emphasis which was reiterated in the socialist notion of women's emancipation.

The entry of large numbers of women into the workforce in both Western and East Central Europe after the Second World War undermined the demarcation of public and private as male and female domains respectively. However, the recognition that entry into the public sphere alone did not eradicate women's subordination led modern feminists to argue that power relations between the sexes needed to be examined in both the public and the private spheres.

The problem was (and is) how to define the boundaries between what is deemed public and what is defined as private. Initially, Western feminists of the so-called second wave wanted to validate women's subjective experience within the family. Using the slogan 'the personal is political', they carried this subjective reality into the public sphere and demanded a hearing for it there. Further, they sought to break through the rigid public/private divide which confined women to a lesser realm by demonstrating that both the state and the economy depend upon the family.[65] The argument that family life is in fact state-regulated is corroborated by legislation concerning marriage and a wife's tax status, sexuality and social welfare, which denies the liberal claim to the inviolable principle of privacy within the family.[66]

Western feminists have had considerable success in demolishing the view that legal regulation stops at the garden gate. State institutions like the police and the judiciary have come to mediate and adjudicate in cases of domestic violence which previously remained confined within the jealously guarded privacy of the marital home. Rape within marriage can in Britain now be contested in court. In a contrary trend, far from 'exploding' the public/private split, state socialism in effect entrenched this divide, with the private sphere being idealized along classical nineteenth-century liberal lines as the source of gender-neutral individualism and anti-state solidarity.

Zsuzsa Ferge addressed this East-West difference in approach when she said in 1988:

> We didn't have feminism also... because feminism in the West really developed an agenda around the issues of the personal as political. But this is adverse to everything which is attractive in East European societies. The reality and the danger is that the private becomes political too often and always. Private life we had and we really would try to stick to it and to enlarge it and not let the political into the private. We have an over-politicized life so we want to defend it.[67]

There is a marked contrast at present between renewed efforts in

Western Europe to promote greater visibility of women in the public sphere of formal politics and the labour market, and the discernible trend in East Central Europe to displace women from the workforce and reinforce their primary responsibility for the private sphere. Indeed, in East Central Europe, many women are welcoming, with a sigh of relief, the opportunity to shed the double or triple burden and 'spend a few years at home with the children'. They wish to indulge a right they never had and imagine Western women enjoying, namely the right to choose whether to go out to work or to stay at home.[68]

In part the rejection of the tractor driver, crane driver, kerchief- or hard-hat wearing labourer image of woman-as-worker is expressed as a positive reclamation of femininity. The widely held view that state socialist 'emancipation' forced women to neglect their maternal role *and* made them unattractive, old before their time, contributes to this sense of women being happy to rediscover their womanhood through their caring role within the family. Miroslava Holubová of the autonomous women's group New Humanity in Prague expressed support for a re-establishment of gender-demarcated role divisions, commenting that men had been 'emasculated' by state socialism and are now blossoming, able to express their masculinity again and to take on responsibility through the entrepreneurial opportunities provided by the market. And women's caring was in her view necessary to the well-being of the family.

Influenced by their cultural heritage, many women in Poland and to an extent in Hungary see their position in the family as one of strength. Historically, in these (until the Second World War) predominantly agrarian societies, women's status was low in public life, but high in the family. Thus some women in East Central Europe consider the need for 'liberation' from this traditionally strong role to be a purely Western concept. They are celebrating their return to the hearth rather than mourning it as defeat or even temporary retreat. From this perspective, current ideology about women's primarily domestic role need not necessarily be interpreted as the state's machiavellian attempt to mask the necessity of making massive cuts in the labour force. Nor does it have to reflect the Catholic Church's restrictive view of women's role in a divinely ordained 'natural' order, nor even nationalism's traditionalist morality and population policies. On the contrary, confinement to the private realm might be re-interpreted by women themselves as offering them space for renewal, and help them in adapting to totally new situations in the aftermath of state socialism.

It should be noted, however, that women's relegation to the hearth is occurring precisely at the moment when the private sphere has lost the significance it inadvertently gained as a substitute civil society. In other words, at the very moment when women are being once again assigned to the private sphere, it is the public sphere which is being revalued, at least for men. So, while former dissident men move out of grassroots anti-political activity into the glare of public life in the structures of mainstream politics, their female counterparts fade into oblivion. There is an echo here of nineteenth-century public/private demarcation leading to a depreciation of the domestic sphere. And the ideological celebration of hearth and home may hamper recognition on women's part that a newly entrenched public/private split plus female economic dependence will ensure only male and not female autonomy.

Newly embraced traditional attitudes to the family were previewed in Czechoslovakia, Hungary, Poland and the former Soviet Union even before the transition. An international survey on attitudes to women's labour force participation in 1988 showed Hungary to be far more conservative than West European countries. The statement that 'a job is all right, but what most women really want is a home and children' was endorsed by 76 per cent of Hungarian respondents (79 per cent of men and 75 per cent of women). While the statement was accepted by 61 per cent of those asked in Austria and 57 per cent in Ireland, the Hungarian figure indicates markedly greater approval for such a traditional attitude to gender roles. The same statement was unambiguously rejected by British, Dutch and American respondents. A clear majority of Hungarian men expressed the view that women should not work outside the home when there were children under school age in the family. But perhaps most striking of all were the 19 per cent of Hungarian men who felt that even before having children, married women should not go out to work at all. In a Polish opinion poll carried out at the end of 1990, 45 per cent of working women's husbands also thought that women should not work outside their homes. This opinion was shared by a high 35 per cent of working women.[69]

Zsuzsa Béres sees women complying, out of exhaustion, with a new nationalistic variant of the patriarchal family:

> Today women are told they must bear more children or else the Hungarian nation will die out ... 'Being told' what to do by people who know better what's good for you than you yourself is what paternalistic socialism was all about. To a majority of Hungary's women today, 'being told' seems to hold out promise of the long-coveted dream: to be provided for forever by men, in the haven of the Holy Family. No more strain, no more sense of guilt.[70]

This ideal model based on the 'family wage' – supported in rhetoric at least by politicians in several East Central European countries – has an air of total unreality about it. Two, and in Poland and Hungary often three, incomes were necessary to maintain the family in the past. The removal of subsidies, and growing inflation make this more, rather than less, true in the present.

In Hungary, young urban families with children are disproportionately represented amongst those falling beneath the poverty line. In these circumstances, as Czech sociologist Hana Navarová notes, the life of young families 'can be characterized as one of constant improvization'. If the past shortage economy made 'institutionally unsecured areas of material needs ... the family's responsibility', today too economic transformation lands the family with problems. Four-fifths of young families in Czechoslovakia, especially those with one child under three, have difficulty meeting their basic material needs, unless they have access to parental help. In this process, uncertainty and ever-increasing 'difficulties with securing the everyday life of the family' have reinforced the traditional family model based on the 'principle of patriarchy'.[71]

As in Western Europe, social policy based on the two-parent family is increasingly obfuscating the reality. The Western-documented phenomenon of the feminization of poverty appears to be taking hold in the societies of Eastern and Central Europe, with lone mothers among the first to become impoverished. Heike Reggentin is the 36-year-old mother of a five-year-old son and a fourteen-year-old daughter in Neustrelitz in the former GDR. When the city administration's central kitchens closed in March 1990, she became unemployed, living for almost two years on a monthly income of DM 690 unemployment assistance plus DM 207 maintenance for the children. In January 1992 she accepted a job for even less, DM 746 take-home pay, cleaning for six hours a day, simply to avoid sitting around at home all day. For her it is a struggle to have 50 pfennig to spare for her son each evening when the ice-cream man comes by her home. 'Bring back the Wall? Sometimes you say that.'[72]

Older women are also particularly prone to poverty, since under state socialism they retired five years earlier than men but have approximately seven years' longer life expectancy. Because of their lower wages, they also form a disproportionate percentage of those on the minimum pension, and perhaps in part because of their duties as grandmothers, they are less likely than men to become re-employed.[73]

While female poverty and domestic violence are on the increase, it seems paradoxically that divorce and the birthrate are both set to decrease in the face of material insecurity and women's widespread loss of independent earning power. Reports from the former GDR and from Moscow speak of women now refraining from divorce proceedings and also of an 'unofficial birthstrike'.[74]

The family's role is at one and the same time being devalued in relation to the public sphere, and enhanced in the search for identity and meaning following the collapse of state socialism. Simultaneously this process is focusing, in its rejection of state socialist notions of egalitarianism and social justice, on individualist enterprise in the market, and autonomy and creativity within the family.

These processes too are marked by contradictions. On the one hand, the search for identity posits the family as the individual unit within the wider ethnic group. Ironically, given the individualism that lies at the heart of liberal views of the family, this is accompanied by an explicit rejection on the part of the Polish Catholic Church of individualism as naked self-interest or greed, in the name of support for the notion of ethnic or national solidarity.

On his 1991 visit to Poland, the Pope deplored individualism as unsuitable for Poland, contrasting the strong traditional values of community and family with the false collectivism of state socialism. The Ministers for Health and Justice, both members of the conservative Christian National Association, were quoted in *Gazeta Wyborcza* on 19 June 1991 as praising the Pope's defence of unborn life and the unity of the family against 'individualistic' tendencies to put private happiness above the collective good. They saw the Pope's defence of private property and entrepreneurial initiative as bound up with human dignity and the consolidation of the family as well as with economic efficiency. Such a line of argumentation treats women and the family as co-terminous. Some Polish feminists have reacted by stressing the value of individualism. They insist that women should have the right to develop their potential as opposed to being subordinated to the family, as envisaged by this 'clerical collectivist authoritarianism'.[75] Neo-liberal market ideology is as adept as was nineteenth-century liberal theory at reconciling individualism with a 'natural' gender-based division of labour.

Furthermore, there is an uncanny resemblance between Tönnies's notion of the household and women's role within it as constituent elements of the *Gemeinschaft* – a community based on 'natural' social relations of kinship and neighbourhood of which 'the outstanding example' is the rural village community – and current visions of women's role in the private sphere, situated within an idealized rural past.[76] Current East Central European desires to annihilate the immediate past and escape from society's problems in the transformation process into the myth of traditional community are equivalent to an abandonment of modern society itself, of the real in favour of the romantic.

The parallels between current discourse on women's domestic mission and the public/private divide as exemplified in Tönnies's ideas of *Gemeinschaft* and *Gesellschaft*, make it clear that new definitions of national identity which rest on the counterposing of private and public, natural and cultural, female and male, in practice weaken women's citizenship rights within the public sphere. The attacks on reproductive rights discussed in the next chapter seem to exemplify this. Mounted in the interests of raising the nation's birthrate, they are ostensibly part and parcel of just such a quest to establish new national moral and ethical norms. Moreover, such moves to abrogate women's right to a termination of pregnancy are being made by male-dominated, albeit democratically elected, governments.

Notes

1. Olga Nikolaevitch, the first-person narrator, research assistant and harassed mother in Natalya Baranskaya, *A Week Like Any Other*, trans. Pieta Monks, Virago Press, London, 1989, pp. 5–8, 49.

2. Eva Hauserová, 'The Cult of Motherhood', in: *Prague Post*, 22–30 March 1992, and reprinted in: *Everywoman*, July/August 1991, pp. 20–21.

3. Olga Lipovskaya, 'New Women's Organizations', in: Mary Buckley, ed., *Perestroika and Soviet Women*, Cambridge University Press, Cambridge, 1992, p. 72.

4. See for example Elemér Hankiss who, in discussing Hungary, describes 'atomization as a basic feature of early socialist (Stalinist, totalitarian) societies' which 'has been analysed by many in detail, beginning with Hannah Arendt's study of totalitarianism', in: Elemér Hankiss, *East European Alternatives*, Clarendon Press, Oxford, 1990, p. 33.

5. Hungarian sociologist Júlia Szalai writes: 'there is a strong and broad opposition in our countries to everything that has the slightest flavour of "statism". It is a long process to get rid of the idea and practice of the totalitarian state and to define a state that is "ours", that is created and controlled by the democratic processes of the civil society,' in: Bob Deacon and Júlia Szalai, eds, *Social Policy in the New Eastern Europe: What Future for Socialist Welfare?*, Avebury, Aldershot, 1990, pp. 34–35.

6. 'Entrance into the socialist labour force was not merely a financial issue, but a matter of social membership as well. Eligibility rights based on citizenship were substituted by ones based on having regular and continuous employment, now the only way of gaining access to basic services like child care, medical care, family allowances, sick benefits, or pensions.' Júlia Szalai, 'Some Aspects of the Changing Situation of Women in Hungary', in: *Signs*, vol. 17, no. 1, autumn 1991, p. 153.

7. For a discussion of the shift from private to public patriarchy, and women's dependence on the welfare state, see Helga Maria Hernes, 'Women and the Welfare State: The Transition from Private to Public Dependence', and Anette Borchorst and Birte Siim, 'Women and the Advanced Welfare State – A New Kind of Patriarchal

Power?' both in: Anne Showstack Sassoon, ed., *Women and the State: The Shifting Boundaries of Public and Private*, Century Hutchinson, London, 1987.

8. Crescy Cannan, 'Active and Inactive Citizens in Europe's Welfare States: The Legacy and Contribution of Beveridge', in: John Jacobs and Peter Squires, eds, *Beveridge 1942–1992*, Avebury, Aldershot, 1992. See also Stephan Leibfried and Ilona Ostner, 'The Particularism of West German Welfare Capitalism: The Case of Women's Social Security', in: Michael Adler et al., eds, *The Sociology of Social Security*, Edinburgh U.P., Edinburgh, 1991, pp. 175–76; and Gösta Esping-Andersen, *The Three Worlds of Welfare Capitalism*, Polity Press, Cambridge, 1990.

9. Prue Chamberlayne, 'Focus on *Volkssolidarität* (VS)', in: *Community Development Journal*, vol. 27, no. 2, April 1992, p. 154, in the second case citing Mary Langan and Ilona Ostner, 'Gender and Welfare: Towards a Comparative Framework', in: G. Room, ed., *European Developments in Social Policy*, SAUS, Bristol, 1991.

10. Mária Adamik, 'Hungary: A Loss of Rights?', in: *Shifting Territories: Feminism in Europe*, special issue no. 39 of *Feminist Review*, winter 1991, p. 170.

11. Szalai, 'Some Aspects', 1991.

12. Wendy Bracewell, 'Problems of Gender and Nationalism', ms. 1992.

13. Ferdinand Tönnies, *Community and Association*, (English translation of *Gemeinschaft und Gesellschaft* by Charles Loomis), Routledge and Kegan Paul, London, 1955, reprinted 1974, pp. 45–46. I am indebted to Katherine O'Donovan's book *Sexual Divisions in Law* for alerting me to the relevance of Tönnies's work in connection with the public/private divide. She should not, however, be held in any way responsible for the way I have applied Tönnies's ideas to current processes of social transformation in East Central Europe.

14. Tönnies, ibid., pp. 174–75, 186.

15. Obviously this was more true of professional women than others. Many women worked in unfulfilling jobs for poor wages, motivated primarily by the necessity of a second income to maintain the family.

16. Zsuzsa Béres, 'A Thousand Words on Hungarian Women', published in: *Budapest Week*, March 1991 and reprinted in: *Trouble and Strife*, issue 23, 1991.

17. This leave comprised five weeks annually in the former GDR as compared with five days in West Germany, until the child's eighth birthday only. (See Eva Kolinsky, *Women in West Germany*, Berg, Oxford, 1989, p. 71; Sabine Berghahn and Andrea Fritzsche, *Frauenrecht in Ost und West Deutschland (Law Relating to Women in East and West Germany)*, Basisdruck Verlag, Berlin, 1991, p. 101.) As of 1990, this sick leave could be taken by either the father or the mother in Czechoslovakia and the then Soviet Union, and comprised seven working days and seven calendar days respectively for every illness of a child under 10 and under 14 respectively. In Poland, mothers of young children were entitled to 30 working days annually. (Source: Alena Kroupová, 'Women, Employment and Earnings in Central and East European Countries', Paper prepared for Tripartite Symposium on Equality of Opportunity and Treatment for Men and Women in Employment in Industrialized Countries, Prague, May 1990.) For the change in the Polish regulations, see Jolanta Plakwicz, 'Between Church and State: Polish Women's Experience', in: Chris Corrin, ed., *Superwomen and the Double Burden: Women's Experience of Change in Central and Eastern Europe and the Former Soviet Union*, Scarlet Press, London, 1992, p. 83.

18. Sources: for the provisions governing such leave in Hungary, which in recent years was available to mothers *or* fathers, see Kroupová, ibid.; for the time spent absent from work, see Mária Adamik, 'Hungary – Supporting Parenting and Child Rearing: Policy Innovation in Eastern Europe', in: Sheila Kamerman and Alfred J. Kahn, eds, *Child Care, Parental Leave, and the Under Threes: Policy Innovation in Europe*, Auburn House, New York and London, 1991, pp. 115–45.

19. Gwyn E. Edwards, *GDR Society and Institutions*, Macmillan, London, 1985, p. 47.

20. Report of the Central Committee of the SED to the Ninth Party Congress in 1976.

21. Barbara Einhorn, 'Socialist Emancipation: The Women's Movement in the GDR', in: Sonia Kruks, Rayna Rapp, Marilyn B. Young, eds, *Promissory Notes: Women in the*

Transition to Socialism, Monthly Review Press, New York, 1989, pp. 288–90, 303, notes 13, 19; Edwards, *GDR Society*, 1985, p. 39.

22. Edwards, ibid., pp. 54–56.

23. For an analysis of children's primers, see Barbara Einhorn, 'Emancipated Women or Hardworking Mothers? Women in the Former GDR', in: Corrin, ed., *Superwomen and the Double Burden*, 1992, pp. 142–43.

24. It is worthy of note that GDR public discourse did not adopt the linguistic suffix introduced to West German discourse by the Greens and feminists, which makes occupational denotations encompass both sexes.

25. One of the targets of anti-militarist campaigning by the GDR Frauen für den Frieden (Women for Peace) in the early 1980s was the glorification of the 'peace-keeping' role of the army evident in these texts. Both books praise the 'workers' of the National People's Army (Nationale Volksarmee – NVA), and the first school reader encourages classes to 'adopt' and correspond with a member of the army.

26. Sources: (for Hungary) Katalin Koncz, 'Results and Tensions of Female Employment in Hungary', mimeo, 1987; (for Poland) Renata Siemieńska, 'Women's Issues in the Transitional Period in Poland', mimeo, 1991; (for the former GDR) Gunnar Winkler, ed., *Sozialreport 90*, Verlag die Wirtschaft, Berlin, 1990, pp. 269–73.

27. For figures on time spent on domestic chores, see Table A2 in the Appendix. On the relatively little time spent on childcare, Hungarian women spent an average of 26 minutes in 1976–77 compared with 12 minutes for men of the total 4h. 16m. and 1h. 04m. respectively; or 1h. 2m. by married women with two children plus 5h. 13m. per day on household tasks (Barnabás Barta, András Klinger, Károly Miltényi and György Vukorich, 'Female Labour Force Participation and Fertility in Hungary', in: Valentina Bodrova and Richard Anker, eds, *Working Women in Socialist Countries*, ILO, Geneva, 1985, tables 29, 30, pp. 52–53). In Poland in 1984, married women with children spent 5h. 55m. per day on household chores compared with 1h. 39m. for men (figures supplied by Renata Siemieńska, from Analysis of Time Budget of Polish Population, mimeo, 1987, p. 60).

28. Valentina Bodrova and Richard Anker, *Working Women in Socialist Countries: The Fertility Connection*, 1985, tables 4, 53, 54, pp. 9, 85.

29. These findings for the former GDR are taken from Hildegard Maria Nickel, 'Ein perfektes Drehbuch: Geschlechtertrennung durch Arbeit und Sozialisation', (A Perfect Screenplay: Gender Division by Work and Socialization) in: Gislinde Schwarz and Christine Zenner, eds, *Wir wollen mehr als ein 'Vaterland'* (We Want More than a 'Fatherland'), Rowohlt Taschenbuch Verlag, Hamburg, 1990, pp. 80–81.

30. Kroupová, 'Women, Employment and Earnings', 1990. For figures on the leisure time available to men and women, see Table A2 in the Appendix. See also Susan Poiznèr, 'The Sorrows of Mother Russia', in the *Guardian*, 30 June 1992. She cites a figure of 31.7 hours per week spent by women on childcare and household chores. Ellen Hume, 'Perestroika Leaves Women in the Political Cold', in the *Guardian*, 22 December 1990, spoke of Soviet women waiting in queues 2½ hours per day for food and other staples.

31. Gwyn Edwards cites evidence that in the former GDR, 'half of the mothers are socially active' (Edwards, *GDR Society*, 1985, p. 32).

32. See Gislinde Schwarz and Christine Zenner, 'Ursprünglich war da mal eine Frau', ('In the Beginning There was a Woman') in: Schwarz and Zenner, eds, *Wir wollen mehr als ein 'Vaterland'*, 1990, p. 12.

33. Béres, 'A Thousand Words', 1991.

34. A. Alvarez, 'Terror: A Muse without Shelf Life', in: the *Guardian*, 21.11.92.

35. Baranskaya, *A Week Like Any Other*, 1989, pp. 1–2, 23.

36. Vera Golubeva from Archangelsk in Russia describes everyday life for women in the northern provinces in: Tatyana Mamonova, ed., *Women and Russia: Feminist Writings from the Soviet Union*, Blackwell, Oxford, 1984, p. 27.

37. Irmtraud Morgner's 'Das Seil' ('The Tightrope') is an integral part of her novel *Leben und Abenteuer der Trobadora Beatriz nach Zeugnissen ihrer Spielfrau Laura* (*The Life and*

Adventures of the Female Troubadour Beatriz, According to the Testimony of Her Accompanist Laura), Aufbau Verlag, Berlin and Weimar, 1974. The story was published in abridged form in English as 'The Rope', transl. Karin R. Achberger, in: Edith H. Altbach et al., eds, *German Feminism: Readings in Politics and Literature*, State University of New York Press, Albany, 1984, pp. 215–19.

38. Baranskaya, *A Week Like Any Other*, 1989, p. 53.

39. In Czechoslovakia, there were 32 divorces for every 100 marriages (Source: Hana Navarová, 'The Lives of Young Families in Czechoslovakia', English version as mimeo, 1990, p. 3). One in three marriages failed in the Soviet Union. In the former GDR, 38% of all marriages ended in divorce (Source: Gunnar Winkler, ed., *Frauenreport 90*, Verlag Die Wirtschaft, Berlin, 1990, pp. 109, 111). In Hungary there were 44 divorces for every 100 marriages (Source: Chris Corrin, 'Magyar Women's Lives: Complexities and Contradictions', in: Corrin, ed., *Superwomen and the Double Burden*, 1992, p. 49).

40. On the link between the relatively low rate of divorce and Catholic mores, see Plakwicz, 'Between Church and State', in: Corrin, ibid.

41. In Hungary, for example, the divorce rate soared, from 11.4 per 100 marriages in 1948 to 44 per 100 in 1988. In Czechoslovakia too the rate of divorces per 100 marriages grew from 9.8 in 1950 to 14.4 in 1960, 19.7 in 1970, 28.7 in 1980, and 32 in 1985. Sources: Corrin, ibid.; Navarová, 'The Lives of Young Families', 1990.

42. GDR statistics in: Winkler, ed., *Frauenreport 90*, 1990, pp. 29, 103. For the Perm survey, see Hilary Pilkington, 'Behind the Mask of Soviet Unity: Realities of Women's Lives', in: Corrin, ed., *Superwomen and the Double Burden*, 1992, pp. 213–14.

43. In 1988 only around 40% of young men and women in the GDR felt sure that they would marry. This represented a marked drop from the 75% who expressed this certainty about marriage in 1982 (Winkler, ed., *Sozialreport 90*, pp. 35, 271, 276). In Czechoslovakia, marriage was the 'main aim of 60–70% of young women and about 40% of young men' interviewed in 1988 (Navarová, 'The Lives of Young Families', 1990).

44. The average age upon marriage in Czechoslovakia was 21.5 for women, and 24 for men (Navarová, ibid., 1990). In the former GDR it rose during the 1980s from 21.3 to 22.7 for women and from 23.4 to 24.8 for men (Winkler, ibid., p. 32).

45. Slavenka Drakulić, *How We Survived Communism and Even Laughed* (1987), Hutchinson, London, 1992, p. 107.

46. An old joke which links supply-side shortages of consumer durables with the power of tradesmen in state socialism goes as follows: A man goes to the garage and says 'I'd like to order a new Skoda (or Lada, or Trabant, or Moskvitch)'. 'A brand new Skoda?' 'Yes, a brand new one.' 'Ah yes,' is the reply, 'well, that will take a very long time.' 'How long?' enquires the customer. 'Twenty-five years, I'm afraid.' 'Twenty-five years *exactly*?' the customer presses. 'Yes, precisely twenty-five years,' comes back the answer. 'Morning or afternoon?' he pursues the question further. 'Why do you ask?' 'Because I've got the plumber coming in the morning.' Bearing in mind that jokes thrive on exaggeration, this one expresses an objective as well as a subjective reality of life under state socialism.

47. Charlotte Worgitzky, 'Hänsel und Gretel: Kein Märchen' ('Hansel and Gretel: Not a Fairy Tale'), in: Worgitzky, *Vieräugig oder blind (With Two Pairs of Eyes or Blind)*, Buchverlag Der Morgen, Berlin, 1978, pp. 133–47 [translations mine, BE].

48. Angela Stachowa, 'Und der steinerne Elefant' ('And the Stone Elephant'), in: Stachowa, *Stunde zwischen Hund und Katz (Twilight Hour)*, Mitteldeutscher Verlag, Halle (Saale), 1976, pp. 189–92 [translations mine, BE].

49. Ekaterina Alexandrova's testimony, 'Why Soviet Women Want to Get Married' is in: Mamonova, *Women and Russia*, 1984, pp. 31–33.

50. Tatyana was quoted by Francine Du Plessix Gray, *Soviet Women Walking the Tightrope*, Virago, London, 1991, pp. 59–60. The Azerbaijan survey is cited by Pilkington, 'Behind the Mask of Soviet Unity', in: Corrin, ed., *Superwomen and the Double Burden*, 1992, p. 213.

51. Hungarian data cited by Corrin, 'Magyar Women's Lives', in: Corrin, ed.,

Superwomen and the Double Burden, 1992, p. 50. On the importance of housing in Poland, see also the article in the *Guardian*, 29.9.92.

52. (On the former Soviet Union) Du Plessix Gray, *Soviet Women Walking the Tightrope*, 1991, p. 54; (on Czechoslovakia) Hana Navarová, 'The Lives of Young Families', 1990; and 'Woman and Family, Woman in the Family', in: Marie Čermáková, Irena Hradecká, Hana Navarová, *K postaveni žen v československé společnosti* (*The Situation of Women in Czechoslovak Society*), publication of the Institute of Sociology of the Czechoslovak Academy of Sciences, Prague, 1991; (on Hungary) Corrin, ibid., 1992, p. 50.

53. (For Poland) Ewa Gontarczyk-Wesoła, interview with Barbara Einhorn, Poznań, April 1990; (for Czechoslovakia) Navarová, 'Lives of Young Families', 1990; (for Hungary) Eminent philosopher and academician Éva Ancsel, Interview with Barbara Einhorn, Budapest, May 1990; and Corrin, ibid., 1992, p. 52; (for the Soviet Union) Du Plessix Gray, *Soviet Women Walking the Tightrope*, 1991, p. 54; and Ekaterina Alexandrova, 'Why Soviet Women Want to Get Married', 1984, p. 39.

54. Zsuzsa Ferge, 'Unemployment in Hungary: The Need for a New Ideology', in: Bob Deacon, ed., *Social Policy, Social Justice and Citizenship in Eastern Europe*, Avebury, Aldershot, 1992, pp. 158–59.

55. For an elaboration of this 'innovation of Kádarism', see Júlia Szalai, 'Social Participation in Hungary in the Context of Restructuring and Liberalization', in: Deacon, ed., ibid., 1992, pp. 42ff.

56. Drakulić, *How We Survived Communism and Even Laughed*, 1992, pp. 91–92.

57. Zsuzsa Ferge is quoted by Chris Corrin, 'The Situation of Women in Hungarian Society', in: Bob Deacon and Júlia Szalai, eds, *Social Policy in the New Eastern Europe: What Future for Socialist Welfare?*, 1990, p. 189. For an analysis of the 'second' economy, its main spheres of activity, its contribution to household incomes and estimated participation rates, see Szalai, 'Social Participation in Hungary', in: Deacon, ed., *Social Policy, Social Justice and Citizenship in Eastern Europe*, 1992, pp. 42–45.

58. Renata Siemieńska, Interview with Barbara Einhorn, Warsaw, 31.3.90; Mira Marody, 'Why I Am Not a Feminist', ms. 1992; and Marody, 'Perception of Politics in Polish Society', in: *Social Research*, vol. 57, no. 2, summer 1990, p. 268.

59. Elżbieta Tarkowska and Jacek Tarkowski, 'Social Disintegration in Poland: Civil Society or Amoral Familism?', in: *Telos*, no. 89, fall 1991, pp. 103–109; Bożena Umińska, 'The Portrayal of Women in Polish Literature', ms., 1991.

60. Mira Marody, 'On Polish Political Attitudes', in: *Telos*, no. 89, fall 1991, pp. 112–13.

61. Tarkowska and Tarkowski, 'Social Disintegration in Poland: Civil Society or Amoral Familism?', 1991.

62. Anna Titkow, cited by Plakwicz, 'Between Church and State', 1992, p. 81.

63. Steven Lukes, *On Individualism*, Blackwell, Oxford, 1973, pp. 63, 66, 123. I am indebted to Katherine O'Donovan's book *Sexual Divisions in Law* for alerting me to the relevance of the ideas of John Stuart Mill and Steven Lukes on privacy as a precondition for individual freedom. Obviously she cannot be held responsible for what I have made of these ideas in this context.

64. Jean Bethke Elshtain, *Public Man, Private Woman: Women in Social and Political Thought*, Princeton U.P., Princeton, and Martin Robertson, Oxford, 1981, pp. 135–45.

65. Katherine O'Donovan points out that 'the ideology of equality which nineteenth-century women relied on in their struggle against discriminatory laws and practices which denied them access to education and employment was formal equality.... The interaction between private and public and the consequent restraints on freedom were ignored. Hidden behind the rhetoric of equality were issues of whether to recognize in the public sphere needs which arise out of the private. This continues today. The conflict reformers face between the values of individualism in the market-place and community in the family has been managed hitherto through reliance on the language of freedom of contract and formal equality'. Feminist scholars have also sought to explode the dichotomy behind the

liberal concept of private and public defined as 'areas of activity and behaviour unregulated or regulated by law' (ibid., pp. 3, 160).

66. For an elaboration of a range of feminist critiques of the public/private divide, see Carol Pateman, *The Disorder of Women*, Polity, London, 1989, pp. 118–141.

67. Zsuzsa Ferge, in: Deacon and Szalai, eds, *Social Policy in the New Eastern Europe*, 1990, p. 43.

68. It is difficult for women in the former state socialist countries to realize that most Western women can no more afford this choice than they could – or can. Similarly, in relation to paid work they tend, understandably after years of juggling full-time work and family, to idealize the choice of working part-time or at home, little knowing that these forms of work are often poorly paid, exploitative and lacking in social protection in the West.

69. The survey was carried out in seven countries, of which Hungary was the only state socialist country, with a representative sample of 1700. It was analysed by Olga Tóth, in 'Conservative Gender Roles and Women's Work', her paper presented at the Conference of the Hungarian Sociological Association, Budapest, June 1991. Opposition to women working outside the home when there were children under school age in the family was expressed by 58% of Hungarian men. The percentage of men in other countries who felt that married women should not go out to work at all ranged from 3% in Britain and the Netherlands to 11% in Italy.

The Polish opinion poll is reported by Małgorzata Tarasiewicz, 'Women in Poland: Choices to be Made', in: *Shifting Territories*, 1991, p. 184. In the former Soviet Union too, a 1990 opinion poll registered a 'tendency … to strengthen the ideology of women's "natural destination"' when 35.8% of those polled supported the idea that 'it is time to make women return home to the family'. This result also showed a discrepancy between men and women, with only 30.8% of female, but 41.8% of male respondents endorsing this view. The poll was analysed by Valentina V. Bodrova, 'Women, Work, Family in the Mirror of Public Opinion', in: Valentine Moghadam, ed., *Democratic Reform and the Position of Women in Transitional Economies*, OUP Clarendon Series, Oxford, 1993.

70. Béres, 'A Thousand Words', 1991.

71. Hana Navarová, 'The Lives of Young Families', 1990; and 'Woman and Family, Woman in the Family', in: *K postavení žen v československé společnosti*, 1991.

72. Heike Reggentin was quoted in *Der Spiegel*, no. 24, 1992, p. 101.

73. Jiřina Siklová, 'Women and Ageing Under Real Socialism', in Deacon and Szalai, *Social Policy in the New Eastern Europe*, 1990, pp. 192–200.

74. The remark about an unofficial birthstrike was made by Christiane Schindler, spokesperson for the Independent Women's Association (UFV) in the former GDR. See the *Guardian*, 1 May 1992, on empty Moscow labour wards; and the *Guardian*, 4 February 1992, on the decreasing German birthrate and the need to import labour massively by the end of the century, ironic postscript to the German hostility to refugees and asylum seekers at present.

75. Nina Gladziuk, interview with Barbara Einhorn, Warsaw, 19.6.91.

76. In the introduction to his translation of Ferdinand Tönnies, *Community and Association (Gemeinschaft und Gesellschaft)* p. xii, Charles P. Loomis points out that although these twin concepts denote 'ideal types', they can be used to compare 'various groups in a given period, or in different periods of history'.

3

Self-determination under Threat:
The State and Reproductive Rights

> As all this [the threat to abortion rights in Poland] has progressed, women
> activists in Poland have learned a lot about how the authorities see us. We
> learned that the government's decision to abolish rights to reproductive
> freedom is justified when it is in the 'national interest', such as when the
> population is declining. We learned that just as women were once seen
> solely as producers, they can now be seen solely as reproducers. We
> learned that ... women ... are to be forced to bear unwanted children.
>
> Jolanta Plakwicz, Polish Feminist Association[1]

The most visible examples of current attacks on women's rights in many
former state socialist countries are the attempts to repeal existing
legislation providing access to abortion. Yet newly democratic
politicians of all shades of opinion seem united in their conviction that
women's issues are of secondary importance in the face of pressing
problems of democratization and economic reform. So why the
prominence accorded abortion? This apparent paradox begs closer
examination. What are the issues at stake here, and for whom? Are they
primarily political, ethical, socio-economic, or demographic? Is abortion
a question of women's reproductive freedom, or is it interpreted as
having a broader social or even national significance?

Reproductive rights have always been on the borderline between the
private and the public domains, encompassing the dual, and sometimes
seemingly incompatible, issues of 'a woman's right to choose' and the
state's responsibility to intervene on behalf of the health and well-being
of its members. Questions of a woman's right to self-determination
through control of her own body, and family planning, here converge
with broader issues of legality, morality and social policy, which in turn
are linked to the role of the state in regulating (in order to safeguard) its

citizens' lives. In this sense, reproductive rights provide a unique illustration of the dilemmas between the rights and responsibilities of the individual as opposed to those of the collective.

The abortion question is no more than the most prominent and most hotly debated of a whole cluster of issues involved in reproductive rights for women. These include the right to safe and affordable birth control, to sex education, to ante-natal and post-natal care, and to choice about sexuality. Such rights in turn presuppose a set of state policies to underwrite them. Reproductive choice requires equal pay legislation, paid maternity leave with one's job held open for the duration, high quality public childcare, and an environment which does not threaten fertility.

It is clear, therefore, that reproductive freedom implies not only the possibility of exercising individual choice, but also the existence of social relations and a social infrastructure that together facilitate and guarantee such choice.

In the past, socialist states did take responsibility for public provision of reproductive facilities. They did this, not so much in the name of women's reproductive freedom, but rather in order to enable women to maximize their contribution to the collective as working mothers. This was reflected in official policy with regard to reproductive rights (encompassing contraception, maternity benefits and childcare as well as access to abortion) which fluctuated in response to labour force requirements and demographic trends. These fluctuations meant that the infrastructure supporting reproductive choice was created patchily and to varying degrees both between state socialist countries and over time within individual countries.[2] Sociologist Jutta Gysi argues that in the GDR, the last act showing genuine official commitment to equality was the promulgation of the Abortion Law in 1972. Thereafter, pro-natalist policies and the juridical and party political emphasis on helping women 'master' their dual role denigrated the 'woman question' to no more than an element of state population policies.[3]

The general commitment to social provision facilitating women's labour market participation was made in response to socially set goals, and not as an outcome of women's demands. Nor did it prioritize individual women's right to choose. There was a deep distrust of claims based on the individual person, which were thought to smack of ideologically suspect 'individualism'. The necessity for fundamental change in the gendered division of labour in both public and private spheres – in the structures of employment (to eliminate occupational segregation), the administration of the state (to increase women's active

75

rather than formal representation), and in the household (through shared parenting) – in order to equalize women's opportunities in each, was scarcely addressed, perhaps not even recognized.

In a Western socialist feminist discussion of reproductive rights, Rosalind Petchesky argues that there are dangers inherent in radical feminist assertions of women's right to exclusive control over reproduction. Presented as an absolute claim, such an assertion is ahistorical in not acknowledging the specificity of social relations and gender divisions within which the claim is made. Hence it runs the risk of being used against women in allotting them sole responsibility for reproduction as their 'natural', biologically given, function. On the positive side of the argument, she stresses the historically radical connotation of liberal notions about the right to privacy. In that context, control over one's own body, the right to 'bodily self-determination', is an integral part of personal autonomy or 'individual self-determination', the denial of which abrogates or seriously impairs an individual's 'ability to function as a fully responsible human being'. While not an absolute claim, therefore, 'a woman's right to choose' forms the inviolable core of any policy for reproductive freedom. It is neither synonymous with, nor should it be reducible to, individual women bearing the entire responsibility for children they bring into the world, nor to their being personally stigmatized, or even criminalized, for a decision not to go through with a pregnancy.

Beyond the argument for 'a woman's right to choose', and inevitably in tension with it, even in a hypothetical ideal society, Petchesky maintains, are society's claims to involvement in the health of its citizens, as well as socialist notions of society's responsibilities in the area of reproduction. For the implementation of reproductive freedom, society must be constructed in a way which is children-friendly. This would involve public provision of those socio-economic conditions listed above. Access to decent health care for all is, claims Petchesky, a moral question, and, one might add, clearly also a political one. Furthermore, there need to be fundamental changes in cultural practice so that childcare is seen as an issue involving both genders and necessitating a high level of social commitment and structural change.[4]

What is happening now in the former state socialist countries is a contradictory process. That there is far greater scope for individual moral decisions is clearly a gain. Yet the imposition of ethical imperatives specified by institutionalized religion appears to deny the very area of individual responsibility for one's own fate that was so absent during the state socialist era. Such moral dictates themselves co-exist with economic arguments and political theories which stress the importance of devolving responsibility on to the individual. In the context of health care more generally and reproductive rights in particular, it seems that the citizens' right to expect certain levels of state provision is in question.

It also appears that there is a link between nationalist desires to raise the birthrate and limitations on legal abortion. During the 1930s and the Second World War, Stalin played on nationalism, on the need to strengthen and defend Mother Russia against her attackers, as well as on the need to build socialism. The 1936 ban on abortion in the Soviet Union would seem to be an example of the subordination of women's reproductive rights to nationalist concerns, reducing women to their breeding function in order to ensure, as suggested more recently in pronouncements by some Serbian leaders during the fighting in former Yugoslavia, that there is a continuing supply of cannon fodder.[5]

Whatever the value ascribed to individual as opposed to collective interests, current debates in East Central Europe clearly entail consequences for women's reproductive rights. The explanation for the past frequency of abortion as a means of contraception, especially in Poland and the Soviet Union, lay in the lack of sex education and the relative unavailability or unreliability of other birth control means. Both sex education and available (and affordable) contraceptives are necessary for the medical and social health of the nation. However, in the Polish case at least, the campaign to criminalize abortion has been accompanied by campaigns to outlaw sex education and to ban contraception. In such a context, the limits on reproductive choice represent a threat to women's citizenship rights. This chapter will cover a range of reproductive rights: health care, sexuality, birth control, and abortion. The particular ferocity of current campaigns around abortion rights in Germany and Poland makes it appropriate to focus in greater detail on those two countries.

Women's Health

The level and quality of health care provision is clearly a major factor in determining the well-being and quality of life enjoyed by the members of any society. Reproductive facilities comprising sex education, access to birth control means, maternity benefits and childcare, are an integral part of any health care system. Rosalind Petchesky argues that only a socialist state is likely to accept responsibility for the provision of public, safe, free reproductive services.[6] Despite overt commitment to this goal, however, the state socialist societies of East Central Europe varied enormously in their delivery of these services.

In the former GDR, a network of polyclinics guaranteed the entire population access to free medical care, including regular gynaecological check-ups and ante- and post-natal care for women. This network is now being dissolved in favour of private medical practices. The present Polish government also favours privatization, which would make health care accessible only to the rich. As of 1992, the average monthly wage in Poland was less than two million złoty (around £80), yet a house call from a private doctor cost the equivalent of more than £7, a tooth-filling up to £23, and a private abortion as much as £192.[7] There are plans to privatize medical services in several other former state socialist countries. This is couched in terms of consumer choice, an advantage not available to citizens of state socialism, unless they belonged to the *nomenklatura* or were prepared to pay bribes in the hope of getting better treatment.[8] In practice, such consumer choice may well mean a deterioration in service, especially for women in rural areas, or urban women who are unable to pay.

Low maternal and infant mortality rates were a tribute to the quality of East German obstetrical care, which has gained West German recognition since German unification.[9] Yet women felt that the quality of reproductive care was sometimes lacking in terms of personal attention. There was little after-care or counselling, especially in relation to abortion or post-natal care. Nevertheless, standards were strikingly higher than in the Soviet Union, where many analysts have pointed to the way initially high levels of medical care were run down during the Brezhnev era with its prioritization of heavy industry, the military and space technology.[10] As a result, Tatyana Mamonova wrote in 1979 in *Women and Russia*, the first feminist samizdat journal, of the 'traumatic' environment in maternity hospitals where 'seven to ten women writhe on their beds and scream with pain', so that 'the experience [of childbirth] was a nightmare'. Mamonova implies a direct connection between the priority accorded defence spending and the 'degrading conditions' in abortion clinics and maternity hospitals when she writes: 'We're always talking about military defence but before defending anyone we've got to assure the vitality of society in and of itself. That means that woman, the giver of life, should come first, and *then* her defenders – not the other way round!'[11]

Despite disparities between countries and over time, health care for women seems to have produced some tangible benefits. While women may have been prematurely aged by their double burden or professionally disadvantaged by their retirement age being set five years lower than men, their life expectancy was on average more than seven years higher than that of men. Women worked full-time, but men in Poland and especially in Hungary often did two or three jobs, one in the 'official' state sector, and the other(s) in the unofficial 'second' economy, since two salaries were insufficient to maintain a family. In Hungary, the resulting gender gap in life expectancy gained a bitter twist during the 1980s. Vitriolic anti-feminist writings 'blame women', writes feminist and sociologist Mária Adamik, 'for the increasing mortality of middle-aged men, the rising divorce rate, the falling birth-rate, and the generally decreasing stability of families'.[12]

However, life expectancy in East Central Europe was around four years lower for both sexes than in Western Europe. Despite women's frequent involvement in heavy manual labour, the gap between women's and men's life expectancy remained somewhat greater in East Cental Europe than in Western Europe, as shown in Table A3. But there is much evidence to show that while women's mortality rates were lower than men's, their morbidity was higher in terms of chronic health problems, often caused by the health risks or poor working conditions associated with their jobs. In Czechoslovakia, for example, in the age group 30–70, women were 15–30 times more prone to chronic illnesses than men. Dr Jaroslava Moserová, a Czech politician and physician, spoke movingly of the women workers in the textile and glass factories, 'the backbone of Czechoslovak export performance', as half deaf from the noise of antiquated machinery and having ulcerated legs. Another report held shift work and pressure to work overtime responsible for the fact that 8.7 per cent of women employed in light industry in Czechoslovakia held jobs exposing them to health hazards. And in Poland, about 35 per cent of women over forty-five suffer from advanced spine and joint degeneration. Amongst women weavers in the textile industry-dominated Polish city of Łódź, for example, 60 per cent of those who have worked longer than ten years have diseases affecting the bones and joints.[13]

Sexuality

The issue of reproductive rights was couched within a context of heterosexuality as the assumed norm in the model of sexual and family relations espoused by state socialism. Congruent with the exclusion of gender issues from the parameters of official discourse was the invisibility of sexuality and identity, sexuality and personal autonomy. The difficulties encountered by ostensibly emancipated women at the level of personal relations were often expressed, as were many other contradictions of daily life under state socialism, in literature rather than in public discussion.

In *Bolero*,[14] the East German author Helga Königsdorf gives a grotesque twist to the portrayal of one woman's reaction to perceived sexual, emotional and professional exploitation by a man. She endures years of 'being there' for her married colleague and lover. She resents being available at his convenience, and at his service, both sexually and domestically – he likes a good meal before sex – but since she has no partner, and fears loneliness, she finds it hard to say no. She feels robbed of initiative and autonomy, dependent on his telephone calls. To add insult to injury, he takes credit at the research institute where they both work for ideas which were originally hers. Thus she feels professionally exploited too, but is unable to protest publicly for fear of exposing their illicit private secret. One fine day, for reasons she cannot fathom when she muses over it later, she acts, quite suddenly and without premeditation. As he is getting his suit jacket from the balcony of her twelfth-floor flat where he had prudently hung it to air, preparing to return to respectability without so much as a whiff of her, she catches hold of his ankles and tips him over the edge. No one ever questioned, she remarks whimsically, why such a fastidious and proper person should have committed suicide in his socks.

Since heterosexuality was the norm, until recent years homosexuality remained at best unmentioned, at worst prohibited. In the former GDR, paragraph 175 of the Penal Code outlawing homosexuality was repealed in 1967.[15] Nevertheless, whilst not stigmatized by being outlawed, homosexuality was regarded as an unfortunate affliction. Attitudes to it were marked by compassion and tolerance, accompanied by distancing. It took until the late 1980s for homosexuality to surface in public discourse. In 1986, the GDR journal *Junge Welt* (*Young World*) printed revelations about gays being discriminated against in employment. Along with peace and women's groups, a gay scene grew under the protection of the Protestant church from the early 1980s. Eventually, but only a short while before the demise of the GDR in 1989, came the establishment of gay bars and cafés in Berlin.

However, the word homosexuality was always assumed in public writings to mean gay men. The specific interests of lesbians, as of other groups of women, remained invisible in the public domain. The dénouement of the story 'I Have Re-married' ('Ich habe wieder geheiratet') by Christine Wolter plays on this lack of acknowledgement with wry humour. The reader is beguiled into assuming that the narrator describing Rosa, the gentle and compliant new 'spouse', is a 'new man', who shares all domestic chores and childcare and is emotionally very supportive. Only a description of what they wear and the dramatic effect their entrance as a couple has at a social gathering, reveal that narrator and spouse are both women.[16] In February 1990, closely following the opening of the Berlin Wall, over thirty lesbian and gay groups formed an umbrella organization, called the Schwulenverband der DDR (GDR Queers' Association). German unification has disadvantaged East German gays. Whereas the law in the former GDR made 14 the unitary age of consent, West German law made sex legal for heterosexuals and lesbians at 14, but for gay men from 18 only.

Lambda Praha, a homosexual rights group launched in 1988, forms the hub of an active gay scene in Czechoslovakia. Lesbian and gay relationships had been legalized in 1961, and lesbian and gay issues had been discussed positively in the media since the mid-1980s. Nevertheless, despite this relative openness, contradictory attitudes are revealed by AIDS education material in Czechoslovakia, which frequently refers to homosexuality as an 'abnormal sexual practice'.

Paragraph 199 of the Hungarian Penal Code still refers to 'illicit sexual practices', despite the fact that anti-gay and anti-lesbian proscriptions were repealed in 1961. Yet Homeros Lambda, the Hungarian association for homosexual rights, was the first lesbian and gay organization to be legalized under a state socialist régime.

The first, unofficial, lesbian and gay group in Poland, ETAP, was formed in the city of Wrocław in 1986, followed by Filo in Gdańsk and WRH in Warsaw. Despite positive media portrayal of same-sex relations, in mid-1990 the American gay weekly *The Advocate* reported Lech Wałęsa as promising during a televized campaign speech to 'eliminate homosexuals and drug users' from Poland if he were elected president. Ryszard Kisiel of *Filo*, the Polish gay magazine, called this an example of 'outdated Catholic morality'. Also in 1991, the Deputy Health Minister, Mr Kapera, was sacked by the then Prime Minister Bielecki for publicly stating not only that he was opposed to contraception, but, when asked: 'What about AIDS?', replying: 'Only sexual perverts catch HIV.'[17]

The first post-revolutionary Soviet Constitution had offered homosexuals equal rights. But Stalinist puritanism in the 1930s put an end to revolutionary rethinking of sexuality and defined male homosexuality as a crime. As of 1990, Article 121 of the Soviet Criminal Code which stipulates five to eight years in prison for those convicted of having gay sex, had yet to be repealed. As late as the 1970s, a leading Soviet filmmaker, Sergei Paradzhanov, had been sentenced to five years' imprisonment for 'deviant' behaviour. Soviet legislation was silent on lesbians. But Tatyana Mamonova reported that those lesbians who came out were forcibly detained in psychiatric hospitals.[18] And one of the first post-*glasnost* discussions of the issue in Russia reveals an alarming logic. In 1987, *Moskovskij Komsomoletz*, then the voice of Moscow's party youth organization, published a letter from a sixteen-year-old gay schoolboy about the agonies of isolation and bullying he suffered. The paper responded with comments, and discussion with a medical 'expert', lambasting discrimination based on ignorance and fear of the unknown:

> For the first time he has experienced the feelings of an outcast, a social leper, whom normal people shun at any cost. . . . Thus they treat a snake, a poisonous insect, or any unusual creature that might mean danger. This can be traced to prejudice, to the mysterious horror that comes from instinct rather than any rational calculation of danger. ... This is understandable, because all information about homosexuality was taboo for a long time . . . [so] distorted rumours and incorrect information filled the vacuum.

Following this comment, however, the journal printed a discussion with Dr Vyacheslav Maslov of the All-Union Sexopathology Council, who implied that homosexuality arose from government policies of gender equality:

> The overwhelming dominance of women teachers in our schools contributes to the growing equalization of sex roles. Who, according to the teacher, is the best boy in class? – a quiet, obedient one. And the best girl? – one who is energetic and active. . . . The common goals and targets that we put in front of our children lead in their minds to a sexually neutral self-evaluation.[19]

Reproductive Rights and Population Policies

Reproductive rights are located on the border between the public and the private. The extent of their implementation, facilitating reproductive *choice* – the availability of birth control means and information, the quality of reproductive facilities and care – could be taken as one measure of the humanity of a particular society. In the state socialist past, the availability and quality of birth control means and health care varied from one country to another, representing deep divisions in attitudes toward the central issue of reproductive freedom.

At different times in their history, all the state socialist countries faced either a gender imbalance in, or a declining, population. This was especially true in the Soviet Union, Poland and the GDR, whose male populations had been decimated by the Second World War. It is within this context that birth control measures, abortion legislation and later pro-natalist policies have to be viewed. It is important to attempt to evaluate how far demographic concerns, in particular the need to replace the labour force, dictated reproductive policies. In several countries, especially Poland, these policies trod a wavering path, in a balancing act between commitment to women's 'emancipation', labour force requirements, and the moral dictates of the Catholic Church.

Largely in response to the pressures of the dual burden, the birthrate in state socialist countries fell dramatically by the mid-1960s, and the one-child family became for many the norm.[20] Governments responded by introducing various material incentives designed to induce women to increase their family size. Prime among these measures was the extension of already generous maternity leave to include an additional 'childcare' leave which lasted, in the case of Poland, Hungary and Czechoslovakia, until the child's third birthday.[21] Several writers have highlighted the way maternity and childcare leave disadvantages women both in the labour market and at home. Hilary Land wrote in 1979 that generous maternity leave provisions were a two-edged sword. She referred to research showing that men are much less likely to help with housework if their wife is at home on maternity leave. For women taking up their entitlement, 'the opportunity to be a full-time mother turns into the "opportunity" to be a full-time housewife'.[22]

Several countries introduced additional material incentives in an effort to boost the birthrate. In the former GDR, for example, young people considering starting a family were eligible for a substantial interest-free loan, for which each child born into the family was considered as part payment! In Czechoslovakia too, new couples could claim interest-free loans. And a family with three children could write off one-third of this loan.[23]

In retrospect, the UFV (Unabhängiger Frauenverband – Independent Women's Association in Eastern Germany, formed in December 1989) has derided what it calls the socialist state's 'Mummy policies' ('Muttipolitik'). Nevertheless, it has to be said that increased child benefit payments and extended maternity leave – the so-called 'baby year' – were introduced in the GDR in 1976 without concomitant restrictions on legal abortion, and in a situation of ever-increasing childcare availability. By contrast, Romania outlawed abortion in 1967 for all women bar those with four or more children. As of 1985, this law was further tightened, allowing abortion only for women with five children under eighteen. Contraceptives were unavailable except for black market supplies of the pill. Even in Bulgaria and Hungary, while abortion was never illegal, it was available only to married women with two or more children, or to single women.[24]

In fact, the only country where there does seem to have been a modicum of real reproductive choice was the GDR. Not only was a woman's job held open for her during childcare leave, as was the case in all state socialist countries, but by the mid 1980s there were enough childcare places to meet demand, and contraception and abortion were freely available. The dismissal of increased maternity and child benefits in the GDR as nothing more than 'Mummy politics', in other words the notion that women were instrumentalized in terms of demographic (and future economic) requirements, needs therefore to be taken with a grain of salt. In Poland, by contrast, where there were never public childcare facilities for more than half of three to six year-olds, and for a tiny number of children under three, and where contraception was unreliable in quality and availability, it would be an exaggeration to speak of reproductive freedom.

The differential level of public childcare provision between countries and over time was discussed above in Chapter 1 and is documented in Table A1 of the Appendix. Public qualms about the chronic health problems suffered by many young children in institutional care elicited inconsistent policy responses. Paid sick leave to care for sick children was an example of state regulation which in effect perpetuated gender divisions. Official ambivalence about gender equality was reflected in the fact that choice about which parent should fulfil this role was not left to individual couples to decide; rather the notion that parental care in such circumstances is exclusively 'women's work' was often decreed in advance by state policy. In Poland, for example, when the regulation was first introduced in 1972 it allowed either parent to take paid leave to care for sick children; but this was rescinded in 1975. Thereafter, it was restricted to mothers unless they themselves were ill or absent.

Hilary Land predicted the implications of this at an early stage when she wrote in 1979 that: 'the problem of combining paid employment with the demands of child care is still seen largely as an issue for women.

... The majority of measures introduced are likely to give more legitimate grounds for discriminating against women in the labour market as well as discouraging men from taking more responsibility in the home.'[25] In countries where paid leave to care for sick children was available to either parent, women were still the ones to take it. Since they were more often than not the lower paid of two parents, where two existed, it followed that they were more 'dispensable' from their place of work. Nevertheless, German unification provides graphic illustration of the problems for working women embodied in the loss or severe reduction of this right. The five weeks of paid leave annually to care for sick children under GDR law shrank upon unification to five working days per year under Federal German Law, and that only until the child's eighth birthday.[26]

The low status attributed to childcare as an occupation was reflected in the gender-segregated workforce and low pay in that sector. These factors demeaned childcare as menial 'women's work' rather than as a responsibility of the whole society for its own future. Despite frequent critiques of childcare *quality*, however, where it was *quantitatively* adequate, it did fulfil a positive function in facilitating choice for women about when to return to work after having a child. Not only did it provide a heavily subsidized service accessible to all citizens regardless of income, it also ensured that children received cheap hot meals every day, as well as early socialization in the positive sense. The nominal cost of 30 marks per month towards meals and milk in the former GDR had by 1 July 1990, just prior to German unification, already risen to DM 250–300 per child per month. In Poland in early 1990, kindergarten charges were approximately 60–80,000 złoty per month or 16–20 per cent of the average monthly salary for women. In view of the fact that fixed monthly payments took another 25 per cent and food bills 75 per cent of this wage, it is clear that single parents found it impossible to live off one salary and pay for childcare. There were reports of women giving up their jobs because they could no longer afford childcare, or sending their children to be cared for by people in the countryside so they could 'afford' to go on working to keep themselves and their family.[27]

While there is understandably debate around the question of the costs and benefits of institutional care for young children in the state socialist countries, it remains true that the length of maternity leave and the level of childcare provided there were but demands in the programmes of most Western feminist movements.

By contrast, current developments in East Central Europe raise questions about the way curtailing reproductive rights may affect women's capacity to act as equal citizens in the new market-based democracies. In a situation where the processes of marketization and privatization create pressures to shed labour, it is ironically the very advantages women enjoyed under state socialism – maternity and childcare leave with their job held open, paid sick leave to care for children, and the often enterprise-financed childcare facilities themselves – which contribute to women being regarded as both expensive and unreliable labour, hence to their being the first to be made redundant.

These developments are the direct outcome of treating reproductive responsibility as something that uniquely affects women, rather than as the responsibility of society as a whole. In the current transformation process, women's needs are again being subsumed under collective imperatives in that reproductive rights are instrumentalized in the name both of restructuring the economy, and of nationalistic population policies.

Birth Control and Sex Education

The point has already been made that reproductive rights need to be understood as a package of issues including contraception, sex education and childcare facilities. High abortion rates in several former state socialist countries were cause for concern about the efficacy of sex education and the availability of other birth control means and need to be examined within this total context. Critical evaluations from both inside and outside the former state socialist countries have suggested that abortion was commonly used as the sole means of birth control. Concern about this stems, among other reasons, from worry about the health implications for women of multiple abortions. Often, however, it has an anti-abortion sub-text, suggesting that freely available legal abortions *inevitably* mean a high rate of abortion, and signal irresponsibility on the part of women who 'choose' to terminate a pregnancy rather than using other forms of birth control.

The availability of contraception varied greatly between countries and over time, as did the existence and quality of sex education. UN data suggest that among the world's developed nations, citizens of the former Soviet Union had the second-lowest access to birth control information after Romania. And outside of Moscow and Leningrad, it was immensely difficult to obtain contraceptives. Even in the main urban centres, according to Francine Du Plessix Gray, only one in ten gynaecologists had access to contraceptives.

In the book *Women and Russia* Tatyana Mamonova clearly links the high rate of abortions to the lack of sex education and contraceptive means:

> Abortion clinics ... are simply production lines. ... They give abortions without anaesthetics to several women simultaneously. ... Yet I know women who have had as many as fifteen abortions. We have no sex education. Contraceptives are in short supply, and those available are crude and ineffective.[28]

Georgian gynaecologist Dr Archil Khomassuridze claimed in 1988 that only 18 per cent of Soviet women used any form of contraception at all, and of those, only 5 per cent used contemporary methods such as the pill or IUDs, a level which he asserted was 'the lowest in the world, lower than Bhutan or India'. In Georgia, however, it was even lower – only 3 per cent. Leningrad feminist Olga Lipovskaya echoes this finding in her account of her friends' two most commonly used methods of 'contraception': '1) Douching with the juice of a lemon after intercourse; 2) Jumping off an icebox when your period is three days late.'[29] (In a further irony, it should be added that one of the notoriously scarce foods under state socialism were lemons.)

By contrast, in the Protestant and heavily secularized society of the GDR, contraception was free of cost and available to all women over the age of sixteen, regardless of marital status.[30] The main method of contraception was the pill, but discussions of the health hazards associated with it were slow to surface. In Czechoslovakia, domestically-produced pills became available in the mid-1960s. Yet by 1977, only 5 per cent of Czech women and 2 per cent of Slovak women used oral contraceptives, as compared with 18 per cent in West Germany, 31 per cent in New Zealand, and 37 per cent in Holland. A 1977 Czechoslovak survey showed 30 per cent of urban and 45 per cent of rural women as having no knowledge of contraception at all, which explains the estimate of 25 per cent of urban and 20 per cent of rural women venturing into marriage pregnant. More recent surveys in Czechoslovakia suggest that despite liberalization of the abortion law in 1987, in 1988 the figure for women who were pregnant on marriage may have been as high as 45 per cent.[31] The birth control technique favoured by 40 per cent of Czech and 50 per cent of Slovak women in the 1977 sample was *coitus interruptus*. Discussions of the possible health risks associated with the pill were absent or conducted at the level of informal friendship networks in Czechoslovakia until the late 1980s, and it seems that alternatives such as the diaphragm were little used.

In Hungary, there was in 1990 a lack of sex education, scarcely any IUDs, and the pill was available only on prescription and for a fee. The diaphragm was banned in 1989 for 'hygienic' reasons. Condoms were in short supply and tended to be rejected by Hungarian men. A common anti-condom joke shared amongst men was: 'You wouldn't wash your feet with socks on, would you?'[32]

In Poland, problems of quality and availability provided yet further irritants to women's already heavily-stressed lives. Women complained that locally produced condoms were thick, and that irregular supplies made using oral contraceptives impossible. In spring 1991 the Ministry of Health withdrew from the market several brands of pill imported from the EC on the grounds that they were dangerous. Not only did irregularity of supply make for unreliable contraception; questionable efficacy of the only reliably available alternative, namely vaginal 'pills' or spermicidal capsules, compounded the problem. In 1990, the magazine *Przyjaciółka* (*Girlfriend*) carried an article entitled: 'The Only Form of Contraception for Men and Women: Be Careful!' Barbara Labuda, founder and chairperson of the Women's Caucus in the Sejm (the Lower House of the Polish Parliament) reported in 1991 that contraceptives were not included on a new government list of subsidized medicines. In June 1991, a pamphlet on methods of birth control, prepared during the state socialist era, was finally published. It mentions the paragraph in the Polish Penal Code prohibiting vasectomy as a form of 'self-inflicted injury'. Abortion does not feature at all. The pamphlet ends with a passage emphasizing the moral superiority of 'natural methods'.

Perhaps not surprisingly, given that problems of supply were complemented by Catholic disapproval of contraception, in Poland too 'natural methods' were the most widely used forms of birth control. Lack of sex education has been blamed for the fact that only 11 per cent of Polish women use modern contraceptives. Compared with the 35 per cent of couples using the rhythm method and another 34 per cent who practise *coitus interruptus*, only 15 per cent use condoms, 7 per cent the pill, 2.5 per cent chemical spermicides and 2 per cent IUDs. Jacqueline Heinen refers to church dignitaries and vigilante groups of young men 'raiding' pharmacies to confiscate all contraceptive supplies. As a result, by the spring of 1991, in most towns outside Warsaw it had become virtually impossible to obtain the pill or an IUD from the chemist. Heinen also interprets the high number of young couples (40 per cent) who use no form of contraception as compared with only 10 per cent of older couples as evidence of the moral pressure of the Church.[33]

The Catholic Church in Poland has waged a fairly sustained campaign to eliminate sex education. One of its successes in this area was to have Family Planning Centres closed in 1989, and the subsidies withdrawn from the Family Planning Association. Sex education 'disappeared' from school curricula in 1988 when the Ministry of Education withdrew a manual on family life which included a chapter on sex education. In a similar vein, a comprehensive family planning programme in the Suwałky district of northeast Poland, financed by the World Health Organization (WHO), the UN and the International Planned Parenthood Federation (IPPF) was quietly ended.

A French-Polish programme of cooperation in the area of birth control and family planning was initiated by the French organization Est à Venir in 1991. The programme was sparked off by a perceived need for solidarity with Polish women. It unites a wide range of women's, pro-choice, and family planning groups in both countries. Current projects include the production of a sex education brochure aimed at teenagers, training courses on family planning, and sending pills, condoms and diaphragms to women's groups in several Polish cities. These projects are being largely financed by the French Foreign Ministry. Est à Venir is proposing to consolidate existing links with other groups like the French Movement for Family Planning to form a federation which would be financed jointly by the European branch of the IPPF, and the American organization Catholics for a Free Choice.[34]

In summer 1992, a new Federation for Women and Family Planning was established from five Polish organizations – the Polish Feminist Association, Pro Femina, the Women's League, NEUTRUM, and the YWCA. The Federation aims to provide contraception, family planning services and educational courses for women and young people.

Abortion

Abortion provides the most visible, contested and controversial focus of reproductive rights policies. As with other aspects of state socialist policies affecting women, it is difficult, in retrospect, to evaluate to what extent these policies were motivated by a genuine commitment to women's right to decide, or by demographic trends and labour force requirements. Previous sections have illustrated the ambivalence that characterized state socialist policies on maternity leave, birth control and sex education, especially in Poland and the former Soviet Union. The latter's record in this respect is particularly contradictory in that the abortion ban of 1936 symbolized a complete turnaround from the earlier commitment to more liberal reproductive and family policies.

Only in 1955 did abortion again become legal in the Soviet Union, closely followed by the other state socialist countries. Hungary and Poland legalized abortion in 1956 and Czechoslovakia in 1957. It is noteworthy that the falling birthrate of the 1960s led several countries subsequently to restrict access to legal abortion (Czechoslovakia, 1962; Hungary, 1973; in 1967 Romania made abortion illegal and promoted a policy of four children per woman). Recently, these countries again liberalized the conditions governing legal abortion (Czechoslovakia, 1987; Romania, 1989; Hungary, 1989). The former GDR legalized abortion relatively late, in 1972. Despite its somewhat patronizing and begrudging tone, however, the preamble to the GDR's Abortion Law conceded that women should have autonomy in the decision:

> The equality of women in education and vocation, in marriage and family makes it necessary to leave it to the discretion of women themselves to decide whether and when to have a child. ... Women have the right to decide on their own responsibility on the number and timing of children they bear and shall be able to decide upon this through a termination of pregnancy.[35]

But legislatively enshrined commitment to a woman's right to choose did not spare individual women from moral lectures with a strongly paternalist flavour. In her novel *Meine ungeborenen Kinder* (*My Unborn Children*), the GDR author Charlotte Worgitzky describes 'what so many women had to suffer – and sometimes still do have to put up with: the contempt of some doctors and nurses for women who abort.'[36] Despite the fact that abortions were free and women had the right to paid sick leave to cover them, social stigmatization was such that many women chose to give fictitious reasons for their absence from work. In Brigitte Martin's short story 'At the Friedrichshain Hospital',[37] the narrator is relieved when she can produce a doctor's certificate for her daughter's supposed illness to avoid workplace gossip. But there is no escape from the didactic homily given by the doctors she encounters. They reprimand her severely, a woman with two children and not using contraception! In fact her sex life is very intermittent, since her married lover appears irregularly and unexpectedly. 'I live alone,' she says, 'should I take the pill day after day, keeping my body in a state of artificial pregnancy year after year, for the one hour which can get me into this situation?'

The fluctuations in official policy in several of the former state socialist countries suggest strongly that abortion has not been treated as an aspect of reproductive rights, but rather has functioned as an extension of population policies.

The rationale for this, at least on the part of the Catholic church in Poland, that abortion is not a matter of women's reproductive rights at all, but an ethical question concerning society and indeed the nation as a whole. On the initiative of the Catholic church it is being turned into a constitutional issue in Poland, Czechoslovakia, Hungary and Slovenia. This involves proposals to extend citizenship rights to the unborn foetus or to include a clause on the sanctity of human life as a fundamental value in society.[38] Invoking the authority of the Constitution is often a means of subordinating women's (reproductive) rights to the putative right to life of the unborn. The Constitution of the Irish Republic expresses this dilemma most directly by equating the right to life of the woman and the foetus. Significantly, current moves in East Central Europe to include the right to life of the unborn are often accompanied by the deletion of women's rights from the democratic constitutions and other new legislation of these countries.

The 1992 Polish Code of Medical Ethics provides in Article 32 for doctors to provide the same quality of medical care to any patient, regardless of 'age, race, nationality, religion, social background, financial status, or political beliefs'. Helsinki Watch reports the Medical College's lawyer as stating that sex was omitted from this clause as an additional category because it was seen as 'too obvious'. Equality of the sexes is retained in the existing Polish Constitution. But a new clause to be added provides for the right to life from conception. And the Polish Church is adamant that 'in no case is the interest of the woman recognized as superior to the life of the child in question'.

Poor quality, non-existent, or only intermittently available contraception and sex education help to explain the extremely high abortion statistics in many of the former state socialist countries. In the former Soviet Union, abortions exceeded the level of live births by a factor of two to one. A far higher estimate which should not be mere alarmism, given that its source is a well-known gynaecologist, Dr Archil Khomassuridze, cites the shocking figure of five to eight abortions for every live birth. The situation is predicted to worsen. The Ministry of Health cannot afford to import contraceptives from the West, the two existing condom factories have closed down because there is no hard currency to import latex, and the only IUD factory closed because the products were of such low quality. Dr Khomassuridze claimed that half of all Soviet condoms broke on first use. In August 1992, it was estimated that contraceptive supplies would run out before the end of the year.[39]

Romania has three times as many abortions as live births. This is thought to be in part the legacy of the Ceauşescu régime, which in 1967 banned contraception and deluged women with propaganda about the health hazards associated with it, in a nationalist effort to increase the population from 23 to 30 million by the end of the century. In Czechoslovakia, there were 56.2 (67.6 including spontaneous) abortions per 100 live births in 1985. After liberalization of the abortion law in 1987 dispensed with the necessity for women to seek medical permission, the rate of terminations increased to the point where, it is estimated, they equalled live births by 1989.

In Hungary there were 126 abortions for every 100 live births during the 1970s, but this rate was almost halved, to 67 per 100 live births in 1990. The decrease can be attributed to a tightening of the law. Until 1974, abortion had been available on demand, but new regulations stipulated that women appear before a commission which had the right to refuse consent. In Poland, there are 500,000–600,000 abortions per year if one includes those carried out in private clinics. This is equivalent to a rate of one abortion for every live birth, and is strikingly high in view of Poland's relatively high birthrate. These statistics make Poland, after Romania, Russia, and possibly also Czechoslovakia, one of the countries with the highest rates of abortions in the industrialized world.[40]

The notion that women 'choose' abortion as a form of contraception is, however, controversial. Data from both East and West suggest rather that abortion is a last resort option spurred by impediments to safe, reliable, freely available contraception. Drawing on the pre-unification German case, it is possible to hypothesize that approximately equal numbers of women resort to abortions, whether they are legally available or not. The main inter-country difference lies in the statistically unverifiable number of deaths caused by backstreet abortions.

The former GDR law made abortion available 'on demand', free of charge and covered by sickness benefit within the first twelve weeks of pregnancy. In combination with freely available contraception and adequate childcare facilities, this led to a falling rate of terminations. Whereas in 1973 – one year after the Abortion Law was promulgated –

there were still two terminations for every live birth, in 1988 there were approximately 80,000 abortions, representing 43 abortions for every 100 live births. Not only was this termination rate under half of that in Poland and less than a quarter of the rate in the former Soviet Union, it also represented an internationally low level.

In the Federal Republic of Germany (FRG), the notorious paragraph 218 of the Penal Code made abortion a criminal offence. Certain medical, eugenic, social and ethical grounds provided for limited exceptions, to be decided upon by a doctor after the woman had undergone extensive consultation with other doctors and welfare agencies. Yet the official statistics suggest that the number of women having legal abortions was quite similar in both German states. This fact can be interpreted in a number of ways. On the one hand, it demonstrates that criminalizing abortion does not lower the number of women obtaining one; nor conversely, that legalization leads to a sharp increase in abortions. Indeed if one takes into account the shadow statistic for those women procuring abortions in Holland to evade the tightly restrictive legislation in West Germany, it seems clear that the total figures would be considerably higher there. On the other hand, the similarity of the figures can be read as confirmation of research findings in both East and West which show that women do not have abortions lightly or as their first choice, but rather as a last resort.[41]

Given the gruesome accounts by many women of the conditions under which abortions were performed in the Soviet health system, without anaesthetic or privacy and in the most unsanitary environment, only a convinced misogynist could imagine that women 'chose' to submit themselves to such an ordeal. A newspaper report by a male Georgian reporter speaks of the screams of women permeating hospital corridors. Shortages of bed linen, drugs, medical gloves and needles contributed to the high number of deaths following abortions (2,000 in the past five years) and to an infertility rate double that in the West. Poet and feminist Olga Lipovskaya relates that when your turn in 'the production line [comes], you go into a hall spattered with blood where two doctors are aborting seven or eight women at the same time; they're usually very rough and rude, shouting at you about keeping your legs wide open et cetera ... if you're lucky they give you a little sedative, mostly valium'.

Lipovskaya herself is 35 years old, has had three children and seven abortions, and suggests that fourteen in the reproductive life of any one woman is the national average. She relates this not only to ignorance about birth control methods, asserting that in addition 'we've been brought up to look on abortion as salubrious, almost "cleansing", and on

93

birth control devices as harmful and unreliable'.[42] Such views suggest a kind of puritanical and ultimately punitive attitude to women's sexuality. Perhaps this is a real life version of the duality of mother and whore, and of female sexuality as both powerful and dangerous, hence requiring suppression. Such imagery is discussed in Chapter 7 on literary representations of women.

The current debate about abortion legislation in many East Central European countries is usually raised and conducted by male politicians or elderly clergymen. This pattern is familiar in the West, but perhaps somewhat unexpected after forty years of the state socialist experiment in which women's rights enjoyed explicit foregrounding in constitutions, legislation, and social policy. Women's intimate responsibility for their own fate and that of children born to them is ignored; women's citizenship rights overlooked or denied. Indeed the debate goes much further. Women are not regarded as responsible, politically mature citizens who weigh up the interests of potential life, in the context of the familial and societal pressures within which they find themselves, when making a decision whether to continue a pregnancy.

Rather, frequent and explicit allusions linking abortion to the Holocaust suggest that women are in fact globally linked in a programme of genocide against future generations. That this is no fanciful conjecture is underlined by a circular from the Polish Episcopate in 1991 which stated: 'We are dealing with systematic genocide – in peace time – via the massive murder of weak beings by strong beings.'

Anti-abortion posters in Croatia in the summer of 1990, juxtaposing pictures of dead foetuses with photos of concentration camp corpses, previewed inflammatory statements by various Catholic Church dignitaries. Joseph Höffner, Cardinal of Cologne, Cardinal Glemp of Poland, and Pope Paul II himself on his June 1991 visit to Poland all equated abortion, that 'vast graveyard of unborn children', with the Holocaust, some of them even designating it as numerically and morally far worse. Hungarian politician Gyula Fekete, president of the conservative Hungarian People's Party, wrote in 1989: 'In the last decades, especially in the highly developed countries, more crimes against life have been committed in the form of abortion than by Hitler and Stalin put together.' He went on to demonize feminism as 'the main contributor to this new wave of crime'.[43]

Ruth Rosen uses a 1990 Czechoslovak opinion poll showing only 52 per cent of women and 40 per cent of men in favour of unrestricted access to abortion to argue that ambivalence is not confined to extreme pro-life proponents, but is more general and widespread. She goes so far as to assert that 'since the [socialist] state sometimes encouraged abortion as a form of birth control, many men and women now regard abortion as part of the state's barbaric and inhumane policies'.[44]

In the summer of 1990, the Hungarian Christian Democratic Party (the smallest partner in the ruling coalition government, with control of the Ministry of Health) attempted to introduce a ban on abortion. This prompted the newly formed Hungarian Feminist Network to collect over 7,000 signatures within ten days, for a petition opposing restrictions on abortion. The Catholic Church has collected more than 10,000 signatures, opposing not only abortion, but also pornography and the glorification of violence in films. On 28 December 1990, pro-life groups prayed for 'the almost five million Hungarian children who could not be born in the last thirty-five years because their environment decided that there was no room for them' and church bells tolled for the 'victims of abortion'. The issue resurfaced in the summer of 1992, with a very conservative pro-life statement by the heads of the Hungarian Catholic Church. FIDESZ, the Young Democrat Party, helped to set in motion a Christian Women's Group in Szeged to formulate an alternative Catholic view.

A new 'Law on the Protection of the Foetus' was passed by the Hungarian Parliament on 17 December 1992. This law was one of two drafts. The one that Parliament rejected would have banned all abortions save those in cases where the woman's life was at risk, the foetus was unhealthy, or the pregnancy was the result of rape. The version that was passed was seen as liberal by comparison. It made termination of pregnancy legal up to twelve weeks, but with severe restrictions. There is a compulsory three-day waiting period after submitting the request for an abortion, and a compulsory pre-termination counselling session. For young women, parental consent is obligatory; indeed a parent must apply for the abortion. Social security will pay for the abortion only if the woman's life or the foetus is at risk. Abortion is only permissible, apart from health grounds or rape, if the woman can show she is in a 'crisis situation'. Pacem in Utero, an anti-abortion group, have appealed against the new law in the Constitutional Court, since they view this as an unacceptable reason for allowing women to terminate a pregnancy. Pro-choice activists in Hungary are pessimistic about the operation of this law in practice.[45]

As early as 1990 abortion was described by Czech women as 'at present, the number one women's social issue'.[46] In Slovakia, the new draft 'law on the protection of human life' would make abortion illegal except in cases of rape, incest, medical complications, or 'social problems that are impossible to resolve'. Its promulgation was postponed until after the June 1992 elections.

Since the liberalization of abortion in 1987 dispensed with the obligatory interview before a commission, the number of abortions in Czechoslovakia has increased. Miroslava Holubová, spokesperson for Nová Humanita (New Humanity), a newly formed group of women professionals – teachers, lawyers, philosophers in the Czech lands – argued in spring 1992 that access to abortion *should* be restricted. Fees should be introduced to discourage what she asserted was young women's feckless use, since the introduction of the vacuum aspiration method, of abortion as a 'regular monthly' form of contraception. This view would seem to be at least tempered by earlier findings that 'less than 17 per cent of women having an abortion in Czechoslovakia are childless, compared to 56 per cent in the US'; indeed that '"sufficient number" of children in a family (three and more) has consistently been the single most frequently cited reason for seeking an abortion and has accounted for 18–19 per cent of all abortions'. Alena Heitlinger maintained that in 1975 only one third of abortions were by vacuum suction method, although it is probable that this technique has become more widely available since then.[47]

In Germany, there was a short period during 1990 when unification itself hung in the balance on the issue of abortion. Laws in the former GDR and in the Federal Republic were diametrically opposed. The 1975 Federal Law and the 1972 East German law have already been described. The impasse between criminal status in the West and abortion on demand in the East was temporarily patched over with a bizarre compromise. According to this the existing laws would remain in force on the territory of each of the two former states until the promulgation of a new all-German law by the end of 1992. This produced the heavily protested possibility of 'prosecution by address' on grounds of 'abortion tourism' for women resident in West Germany who chose to avail themselves of legal abortions in the East. In 1990, the Federal German government had prosecuted a former East German woman, then resident in West Germany, when she re-entered the Federal Republic after obtaining an abortion in the Netherlands, something which had long been common practice for West German women. And the so-called 'witch-hunt' trials in Memmingen humiliated women forced to testify against a doctor who was ruined professionally and hunted down juridically for his support in helping women obtain a legal abortion in the fervently Catholic state of Bavaria.

A 1991 opinion poll showed that 55 per cent of West Germans and 75 per cent of East Germans favoured either complete legalization, or the extension of the East German time-limited law to the whole of Germany. The debate raged throughout 1991 and the early part of 1992, threatening at times to tear apart the ruling government coalition of Christian Democrats (CDU), their fiercely Catholic equivalent in Bavaria, the Christian Socialists (CSU), and the smaller liberal party, the Free Democrats (FDP).

The Christian Democrats favoured a ban on abortion accompanied by generous state maternity allowances and the provision of childcare facilities to ease the burden of child-rearing. A social package contained in the Unification Treaty had provided for the contraceptive pill to be available free of charge on prescription, for an increase in child allowances, and for the right to a kindergarten place. All of these measures implied billions of marks being invested, especially since complete kindergarten availability for three- to six-year-olds in the former GDR had already been severely eroded by the closure of childcare facilities since unification. Moreover, nothing like this level of provision had ever been reality in the Federal Republic. Women's Minister Angela Merkel in 1991 estimated a shortfall of 600,000 kindergarten places.[48] Referring to the strain on the state coffers of the unification process, Federal Finance Minister Theo Waigel, coincidentally also head of the staunchly Catholic Bavarian CSU, refused to fund the social package.

In summer 1991, six disparate draft laws were submitted to the Bundestag. These ranged across a predictable spectrum. At one end were two laws, one entitled 'On the Protection of Unborn Life', from the CDU/CSU (the two leading parties in the governing coalition), which portrayed abortion as a crime and provided for almost no exceptions, the other an even more extreme version from a group of forty-six independent members of the Bundestag (of whom only two were women), which proposed to insert their conditions into the Penal Code under the title 'Killing an Unborn Child'.

At the other end of the spectrum lay the draft from Alliance 90/The Greens/UFV (a coalition in the new Federal states of former GDR dissident groups including the Independent Women's Association [UFV]), and that from the PDS/Left List coalition (the PDS, the Party of Democratic Socialism, is the successor to the ruling Socialist Unity Party of the former GDR). Both of these proposed to eliminate paragraph 218 from the Penal Code and to give every woman the legal right to decide on an abortion. Between these two extremes lay the drafts from the opposition Social Democrats (SPD) and the Liberals (FDP), both providing for abortion to remain within the Penal Code, but to be exempt from criminal proceedings within the first twelve weeks of pregnancy. Their difference lay in the issue of counselling, which the SPD saw as a right, while the FDP wished to impose it as an obligation, with a three day 'period for reflection' between counselling and an abortion itself.[49]

It became ever clearer during the early months of 1992 that none of these six drafts could hope to gain the necessary two-thirds majority in the Bundestag. Consequently, women members of the Bundestag formed an unprecedented supra-party alliance of politicians from the SPD, the FDP, Alliance 90/Greens/UFV and, most significantly, from the CDU, especially those members representing the former GDR. This group presented a seventh draft law, based on a compromise between the SPD and FDP drafts. Their compromise pleased almost no one, angering the CDU/CSU with its legalization of abortion, and the UFV and many West German women with what they saw as its paternalistic insistence on compulsory counselling. They regarded this as inscribing in law women's lack of majority as political subjects, their inability to make responsible and informed decisions, based on ethically considered reasoning and morally sound powers of judgement.[50]

During late May and early June the media reported heavy pressure being brought against those CDU politicians seen as likely to vote for the compromise solution. Such pressure contravened the provisions of the Unification Treaty, which provided in the matter of the abortion law for politicians' right to vote according to their conscience rather than along party lines. Nevertheless the pressure was such that even the Minister for Women and the Family, Angela Merkel, a CDU politician from the former GDR, was reported as having been 'persuaded' not to vote in favour of legalizing abortion against the wishes of her party.

Despite attempts to intimidate CDU rebel politicians, 32 of them (20 from the former GDR) crossed the floor of the Bundestag on 26 June 1992, helping to form a clear majority for the new abortion bill. It was passed by 356–283 with 18 abstentions. This made abortion legal within the first three months of pregnancy, provided a woman 'in distress' underwent compulsory counselling at least three days before termination. The ultimate right of decision was to be the woman's. Christina Schenk, the only MP representing the UFV (the East German *Unabhängiger Frauenverband* – Independent Women's Association) in the Bundestag stated triumphantly: 'Paragraph 218 belongs on the garbage dump of history and it is certain to wind up there.'

Jubilation was, however, shortlived. No sooner was the law passed than a group of 247 conservative politicians, including Chancellor Kohl, signed an appeal demanding that the Federal Constitutional Court rule on whether it contravened the German Basic Law (Germany's equivalent of a Constitution). The Court, made up of one female and seven male judges, granted a preliminary injunction preventing the new law coming into force. This meant that Germany reverted to its paradoxical and anomalous position of having two irreconcilable laws within the territory of one country. Had the defeat of paragraph 218 been final, it might have set a standard influencing the outcome of the abortion debates simmering in most former state socialist countries of Eastern and Central Europe. As things stand, the apparent historic victory for women's reproductive rights in Germany was not the end of the story, but merely one chapter in an ongoing saga with an unknown outcome.[51]

On 28 May 1993, in a 6–2 decision, the Court pronounced the new abortion law unconstitutional. Pending Bundestag endorsement, the Court stipulated that although abortion was now illegal, criminal proceedings would not be instigated within the first three months of pregnancy if the woman had undergone compulsory counselling. However, abortion would not be available under state health insurance schemes, thus provoking a situation whereby legal abortions will now be available only to those who can afford them.

It is in Poland that the fiercest battles have raged over the abortion issue. As early as October 1988, a team of experts from the Polish Episcopate drafted a new Law on the Protection of the Unborn Child. This banned abortion with no exceptions whatsoever, and provided for a three-year prison term for the woman and for the doctor who performed the abortion. This draft law was discussed in the Sejm in April and May of 1989, sparking off mass demonstrations in the spring and summer, and the creation of several grassroots groups devoted to preserving the legal right to abortion. Indeed one analyst has asked ironically whether the attack on abortion rights should be welcomed as a catalyst for a new women's movement in Poland.[52] Sociologist Ewa Gontarczyk-Wesoła saw the draft law as a Machiavellian move to keep women at home in order to ease projected unemployment. At the same time, in Warsaw, a city of two million, there were only twenty incubators at the maternity hospital. This led activists of the pro-choice Pro Femina to remark that prohibiting abortion would be hypocritical in a situation where there are insufficient facilities for already born children.

The Polish Women's League tried an indirect approach, in July 1991 raising the question with government ministers of how they foresaw the care of mothers and children in a time of economic crisis, with special reference to the 800,000 babies likely to be born from a total ban on abortion. As of summer 1992, free market transformation had brought some stocks of contraceptives to Polish pharmacies. Yet in the absence of information, both about where to find them and how safe they are, usage remains low, especially since they must be paid for.[53]

The first draft of the anti-abortion law had been rejected as too draconian by the Polish Senate and sent back for redrafting. Widespread protests, demonstrations and petitions in the summers of 1989 and 1990 succeeded in getting eliminated the clause that provided for women convicted of having a termination to be imprisoned. But they could not reverse the Church-impelled tide surging towards a total ban. A second draft law, permitting abortion only in cases of rape and danger to the woman's life, was approved by the Senate in September 1990 and considered by the Polish Sejm in the early spring of 1991. A statement by Pro Femina condemned the draft bill's lack of any economic or social indications as grounds for abortion. 'In our country's reality, it means that many women will return to self-induced abortions or back-alley butchers.' From February until March of 1991, citizens and organizations had the right to send their opinions on the draft bill to the parliament. There were reports that people attending Sunday mass were asked to sign petitions against protesting the 'killing of innocent children'. As a result of its country-wide infrastructure, the Church was able to create a situation in which 80 per cent of the signatures received by the Parliament were in favour of the draft anti-abortion bill. Nevertheless, in the summer of 1991 and two drafts later, the issue was deferred.

Opinion surveys between 1990 and 1992 indicated that a referendum on the issue would show approximately 60 per cent of the population opposing criminalization.[54] These survey results led the Catholic Church to change tack, declaring that an ethical and moral issue of this nature could not be decided by politicians. There were many reports of Church pressure, including threats to withhold a Christian burial from parishioners who favoured retaining the 1956 law legalizing abortion. Informants maintained that parents wanting first communion for their child were required to supply the priest with a doctor's document certifying that they did not use an IUD. A reader's letter to the women's magazine *Kobieta y Życie* (*Women and Life*) at the end of 1992 expressed the commonly held view that swallowing the pill daily was considered by the Church to be a worse sin than an annual abortion which could be forgiven in confession. Hence some women in small towns would remove the spiral before going to confession, in order to be able to say with a clear conscience that they used to use the IUD, but that this was no longer the case![55]

In the interim period, the Polish Medical College promulgated a Code of Medical Ethics in December 1991, which forbade doctors to perform abortions. The Code was pushed through despite the findings of an unpublished survey, carried out by the *Doctors' Gazette* in 1991, which showed that 63 per cent of doctors were opposed to any change in the law, and only 7 per cent supported a total ban on abortion.[56]

The Code of Ethics, which came into force in May 1992, in effect made legal abortions unavailable in public hospitals in Poland, despite the fact that the Abortion Law of 1956 is still legally valid. It also deprived women of certain types of ante-natal tests such as amnio-centesis. In practice therefore, the Code blatantly contravened international law in its failure to observe legislation still on the statute books. The Ombudsman appealed against it to the Constitutional Tribunal in January 1992, yet the Code remained in force while the case was pending. This anomalous situation raised serious questions about the treatment of women's reproductive rights.

On 24 July 1992, the latest law banning abortion in Poland was approved at its first reading in the Sejm by a majority of 212–106. This majority reflects the current parliamentary dominance of rightwing nationalist and Catholic forces centred on the Christian National Union. The new law stipulates two-year sentences for doctors performing abortions. In its exclusion of any medical, legal or eugenic grounds, the draft bill is more restrictive than the abortion clauses of the 1932 Penal Code which predated the present 1956 law. In theory, it could also lead to the outlawing of intra-uterine devices and the 'morning-after' pill. At the same time, a bill calling for a referendum on the issue was thrown out by a more narrow majority of 188–136, with 18 abstentions. A third draft backed by the women's caucus within the Sejm was modelled on the West German 'indications' legislation. It would have allowed abortions up to 12 weeks for family or social reasons, up to 20 weeks where the mother's life was endangered or the pregnancy was the result of rape, and up to 24 weeks if the foetus was incurably handicapped. In the closest vote of the three, this draft was also thrown out, by a vote of 175–149, with 19 abstentions.[57]

The Unborn Child Protection Bill was sent to a special commission for redrafting in September 1992. Of the 25 members present at the Commission's first meeting on 24 September, fourteen were known to be pro-life, as against nine pro-choice, with the views of the remaining two unknown.

Nevertheless, subsequent developments were encouraging in that a more broadly based Social Committee for a Referendum was established in November 1992. Significantly, however, its proposed referendum did not intend to address women's right to reproductive freedom in the form of access to abortion, but was to focus merely on the issue of prison terms for those performing abortions. In a comment on this limited goal, Wanda Nowicka, a leading committee member and head of the pro-choice Federation for Women and Planned Parenthood said: 'Here in Poland, we know we have to go step by step – campaign by campaign. We cannot achieve everything in one day.'

The issue threatened to undermine the ruling coalition, since the National Christian Union is fiercely anti-abortion and anti-referendum, while most members of the Democratic Union (UD) favour a more liberal abortion law and a referendum. On 7 January 1993, the Sejm reached a 'compromise' solution. The bill providing for abortions only in cases where there is a threat to the life or health of the mother, if the pregnancy is the result of incest or rape, or ante-natal tests show the foetus to be irreparably damaged, was passed by a majority of 42. The proposal to hold a referendum was rejected, so that the clause providing for two-year prison terms for doctors performing an abortion under any other circumstances still stands. The new law was interpreted, even by pro-choice activists, as a relative liberalization. On 1 February 1993, the Polish Senate approved the Bill by one vote, without further amendments. Many commentators had expected the Senate to restrict further the admissibility of abortion, since the Christian National Union had pressed for women to be punished and for a total ban, without exceptions. But opinion polls showed that the Catholic Church's popularity had waned by up to 40 per cent during the abortion debate. As a result, the Church announced its temporary approval of the 'compromise' Bill. And despite President Lech Wałesa's announcement that he would refuse to put his name to any law which permitted the 'killing of unborn children', he duly signed the new law on 15 February 1993. The new law came into effect on 16 March 1993.[58]

During an earlier Senate consultative meeting on abortion in June 1990 (after protests, this meeting included women's groups as well as representatives of the clergy), practising Catholics opposed to the criminalization of abortion like Zofia Kuratowska, then vice-president of the Senate, were denounced as being 'neither good Catholics nor Polish patriots'. It is noteworthy that patriotism was invoked in this context, suggesting the subordination of women's reproductive function to Polish national interest. Kuratowska's view of the proposed anti-abortion bill was that it 'completely take[s] away women's right to determine their own destiny'. She added: 'Today there are already . . . a large number of abandoned children. We should exert every effort to change this unfavourable situation before we discuss restrictive laws.'[59]

The sacking of Anna Popowicz, Under-Secretary of State for Women, and the squeezing out of Solidarity's Women's Commissioner, Małgorzata Tarasiewicz, both of which occurred in 1991 on the issue of reproductive rights, meant that the political infrastructure for supporting a pro-choice stance on abortion was destroyed in advance of the law passing through its first reading on 24 July 1992.[60] Meanwhile, abortions were available in Poland only at private clinics in large cities. The price of an abortion had risen sharply in 1992 and was equivalent to two average monthly salaries (many women earn less than the average wage). There were reports of 'abortion tourism' to Czechoslovakia, Russia, Ukraine and Germany. The ex-government daily *Rzeczpospolita* carried advertisements for a German clinic which offers 'gynaecological interventions', contraception and sterilization. Sterilization is also illegal in Poland.[61]

The contrasting trends exhibited by the passage of the two laws in Poland and Germany, the one likely to ban abortion, the other almost succeeding in de-criminalizing it, suggest that moves to restrict women's autonomy in the sphere of reproductive rights are neither all one-way, nor uncontested. However, a sombre and even macabre note is struck in a 1992 report that young women between the ages of nineteen and thirty-three in the former GDR were having themselves sterilized as a means of improving what they perceived as their otherwise zero-level chances in the labour market. This grotesque connection between the labour market and the female body is made possible by the practice of granting a certificate after the operation, which, the report claims, was at times demanded by potential employers in job interviews. The certificates are to be discontinued. In the meantime, however, the Government Spokesperson for Equal Opportunities in Magdeburg, Edita Beier, reported a staggering increase in one Magdeburg clinic alone of 1,200 sterilizations in 1991 compared with eight in 1989. 'Many women, especially those living alone with their children, see sterilization as the only means of getting a job at all,' she said. 'Their chances otherwise at the moment are zero. They have themselves sterilized out of anxiety for the future.' Abortions at the same clinic had increased 150-fold in 1991 as compared with the 1989 level, presumably for similar reasons.[62]

In a parallel reaction to the transition process, Christiane Schindler, official spokesperson of the Independent Women's Association (UFV) in the former GDR, spoke of an 'unofficial birth strike' in the face of economic uncertainty and high unemployment. This would seem to be endorsed by a report in the *Guardian*, which pointed to the fact that East German women, formerly more fertile as a result of government subsidies and social provision, are now producing fewer babies than their Western sisters. The drop in the birth rate, already lower than that in Britain and France, means that by the year 2030, there will be 20 million fewer Germans than there are today. This will necessitate, according to the German Economic Research Institute (IW) at least 300,000 immigrants annually, just to fill the gap in the labour market.[63]

The evidence of women going on 'birth strike' or indulging in sterilizations would appear to counter the notion that the market maximizes individual choice and initiative. Rather it suggests that market freedoms in the current transition mean for women the 'freedom to lose'.[64] And it is ironic that the denial of the principle of 'a woman's right to choose' in terms of abortion is occurring concurrently with the withdrawal of state provision in other fields of reproductive policy such as childcare.

Citizenship implies not merely the right to individual autonomy in terms of non-interference from the state, but also the expectation of or indeed the right to certain state services. Without sufficient incubators in Warsaw, or childcare facilities in Germany, for example, the abstract 'right to life' so enamoured of anti-abortionists loses concrete meaning. The non-provision of such facilities and the criminalization of abortion will affect most acutely those women who are already suffering from unemployment. Such women's chances of getting another job are hindered by the lack of relevant skills or retraining programmes, the loss of childcare facilities, the fact that they are young women beginning their working life, or because they are the mothers of young children. It is such women who are most prone to the grave health risks associated with backstreet abortions.

Finally, the way in which women's reproductive role is currently being hitched to the nationalist waggon in some East Central European countries has severe implications for women's right to self-determination as citizens enjoying equal rights with men.

At times this link with nationalism also has overtly racist overtones. These were already to be heard in the pre-1989 period, with Russian women being urged to produce more children to neutralize the effect of the high birthrate in the Central Asian Soviet republics. Similarly, abortion and contraception were denied Romanian women defined as 'breeding chambers for the Greater Romania'.[65]

Calls to Hungarian women to have more babies have an unspoken racist sub-text which reads: lest the Hungarian nation be over-run with gypsies. Hungarian feminist and sociologist Mária Adamik warns against this cooption of women's reproductive rights:

> Another case of male logic is the belief that banning abortion will lead to a rise in the birthrate. As if the examples of Hitler and Ceausescu weren't enough to ward us away from the notion of 'giving birth for the nation'. Such a medieval approach treats the intimate sphere of sexuality as something that can be put to the nation's service. Pornography, brothels and forced birth are all part of the same world-view that is shockingly hostile towards women. On the one hand women are just sexual objects, on the other they are caught up in male myths of mother and nation.[66]

Serbian women were also being urged to produce babies 'for the nation' in 1990. And in Kosovo, Serbian women were exhorted to have more babies in order to counterbalance the breeding habits of 'ignorant' Albanian women who 'know no better' than to have large families.[67]

In an extreme version subjugating women as reproductive vessels to a joint imperative of nationalism and militarism, Rada Trajković, a Serb politician in Kosovo, stated in June 1991 that 'for each soldier fallen in the war against Slovenia, Serbian women must give birth to 100 more sons'. The 'Women in Black', silently protesting against the ethnically-based war in the former Yugoslavia in weekly Belgrade demonstrations, saw the link between nationalism and militarism as the outcome of their traditional, patriarchal society. They spoke of declarations by Serb and Croat leaders of both church and state, expressing concern at the low birthrate. By late 1991 there was growing pressure on women to fulfil their 'duty to the nation' by giving it sons.

Sociologist Maja Korać writes:

> The basis of nationalist madness in the former Yugoslavia is the patriarchal matrix of values. .... As is common in the patriarchal order, women are regarded as mothers who will have to give birth to sons, tomorrow's soldiers of their nation, and as wives who will have to take care of 'their men'. Although important for the nation, their role is passive and static.[68]

The grotesque contradiction within such a concept of nationalism seems to have escaped the warmongers. The ultimate duty of citizenship as traditionally conceived is to lay down one's life in defence of family and nation, in other words for men to go to the front to 'protect' their wives and children at home. This context reveals as absurd the demand that these same wives should produce more sons who can then be expended as cannon fodder. It implies that women's national duty is to bear sons whose destiny is to get themselves killed in the name of the nation.[69]

The systematic rape of Bosnian women during the hostilities in Bosnia reveals itself as the ultimate expression of this subjugation of women and reproduction to rabid nationalist objectives. Separated from their menfolk, Muslim and Croatian women in Bosnia have been held in special 'rape camps' like that housing 2,000 women in Doboj in northern Bosnia. The women's organization 'Tresnjevka' in Zagreb has estimated that there were 16 such camps on Serb-occupied territory; the Islamic community in Sarajevo has named a further 20. The International Red Cross, which initially dismissed the allegations, subsequently produced its own list of 42 suspected camps.

The Bosnian Interior Ministry has estimated that 50,000 women have been raped, most of them several times. Later reports claim that the number is nearer 20,000. Eye witnesses report that only those women in the camp who became pregnant were given milk to drink and permitted to wash, kept alive to bear 'little Chetniks'. Many reports maintain that pregnant women were deliberately held until such time as their pregnancy was too advanced for abortion to be possible.

Drs Narcisa Sarajlić and Mladen Loncar, two Croatian psychiatrists, told reporters that in their view, Serbian irregular troops were using rape as a public spectacle, a tactical weapon to promote the strategy of ethnic cleansing. Asija Armanda of the Zagreb women's group 'Kareta' described the rapes as a 'war tactic'. Nihada Kadić of 'Tresnjevka', a group which tries to help the women, said: 'Even if they get out [of the camps] alive, these women will never again be able to enjoy normal sexual relations. This is part of the genocide against Muslims.' Meanwhile silence reigns on the topic in Croatia, where the Catholic ruling party (HDZ) of President Tudjman has made moves to ban abortion. Figures showing 1,000 more pregnancies registered in Croatian hospitals during 1992 than in 1991 – 75 per cent of them among Bosnian women – would appear to corroborate the stories of mass, systematically organized, rape as a weapon of war.[70]

In conclusion, it should be said that defining women as mothers with a 'sacred duty' to reproduce the nation is occurring concurrently with and hence underwriting the economic need to shed labour. But this convenient concurrence is likely to clash with material reality. The necessity of (at least) two incomes in the past, amplified by the possibility that the male breadwinner may (have) become unemployed, will in all likelihood recreate the need, purely in terms of the family's survival, for female labour force participation. The 'Holy Family' with women as glorified breeders in a harmonious national community is probably destined to remain a myth. An examination of women's past and present labour force participation should help to throw some light on the extent to which the worker side of the worker-mother equation – with all its contradictions – has become, over the forty plus years of the state socialist period, an integral part of women's self-image.

Notes

1. Jolanta Plakwicz, 'Between Church and State: Polish Women's Experience', in: Chris Corrin, ed., *Superwomen and the Double Burden: Women's Experience of Change in Central and Eastern Europe and the Former Soviet Union*, Scarlet Press, London, 1992, p. 90.

2. On fluctuations in state policy with regard to reproductive rights, depending on whether the state needed women as mothers more than it needed them as workers, see (for Poland) Jacqueline Heinen, 'The Impact of Social Policy on the Behaviour of Women Workers in Poland and East Germany', in: *Critical Social Policy*, issue 29, vol. 10, no. 2, autumn 1990, pp. 79–91; and (for Hungary), Júlia Szalai, 'Some Aspects of the Changing Situation of Women in Hungary', in: *Signs*, vol. 17, no. 1, autumn 1991, pp. 152–70.

3. Jutta Gysi, 'Women in Relationships and the Family' ('Frauen in Partnerschaft und Familie'), in: Gislinde Schwarz and Christine Zenner, eds, *Wir wollen mehr als ein 'Vaterland' (We Want More Than a 'Fatherland')*, Rowohlt Taschenbuch Verlag, Hamburg, 1990, pp. 90–120.

4. Rosalind Petchesky, *Abortion and Women's Choice: The State, Sexuality and Reproductive Freedom*, Longman, New York, 1984; reprinted Verso, London, 1986, especially Introduction and Conclusion.

5. A statement by Rada Trajković of the Kosovo Serbs which exemplifies this attitude is cited later in this chapter. See note 69 below.

6. Petchesky, *Abortion*, 1986, ibid.

7. Sheila Malone, 'Women's Rights in Poland', in: *Labour Focus on Eastern Europe*, no. 42, 1992, p. 43.

8. In Hungary for example, people paid between 4,000 and 10,000 forints for operations in what one informant called the 'vain hope' of extra attention. Childbirth cost 10,000 forints. This 'voluntary' payment was in effect compulsory, and one informant reported in 1990 that a friend had gone to the pawnshop the previous week in order to raise the cash for an operation. (Source: Barbara Einhorn, key informant interviews, Budapest, May 1990.)

9. In 1987, 27 women died in East Germany as a result of pregnancy or in childbirth, representing a rate of 1.2 women for every 10,000 births; infant mortality had fallen from a rate of 21.7 per 1,000 live births in 1950 to 5 per 1,000 births in 1988. (Source: Gunnar Winkler, ed., *Sozialreport 90*, Verlag Die Wirtschaft, Berlin, 1990, table 1.12, p. 29.)

10. Francine Du Plessix Gray points out that between 1914 and 1925, infant mortality rates were cut in half; now, however, falling standards were in part attributed to the low pay in this sector: doctors at the end of the 1980s earned on average 250 rubles per month compared with 450 for a skilled worker in industry (Du Plessix Gray, *Soviet Women Walking the Tightrope*, Virago, London, 1991, p. 26).

11. Tatyana Mamonova, ed., *Woman and Russia: Almanach for Women about Women*, Sheba, London, 1980, pp. 22–23; and *Women and Russia: Feminist Writings from the Soviet Union*, Blackwell, Oxford, 1984, p. xix.

12. On the gender gap in life expectancy and the East-West comparison, see table A3 in the Appendix. For examples of Hungarian anti-feminist attacks, see the writings of Dávid

Biró (1982) and Löcsei Pál (1985), referred to in: Marilyn Rueschemeyer and Sonia Szélenyi, 'Socialist Transformation and Gender Inequality: Women in the GDR and Hungary', in: David Childs, Thomas Baylis, Marilyn Rueschemeyer, eds, *East Germany in Comparative Perspective*, Routledge, London, 1989, pp. 99–100. The exchange between Gyula Fekete and Enikö Bollobás in 1989, described in Chapter 6 below, is alluded to in the quote from Mária Adamik, 'Hungary: A Loss of Rights?', in: *Shifting Territories: Feminism in Europe*, special issue no. 39 of *Feminist Review*, winter 1991, p. 169.

13. Dr Moserová's views were expressed in an interview with Barbara Einhorn, Prague, September 1990. The percentage of women in light industry exposed to health hazards is cited from Alena Kroupová, 'Women, Employment and Earnings in Central and Eastern European Countries', Paper prepared for Tripartite Symposium on Equality of Opportunity and Treatment for Men and Women in Employment in Industrialized Countries, Prague, May 1990, pp. 15–16. Other sources cited on work-associated health problems: (for Czechoslovakia) Mít'a Castle-Kaněrová, 'A Culture of Strong Women in the Making?' in: Chris Corrin, ed., *Superwomen and the Double Burden*, 1992, pp. 109–10; (for Poland) Zofia Kuratowska, 'The Present Situation of Women in Poland', in: *The Impact of Economic and Political Reform on the Status of Women in Eastern Europe and the USSR*, Proceedings of United Nations Regional Seminar, Vienna, 8–12 April 1991, ST-CSDHA-19-UN, New York, 1992.

14. Helga Königsdorf, 'Bolero', in: Königsdorf, *Meine ungehörigen Träume* (*My Outrageous Dreams*), Aufbau Verlag, Berlin and Weimar, 1978, pp. 7–16.

15. Information taken from Chris Bull, 'No Glasnost for Gays', in: *The Advocate*, 14 August 1990.

16. Christine Wolter, 'Ich habe wieder geheiratet' ('I Have Re-married'), in: Wolter, *Wie ich meine Unschuld verlor* (*How I Lost My Innocence/Virginity*), Aufbau Verlag, Berlin and Weimar, 1976, pp. 26–35. A translation of this story by Friedrich Achberger was published in: Edith H. Altbach et al., eds, *German Feminism: Readings in Politics and Literature*, State University of New York Press, Albany, 1984, pp. 220–25.

17. Wałesa's remark is quoted by Bull, 'No Glasnost for Gays', 1990. Kapera was quoted in the Polish media, and the information was relayed to Barbara Einhorn by Nina Gladziuk, Warsaw, 19 June 1991.

18. Tatyana Mamonova, Introduction to *Women and Russia*, 1984, p. xxii; and *Russian Women's Studies: Essays on Sexism in Russian Culture*, Pergamon Press, Oxford and New York, 1989, p. 131.

19. The bulk of the details of legislation on gay and lesbian rights, and on gay organizations in East Central Europe, is taken from Peter Tatchell, *Out in Europe: A Guide to Lesbian and Gay Rights in Thirty European Countries*, Channel 4 Television, London, 1990. The 1987 Soviet journal discussion is cited in: the *Guardian*, 25.3.87.

20. Poland remained an exception, probably as a result of Catholic mores. In 1990, rural women still had on average 3–4 children, whilst urban intellectuals tended to have only 1–2 children.

21. In Hungary, women had the option from 1967 of extending their six months of fully paid maternity leave by taking up the protected childcare grant (GYES). This flat-rate grant enabled mothers to stay at home until their child was three, with their job being held open for them. As of 1982, access to the grant became a parental right available to fathers too in the second and third years of the child's life, but in practice men rarely took it up. The value of the grant was quickly eroded: by 1980 it represented only 30% of the average national wage. Hence while in 1973 80% of women eligible for the grant took advantage of it, by the early 1980s, many women felt unable to afford to take it. In 1985, the earnings-related child care allowance (GYED) was introduced, which paid women (or either parent after the child's first birthday) 66–75% of their previous average earnings. By 1986, the proportion of women choosing to stay home until the child's third birthday was over half of those entitled to do so. (Sources: Mária Adamik, 'Hungary – Supporting Parenting Policy and Child Rearing: Policy Innovation in Eastern Europe', in: Sheila Kamerman and

Alfred J. Kahn, eds, *Child Care, Parental Leave, and the Under Threes: Policy Innovation in Europe*, Auburn House, New York and London, 1991, pp. 115–45; Júlia Szalai, 'Some Aspects of the Changing Situation of Women in Hungary', 1991, pp. 162–69.)

Maternity leave in Poland is 16–18 weeks (depending on the number of children in the family). Fathers or mothers are entitled to parental leave for a further two years, but at the low rate of only 25% of average monthly wages. (Source: Jolanta Plakwicz, 'Between Church and State: Polish Women's Experience', in: Corrin, ed., *Superwomen and the Double Burden*, 1992, pp. 82–83.)

In a clear attempt to halt the decline in the birthrate, the former GDR introduced its so-called 'baby year' in 1976. Later improvements meant that 26 weeks fully paid maternity leave was supplemented by a second six months on 70% of average net earnings. During this time, as in Hungary, a woman's job or equivalent had to be kept open for her. As of 1986, the second six months could be regarded as parental rather than maternity leave since it was available to fathers or grandmothers as well as mothers. The immediate 'baby boom' noted in several state socialist countries after the introduction of extended childcare leave is evident in the GDR case. Births per thousand population had reached an all-time low of 10.8 in 1975, but after the introduction of the 'baby year' in 1976, reached a high of 14.6 by 1980. This level did not hold. Nevertheless, an East-West comparison illuminates the effectivity of 'Mummy policies' ('Muttipolitik') in the GDR. In 1960, the rate of births per thousand inhabitants was 17.7 for West Germany and 17 for the GDR. This had fallen still further by 1970 but remained similar, with a rate of 13.3 and 13.9 respectively. However, the 1985 figures diverge significantly, with the GDR back up to a rate of 13.7 per thousand while the West German rate had fallen further to 9.6. (Sources: Barbara Einhorn, 'Socialist Emancipation: The Women's Movement in the GDR', in: Sonia Kruks, Rayna Rapp, and Marilyn B. Young, eds, *Promissory Notes: Women in the Transition to Socialism*, Monthly Review Press, New York, 1989, p. 303, note 16; Einhorn, 'Emancipated Women or Hardworking Mothers? Women in the Former German Democratic Republic', in: Corrin, ed., *Superwomen and the Double Burden*, 1992, p. 135; and Winkler, *Sozialreport 90*, table 1.8, p. 24.)

22. Hilary Land, 'The Changing Place of Women in Europe', in: *Daedalus*, vol. 108, no. 2, spring 1979, p. 87.

23. Sources: (for the GDR) Winkler, ed., *Frauenreport 90*, p. 149; (for Czechoslovakia) Castle-Kaněrová, 'A Culture of Strong Women in the Making?', 1992, p. 119.

24. Source: HCA Women's Commission, *Reproductive Rights in East and Central Europe*, Helsinki Citizens' Assembly Publication Series no. 3, Prague, June 1992, pp. 15, 24, 31.

25. Land, 'The Changing Place of Women in Europe', 1979, pp. 87–88.

26. Eva Kolinsky, *Women in West Germany: Life, Work and Politics*, Berg, Oxford, New York, Munich, 1989, p. 71. The number of weeks of paid sick leave in the GDR varied according to the number of children. Nevertheless, it was markedly higher, as it was in the other state socialist countries, than the five days paid for in the Federal Republic. Post-unification there was also a sharp drop in paid maternity leave for East German women, from 26 weeks plus an additional six months childcare leave, to 14 weeks under Federal German law. For the details of these and other differences in the juridical status of women, see also Sabine Berghahn and Andrea Fritzsche, *Frauenrecht in Ost und West Deutschland (Law Relating to Women in East and West Germany)*, Basisdruck Verlag, Berlin, 1991, p. 92.

27. For the information on German childcare fees, see Irene Dölling, 'Between Hope and Helplessness', in: *Shifting Territories*, 1991, p. 8; the Polish information comes from interviews conducted by Barbara Einhorn with sociologist Ewa Gontarczyk-Wesoła, Poznań, April 1990.

28. Mamonova, ed., *Women and Russia*, 1984, p. xix.

29. Information about birth control availability in the former Soviet Union, and the quotations from Dr Archil Khomassuridze and Olga Lipovskaya are in Du Plessix Gray, *Soviet Women Walking the Tightrope*, 1991, pp. 15, 19–20, 59.

30. Dölling, 'Between Hope and Helplessness', 1991, p. 7, points out that following unification, women from the former GDR will have to pay for contraception, as West German women have always had to do.

31. Alena Heitlinger, 'Passage to Motherhood: Personal and Social "Management" of Reproduction in Czechoslovakia in the 1980s', in: Sharon L. Wolchik and Alfred G. Meyer, eds, *Women, State and Party in Eastern Europe*, Duke University Press, Durham, 1985, pp. 287–88; Hana Navarová, 'Lives of Young Families in Czechoslovakia', mimeo, 1990.

32. Sources: Chris Corrin, 'Magyar Women's Lives: Complexities and Contradictions', in Corrin, ed., *Superwomen and the Double Burden*, 1992, pp. 63–64; Barbara Einhorn, Interview with Antonia Burrows of the Hungarian Feminist Network, Budapest, July 1990.

33. Sources: Hanna Jankowska, 'Abortion, Church and Politics in Poland', in: *Shifting Territories*, 1991, p. 178; Sheila Malone, 'Abortion Rights in Poland', in: *Labour Focus on Eastern Europe*, no. 41, 1992, p. 48; Jacqueline Heinen, '"Polish Democracy is a Masculine Democracy"', in: *Women's Studies International Forum*, vol. 15, no. 1, 1992, pp. 134–35.

34. Jacqueline Heinen, 'Linking Women East and West: French-Polish Cooperation', in: HCA, *Reproductive Rights in East and Central Europe*, 1992.

35. For further details on the abortion legislation and practice of each country, see (for Czechoslovakia and the former Soviet Union) Castle-Kanerová, 'The Culture of Strong Women in the Making?', 1992, pp. 97–125; Heitlinger, 'Passage to Motherhood', 1985; Hilary Pilkington, 'Behind the Mask of Soviet Unity: Realities of Women's Lives', in: Corrin, ed., *Superwomen and the Double Burden*, 1992, pp. 180–235; Hilda Scott, *Women and Socialism: Experiences from Eastern Europe*, Allison and Busby, London, 1976; (for Hungary) Júlia Szalai, 'Abortion in Hungary', in: *Feminist Review*, no. 29, spring 1988, pp. 98–101; Chris Corrin, 'Magyar Women's Lives', 1992, pp. 27–75; (for the former GDR) Barbara Einhorn, 'Emancipated Women or Hardworking Mothers?' in: Corrin, ed., *Superwomen and the Double Burden*, 1992, pp. 125–55; Dorothy Rosenberg, 'Shock Therapy: GDR Women in Transition from a Socialist Welfare State to a Social Market Economy', in *Signs*, vol. 17, no. 1, autumn 1991, p. 135; (for Poland) Małgorzata Fuszara, 'Will the Abortion Issue Give Rise to Feminism in Poland?', in: Mavis Maclean and Dulcie Groves, eds, *Women's Issues in Social Policy*, Routledge, London and New York, 1991, pp. 205–21; Fuszara, 'Legal Regulation of Abortion in Poland', in: *Signs*, vol. 17, no. 1, autumn 1991, pp. 117–27; Heinen, '"Polish Democracy is a Masculine Democracy"', 1992; Hanna Jankowska, 'Abortion, Church and Politics in Poland', in: *Shifting Territories*, 1991, pp. 174–82.

36. Charlotte Worgitzky, *Meine ungeborenen Kinder* (*My Unborn Children*), Buchverlag Der Morgen, Berlin, 1982, pp. 121–22 [my translation, BE]. The subject of this novel is the narrator's six abortions, which she had in order neither to compromise her acting career nor to deprive her one wished-for son. The novel was controversial at the time of its publication, and is under renewed discussion in the present context of disputed abortion rights in the united Germany.

37. Brigitte Martin, 'Im Friedrichshain', in: Martin, *Der rote Ballon* (*The Red Balloon*), Buchverlag Der Morgen, Berlin, 1978, pp. 16–34 [my translation, BE].

38. In Czechoslovakia, the Federal Constitution was amended in January 1991 by the addition of a Catalogue of Fundamental Rights and Liberties. Article 6 of this states that human life is 'worthy of protection', 'even before birth'. Slovenia represents an exception, in that pressure from the women's movement and women politicians was able to avert such a move. For the present, women in Slovenia are assured continued access to abortion until the tenth week of pregnancy. In Hungary, a group of pro-lifers called Pacem in Utero took the existing abortion law to the Constitutional Court in May 1991. In December 1991, the Court declared the law invalid, since it didn't specify when life begins. They charged the parliament with deciding before the end of 1992 'when life begins'. If parliament failed to

promulgate a decision by that date, the Court's ruling was to become law, making abortion illegal. In fact the Hungarian parliament passed a new law on 17 December 1992 – see main text. (Sources: HCA, *Reproductive Rights in East and Central Europe*, 1992; Commission for Women's Politics, Assembly of the Republic of Slovenia, *Report on the Position of Women in Slovenia*, Ljubljana, November 1992, p. 12.)

39. Dr Khomassuridze, quoted by Du Plessix Gray, *Soviet Women Walking the Tightrope*, 1991, p. 14.

40. Source (for Romania and some of the information on the former Soviet Union), survey article entitled: 'Abortion: Who Believes in a Woman's Right to Choose?', the *Guardian*, 11.8.92; (for Czechoslovakia) Hana Navarová, 1991, personal estimate using data from the Czechoslovak Statistical Bureau; Castle-Kanerová, 'A Culture of Strong Women in the Making?', 1992, p. 119; (for Hungary) Corrin, 'Magyar Women's Lives', 1992, pp. 63–64; (for Poland) Heinen, ' "Polish Democracy is a Masculine Democracy" ', 1992, p. 37.

41. Fuszara, 'Will the Abortion Issue Give Rise to Feminism in Poland?', 1991; and 'Legal Regulation of Abortion in Poland', 1991; *Der Spiegel*, no. 20, 1991.

42. For descriptions of this ordeal, see J. Peers, 'Workers by Hand and Womb – Soviet Women and the Demographic Crisis', in: Barbara Holland, ed., *Soviet Sisterhood: British Feminists on Women in the USSR*, Fourth Estate, London, 1985, p. 134; M. Akchurin, in the *Guardian*, 7.8.92; Olga Lipovskaya quoted in Du Plessix Gray, *Soviet Women Walking the Tightrope*, 1991, p. 19.

43. Statement from the Polish Episcopate's letter cited in Heinen, ' "Polish Democracy is a Masculine Democracy" ', 1992, p. 136. On the equation of abortion with the Holocaust in various countries, see further: (for Poland) Heinen, ibid., 1992, p. 129; (for Croatia) Ruth Rosen, 'Male Democracies, Female Dissidents', in: *Tikkun*, vol. 5, no. 6, 1990, p. 100; (for Germany) *Der Spiegel*, no. 29, 1991; (for Hungary) Corrin, 'Magyar Women's Lives', 1992. Gyula Fekete's vitriolic article 'Mother's Day Greeting with Thorns' initiated an exchange with Hungarian feminist Enikö Bollobás in the literary-political bi-weekly *Hitel* in June 1989.

44. Rosen, 'Male Democracies, Female Dissidents', 1990, pp. 100–101.

45. The situation in Hungary with regard to abortion was taken from the following sources: Corrin, 'Magyar Women's Lives', 1992, and 'Women in Eastern Europe', in: *Labour Focus on Eastern Europe*, no. 41, 1992, p. 46; Zsuzsa Béres, 'A Thousand Words on Hungarian Women', published in *Budapest Week*, March 1991, and reprinted in: *Trouble and Strife*, issue 23, 1991; HCA, *Reproductive Rights in East and Central Europe*, 1992, p. 24; Rita Szilágyi, personal letter to Barbara Einhorn about the situation in Szeged, summer 1992; Antonia Burrows, information relayed to Barbara Einhorn from Budapest detailing the terms of the new 'Law on the Protection of the Foetus', 5.2.93.

46. Rosen, 'Male Democracies, Female Dissidents', 1990.

47. Miroslava Holubová's views were expressed in an interview with Barbara Einhorn, Prague, April 1992; Heitlinger, 'Passage to Motherhood', 1985, pp. 289–90.

48. Details cited from reports in: *Der Spiegel*, no. 20, 1991; and no. 32, 1991.

49. Source: text of draft laws, June–September 1991.

50. Report in: *Der Spiegel*, no. 21, 20.5.92. On the implied treatment of women as political minors, see veteran feminist and pro-choice campaigner Alice Schwarzer, in: *Emma*, no. 1, January/February 1993, pp. 68–69.

51. The passing of the new law legalizing abortion and the subsequent appeal against it were reported in: the *Guardian*, 26.6.92, 27.6.92, 5.8.92, 11.8.92, and 29.5.93. The Constitutional Court met on 8–9 December 1992, and had been expected to pronounce in February 1993, but the decision was delayed until May 1993.

52. Fuszara, 'Will the Abortion Issue Give Rise to Feminism in Poland?' 1991.

53. Ewa Gontarczyk-Wesoła, interview with Barbara Einhorn, Poznan, April 1990; Hanna Jankowska, interview with Barbara Einhorn, Warsaw, June 1991; Polish Women's

League tactics cited from an interview by Barbara Einhorn with Izabela Nowacka, President, Warsaw, May 1991.

54. For Polish public opinion on abortion, see Fuszara, 'The Legal Regulation of Abortion in Poland', 1991; Jankowska, 'Abortion, Church and Politics in Poland', 1991; Heinen, '"Polish Democracy is a Masculine Democracy"', 1992.

55. Information from interviews by Barbara Einhorn with Bożena Umińska, spokesperson for the Polish Feminist Association, and Professor Renata Siemieńska, sociologist working on the status of women in Poland, Warsaw, June 1991. The reader's letter to *Kobieta i Życie* was cited by the magazine's editor Anna Brozowska at an international conference of women journalists in Germany and reported in the German feminist magazine *Emma*, no. 12, December 1992, p. 26.

56. Survey results cited by Malone, 'Women's Rights in Poland', 1992, p. 48.

57. Information on the progress of the abortion law through the Sejm from the *Guardian*, 25.7.92; interview by Barbara Einhorn with Barbara Labuda, chairperson of the women's caucus in the Sejm, Warsaw, June 1991; Malone, 'Women's Rights in Poland', 1992, p. 43.

58. For reports on these recent developments, see the *Guardian*, 27.12.92; Krzysztof Leski in: *Daily Telegraph*, 1.2.93; *Frankfurter Rundschau*, 1.2.93.

59. For the abusive description of Senator Kuratowska as unpatriotic, see Heinen, '"Polish Democracy is a Masculine Democracy"', 1992, p. 135. Kuratowska's views are part of an interview with her in: *Labour Focus on Eastern Europe*, no. 41, 1992, p. 23.

60. These political moves are discussed in detail in Chapter 5 below.

61. I am grateful for much of the Polish information to Hanna Jankowska, spokesperson for the pro-choice organization Pro Femina, in a letter to Barbara Einhorn, October 1992; and in: Hanna Jankowska, 'The Reproductive Rights Campaign in Poland', paper presented to the conference on 'Mary Wollstonecraft and Two Hundred Years of Feminism' held at Sussex University, England, 5–6.12.92.

62. Report in *The German Tribune*, 12.6.92.

63. Cited from David Gow, 'The Dwindling Patter of Little German Feet', in the *Guardian*, 4 February 1992.

64. *Free to Lose* is the title of a book by John Roemer (Polity Press, Cambridge, 1986).

65. Quotation taken from C. Stephen, in the *Guardian*, 11.8.92.

66. Mária Adamik, writing in the FIDESZ-associated weekly *Magyar Narancs*, excerpted in: *East European Reporter*, vol. 4, no. 4, spring/summer 1991.

67. See Wendy Bracewell, 'Problems of Gender and Nationalism', manuscript, 1992.

68. Maja Korać, 'Nationalism and War in the Balkans: The Place and Role of Women', paper presented at the conference on 'Mary Wollstonecraft and 200 Years of Feminism', December 1992.

69. Sources on the former Yugoslavia, including the quotations by Rada Trajković,: Staša Zajović, 'Patriarchy, Language and National Myth: The War and Women in Serbia', in: *Peace News*, March 1992; Branko Milinković, 'Yugoslavia: Women at the Forefront of the Peace Movement', in: *Lutherische Welt-Information*, no. 34, 1991.

70. Information on the rape of Bosnian women was taken from Alexandra Stiglmayer, 'Rape as a Weapon: The War against Women', in: *Stern*, no. 49, 26 November 1992, pp. 22–28 [my translations, BE]; Linda Grant, 'Secret Shame That the Rape Victims of Bosnia Will Take to the Grave', in: *Daily Telegraph*, 1.2.93, p. 8; and Slavenka Drakulić, 'The Rape of Bosnia', in *The Nation* (US), February 1993 and *Elle*, May 1993, pp. 36–40. The Chetniks were a right-wing anti-Communist para-military Serbian organization in the Second World War which has been revived during the present conflict in the former Yugoslavia.

4

Right or Duty?
Women and the Economy

Socialism liberated women from wage exploitation *and* enslaved them by compelling them to work. But the end of socialism hasn't meant gains for women. We fear that we will lose maternity leave *and* our jobs.

Lolita Alimova, Samarkand[1]

Paid employment has been the norm for women in East Central Europe for the past forty years. Now they are the first to be dismissed. A West German commentator has suggested that most of them will never work again. Indeed the idea that around 90 per cent of women of working age could be economically active was simply 'unrealistic'. In Western Europe, less than 50 per cent of working-age women are economically active. This level is 'normal'.[2]

Why do women currently form the majority of the unemployed in many of these countries? In 1990, Czech National Assembly delegate Dr Moserová saw a paradox here: it would seem obvious that the unwieldy heavy industry conglomerates with their outmoded machinery, top-heavy administrative structures and male-dominated workforce would be prime candidates for closure – as would the open-cast mines which have transformed parts of Bohemia into a moonscape of environmental devastation. Yet it was textiles – together with glassware (and armaments) Czechoslovakia's best export – with a heavily female-dominated workforce, which were the first to go under in the process of marketization. Dr Moserová claimed that without the female textile workers, Czechoslovakia would have gone bankrupt in the past. Deafened by machine noise and with ulcerated legs from standing at their work stations, these women had kept the country alive, she maintained, at high cost to themselves.

113

Yet women in the former state socialist countries are not objecting vociferously to their high redundancy levels. They fail to see their jobs as an unambiguous benefit worth defending. What, then, did labour force participation mean to women in East Central Europe? For many of them, the right to work was degraded by state compulsion into an obligation to be endured. It subjected them to the rigours of the double burden – long days, exhaustion, feelings of guilt and inadequacy towards their children, lack of career satisfaction. Małgorzata Tarasiewicz, former leader of Solidarity's Women's Section and current president of Amnesty International in Poland, maintains that 'the motivation for most of them was not the hope of fulfilling career ambitions or the intention of being financially independent but a much more mundane need to make ends meet'.[3] Their attitude was therefore marked by ambivalence and hesitation.

So what was wrong with the worker-mother? Chapter 2 examined the persistently unequal gendered power relations within the family. An analysis of the woman-as-worker side of the equation may help to illuminate women's current lack of enthusiasm for the right to work. Did the problem originate in their conditions of employment? In patterns of occupational segregation within the workforce? Or in the very fact of the onerous double burden?

It is not clear whether state socialism's ideological emphasis on women's labour force participation demonstrated commitment to women's 'emancipation', as they called it, or simple expediency dictated by economic need and demographic imbalances. Whatever the state's intentions, the meaning of work obviously differed for in-dividual women, depending on whether they worked in a profession, or performed physically strenuous or repetitive unskilled work on the production line. Even within state socialism's reductionist paradigm which equated labour force participation with women's emancipation, there were yawning gaps between rhetoric and reality. Legislation for, and the implementation of, equality of opportunity in education and vocational training, women's rights at the work-place, or equal pay for work of equal value, were very different matters. And what got irretrievably lost by state socialism was the need to ameliorate the conditions of work. Rather than humanizing the social relations of production for *all* workers, they promul-gated compensatory protective legislation.[4] This emphasized women's reproductive function rather than their productive capacities, thus entrenching the worker-mother duality. It is not surprising that women are now reacting in such disparate ways to current economic and ideological pressures pushing them out of the workforce.

Socialist feminists and many others in the West have seen labour force participation as a necessary (if not sufficient, as in the crude state socialist model) precondition for the achievement not only of economic independence, but of improved status, meaningful social contacts, job fulfilment and through these, both an enhanced life experience and a greater sense of self-esteem, a more autonomous self-image. Western socialist feminists have also stressed the importance of analysing the gendered stratification of the workforce.

Both the life-enhancing and the discriminatory aspects of paid work make an analysis of the impact of labour force participation on at least two generations of women in East Central Europe all the more compelling. Was their working life an integral part of their self-image? Did they in fact achieve economic independence? If so, did this give them greater autonomy in terms of decision-making? Did they enjoy a better social status than women in Western Europe? Did they have an enhanced self-esteem? In short, were they autonomous subjects more able to articulate their needs and aspirations, and to act on their own behalf, than their Western sisters? Or did they suffer from 'too much' emancipation,[5] wearing themselves out prematurely in the effort to achieve a seamless integration of their two roles? Were they stretched on a rack of eternal guilt about their shortcomings in both, their inadequacies as mother and lack of perfection as worker?

The double load is currently being lightened by confining women to their maternal role, supplanting the Janus-headed worker-mother with the doleful visage of the suffering mother. Current ideology has underwritten the economy's need to shed labour in the transition to the market by reintroducing the notion of the 'family wage'. Opinion polls in the former Soviet Union showed support for this notion, espoused too by the Hungarian Free Democrats (SZDSZ) and (although not implemented!) by Solidarity in Poland under Wałeşa.[6] Interviews conducted by this author reveal a widespread subjective tendency on the part of women themselves to reinterpret their redundancy as the embodiment of a 'choice' previously unknown, enabling them to spend time at home with the children. Yet in the longer term, confining the parameters of female rights and duties to the private domain curtails women's freedom in terms of choice about the ways in which they wish to develop their potential. It also undermines their ability to exercise citizenship rights in the public sphere of work and politics.

Levels of Labour Force Participation

Under state socialism, female labour force participation was extremely high, with women accounting on average for 45–51 per cent of the total labour force in 1989–90. Over 70 per cent of women of working age were employed or undergoing vocational training. This number reached more than 91 per cent in the former GDR in 1989, as compared with 55 per cent in the Federal Republic of Germany (FRG). There was a dramatic growth in the numbers of women who were economically active during the state socialist period, providing a marked contrast with the figures for Western Europe.[7] While there was also a substantial increase in the numbers of economically active women in some Western European countries during the post-Second World War period, the figures remained both significantly lower than those in Eastern Europe, and crucially differentiated in one important respect. The great majority of women in East Central Europe worked full-time, whereas the growth in female labour force participation in, say, Britain and West Germany has been due largely to increases in part-time work.[8]

The reasons for the past predominance of full-time work among economically active women in East Central Europe were twofold. There was considerable government pressure for this, since the decimation of the male population in the Second World War and the inefficiencies of socialist production combined to produce ongoing labour shortages, exacerbated in the case of the GDR by people escaping to the West. The demographic imbalance which favoured, indeed required, women's employment was then perpetuated by the subsequent downward trend in the birthrate, itself influenced by women's double burden of full-time work and household responsibilities.

A second reason for full-time work dominating female employment was the necessity in most East Central European countries for at least two wages in order to fulfil basic household needs, despite subsidies on rents, public transport and many essential foodstuffs and clothing items, especially children's clothing. Financial pressure was especially acute for the high number of female-headed households in these countries, resulting from the almost uniformly high divorce rate discussed in Chapter 2.

Despite this double, material and ideological pressure, however, many women longed for the opportunity to work part-time in order to combine with greater ease their paid employment and their domestic role. This desire is evident, for instance, in the preference for part-time work expressed by a substantial proportion of women workers,

116

concurrent with a marked increase in the number of women actually working part-time, in Czechoslovakia between 1986 and 1989.[9]

Natalya Baranskaya's novella *A Week Like Any Other*[10] provides a graphic example of the way work time was invaded by a collective self-help system devised to ease, by sharing, the difficult feat of acquiring scarce foodstuffs. The time-consuming tasks of standing in the queue, and dragging home heavily laden shopping bags, were overwhelmingly performed by women. Travel alone takes three hours per day for the young working mothers in Baranskaya's novella. And time-budget studies have verified this fictional account of the fact that women enjoyed far less leisure time for relaxation, further study, or recreational activities than men.

In fact, women in East Central Europe and the former Soviet Union worked longer hours than anywhere else in the world, taking into account their paid work time and the time spent on household tasks. And in terms of hours worked per week, the gender gap was greater in those countries than in any other industrialized region of the world. Despite men's higher participation in the second economy – in, for example, Poland or Hungary – the enormous differential in time spent on domestic labour meant that women worked on average seven hours more per week than men.[11]

Furthermore, state socialist régimes exerted considerable pressure on women to involve themselves in the wider concerns of society. This meant participation in local or central government, union politics, school or neighbourhood committees. The resulting triple burden caused severe stress, overburdening women to the point that it is understandable if many of them perceived – or perceive, in retrospect – the right to work as yet another obligation, rather than a right on which they might pride themselves.

There were both benefits and costs in state socialism's emphasis on female labour force participation. However, the need to shed labour in the current economic restructuring process will tend to render anachronistic the notion of paid work as the norm for women. Relegation to primary responsibility for the family will inevitably have profound repercussions. Not only will it undermine women's economic independence, it is also likely to have adverse effects on their self-esteem and their perception of their role in society. This in turn must have ramifications for gender relations within the family, as well as attitudinal and behavioural implications for the education of the next generation. What was the reality behind the much-vaunted pre-1989 levels of women's education?

Education and Training

Would-be investors in the newly marketizing economies of East Central Europe have noted with surprise the high level of training and education of the workforce. This was particularly true of the female labour force compared with levels in Western Europe. Equal access to tertiary education was attained by young women in the Soviet Union and East Central Europe much earlier than women in Western Europe or the USA. Ireneusz Bialecki and Barbara Heyns document the fact that university training in Eastern and Central Europe was close to 50 per cent female by the early 1970s, but that 'it took the more economically "developed" West at least a decade longer'.[12] Such a high level of education among the female workforce would appear to lend credence to state socialism's genuine commitment to 'emancipating' women, rather than simply requiring their labour power.

The opposite case is put by Hungarian sociologist Júlia Szalai. She argues that women's involvement in the labour force was actually necessitated by state policies making it a prerequisite for 'access to social services', indeed that 'eligibility rights based on citizenship were substituted by ones based on having regular and continuous employment'.[13] In addition, it has already been noted that the 'two-earner family model' was an 'economic imperative' owing to the fact that most men did not earn a 'family wage'. Hence women's labour force participation during the state socialist period could not be regarded as 'fully voluntary'. Indeed Mária Ladó claims that 'for the past four decades there has not been any real choice for women'.[14]

Nor is the general observation that the female workforce in East Central Europe was highly qualified without its problems. On the one hand, women were generally better educated than men, and by 1985 even outnumbered men at post-secondary educational institutions in Bulgaria, East Germany, Hungary and Poland.[15] On the other, it can be shown that most women were employed in jobs involving lower skill levels and commanding lower pay than men. This statement was true to a differing degree of most state socialist countries and raises the question: did the socialist state foster women's education as a means to 'emancipation', or with the more narrowly expedient perspective of a well-qualified workforce as the precondition for increased productivity?

In the former GDR, all schooling was gender neutral, with a unified compulsory curriculum throughout the ten to twelve years of schooling. In the early years, girls were encouraged to enter technical colleges and scientific and mathematical disciplines at university. High numbers of female students in economics, the natural sciences and mathematics in the mid- to late 1980s across all of East Central Europe show the success of this policy.[16] Once at work, there was positive discrimination in favour of women, at least in the GDR case, with Measures for the Promotion of Women (*Frauenförderungsmaßnahmen*) enabling them to improve their qualifications by attending further education or training courses on day release from their jobs or on other paid leave schemes. This meant that by 1988 in East Germany, 'entry-level skill or professional qualifications had reached gender balance in age cohorts up to age forty'.[17]

In Poland, Hungary and Czechoslovakia on the other hand, secondary schooling remained divided along traditional lines between technical and humanities-based schools. The fact that boys tended to enter technical schools whilst girls opted for the humanities meant that gender imbalances were already entrenched at the point of entry to the labour market. Boys began their working lives after completing some form of vocational training integral to their schooling, while girls, despite relatively higher levels of general education, entered the workforce as unskilled labour.

Bialecki and Heyns have illustrated this trend in their study of educational policy and practice in Poland. They argue that the high levels of female educational attainment, and indeed the feminization of many professions, happened by default. Because class and not gender was prioritized in state socialism's form of egalitarianism, these outcomes were actually the unintended by-product of educational policies formulated in the late 1950s and early 1960s to expand technical and vocational education for the proletariat and the peasantry.[18] The fact that increases in vocational education were most evident among males from a working class or rural background reinforced the gender imbalance in the skilled workforce.

Júlia Szalai confirms the same pattern for Hungary, where girls chose 'less vocational, more academic forms of secondary education' and hence entered the workforce less skilled than boys. She argues that 'women provided the great bulk of investment-saving semi-skilled and unskilled labour: their proportion in this segment of the labour force doubled from 27 per cent in 1949 to 54 per cent in 1984', while unskilled and semi-skilled jobs had 'dropped to 31 per cent of total available jobs by 1990.... Even now, as many as 37 per cent of women in the workforce are unskilled and semi-skilled workers. In other words, despite their rising level of education, women were ... heavily over-represented in the least skilled segments of the labour market.'

Under new market conditions, these basic patterns are borne out. The high proportion of women among unskilled and semi-skilled workers is reflected in Hungarian unemployment statistics for May 1992, according to which women form 41 per cent of the total unemployed, but 40 per cent of unskilled and 54.5 per cent of semi-skilled workers who are unemployed. This imbalance also contributes to wage differentials, since it reinforces 'the prevailing dominance of men in well-paid, more mobile jobs in all industries, whereas women (even with broader, though less job-oriented education) are increasingly caught in the lower-paid, more monotonous blue- and white-collar jobs'.[19]

The fact that women were if anything over-represented in tertiary level education is also two-edged. Polish sociologist Renata Siemieńska points out that there was under state socialism little motivation for men to go to university (for which the humanities-based secondary school or lyceum formed the prerequisite). The industrial bias of state socialist countries meant that a man's earning potential was far more favourable as a skilled blue-collar worker than as a university graduated professional. In Poland, what was seen as the 'excessive' feminization of medicine resulted in the imposition of quotas favouring male medical students. Yet comparable quotas were never applied to encourage men to enter other traditionally feminized professions such as nursing or the care of young children. These quotas were removed after they were successfully challenged as discriminatory by the Ombudsman in 1987.[20] In East Germany too, girls' higher performance at secondary level and the ensuing disproportion of women entering universities had caused the introduction of a form of positive discrimination to boost the numbers of boys gaining university places.

The high proportion of female university students was common to all the former state socialist countries. This in turn explains the phenomenon of women dominating the lower levels of academic and particularly research positions – a large sector of the labour force in the state socialist countries – as well as such occupations as sociologist, psychologist, editor, journalist. And a disproportionate number of students in humanities subjects and teacher training were women.[21] In Czechoslovakia for example, a Civic Forum spokeswoman for higher education stated in 1990 that women comprised 80 per cent of students in Arts Faculties and 90 per cent of those studying education.

Despite the high level of general education among young women, there is evidence that even before 1989, many of them tended to opt for training in occupations traditionally deemed 'suitable for girls' or seen as 'women's work'. It seems therefore that educational means alone do not necessarily guarantee the overcoming of gender-specific stereotypes and preconceptions about work. In the former GDR for example, in 1987 over 60 per cent of female school leavers opted for training in a mere 16 out of a total of 259 occupations. Young women comprised 95 per cent of trainee textile and 99 per cent of trainee garment workers in 1989. And close to 100 per cent of trainee secretaries and salespersons were women. Very similar patterns operated in Hungary, where in vocational schools in 1990-91, only 0.7 per cent of apprentices in metallurgy and 1.1 per cent in engineering were women, but 98 per cent of apprentices in the textile and garment industries were women.[22]

Pre-transition Patterns of Employment

Female employment under state socialism was marked by paradox. On the one hand, women did succeed in entering several traditionally male-dominated occupations, professions and sectors of the economy. On the other, there was marked and continuing occupational segregation of a kind not dissimilar from that obtaining in Western Europe. Contradic-tions were not confined to the situation of women within the labour force. Rather it was the complicated inter-relationship between their productive and their reproductive roles which was problematic. The attempt to regulate this relationship through gender-based prohibitions has been criticized by the authors of a 1992 World Bank report as both inefficient, in that such regulations may distort the functioning of the labour market, and discriminatory. In cases where women are banned from night-shifts or overtime work, this reduces their flexibility in seeking new employment in the transition period. It is also unclear why any such protective measures should not apply equally to men and women.[23]

In the past, socialist realist stereotypes of a woman tractor driver or women wearing hard hats on a building site did mirror real changes. In comparison with Western Europe, women were well represented in the heavy industry, construction and mining sectors of the economy. But most women employed here worked in the over-staffed clerical and low-level administrative areas. And in absolute terms, the level of female representation was low in heavy as opposed to light industry, such as chemicals, clothing, food processing and textiles. And the retail and service sectors were heavily female-dominated. The disproportion in centrally planned economies between the industrial and service sectors might have been assumed to protect women's employment relative to

121

men's in the current transition period. In fact whilst heavy industry and mining are indeed amongst the hardest hit by collapse due to pollution or old technology, the top-heavy clerical and administrative structures in these industries make for a surprisingly high level of female redundancies in, for example, the Polish coal mining industry.[24]

Women were therefore concentrated in lower status, low-paid jobs within lower status, low-paid sectors of the economy. Although they constituted a high proportion of workers in industry overall, they remained clustered in female-dominated light industrial production and in the clerical and administrative branches of both light and heavy industry. Hungarian economist Mária Ladó cites more than 90 per cent female domination of occupations such as typists, accountants, pay-roll clerks, financial clerks, cashiers and ticket-office clerks. In the mid-1980s in Hungary, women accounted for over half of all office workers in central public administration, and two thirds in local councils.[25]

Heavy industry was prioritized by state socialism, but women's participation as production workers in heavy industry was low, thus privileging the male blue-collar worker. Júlia Szalai points out as 'one of the ironies of the socialist economy ... [the fact] that better-educated white-collar women tend to have relatively lower incomes than blue-collar men'.[26]

Therefore, despite some of the earliest equal pay legislation, the state socialist economies were characterized by a gender gap in incomes which was not dissimilar to that in Western Europe. Women earned on average 66–75 per cent of men's salary, across all branches of economic activity.[27] Skilled workers in heavy industry and mining comprised the elite of these economies in terms of earning power. The concentration of women in clerical or low-grade administrative occupations meant that even women employed in the prioritized sectors of the economy earned a fraction of the wages commanded by male workers.

Female production workers in industry or in construction in the former GDR took home an average 12 per cent lower pay than their male counterparts. Nevertheless, the wage gap was not as wide as in the Federal Republic, where women earned on average 65–70 per cent of male incomes as compared with 76–84 per cent on average in the former GDR. In Poland, studies conducted in the early 1980s established that in all occupational categories barring the professions, gender was a far more decisive factor in wage differentials than level of education, occupational position, age, job tenure, or membership of the Communist Party. Amongst industrial workers in Poland in 1989, women earned only 70 per cent of men's wages. Yet the wage gap is equally marked in the feminized professions. Hence in May 1990, while female lawyers earned 98 per cent as much as male lawyers, female doctors and social workers brought home only 72 per cent, women in administration and management earned 68 per cent, and women bookkeepers scraped together a mere 66.3 per cent of men's pay.[28]

In Hungary, startling figures show that three quarters of women actually earned less than the national average wage, compared with only one third of men. And although the number of female workers who remained unskilled by 1980 was only marginally higher than the number of male unskilled workers, the gender gap among semi-skilled and especially skilled workers was still very marked. Around 59 per cent of women workers were engaged in manual work; half of those were semi-skilled and another quarter were unskilled.[29]

In part these gender imbalances were attributable to discriminatory hiring practices reflecting a view of women as 'unreliable' labour because of their high level absenteeism on maternity and sick leave to care for children. Female choice also contributed, with maternal responsibilities leading women to choose jobs which were convenient but less demanding. Such jobs tended not to exploit fully their education and training, and were therefore also badly paid. Despite a degree of positive discrimination such as privileged access to childcare facilities and longer annual leave, single mothers were more likely than other women to choose less demanding jobs. Alena Kroupová has calculated that over 30 per cent of all Czechoslovak women workers were employed in jobs which under-utilized their skills and qualifications.[30]

Those industrial branches with a high level concentration of female production workers were also lower-status and hence less well-paid. In light industry, these include electronics, chemicals, pharmaceuticals, optics, lighting, textiles, clothing and the food industry. Weavers, spinners, tailors and other manual workers in the textile and garment trades in Hungary were four-fifths female.[31] The poor earning capacity of women in light industry and textiles notwithstanding, these sectors will still be hard hit in competition on the world market. In their World Bank report, Monica Fong and Gillian Paul distinguish between the real and perceived cost of female labour.[32]

Nevertheless, the social provisions available to women under state socialism did make them relatively expensive to employ. In future the decisive factors will be purely market-driven, and women stand to lose their jobs or social provisions, or both.

Female domination of the caring professions and the retail and service sectors, in jobs involving catering, cleaning, serving, was extremely marked. Qualitatively speaking, it could be said that in the centrally planned economies of state socialism, in a manner different only in degree from that typical of Western market economies, a gendered division of labour made women perform, in their paid work, jobs which can be seen as an extension of their unpaid domestic roles, namely feeding, caring for, serving, or cleaning up after, men and children.

Women were under-represented towards the top of career hierarchies even in female-dominated professions. Pre-school facilities were exclusively staffed by women in the former GDR, but although in 1985 77 per cent of all teachers were women, only 32 per cent of head teachers were female. Women accounted for almost half of all employees in higher education in the former GDR, yet scarcely 3 per cent of those were in top positions, such as full professors, departmental heads or institute directors. Bialecki and Heyns have shown that although women in Poland accounted for 81 per cent of the workforce in education and science, they comprised only 13 per cent of full professors in 1987–88, and there was only one female university rector. The situation was similar in Hungary. In 1984, 80 per cent of primary school teachers, 50 per cent of secondary level teachers and 33 per cent of university teaching staff were women. In a 1976 survey conducted by the then Karl Marx University of Economics (now the Budapest University of Economics), although more than 50 per cent of instructors and 33 per cent of assistant professors were women, only 20 per cent of associate professors and 4 per cent of full professors were women.[33]

Nevertheless, it should not be overlooked that women *did* make inroads into formerly male-dominated professions. This was especially true in medicine and law.[34] But as they became feminized, these professions tended to become devalued in terms of both status and remuneration. Mária Ladó identifies a vicious circle whereby those sectors which employed large numbers of women offered less favourable wages, and vice versa. She maintains that 'the feminization of a career starts when, following technical, economic and social changes, the status and prestige of a given career begins to fall. Thus cause and effect are interwoven in a self-maintaining and self-reproducing mechanism'. As a consequence of feminization in the 1980s, around 80 per cent of all Hungarian women workers were in occupations in which female workers constituted the majority. Even within feminized professions, the apex of career hierarchies was dominated by men. In medicine, the senior hospital consultants tended to be men, whilst in

1989 in the former GDR, 95.5 per cent of trainee nurses were women. In Bulgaria in 1989, 90 per cent of paramedical personnel but only 35 per cent of doctors and dentists were women. Within specializations, there was a stereotypical gender divide: surgery, neurology, and psychiatry were 80 per cent male, whilst gynaecology and paediatrics were female-dominated.[35]

On the other hand, it was not unusual for a woman to be the chief engineer or architect on a male-dominated building site. Brigitte Reimann's novel *Franziska Linkerhand*[36] about the construction of a new housing estate in the former GDR is one of several to fictionalize such cases. A socialist realist stereotype from this scenario is that of the female crane driver. One might be forgiven for feeling that this job involves the kind of manual dexterity, albeit at considerable spatial remove, for which women have always been noted. At the end of the day, it seems that what was achieved under state socialism was 'a high degree of female representation in the professions alongside continuing gender segregation of the rest of the labour force'.[37]

Even within female-dominated sectors of the economy such as light industry or textiles, the managers still tended to be male.[38] The under-representation of women at the top of career hierarchies is illustrated by data on management. In 1989, only 14 per cent of the total female labour force in Czechoslovakia held management positions. Of those, 65 per cent were in lower-level, 25 per cent in mid-level and only 10 per cent in top management. The proportion of women holding top management positions in Poland in 1988 was even lower at 4.5 per cent. In Hungary in 1980, only 12 per cent of managers of enterprises or directors of institutes were women. Even more telling perhaps because of women's traditionally strong involvement in agricultural labour, only 5.6 per cent of directors of agricultural cooperatives were women in the same year. By 1991, only 5 per cent of large Hungarian companies were headed by women.[39]

In the former GDR, a breakdown of women's share of leading positions by industrial sector shows that although the level of women managers in female-dominated sectors like light industry and trade was quite high, the figures were not commensurate with the high overall female share of employment in those sectors. Hence in light industry, women formed 56 per cent of the labour force, but accounted for only 44 per cent of leading positions, and in retail and trade 72 per cent of the workforce, but only 62 per cent of leading positions. In industry overall, they formed 41 per cent of the workforce, but only 21 per cent of those in management, and less than 5 per cent of those in top management.[40]

What explains the diminishing presence of women towards the top of career hierarchies? *Frauenreport 90*, the first ever statistical report on women in the former GDR, compiled by Dr Marina Beyer, Secretary of State for Women's Affairs in the 1989–90 GDR transitional government, evaluates state socialism's record as contradictory. The report cites as positive the legislative and educational equality enjoyed by women. Against that, it lists gender inequalities within the family, lack of equality of career opportunity, and continuing prejudices against women as managers.[41]

Further, it could be argued that even prior to 1989, some of the affirmative action measures promulgated in favour of women in fact mitigated against their being promoted to managerial posts. Chapter 1 documented the state socialist system of paid leave to look after sick children which, even in those countries where it was available to either parent, was usually taken by women. According to working-class women interviewed in the former GDR in 1988, it was they who took this leave in around four fifths of cases.[42] The fact of their frequent absenteeism led to their being defined by employers as 'unreliable' workers, which in turn mitigated against their promotion to positions of responsibility, thus reinforcing patterns of occupational segregation.

A further explanation for the under-representation of women at the top of career hierarchies can be found in women's own reluctance to take on responsible positions at work. This tendency was reflected in a survey conducted for the ILO in the Russian city of Naberejnye Chelny. The results revealed pronounced reluctance on the part of both men and women to take on management roles, but a substantial gender gap in responses. Only 8 per cent of men and 3 per cent of women in the sample aspired to become managers. Even against a background of work degradation and devaluation of individual initiative, men still showed greater willingness to take on positions of responsibility, though 68 per cent of men and 72 per cent of women interviewed stated baldly that they would not dream of becoming managers.[43]

Women in Poland displayed far less willingness than men to accept promotion. And in Czechoslovakia, a 1989 study carried out in the Škoda heavy engineering factory in Plzeň showed similar results. Of the plant's total workforce of 34,000, women numbered 35 per cent: 42 per cent of whom were on the shop floor, and 58 per cent in administration. Asked whether they would wish to work in management, 49.8 per cent said no; only 3.3 per cent expressed positive interest in the prospect.[44]

Further reasons for the invisibility of women in top positions were state enterprise managers' reluctance to promote women in view of the extended maternity leave and paid sick leave provisions already mentioned, and the differential retirement age. Women in most state socialist countries were entitled to retire at fifty-five (sixty in Poland), men five years later. Structural as well as socio-cultural reasons thus contributed to the vicious circle whereby women themselves were less likely to take on management positions, for which male managers anyway tended not to consider them suitable.

Although women's employment was central to the state socialist project, it is unclear in retrospect whether this followed a real commitment to the 'emancipation' of women, or merely an economy-led demand. Further, motivation aside, the record on equality of opportunity is highly contradictory. On the one hand, legislation, educational access and positive discriminatory measures mobilized women and supported them in improving their qualifications and skill levels. On the other, the structure of the labour force featured marked occupational segregation and wage differentials. Will the female labour force fare better in a market economy? An analysis of the present transition period will illuminate some of the opportunities and the costs of marketization for women.

The Transition to the Market: Gender-Specific Implications

The transition from centrally planned to market economies in East Central Europe represents a moment of opportunity, but also of high costs, at least in the short term. Spiralling inflation is compounded by high unemployment, and a decline in real wages. The highest price rises have been registered in those basic necessities which were previously subsidized, such as rent, foodstuffs, public transport, childcare, and children's clothes. Taken together, these factors make the management of household budgets extremely problematic.

Real wages declined by 28 per cent in Poland and 15–20 per cent in Hungary during 1990, and by a further 10 per cent in Hungary during 1991–92.[45] Food prices in Hungary went up by an average 35 per cent in 1990, with meat and milk up 40 per cent, and butter up 50 per cent. In Bulgaria, prices jumped 1,200 per cent when they were freed in February 1991, with wages remaining static. Prices rose 600–700 per cent in Poland during 1990. A Polish government survey as early as January 1990 showed that families were spending 60–65 per cent of household budgets on food, and another 20 per cent on regular bills, leaving only 15–20 per cent for other expenditure. This trend

127

inevitably meant a marked decline in consumer demand with a knock-on effect which magnified the problems of, for example, the textile and shoe industries. In Hungary too, the drop in domestic demand as a result of falling real incomes and reduced consumption was noted in 1992.[46]

The removal of subsidies on childcare facilities meant that already in spring 1990, many women in Poland were reputedly having to give up their jobs because they could not afford the cost of childcare. Women's average salary at that time was 400,000 złoty per month, of which rent, phone, electricity etc. took 25 per cent, and the basic food bill the rest. Yet at the same time, kindergarten charges were 60–80,000 per month per child. There were reports of lone mothers sending their children to board with someone in the countryside in order to be able to continue going to work so as to maintain themselves and their children. Izabela Nowacka, President of the Polish Women's League, reported in June 1991 that 50 per cent of kindergartens in Łódź had already been closed down because the sharp price rise had led so many mothers to remove their children. The loss of childcare facilities compounded the already acute female unemployment in Łódź, resulting from the closure of the textile industry which had dominated the city.

In East Germany too, the textile industry is collapsing. Women comprised 75 per cent of the textile workers in the past. The Saxon Cotton and Thread Spinning Works, for example, used to employ 13,000 workers. In 1992, while production was being wound down, the workforce had shrunk to 1,300 and was set to fall to a mere 300. Its products used to be exported to over thirty countries.[47]

Understandably, these abrupt and acute changes have brought general despondency in their wake. A survey of 6,000 families conducted by the Institute of Economic and Social Studies of the Hungarian Trade Unions in December 1990 established that 48.8 per cent of them felt their financial situation had substantially worsened. A June 1992 EMNID poll for *Der Spiegel* in Germany reported that 70 per cent of East Germans thought the economic situation was either bad or very bad. Monika Lopez, a 35-year-old married mother of four in the new Federal states, expressed a widespread sense of hopelessness:

> It's shit now. My husband commutes, working in West Germany. I was one of the first to lose my job in November 1990. ... It's better for your kids, they said. You can fetch coal to heat for them in the mornings and make school lunches in peace. How hypocritical can you get! With four children, every employer will think: No thanks. Now I do any kind of shit job: cleaning, scrubbing, painting windows, mending fences, shovelling

rubble. The main thing is not to become a case for social security. If that happens, I'll turn on the gas and kill all of us.[48]

In summer 1992, a survey of attitudes conducted by Mintel International in Bulgaria, Czechoslovakia, Hungary, Poland and the European part of Russia showed that more than three out of four Poles thought things were 'a lot better' under state socialism, and that well over half of respondents in every former state socialist country said there were too many changes. The survey documented a fall in GDP and a widening gap between rich and poor throughout these countries. It concluded that Portugal, poorest country in the EC, was nevertheless richer than Poland, Romania and European Russia, and raised doubts about the survival of optimism in the face of a continuing decline in economic conditions.[49]

Unemployment, Retraining, Re-employment Opportunities

The struggle to survive in the market, accompanied by the pressures of the privatization process, creates an inexorable logic for the need to shed labour. The unproductive over-employment of the state socialist period has been well documented. So too the archaic technological base and poor infrastructure operating in those economies have been much cited as barriers to foreign investment. Privatization, marketization more generally, and the introduction of new technology therefore combine to force high levels of redundancies and unemployment.

In this process, it seems that women are the first to go. It is striking that in all of the former state socialist countries of East Central Europe bar Hungary, they currently form the majority of the unemployed, constituting 50–70 per cent of the current total. As of mid-1992, women were estimated to make up 70 per cent of the unemployed (80 per cent in Moscow) in post-Soviet Russia. In Brandenburg, one in five women were out of work, and in the new Federal German states overall, women accounted for 67 per cent of the total number unemployed in early 1992. In Poland in April 1991, women accounted for 52 per cent of the unemployed, and in Bulgaria in the same month, for 62 per cent. At the end of March 1992, 52 per cent of the total unemployed in Czechoslovakia and 56 per cent in the Czech lands were women.[50]

Why is it that women constitute the majority of the unemployed in all of these countries except Hungary? For at least two generations of women, it was the norm to be employed in the labour force. Women could scarcely be construed as a 'reserve army of labour', but rather

129

constituted a permanent and very substantial section of the workforce. In this situation it is not immediately evident why, faced with the need to shed labour, women should be the first to be dismissed.

What does become obvious on closer examination is that the very rights that women did enjoy under state socialism, and the policies of positive discrimination which underwrote those rights, are now operating against their interests as employees. So, for example, women are dismissed as 'unreliable workers', precisely because of the extended childcare leave and the paid leave to look after sick children which they still enjoy.

Legislation which is still legally valid, such as maternity leave, is currently being disregarded by enterprises struggling to survive in the new market conditions. In Russia, this legislation is in practice being 'violated all the time', maintains Anastasia Posadskaya, Director of the Institute for Gender Studies at the Russian Academy of Sciences, 'because either the job doesn't exist any more, or the enterprise has been privatized and the new owners feel no responsibility to take the women back'.[51]

There are many instances of massive regional concentrations of female unemployment. One reason for this is the dismantling of the enormously top-heavy central and local government bureaucracies of state socialism, in which most of the lower-level technical, clerical and administrative staff were women. Another is the massive level of university department and research institute closures within the formerly enormous scientific and research sectors of state socialism. These closures are partly accounted for by the discrediting of entire subject fields such as philosophy, Marxism-Leninism, and often history and economics, but partly by lack of government finance. As in the state administrative sector, a high proportion of lower-level researchers and university teachers, and almost all administrative and clerical staff in these institutions, were women. Recent Hungarian unemployment data echoes the predominance of women in administration. A breakdown according to professional groups in May 1992 shows women as constituting 41 per cent of the total number registered unemployed, but within that, a high 66.5 per cent and 88.9 per cent of two levels of administrators, and 63.4 per cent of the total non-manual workers.[52]

A further cause of high female unemployment is to be found in the collapse of the textile and clothing industries which were very important in the state socialist period but with very few exceptions cannot compete in the world market on the basis of quality or price against imports, particularly from the developing countries and the DAEs

(Dynamic Asian Economies). This is the outcome in the first instance of the loss of bilateral trading agreements with the former Soviet Union and the transfer to hard currency trade under newly liberalized foreign trade régimes.

In Slovakia, however, the textile industry seems to be surviving with export markets to Italy assured. In Martin in Slovakia, plans are underway to establish an entirely new, high-tech textile enterprise in a project to convert and diversify the town's heavily concentrated arms industry. In Trenčín, which had 5,000 registered unemployed at the time, of whom 102 were qualified machinists, a clothing factory advertised in March 1992 for machinists. None of the local qualified workers applied, due to the fact that the wages were not sufficiently differentiated from unemployment benefits. As a result, the jobs were offered to workers from neighbouring Ukraine, for whom apparently a low Slovak salary would appear high.

These kinds of pay and living standard differentials between the former state socialist countries will have enormous repercussions in terms of the movement of labour between countries, with ramifications for issues of nationality, social welfare and citizenship. It is not unlikely that a new breed of 'guest workers' will be born, including the Russians who drive to Poland to set up stalls in the world's largest street market underneath the former Palace of Culture in Warsaw. By spring 1991, there were already 20,000 East Germans a month seeking work in the Western part of the country,[53] and there were reports of many more who commute weekly to the West. This emerging trend could create major gender-skewed demographic distortions, with fit and skilled men becoming weekly commuters westwards or longer term 'guest workers' while women remain behind to care for the elderly and the young in the industrial and environmental wastelands of the former state socialist countries.[54]

One of the disturbing phenomena of the present transition period is the lack of forward planning, particularly in relation to the specific employment needs of women. There is no consciousness on the part of politicians that regional concentrations of high female unemployment, for example, or the widespread closure of childcare facilities, could have gender-specific implications for which one should plan in terms of retraining opportunities. Part of the problem here is that state intervention and the notion of planning are themselves in disrepute as a legacy of the over-planned and -centralized economic management of state socialism. Retraining is haphazard and non-focused, and in most of these countries seems to consist, as far as women are concerned,

131

almost exclusively and universally of computer training courses. This may represent a skilling process for secretarial, clerical or administrative workers, but for highly skilled female industrial workers, fully qualified women engineers, or researchers, it must mean a level of de-skilling.

In the future, it is possible that the introduction of new technology, or the much-needed expansion of the retail and service sectors may create new opportunities which will favour women's employment. In their World Bank discussion paper, Monica Fong and Gillian Paul suggest this, noting that 'many women – because of experience and education – have acquired strong positions in potentially expanding sectors, such as consumer goods and service industries, particularly financial services, commerce and trade, and information technology. They have also developed entrepreneurial skills that could prove advantageous in the private sector'.[55]

However, at least one set of professions which were feminized and of course relatively unimportant in state socialism's command economy may well become 'masculinized' under market conditions. It is in the banking, finance and insurance sector perhaps more than any other that marketization has produced an enormous growth in size and prestige. It will be interesting to monitor whether the market-induced enhance-ment in the prestige of accountants, bank and insurance clerks will lead to increased salary levels and the consequent displacement of women by men. Fong and Paul point out that policymakers' neglect 'during transition of the particular employment needs and requirements of women ... would have negative consequences, not only for parity between men and women, but also for reform'. This important insight, namely that to neglect the gender implications is shortsighted and ultimately inefficient in terms of the success of the economic reform process itself, leads Fong and Paul to recommend a series of 'pro-active measures', including retraining programmes for women and the provision of childcare facilities.

In the shorter term, however, the process of marketization is marked by the closure of old industries rather than investment in new branches, by the closure of childcare facilities and a dearth of retraining programmes specifically geared to women's needs, so that women are particularly badly affected. There is also evidence to suggest that the introduction of new technology itself, even prior to the current rapid and fundamental economic reform, was linked with the displacement of women. Despite the fact that new production aids such as information technology, flexible automation, or robotization can mean a qualitative improvement in working conditions, which might suggest the creation of a more woman-friendly working environment, women's share of these sectors in the former GDR showed a continuous decline during the 1980s, even taking into account the creation of female jobs in microelectronic and chip production.[56]

This would seem to suggest what might be deemed a reversal of gender stereotypes. As new technology makes jobs cleaner and more highly skilled, men opt to move into them, leaving women to perform the simple and repetitive tasks or the lower status jobs which do not offer career-enhancement opportunities. In *Frauenreport 90*, Dr Marina Beyer considers a set of different explanations for this phenomenon. First, the introduction of new technology often requires relevant or specialist training, for which women are less likely to volunteer because of their family responsibilities. The same constraint operates against women taking up such jobs, since for example robotization in the car industry often involves shift work. Finally, and even more gender-specifically, the report notes that jobs involving the most modern technologies often command higher wages, and are therefore more likely to be offered to men. This tendency for women to be pushed out of formerly female-dominated occupations by the introduction of new technology is confirmed by figures showing substantial decreases in the percentage of young women in the GDR beginning vocational training in data processing and electronics between 1980 and 1989.[57]

Mária Ladó has registered a parallel tendency in Hungary. Margaret Sutherland notes that this trend operates in both Eastern and Western Europe. For example, in computers, software tends to be viewed as women's domain while hardware is male-ascribed, and salaries get adjusted accordingly. Sutherland cites a report of the Commission of the European Community showing a similar pattern of gender-based segregation operating in the field of information technology.[58]

A number of Polish economists now accept large-scale unemployment as inevitable, according to the Darwinian notion that 'there will be winners and losers' in the transformation process. Professor Antoni Kukliński feels that the urgent need is for Polish society to develop a psychology of competitiveness, 'an élite that will be competitive on the European scene'. To this end, he proposed that what he deemed the stifling egalitarianism of socialist educational policy be rejected and that Warsaw University become a training school for the élite along the lines of the French '*hautes écoles*'. In economic terms, he claimed that 'the dilemma "equality versus efficiency" must be solved in favour of efficiency. ... In order to develop the mechanism of individual motivations we need an "optimum" amount of inequality.'[59]

A significant impediment to women's re-employment prospects is that neither sex discrimination in employment opportunities, nor such issues as sexual harassment at work were on state socialism's agenda. The result is that now, advertisements for jobs are frequently blatantly gender-specific. 'Men only' advertisements are widespread. For example, in the Slovak Republic in February 1991 there were 7,563 vacancies, but only 29 per cent of them were for women. In Hungary in 1988 and 1989, between 65 per cent and 71 per cent of vacancies for manual jobs were men-only. Mária Ladó reported that the better the job offered, the more likely it is to specify men-only. Foreign joint ventures openly prefer men to women in their job advertisements and many companies specify men for their higher managerial positions. Women in Poland reported that the length of skirt to be worn to interview or the shape of legs favoured for the job has been included in some advertisements. The state-run employment agency initially had different departments for men and women, which inevitably meant gender-specific job vacancy advertisements.[60]

Another problem is the requirement, often stated in job advertisements or by employment agencies, that a person seeking work be 'available' to take up a job at a moment's notice. Women with young children are less likely to be immediately available, and are thus disadvantaged from the outset. Getting a job is predicated on having one's children placed, yet finding a childcare place is often dependent on having a job.

In January 1990 there were three unemployed women, but just one unemployed man, for every job offer in Poland. By April 1991, there were 17 unemployed men for each vacancy for men, but 59 unemployed women for each vacancy for women. In December 1991, despite the fact that over 50 per cent of unemployed people in Poland were women, there were job offers for only 0.83 per cent of unemployed women. In this situation, Fong and Paul have calculated that the probability of obtaining new employment in East Central Europe is over three times greater for a man than for a woman.[61]

One of the positive job opportunities for women in East Central Europe is as an entrepreneur, owner of a small food or fashion retail outlet, private hairdresser, provider of a service. There is considerable interest in this area. In Brandenburg, one of the 'new' Federal German states, a women's organization named OWEN is setting up plans for a 'train the trainer' scheme. Unemployed female academics from the former GDR with the necessary languages would train women in Moscow and Warsaw in the essentials of setting up small businesses.

The latter would then disseminate this training more widely in their own country. A recent report on privatization in Bulgaria noted that one fifth of new entrepreneurs were women, but many of these, it was thought, were simply providing cover for their men as the real owners. This is regarded in more than one country as one of the ways in which members of the old *nomenklatura* are remasking their move sideways into new positions of – this time capitalist as opposed to state socialist – power. A public opinion poll carried out by the Bulgarian Centre for the Study of Democracy in October 1991 found that 42.7 per cent of women have neither the intention nor the desire to start a private business of any kind (compared with 35.8 per cent of men).[62]

In Moscow, the Women's Association 'Mission' founded in 1990 by Dr Tatiana Lukianenko promotes training courses for women wanting to set up in business. By autumn 1992 it had created 189 jobs. Júlia Szalai has remarked on the utilization of women's 'former informal market experiences', namely in the Hungarian 'second' economy. Thus their participation rates in trading (65 per cent) and new small cooperatives (43 per cent) is high, and '32 per cent of the owners, managers, and members' of 'new privatized businesses' are women. This optimistic view counters the findings of a 1988 survey, which documented the relative unwillingness of women in Hungary to go into business. Whilst 36 per cent of men expressed the wish to become an entrepreneur, only 16 per cent of women echoed this.[63]

Self-employment is much favoured by policy makers right across Europe, and in the case of former state socialist countries has the advantage of encouraging talents not rewarded in the past, namely enterprise, individual initiative, resourcefulness. However, it would be naïve to imagine that this could have a major impact on female unemployment in the current marketization process. Rather, it must remain a minority solution. The small-scale example of Artemis B.T. in Szeged in Hungary, a three-woman language-teaching, translation and interpretation agency, is more likely to be typical.[64]

One successful example of female entrepreneurship appears to be the current boom in prostitution, which had always been a source of hard currency earnings in Berlin or Moscow. In a slightly bizarre illustration of the transition to the market, politicians from Rostock in East Germany paid a visit to legalized 'Eros Centres' in West Germany's Bielefeld and Düsseldorf. They wished to learn how to bring order into the chaos of Rostock, a port city where prostitution has burgeoned since unification, but without West German-style health checks and insurance policies for the women. Now there are plans to build a 'hostel' along West German lines, to eliminate the disorderly caravans of the new female entrepreneurs.[65]

Prostitution could be viewed as the *non plus ultra* of entrepreneurship, with women selling their body rather than – in alienated Marxist form – their labour power! Even before the notion of prostitution emerged as the expression of a specifically female form of business enterprise, it had sometimes been seen as a strike for self-determination in contrast to the reality of women's harsh working lives. In a first-person narrative documenting the involvement of women in heavy labour of the type officially banned by law, a woman from Petrozavodsk in Karelia (in the former Soviet Union), who works lifting heavy mail bags, says:

> It should not be surprising that some women leave this 'women's work' for prostitution ... preferring even that humiliating 'profession' because it gives a woman at least some measure of freedom, some degree of choice. ... Of course prostitution is ruinous for women. I do not want to justify it. ... Yet, ironically, prostitution has become a euphemism for women's freedom, a freedom that society condemns.[66]

Russian women report that a current joke amongst mothers of young daughters about their prospects in life postulates a choice between 'getting married, which is not very attractive, or becoming a prostitute, which is much more attractive'. 'Sex tourism' is one of Albania's main sources of income. Once hermetically sealed against the world, Albania has now become what the German feminist magazine *Emma* describes as the 'bargain-basement brothel of the West'. In a country where every second child suffers from malnutrition and where 80 per cent of the population is unemployed, the fact that the family is the ultimate value does not prevent mothers from selling their daughters to neighbouring Greece in exchange for food, coal or petrol.[67]

It is understandable that the double burden of the past, and the difficulties of the present combine to make women favour staying at home or working part-time or from home. Indeed Solidarity has proposed introducing a 'family wage', by which men would collect substantial supplements to their salary for each child if their wives did not work, thus providing financial incentives for women to stay at home and simultaneously to raise the birthrate. Yet the budgetary constraints that have hindered implementation of the policy in Poland also operate in the other former state socialist countries. Moreover, the experience of the past and the inflationary pressures of the present suggest that one wage, however enhanced, is unlikely to be sufficient to keep a family. Even single-headed households were and often are dependent on the parent holding two to three jobs to make ends meet in Hungary.

Long before *perestroika*, the central character in Natalya Baranskaya's *A Week Like Any Other* responded angrily to her husband's suggestion that she should give up her job and stay at home with the children, pointing out that 'there's no way we could live on your salary', and adding a defence of her job as crucial to her self-respect and fulfilment:

> No, No! 'Dima,' I say, 'You want me to do all the routine stuff, while you do your interesting work, because you think my work isn't worth it. You're just a rotten capitalist.'
>
> 'Maybe I am,' says Dima with an unfriendly smile, 'but it's not just a question of money. It would be better for the children as well...'
>
> 'Dima, do you really think I don't want what's best for the children? You know I do, but what you're suggesting would kill me. What about my five years at university, my degree, my seniority, my research? It's easy enough for you to dismiss it all, but if I didn't work, I'd go mad, I'd become impossible to live with.'[68]

In addition, women in East Central Europe have little notion of part-time or home-based work, since these forms of employment were rare or did not exist under state socialism. Already there are signs in Czechoslovakia that in the process of privatization of small retail units for example, family members, especially women, tend to work long, unregulated hours for very small remuneration. The lack of protection in terms of low rates of pay or lack of holiday entitlement, sick pay and pension rights, standard features of much part-time work in the West, is unknown. Similarly, the exploitative conditions characteristic of casualization and home-based work will be new to East European women.

Western findings on the feminization of poverty seem already to be echoed in the transitional economies. This especially affects the high number of lone parents, of whom the vast majority are women. A report in the newsletter of the East German-based Independent Women's Association compares the social support amd employment which enabled lone mothers to support themselves and their children in the past in the former GDR with lone mothers in the West who are dependent on social welfare and threatened with poverty. In the new Federal states, 20 per cent of all families with school-age children have only one parent, compared with what is already considered a high 13 per cent in the old Federal states. As of the end of July 1991, East German women were edging closer to poverty as a result of unemployment and the closure of childcare facilities. Every tenth unemployed woman in the new Federal states was a lone parent and their bargaining position in terms of re-employment was clearly weak. When Ute Pust, a 27-year-old lone mother of two, wanted back her job in a hotel kitchen after her maternity leave, as was her right under earlier GDR law, her boss said simply: 'Either you work on the late shift, or not at all.' In Russia, although state support for single mothers more than doubled after price reforms began in January 1992, these increases were pitifully inadequate in the face of prices, which rose between ten- and thirty-fold between January and June 1992.[69]

In Czechoslovakia, the term feminization of poverty is also currently in use to describe 'the negative effects that the economic reforms have had on women'. Young women especially are disadvantaged in Poland and East Germany. It is particularly difficult for young female graduates and school-leavers to get jobs, apprenticeship placements, or further training.[70]

Another group especially prone to poverty are older women. The allegedly positive discrimination in favour of women in the form of their five years earlier retirement age in effect operated against their interests even under state socialism, but even more so in the current situation of surplus labour. Now, one of the largest groups of unemployed people are women around the age of fifty, in the so-called pre-retirement bracket, whose chances of finding new employment are almost zero. An example is Heide Haack, who worked for fifteen years as a shepherdess on a collective farm in the GDR, and then took on her own herd of 550 sheep together with her husband. In the past, she was publicly lauded, and given medals and bonuses. Sheep-breeding was the money-spinner of the farm. In November 1991, the sheep were slaughtered. Now she is suddenly 'ancient', aged forty-nine. The job centre has told her she won't ever find another job, and she's 'too old' for it to be worthwhile sending her on a retraining course.[71]

Women, who form the majority of the older age group, are also more prone to poverty because they live longer on smaller pensions, due to the wage differentials which operated during their working lives. Thus in Czechoslovakia, the 'relation between men and women in the post-productive group is 34 per cent men and 66 per cent women, with seven times more women than men in the over-80 age group'. A greater number of women are dependent on the pension as their sole source of income, because of their earlier retirement age and because a lower number of female pensioners work after retirement. Wage differentials during their earning life coupled with their earlier retirement age mean

138

that 'women have on average 5.6 per cent smaller pensions than men under the same conditions.' Retirement pensions in 1985 were 53 per cent of average net wage, whereas the officially defined socially acceptable minimum income was 56 per cent of average per capita income. In 1982 in Czechoslovakia, 15.3 per cent of all pensioners were on the so-called socially acceptable minimum pension; of these, 89 per cent were women. Recipients of this minimum pension spent four fifths of their income on basic needs (food, housing, heat). Czech sociologist Jiřina Šiklová has characterized this as the failure of the supposed strength of socialism, namely in social welfare policy.[72]

Since unification many women of retirement age in the former GDR have been discriminated against: 'In an unprecedented move, the Bonn government has reduced and capped the pensions of doctors, lawyers, judges, teachers, college professors, and public administrators, along with other public employees in the former GDR. . . . Women, who were concentrated in public administration, education, medicine, and the judiciary, are especially affected.'[73]

Under state socialism, women's labour force participation was taken for granted as the norm, yet it was marred by a high degree of occupational segregation and a gender gap in pay levels. The double or triple burden exacerbated these contradictions so that many women experienced their working lives as an obligation to be endured rather than a right they enjoyed.

The 'norm' which appears to be emerging during the current transition to the market is precisely the opposite side of the coin. Full-time motherhood is being posited as women's destiny and sacred duty, almost as though the life experience of two generations of working women was a mirage, or had not existed at all. Moreover, this new ideology is also fraught with paradox and pitfalls. Both models tend to instrumentalize women in the name of the collective.

Will the future bring a synthesis of the two models, or at least a compromise between the two imperatives, that women 'ought' to be workers as well as mothers, or alternatively 'ought' to sacrifice their working lives to family responsibilities? Is there a middle way between the duty to be a worker, and the right to be unemployed, sanctified in motherhood? And where in these 'oughts' is the autonomous choice of women themselves?

It is as yet unclear what the future patterns and levels of female employment will be. Whether economic restructuring could ultimately favour women's employment opportunities remains to be seen. And only time will tell whether women, at this point in time apparently content to shed the double burden for 'a few years at home with the children', might not in the medium term mobilize in support of the right to work. Even now, there is some evidence to suggest that women did not work solely for reasons of economic necessity, but for the social solidarity with other women it gave them, and the sense of pride in their work. Indeed there are many voices which suggest that women's self-esteem and even their sense of self was integrally bound up with their working lives. Surveys in several countries have indicated that, even if their husband did earn enough to keep the family, most women would still want to go out to work.

While inconclusive, then, the evidence seems to point in the direction of women themselves, given the choice, preferring the contradiction-laden option of participation in the public sphere to that of self-fulfilment confined to the private sphere. The following voices and survey results give credence to such an interpretation of likely future aspirations. What is also clear, as stated at the outset of this chapter, is that women's attitudes to defending the right to work will inevitably be influenced by the nature of the work they performed under state socialism, and the career opportunities they had.

In interviews, many women in the former GDR and Czechoslovakia say that work and a rewarding job is part of their sense of identity, or in the case of Russia, their only real aspiration apart from having a child. In contrast, some young women in Poland and Hungary feel unable to see their mothers as role models, old before their time, worn out with work but without much career status to show for it. And the high take-up statistics for extended childcare leave in Hungary documented in Chapter 2 suggest there is a definite backlash on the part of young mothers against putting their children into nurseries before the age of three. As the generation who themselves spent their childhood in state childcare facilities, they have no wish to subject their children to impersonal nurseries with overlarge classes, excessive resultant regimentation, proneness to infection, and general lack of individual attention.

On the other hand women 'choosing' or welcoming unemployment as an opportunity to spend a few years with the children have no past experience which would suggest to them that such a choice may well mean long-term unemployment. In the state socialist past, these extended childcare leave measures were associated with the right to have one's job held open.

Studies on the former GDR and Russia suggest that women for whom working outside the home was the norm would not voluntarily choose the option of domesticity. In Hungary too, Júlia Szalai cites women's 'desire for a more flexible combination of employment, (*which most women definitely want to maintain* – [my italics])' with domestic duties. An INFAS poll in autumn 1990 in East Germany threw up only 3 per cent (of 1,423 women between the ages of 16 and 60) who described being a housewife as their ideal, as against 65 per cent who said that even if they didn't need the income, they would still choose to go to work. An earlier Polish study had shown that between 68–92 per cent of women (depending on socio-occupational category) 'would continue working, even if they were not under financial pressure to do so'.[74] And that study was conducted at a time when jobs were not yet under threat.

Further studies suggest that women did derive a sense of identity and worth from their working lives, in addition to the relative economic independence which their jobs brought them. Dr Regine Hildebrandt, Social Democrat Minister for Women, Labour and Health in the East German state of Brandenburg, points out that women contributed 30–40 per cent of family income in the past, compared with 18 per cent in West Germany. 'We did not have equality in the way they made us believe, but self-awareness was forged by participation in the work process.' Despite the lack of real gender equality in the former GDR, at least 'women were economically independent', says Hildebrandt, voted German Woman of the Year in 1991.[75] This claim may have been relatively more true for women in East Germany than in other state socialist countries.

Hana Navarová, for example, speaks of women's labour force participation in Czechoslovakia producing 'a proclaimed rather than real economic independence from men'. Navarová also introduces the interesting idea that there was a dialectical process whereby women were not only hindered in their career development by their responsibilities as workers and mothers, but that their maternal roles were equally modified by the 'norm' of labour force participation, such that they went to work, not only for reasons of economic necessity or job satisfaction, but also because they perceived it as their 'family duty'. This 'duty' appears to have had positive spin-offs, Navarová asserts, for 'women obtain status, experience, skills in their jobs, they find financial independence, many of them fulfil themselves in and identify with their work'. The evidence on job satisfaction, like the reality of women's working lives under state socialism, is contradictory: Alena Kroupová maintains that 'a professional career does not rank supreme in the scale of values of Czechoslovak women. ... Very often, mothers do not conceive employment as a means of self-realization, but rather as an economic necessity to ensure the family's adequate standard of living.'[76]

However, even where women performed ostensibly dreary or repetitive jobs on the production line, there is some evidence that the social contact and solidarity with other women at work, plus a certain pride in their product, may have contributed to women's sense of self being constructed around their working lives. In a 1991 television documentary on the Narva light bulb factory in East Berlin, the woman worker and single mother on whom the film focused not only prided herself on being able to fend for herself and her three small children, but also said that when she walked through Berlin at night she felt a personal sense of pride and achievement at seeing 'her' lights in the city at night.

It is therefore by no means clear yet whether women will continue to collude with their retrenchment from the workforce and assigned responsibility for the private sphere, or whether they may yet fight to defend or regain the right to work. 'In view of the social norm of "the employed woman" which has existed for a few generations,' concludes Navarová, 'their return to the household is unrealistic, or realistic only for a certain period of time.'

For women to defend the right to work as one of the equal citizenship rights guaranteed them at least in principle by the new democracies, the role of formal and informal political involvement on their own behalf will be central. The next two chapters analyse the mismatch between formal democratic rights and women's voices being heard; and the potential of, and the difficulties facing, new grassroots groups.

Notes

1. Lolita Alimova, b. 1956 in Samarkand, quoted in *Der Spiegel*, no. 21, 1992.

2. Dr Dieter Angst, a West German working as State Secretary for Planning and the Environment in Saxony in the eastern part of Germany, was quoted by Quentin Peel, in: 'Symbols of Hope and Hardship', *Financial Times*, 11.8.92.

Angela Merkel, the East German Federal Minister for Women, reflected a similar view when she said, in retrospect, that the GDR had lulled women into an 'illusory life situation'. She justified the hardships of the transition which, as Dr Angst had maintained, fall mainly on women, by asserting that the level of state welfare provided by the GDR 'could not be guaranteed in any society governed by competition' [my translation, BE]. Merkel was quoted in *Der Spiegel*, no. 24, 1992, p. 101.

3. Małgorzata Tarasiewicz, 'Women in Poland: Choices to be Made', in: *Shifting Territories: Feminism in Europe*, special issue no. 39 of *Feminist Review*, winter 1991, pp. 182–87.

4. For further discussion of the issue of protective legislation, see Chapter 1.

5. Francine Du Plessix Gray, *Soviet Women Walking the Tightrope*, Virago, London, 1991, p. 37.

6. On the hypothetical notion of the 'family wage' (in the former Soviet Union), Maxine

Molyneux, 'The "Woman Question" in the Age of Perestroika', in: *New Left Review*, no. 183, 1990, p. 36; (on Hungary) Ruth Rosen, 'Women and Democracy in Czechoslovakia', in: *Peace and Democracy News*, fall 1990; Chris Corrin, 'Magyar Women's Lives: Complexities and Contradictions', in: Corrin, ed., *Superwomen and the Double Burden: Women's Experience of Change in Central and Eastern Europe and the Former Soviet Union*, Scarlet Press, London, 1992, p. 34.

7. For comparative details on levels of labour force participation between countries and over time, including the East-West comparison, see Table A4 in the Appendix. The GDR figure of 91.3% includes 8% of women involved in vocational training. The dramatic increase in female labour force participation during the state socialist period can be illustrated by the Czechoslovak case, where in 1947, women represented 35% of the labour force, and only 27% of the non-agricultural labour force, compared with 47% of the total workforce in 1991 (Source: Liba Paukert, 'The Changing Economic Status of Women in the Period of Transition to a Market Economy System: The Case of Czechoslovakia after 1989', in: Valentine Moghadam, ed., *Democratic Reform and the Position of Women in Transitional Economies*, OUP Clarendon Series, Oxford, 1993).

8. In the Federal Republic of Germany (FRG), 95% of new labour contracts formed since 1970 have been for part-time positions filled by women. In 1986, 90.3% of all part-time workers were women. By contrast, in 1986 only 3% of Hungarian, 6% of Polish and 7.6% of Czech and Slovak women workers were part-timers (Sources: for the FRG, Dorothy Rosenborg, 'The New Home Economics: Women, Work and Family in the United Germany', ms., 1992; for Hungary, Mária Ladó, 'Women in the Transition to a Market Economy: The Case of Hungary', in: *The Impact of Economic and Political Reform on the Status of Women in Eastern Europe and the USSR*, Proceedings of United Nations Regional Seminar, Vienna, 8–12 April 1991, ST-CSDHA-19-UN, New York, 1992; for Poland and Czechoslovakia, Alena Kroupová, 'Women, Employment and Earnings in Central and East European Countries', Paper prepared for Tripartite Symposium on Equality of Opportunity and Treatment for Men and Women in Employment in Industrialized Countries, Prague, May 1990).

9. The number of female workers working part-time in Czechoslovakia increased from 7.6% in 1986 to 11.6% in 1989. The proportion of women workers expressing a preference for part-time work increased from 19% in 1986 to 23–27% by 1989. Of the roughly 400,000 women who return to their jobs annually after maternity leave in Czechoslovakia, 40% of women would like to work part-time (Source: Kroupová, 'Women, Employment and Earning', 1990).

10. Natalya Baranskaya, *A Week Like Any Other* (1969), translated by Pieta Monks, Virago, London, 1989. For an extract illustrating these difficulties and the resulting stress levels of women, see Chapter 2 above.

11. See Table A2 in the Appendix. The information conveyed in this paragraph is based on a graph in *The World's Women 1970-1990*, UN document cited in the *1992 World Labour Report 5*, ILO, Geneva, 1992, Chart 1.3, p. 25.

12. The share of women in post-secondary education is detailed by Ireneusz Bialecki and Barbara Heyns, 'Educational Attainment, The Status of Women, and the Private School Movement in Poland', in: Moghadam, ed., *Democratic Reform and the Position of Women in Transitional Economies*, 1993.

13. Júlia Szalai, 'Some Aspects of the Changing Situation of Women in Hungary', in: *Signs*, vol. 17, no. 1, autumn 1991, p. 153.

14. Ladó, 'Women in the Transition to a Market Economy', 1992.

15. Bialecki and Heyns, 'Educational Attainment, the Status of Women', 1993.

16. See Table A5.2 in the Appendix for detailed figures. Yet it must be noted that the numbers of women studying technical sciences remained low.

17. Dorothy Rosenberg, 'Shock Therapy: GDR Women in Transition from a Socialist Welfare State to a Social Market Economy', in: *Signs*, vol. 17, no. 1, autumn 1991, p. 13, based on Gunnar Winkler, ed., *Sozialreport 90*, Verlag Die Wirtschaft, Berlin, pp. 41–44.

18. Bialecki and Heyns, 'Educational Attainment, the Status of Women', 1993. See also Renata Siemieńska, 'Poland' in: Gail P. Kelly, ed., *International Handbook of Women's Education*, Greenwood Press, Westport, Conn., 1989, pp. 323–47. Data from December 1990 on unemployed school leavers in Poland illustrates the knock-on effect of this educational gender imbalance in type of secondary school: 82% of unemployed school leavers from general secondary schools were girls, as were 66% of those from vocational schools (Source: Monica S. Fong and Gillian Paul, 'The Changing Role of Women in Employment in Eastern Europe', World Bank, Europe and Central Asia Region, Population and Human Resources Division, Report no. 8213, February 1992, table 8, p. 44).

19. Szalai, 'Some Aspects', 1991, p. 158. See also Tables A5 and A7 in the Appendix. Girls' clear preference for 'gymnasium'-type secondary over technical vocational secondary schools in Hungary is documented in detail by Mária Ladó, Mária Adamik and Ferenc Tóth, 'Training for Women under Conditions of Crisis and Structural Adjustment: The Case of Hungary', draft paper for the ILO, 1991. For skill differentials in the workforce in Hungary, see also Katalin Koncz, 'The Position of Women in Decision-Making Processes in Hungary', Paper prepared for East-West Conference: 'Building a Europe without Frontiers: The Role of Women', Athens, 27-30 November, 1991: Referring to micro-census data from 1984, she claims that only 40% of women in the workforce were qualified, as compared with 75% of men.

20. Renata Siemieńska, Interview with Barbara Einhorn, Warsaw, 31.3.90; and 'Hidden Victims: Women in Post-Communist Poland', *News from Helsinki Watch*, vol. IV, issue 5, March 1992.

21. See Table A5.2 in the Appendix.

22. See Table A5.1 in the Appendix. See also (for the former GDR) Hildegard Maria Nickel, 'Ein perfektes Drehbuch: Geschlechtertrennung durch Arbeit und Sozialisation' ('A Perfect Script: Gender Divisions Through Work and Socialization'), in: Gislinde Schwarz and Christine Zenner, eds, *Wir wollen mehr als ein 'Vaterland'*, Rowohlt, Hamburg, 1990, p. 76; and (for Hungary), Mária Ladó et al, 'Training for Women', draft paper for the ILO, 1991.

23. Fong and Paul, 'The Changing Role of Women in Employment', 1992.

24. Małgorzata Tarasiewicz, Interview with Barbara Einhorn, Warsaw, June 1991.

25. Ladó, 'Women in the Transition to a Market Economy', 1992.

26. Szalai, 'Some Aspects', 1991. Recent Hungarian unemployment data echoes the predominance of women in administration. A breakdown according to professional groups in May 1992 shows women as constituting 41% of the total number registered unemployed, but within that, a high 66.5% and 88.9% of two levels of administrators, and 63.4% of total non-manual workers. (Source: *Labour Market Monthly Survey*, 1992, Országos Munkaügyi Központ, Budapest).

27. See Table A6 in the Appendix.

28. For the GDR figures, see Gunnar Winkler, ed., *Frauenreport 90*, 1990, pp. 91–92, and Rosenberg, 'The New Home Economics'; for the observation about Poland, Renata Siemieńska, 'Women's Issues in the Transitional Period in Poland', mimeo, 1991; for the Polish figures, see Zofia Kuratowska, 'The Present Situation of Women in Poland', in: *The Impact of Economic and Political Reform on the Status of Women*, UN, 1992.

29. See Table A7 in the Appendix. For the GDR, see *Frauenreport 90*, ibid.; for Hungary, cf. Ladó, 'Women in the Transition to a Market Economy, 1992.

30. Kroupová, 'Women, Employment and Earnings', 1990.

31. See Table A8 in the Appendix. On Hungary, see Katalin Koncz, 'Results of and Tensions in Female Employment in Hungary', Budapest University of Economics, Budapest, mimeo, 1987.

32. Fong and Paul, 'The Changing Role of Women in Employment', 1992.

33. For information on the GDR, see Barbara Einhorn, 'Socialist Emancipation: The Women's Movement in the GDR', in: Sonia Kruks, Rayna Rapp, Marilyn B. Young, eds,

Promissory Notes: Women in the Transition to Socialism, Monthly Review Press, New York, 1989, pp. 282–306; and Winkler, ed., *Frauenreport 90*, pp. 94–95. On Poland, see Renata Siemieńska, 'Women in Leadership Positions in Public Administration in Poland', Paper prepared for Friedrich Ebert Stiftung/UNESCO Conference, Bonn, July 1987; and Siemieńska, 'Polish Women and Polish Politics Since World War II', in: *Journal of Women's History*, vol. 3, no. 1, spring 1991, p. 112. On Hungary, see Katalin Koncz, 'Results of and Tensions in Female Employment', 1987; Koncz, 'The Position of Women in Decision-Making Processes in Hungary', 1991.

34. For the former GDR, see Dorothy Rosenberg, 'Shock Therapy', 1991, p. 13, who cites 1978 figures of 8.5% tenured professors, 49% doctors, 52% dentists, 64% pharmacists, and for 1986, 52% judges who were women. Einhorn, 'Socialist Emancipation', 1989, pp. 289–90, gives 57% of dentists and 52% of doctors who were women in 1983. These figures compare favourably with Western figures for 1987, showing 4% of lawyers and 16% of doctors who were women in the UK; 15% of judges, 14% of lawyers, 23% of doctors, and 20% of dentists who were women in West Germany; but only 8% of lawyers, 6% of dentists, and 17% of doctors who were women in the US. Siemieńska, 'Women in Leadership Positions', 1987, gives a figure of 54.5% of Polish judges who were women in 1986; and according to an ILO Report II, 'Equality of Opportunity and Treatment between Men and Women in Health and Medical Services' (ILO, Geneva, 1992, p. 9), 67.6% of Polish doctors were women in 1980.

35. Ladó, 'Women in the Transition to a Market Economy', 1992; Winkler, ed., *Frauenreport 90*; ILO, 'Equality of Opportunity', 1992, ibid.

36. Brigitte Reimann, *Franziska Linkerhand*, Verlag Neues Leben, Berlin, 1974.

37. Rosenberg, 'Shock Therapy', 1991, p. 139.

38. See Tables A9.1 and A9.2 in the Appendix.

39. For Czechoslovakia, Kroupova, 'Women, Employment and Earnings', 1990, and Ludmila Venerová, 'Brief Survey of the Situation of Czechoslovakian Women at the Beginning of the Transitional Period from Centrally-Planned to Market Economy', in: *The Impact of Economic and Political Reform on the Status of Women*, UN, 1992, who gives a figure of 16% total women in business management positions, of which 10.56% are in lower, 3.98 in middle and only 1.46% are in top management; for Poland, see Ewa Gontarczyk-Wesoła, Country Report on Poland, 1989, mimeo; for Hungary, see Rózsa Kulcsár, 'The Socio-Economic Conditions of Women in Hungary', in: Sharon L. Wolchik and Alfred G. Meyer, *Women, State and Party in Eastern Europe*, Duke University Press, Durham, 1985, p. 199, table 11.3; and Katalin Koncz, 'The Position of Women in Decision-Making Processes', 1991.

40. Winkler, ed., *Frauenreport 90*, pp. 94–5.

41. Ibid., pp. 95–6.

42. Ibid.

43. Anastasia Posadskaya and Natalia Zakharova, 'To Be a Manager: Changes for Women in the USSR', ILO, Geneva, 1990.

44. Renata Siemieńska, 'Women, Work and Gender Equality in Poland: Reality and its Social Perception', in: Wolchik and Meyer, eds, Women, State and Party in Eastern Europe, 1985, p.314; and Siemieńska, Peć, Zawód, Polityka: *Kobirty w Życiu Publicznym w Polsce (Gender, Profession, Politics: Women in Public Life in Poland*, Warsaw University: Institute of Sociology, 1990, tables 6, 7, pp. 108, 111. Czechoslovak figures are cited by Míťa Castle-Kanerová, 'A Culture of Strong Women in the Making?', in: Corrin, *Superwomen and the Double Burden*, 1992, p. 104.

45. Polish information in: *Financial Times*, 30.1.91; For Hungary, see Szilvia Borbély, 'Panes et Circenses: The Decline in Living Standards in Hungary', mimeo, 1991; ITOR, Leading Economic Indicators for Hungary, 1992.

46. For some of this information on inflation, wages and prices in the transition period, see Barbara Einhorn and Swasti Mitter, 'A Comparative Analysis of Women's Industrial Participation During the Transition from Centrally-Planned to Market Economies in

East Central Europe', in: *The Impact of Economic and Political Reform on the Status of Women*, UN, 1992. On Hungary, Borbély, ibid.; ITOR, ibid. On Bulgaria, see the *Guardian*, 18 February 1991. Polish information from Barbara Einhorn, Interview with Professor Jerzy Osiatyński, at the time Minister of Planning, as of 1992 Poland's Finance Minister, Warsaw, 1 April 1990; also *Independent*, 31 January 1991.

47. Ewa Gontarczyk-Wesoła, Interview with Barbara Einhorn, Poznan, April 2–3, 1990; Izabela Nowacka, Interview with Barbara Einhorn, Warsaw, June 1991. For the East German examples, see 'Frauen in den neuen Bundesländern: Die Verliererinnen der Einheit?' ('Women in the New Federal States: The Losers of Unification?'), in *Stern*, no. 46, 1992.

48. Monika Lopez was profiled and quoted in: 'Frauen in den neuen Bundesländern', ibid., 46/92, p. 122 [my translation, BE].

49. Borbély, 'Panes et Circenses', 1991. Two polls, cited in the *Guardian*, 2 July 1992 and 23 July 1992.

50. For data on female unemployment rates in the former GDR, see IAB (Institut für Arbeitsmarkt und Berufsforschung der Bundesanstalt für Arbeit), *Aktuelle Daten vom Arbeitsmarkt* (*Current Data on the Labour Market*). This is a regularly updated publication. See also the *Guardian*, 6 May 1992. For data on Hungary, Poland and Bulgaria, see Fong and Paul, 'The Changing Role of Women in Employment', 1992, tables 7A, 7B, pp. 42–43. For Czechoslovakia, data supplied by sociologist Hana Navarová, Prague, September 1992.

51. Posadskaya is quoted in the *Guardian*, 30.6.92.

52. Source: *Labour Market Monthly Survey*, no. 5, 1992, Országos Munkagyi Központ, Budapest.

53. This figure was quoted in *Financial Times*, 26.3.91.

54. The move westwards is a continuous wave. As Hungarian historian István Rév said, there is no former state socialist country for whom there is not another which constitutes the 'East' (lecture on 'Post-Communist National Identity' at Sussex University, 18.1.93).

55. Fong and Paul, 'Women's Employment in Central and Eastern Europe: The Gender Factor', article in *Transition*: Newsletter about Reforming Economies, vol. 3, no.6, June 1992, based on the authors' World Bank Report no. 8213, February 1992.

56. Winkler, ed., *Frauenreport 1990*, pp. 49–50.

57. See Table A5.1 in the Appendix.

58. Mária Ladó and Ferenc Tóth, 'Zwei verschiedene Welten: Die neuen Technologien und Frauenarbeit', ('Two Distinct Worlds: New Technologies and Women's Work'), in: G. Aichholzer and G. Schienstock, eds, *Arbeitsbeziehungen im technischen Wandel* (*Labour Relations and Technological Change*), Edition Sigma, Berlin, 1989, pp. 201–14; Margaret Sutherland, 'Women's Studies and the Social Position of Women in Eastern and Western Europe', ENWS (European Network for Women's Studies) Seminar Report, The Hague, November 1990.

59. Antoni Kukliński, 'Poland – The Difficult Stage of Transformation', in: Antoni Kukliński and B. Jałowiecki, eds, *Local Development in Europe: Experiences and Prospects*, *Regional and Local Studies*, no. 5, Warsaw, 1990, p. 37.

60. Sources: Ladó, 'Women in the Transition to a Market Economy', 1992; Małgorzata Tarasiewicz, Interview with Barbara Einhorn, Warsaw, June 1991.

61. Statistics on Polish women, cited by Helsinki Watch, 'Hidden Victims', 1992, p. 7; Fong and Paul, 'The Changing Role of Women', 1992, table 10, p. 45; Kuratowska, 'The Present Situation of Women in Poland', 1992; Małgorzata Tarasiewicz, 'Women in Poland', 1991; and her presentation to the Workshop on the Economic Implications of Transformation for Women in East Central Europe at the Helsinki Citizens' Assembly, Bratislava, March, 1992.

62. On the 'train a trainer' scheme, information from documents prepared by OWEN in Berlin; on Bulgaria, see Dimitrina Petrova, 'The Farewell Dance: Women in the

Bulgarian Transition', Paper presented to the conference on 'Mary Wollstonecraft and 200 Years of Feminism', Sussex University, 5–6 December 1992; and T. Davidkov, 'The Bulgarian and His Business', *Bulgarian Ouarterly*, no. 3, 1991, p. 125.

63. Information about Women's Association Mission from the organization's brochures and verbal reports. On Hungary, see Júlia Szalai, 'Some Aspects of the Changing Situation of Women in Hungary', in: *Signs*, vol. 17, no. 1, 1991, p. 162; Einhorn and Mitter, 'A Comparative Analysis of Women's Industrial Participation', 1992.

64. Rita Szilágyi, letter to Barbara Einhorn, Summer 1992.

65. *Der Spiegel*, no. 48, 1991.

66. Valentina Dobrokhotova, in: Tatyana Mamonova, ed., *Women and Russia: Feminist Writings from the Soviet Union*, Blackwell, Oxford, 1984, p. 7.

67. 'Verkaufte Kinder' ('Children for Sale'), report in *Emma*, no. 12, December 1992, p. 25 [translation mine, BE].

68. Baranskaya, *A Week Like Any Other* (1969), 1989, pp. 59–60.

69. Petra Drauschke and Margit Stolzenburg, 'Are Lone Mothers Slipping into Poverty?' in: *Weibblick*, newsletter of the Independent Women's Association (UFV), 2/92, pp. 13-15. The case of Ute Pust was cited in an article pointing out that long-term unemployment affects lone mothers particularly in the new Federal states, in: *Der Spiegel*, no. 24, 1992, p. 99. On Russia, see the *Guardian*, 30 June 1992.

70. Szalai, 'Some Aspects', 1991, pp. 155, 169. Castle-Kaněrová, 'A Culture of Strong Women in the Making?', 1992, p. 122.

71. Heide Haack's story was quoted from: 'Frauen in den neuen Bundesländern', *Stern*, no, 46, 1992, p. 126 [my translation, BE].

72. Jiřina Šiklova, in: Bob Deacon and Júlia Szalai, eds, *Social Policy in the New Eastern Europe: What Future for Socialist Welfare?*, Avebury, Aldershot, 1990, pp. 194–199.

73. Rosenberg, 'Shock Therapy', 1991, pp. 12–13.

74. Rosenberg, ibid., p. 13; Szalai, 'Some Aspects', 1991, p. 160; Siemieńska, 'Women, Work and Gender Equality in Poland', 1985, p. 312.

75. The *Guardian*, 6 May 1992.

76. Navarová, 'Impact of the Economic and Political Changes in Czechoslovakia on Women', Paper to EC Workshop on 'The Impact of Economic and Social Changes on the Position of Women in Eastern and Central Europe', Brussels, 24–25 January 1991; Kroupová, 'Women, Employment and Earnings', 1990, p. 21.

5

Where Have All the Women Gone?
Politics and Participation

The Communists said that in the first place a woman is a worker, then she should be active in political life, then in the third place have a family. . . . We are sick and tired of equality. We want to be women in the first place and then to join in other activities.

Rut Kolínská of the group Prague Mothers[1]

'When we were dissidents,' said prominent ex-Charter 77 activist Jiřina Šiklová, 'the men needed us and treated us well.' Now, by contrast, she claimed in 1990, using a concept coined by sociologist and member of the Belgrade Women's Lobby Sonja Licht, there is a danger of 'male democracies' ignoring women's needs.[2] In Poland too, women activists within the Democratic Union (UD) assert in their platform that 'Polish democracy is a masculine democracy'. Their statement adds: 'Women are not allowed to take a full part in decision-making, whether it concerns their country, or women's own lives.'[3] Yet in what Hanna Jankowska cites as 'another Polish paradox', a public opinion poll of 15–16 July 1992 showed that 68 per cent of Poles think that women are as able to fill the highest government posts as men. Indeed 23 per cent saw women as better suited! Only 9 per cent of respondents felt that women were less suited to political life.[4]

The suggestion that women activists from the pre-1989 opposition have been elbowed aside by male ex-dissidents who were catapulted into the corridors of democratic power in East Central Europe echoes a trend observed in the transition from authoritarian or military to democratic rule in Latin America.[5] The shift from opposition 'anti-politics' to democratic 'normalization', this view suggests, is marked by a tendency to oust women. Jiřina Šiklová has pointed out that women were more likely after 1989 to return to their careers and 'normal' life, whereas male dissidents felt a need for political prominence to gain public acknowledgement retrospectively for their dissident credentials.

Indeed some people have suggested that men felt the need to become prominent in dissent during state socialism as a way of endowing their lives as stokers or janitors with meaning, whereas women – because of their multiple roles – did not need such affirmation. Šiklová argues that the maternal role provided an 'out' for women from state socialist pressure to participate in mainstream politics, and that 'as a result, women are today nowhere near as compromised by having collaborated with the previous régime as men are'.[6]

This hypothesized gender difference in political behaviour indirectly reinforces the notion that women are more likely to take an active part in autonomous social movements than in mainstream political parties and electoral processes.[7] Such a factor might favour the emergence of a strong feminist movement in East Central Europe in the years to come, a possibility examined in the next chapter. For the present, however, it suggests a symbiosis between the process of democratization and the marginalization of women from the public sphere of formal politics, with obvious implications for women's citizenship rights.

Electoral advertising in the 1990 Hungarian elections appeared to reinforce this sidelining of women's citizenship rights, subordinating them to the maternal role in the name of the national interest. In the last days of the election campaign, the Hungarian Democratic Forum (MDF), which emerged from the election as the strongest partner in the governing coalition, 'angled for the "women's vote" with a poster showing its ideal of new Hungarian womanhood – a heavily pregnant woman gazing at the sky. The MDF believes Hungary is in need of more babies if it is to be strong.'[8] Such imagery not only reduces women to their maternal role, but reinforces an instrumental link between this role and nationalist aspirations.

This chapter examines in greater detail the proposition that women's citizenship rights are deemed to be of secondary importance in the current democratization process in East Central Europe. In seeking explanations, it poses the further question of whether the subordination of women's interests represents a change from, or continuity with, the past. Was women's citizenship and political representation central to the state socialist project, or does the record point rather in the direction of a shared instrumentalization of women, on the part of state socialists and former dissidents alike?

Current evocations of the past in the search for an untainted national identity and new ethical and political values often focus on the nineteenth century. This period was marked by an upsurge in nationalist sentiment, with aspirations for national self-determination and independence, at least in the case of Poland. In Czechoslovakia, the idealized era of nationhood is identified with the interwar period and the first Czech Republic under Thomas Masaryk. But nineteenth century-style nationalism also incorporated the doctrine of separate spheres in which men and women were allotted different roles. It is significant that only Poland and Czechoslovakia gave women the vote on the achievement of national independence in 1918. In the other East Central European countries, women had to wait for the advent of state socialism after the Second World War before achieving voting rights.[9]

Thus state socialism can be seen as having conferred formal citizenship rights on women. However, it simultaneously negated those rights for all citizens by instituting purely token elections with single candidate lists. Women's citizenship as embodied in political rights is a problematic issue for state socialist and traditional societies alike. To encourage women to become more involved in the political process would require a political climate not favoured by either of them. Such a climate would be facilitated by a state structure that is able and willing to respond to the initiatives of many non-governmental organizations. The present era is dominated in the ex-state socialist countries not so much by efforts to create the substantive conditions for truly participatory democracy as by an almost obsessive concern with new legislation as the preeminent symbol of the rule of law, especially as regards formal legal guarantees for re-instated private property rights. Since land- and other property owners in the pre-state socialist period were usually male, this does little to make active citizenship rights more real or accessible to women.

The Disappearing Woman Trick: The New Democratic Parliaments

In democratic governments in place since the 'revolutions' of 1989, women are almost invisible. Nor is there any political party which boasts a programme for protecting or enhancing women's rights. Election results have revealed what Mira Janova and Mariette Sineau have called 'a spectacular loss of women representatives in the new parliaments'.[10] The average of less than 10 per cent female representation in the new parliaments is not so remarkable in West European terms. Table A10 in

150

the Appendix illustrates just how closely the new East Central European levels of female political representation mirror those pertaining in most of Western Europe. Only Germany and Scandinavia represent exceptions, the Scandinavian countries reaching levels of female representation of 30–40 per cent, as compared to the average 33 per cent achieved by state socialism. The German figures reflect the influence of the Greens' insistence on quotas and gender parity, despite the fact that the Greens themselves failed to clear the 5 per cent hurdle in the December 1990 elections and did not enter the first all-German parliament. Thus the first unified Bundestag was 20.5 per cent female, not markedly different from the 20.2 per cent women in the first and short-lived democratic GDR parliament between March and September 1990.

The more relevant comparison to be made here, however, is not that between East and West, but between the heavily politicized state socialist past and the political opportunities arising from the current democratization process. This comparison between past and present within East Central European countries reveals an absolute drop in female representation. On average, women held about one third of the seats in state socialist parliaments. By contrast, they account for less than one in ten parliamentarians in most of the democratically elected parliaments. The fall is most starkly illustrated in Romania, where the percentage of women representatives fell from 34.4 per cent in 1985 to 5.5 per cent after the elections of May 1990. Mary Buckley has documented the way *perestroika* in the Soviet Union emulated this trend at federal, national and local level. Female representation, she said, both in the Supreme Soviets of individual Soviet republics, and in local soviets, 'came crashing down'.[11]

Yet what did female representation in the state socialist parliaments mean in practice? Past studies and present commentary commonly assert that the ostensibly or at least numerically impressive levels of female representation in the pre-1989 parliaments of East Central Europe stood for no more than tokenism of the worst kind. Much has been made of the 'milkmaid' quota system designed to ensure representation across the social spectrum. This is widely thought to have resulted in unqualified and passive women filling the quotas allocated to the official women's and other mass organizations, trade unions and ruling Communist parties. Mary Buckley cites, in response to the drop in female political representation in the former Soviet Union, the widely held view that 'fewer energetic women were preferable to a higher percentage' of 'the old "yes-women" of the past'.

This echoes the assertion by Gail Lapidus that despite strikingly lower numbers of female deputies right across East Central Europe, 'those who have gained political prominence are more likely to be genuine political actors rather than token appointees'.[12]

In 1990, Anna Petrasovits, the only woman leader of a new political party in Hungary, the Social Democrats, stated that 'we don't want token women like the Communists had, stupid silly little women who sit there. ... We want real, strong women politicians, who have to be born themselves.' Unfortunately, the chances of finding such women in the current situation were, in her view, not high, since 'this is not a civil democratic society. These are half-feudalistic, agrarian societies which have then had forty years of socialist dictatorship. You cannot see women leaders in either form of society.' As if to prove the point, Petrasovits came sixth in her constituency. And her party failed to qualify for the second round of voting in the 1990 elections. Social democracy and all left-of-centre parties are seen as discredited by proximity with the totalitarian past of state socialism.[13]

The state socialist parliaments were themselves token institutions, while the real decision-making bodies were the Central Committees and Politburos of the various ruling Communist Parties. Significantly, women's membership of the ruling parties was relatively high, but their visibility decreased markedly in the higher echelons of party hierarchies. In 1975, women accounted for between 24 per cent and 30 per cent of members of the Communist Parties of the Soviet Union and Eastern Europe.[14] Approximately similar levels of participation appear to have continued until the demise of state socialism. Women's representation on the Central Committees of these parties in no measure reflected their level of membership. In 1976, the percentage of women on the Central Committees of the ruling parties ranged from a high of just 15 per cent in Czechoslovakia to little more than 3 per cent in the Soviet Union.[15]

Despite the nepotism which gave power to visible female figures such as Ceauşescu's wife in Romania, Honecker's wife in the former GDR, or Todor Zhivkov's daughter in Bulgaria, women were, in the late 1980s, conspicuous by their absence from the Politburos of Bulgaria, Czechoslovakia, and Yugoslavia. In the Politburo of the ruling PUWP (Polish United Workers' Party) in Poland, there was one woman in 1987. Two women members graced the Politburos of ruling parties in Hungary and Romania, but it is unclear whether they were full or candidate members. In the former GDR, no woman ever became a full member of the all-powerful Politburo: Inge Lange and Margarete Müller remained non-voting candidate members from 1973 and 1963 respectively, until 1989, the former as the much-hated State Secretary for Women's Affairs. Aleksandra Biriukova was, in 1988, the second woman ever to be nominated to sit on the Politburo of the CPSU, an entire thirty years after the first, Ekaterina Furtseva, who lasted only three years. But like her GDR sisters, Biriukova had only non-voting status. The third woman to join was Galina Semenova, who was appointed in 1990, and thereafter remained as the sole woman member.[16]

However one evaluates the role and impact of women in state socialist parliaments, the fact that currently fewer than one in ten deputies in the formal political structures of East Central Europe are women poses an objective handicap in terms of promoting, or even defending, existing women's interests. Janova and Sineau argue that the low levels of female representation in Western European parliaments from the 1950s on provides one explanation for early post-war uncritical admiration of the state socialist project by many Western feminists. Slight improvements in the percentage of female politicians in most Western democracies have come about, they note, only as a result of the exertions of second-wave feminists.[17] This underlines the necessity for grassroots groups, and hints at a long process yet to be initiated if the visibility of women in East Central European politics is to increase over the next few years.

Currently, it appears that the downward trend is continuing, with those countries which have had a second election since the turning point of 1989, registering a yet further drop in the level of female representation. Thus in Poland, the percentage of women dropped from 13 per cent in the Sejm and 6 per cent in the Senate in 1989, to 9.13 per cent and 8 per cent respectively after the 1991 elections.[18] In the Polish case, the drop in the parliamentary representation may have been in part affected by the circumstances of the June 1989 Polish elections. These are generally classed as having been only partially free elections, since the March 1989 round-table talks had guaranteed the ruling PUWP a quota of 63 per cent of all parliamentary seats. The system of allocating part of the Party quota to women may well have resulted in a relatively higher level of female representation. This would also help to explain the subsequent fall between the elections of 1989 and 1992.

In Czechoslovakia, the drop in representation between 1990 and 1992 was more marginal. In the Federal Assembly, there was a dip from 8 per cent in the Chamber of the People in 1990 to 7.3 per cent (11 women out of 150 members) in 1992; in the Chamber of the Nations, the level dropped from 11 per cent in 1990 to 9.3 per cent in 1992 (14 of 150 members).[19] If one compares this current overall average of

8.3 per cent female representatives with the 7 per cent in the British Parliament after the 1992 elections, the level of female representation in Czechoslovakia may not appear so bad. One should bear in mind, however, that Britain's record, even after the slight improvement in 1992, is one of the lowest in Western Europe, especially conspicuous in a country neither recently industrialized, nor predominantly agricultural, nor Catholic-dominated, and which vaunts its record as a model of parliamentary democracy, the 'Mother of Parliaments'. (Portugal, Greece, Turkey and France, to cite such examples, have also never yet reached 10 per cent female representation.)

Intra-country differences raise questions about national difference. The Polish example also throws up a second phenomenon documented in relation to Western European politics. This is the question about whether left-of-centre political parties have at least in formal terms a greater commitment to getting women elected. An analysis of the 1992 Czech and Slovak national (as opposed to federal) electoral results addresses both the question of nationally-attributed divergences in electoral results and the record of left-leaning parties on electing women. Both Czech and Slovak national parliaments showed slightly better results than the Federal Assembly, with 10.5 per cent women elected to the Czech National Council and 14.6 per cent women to the Slovak National Council.[20]

However, apparent differences between the Slovaks and the Czechs are probably a symptom not so much of national difference as of the same political phenomenon that accounted for the drop in female representation in Poland between 1990 and 1992. It derives from the relatively higher representation of Centre to Left parties in Slovakia, and the tendency for left-wing parties to place women higher on electoral lists.[21]

Perhaps more serious in its implications is the fact that at ministerial level in the new governments, women are almost totally invisible. Janova and Sineau's assertion that in post-1989 East Central Europe 'there may be fewer women in politics ... but they have gained positions of power in government and elsewhere' can surely be validated only by the exceptional case of East Germany. In the March 1990 democratic GDR elections, women's overall representation in parliament fell, but a number of highly visible posts went to women, including Minister of Labour and Social Policy (Regine Hildebrandt), Minister for Women and the Family (Christa Schmidt), State Secretary for Foreigners (Almut Berger) and State Secretary for Gender Equality (Marina Beyer).[22] After unification and the December 1990 elections, a total of four women ministers made up 20 per cent of the German government, equalling the 20.5 per cent women elected to the Bundestag.

By contrast, there was only one female minister without portfolio in the Hungarian cabinet. There was only one woman minister, the General Auditor, in the 1990 Czechoslovak Federal Government, but no Minister for Women's Affairs. There was also one woman minister in the national Czech, but none in the Slovak government. The Slovak Republic instituted a Government Committee for Women and the Family in June 1990, but by spring 1991 this was being referred to as 'inoperative'. As of June 1992, there were no women ministers in either the Federal or the Czech governments, but two (both from the HZDS), representing 14 per cent, in the Slovak government.[23]

In Poland there was one female minister – the Minister for Culture – until the government reshuffle of December 1990, after which there were none. As in Czechoslovakia, there are no political parties headed by women. And the Polish Plenipotentiary for Women's Affairs, a post at deputy ministerial level, was in April 1991 (Resolution no. 53/91 of the Council of Ministers) diluted to Under-Secretary of State for Women *and* Family Affairs, and moved sideways from the Ministry of Labour and Welfare to the Prime Minister's Office. Anna Popowicz held this post for its entire short-lived existence, from April 1991 to February 1992. Many Poles saw the creation of this post as 'merely a figleaf for the Western media ... to prove that Poland is European'.[24] The fact that the office was starved of funds other than for youth activities was seen as confirmation of its marginal position in the government. Polish feminists were also shocked that the office of the Under-Secretary was headed by a man. Popowicz herself related how limited were her possibilities in terms of affecting government policy, in that she had no directive powers, merely the possibility of influencing ministers by making recommendations.[25]

On 28 February 1992, Popowicz was dismissed and her post abolished, significantly over the issue of reproductive rights. Ostensibly, she was dismissed on grounds of 'lack of thrift in office', but implicitly, according to the Polish media, it was because of her attitude to family planning and abortion. Popowicz had been so rash as to declare, on a June 1991 visit to Paris, that she 'did not accept' the Pope's analogy between abortion and the Holocaust. Earlier, she had experienced considerable difficulty in 'trying to extract from the Ministries of Health and Education a promise that they will take action over information and sex education' in order to improve birth control practices.[26]

The significance of Popowicz's dismissal was further highlighted by the surprise instatement, in July 1992, of Poland's first woman prime minister. Hanna Suchocka was elected to the post as a compromise candidate, not because she is a constitutional lawyer, nor because of her term as Poland's representative on the Council of Europe, but precisely, it seems, because of her uncompromising stance in opposition to abortion. Plagued by no such qualms as led Germany's Minister for Women Angela Merkel not to vote for legalizing abortion in opposition to her party, the Christian Democrats (CDU), Suchocka broke party ranks with the Democratic Union (UD) to support a strict draft anti-abortion bill. Further, she seems both to epitomize and to laud the traditional view of women's qualities currently espoused by so many political ideologues in East Central Europe. To the media, she stressed women's special talents for smoothing the waters. 'I think that as a woman I have a better chance of forming a government because women very often eliminate conflicts,' she told reporters.[27]

Nevertheless, some pro-choice activists in Poland saw Suchocka initially as a pragmatist, representing 'moderation, common sense and the independent thinking which we badly need in this country. Being a single, self-made career woman, she is the very opposite of the model propagated by the Christian politicians who support her. It is one of many Polish paradoxes.'[28] This view of Suchocka was endorsed by an interview she gave to *Gazeta Wyborcza* in late June 1992, before the Sejm debate on the new anti-abortion bill, where she was quoted as saying that she opposed the punishment of women who have abortions, and hoped that the terms of the bill would be improved upon by the parliamentary re-drafting commission.

Hungary does not have a government ministry for women's affairs. And in East Germany, the post of State Secretary for Gender Equality of the transitional GDR government was in early 1990 subsumed under the authority of the Minister for Women, the Family and Youth, and then abolished shortly prior to German unification. Its incumbent, Dr Marina Beyer, was summarily made redundant in September 1990.

There are multiple reasons for the current lack of visibility of women in political élites. One is the unwillingness of parties to place women candidates near the top of electoral lists. In the run-up to the June 1992 elections in Czechoslovakia, Jiřina Šiklová reported a poll conducted amongst party colleagues by a woman deputy in the Federal Assembly, in which 89 per cent of them voiced the opinion that the party would lose votes if they were to put a female candidate at the head of the electoral list.[29]

In the March 1990 elections in the GDR, the UFV (Independent Women's Association) ran a joint electoral slate with the Greens. The coalition won eight seats in the new GDR parliament, but because of the UFV candidates' placing, third on the voting lists, none of these seats went to the UFV. The Greens had interpreted their organization's larger size as entitling them to nominate the first two names on each list. And the coalition agreement stipulated a 2:1 division of seats. When it came to the outcome in which no more than two seats were won in any one electoral district, the Greens claimed it would be illegal to distribute the total number of seats according to the overall 2:1 principle. Rather they insisted on giving all eight seats to those candidates whose names had featured first on the relevant district voting list.[30]

A further cause of women's invisibility is the lack of affirmative action in favour of female candidates in the form of quotas. The idea of quotas was seen as discredited by the passive or token women representatives typical of the state socialist era. State socialism's method of ensuring that all sections of society had a voice was to allocate block quotas for women, peasants, workers. The rejection of this method as a travesty of democratic rule meant that the notion of quotas as a move towards gender parity was not countenanced. Only in the former GDR, influenced by the record of the West German Greens, were quotas one of the first demands in the UFV's election programme. This makes their relegation to third place and consequent electoral oblivion in the GDR all the more ironic.

Another reason for the dearth of female politicians appears to lie in a rejection of politics and the public sphere as a 'dirty' business best left to men. Perhaps most significant as a cause is the current, apparently ubiquitous view in East Central Europe that women's issues constitute a second rank or even superfluous political agenda. This is partly the legacy of state socialism's designation of the 'woman question' as a separate and discrete set of issues, rather than as something integral to, both affected by and in turn directly impinging on, all social and economic policy decisions. One hears politicians of both sexes asserting that it is not an issue, that men and women are equal (but different), or that women had *too many* rights under state socialism. They are adamant that what women want now is to rediscover their essentially feminine role in the private realm and have men look after their interests in the public sector. Politics, they aver, is not for women.

In the view of Magda Kučerová, an OF (Civic Forum) official in Prague, women tended not to get involved in politics and responsible public posts because of lack of time, since they had to care for the children and their own parents, queue for food, manage in inadequate living conditions. And in her personal opinion, Kučerová added: 'For a woman to be elected as prime minister here, she would have to be twice as clever as a man.' Nevertheless, someone had to look after the family, and 'frankly I don't like those women who are fighting for independence – they should fight for improvements in the economy, better services, since women would then automatically be better off'.

Asked about Václav Havel's position on women's issues, a female aide responded: 'He likes women very much and treats us all very well.' As early as 1985, Havel had ended a (written and published, not merely verbal) diatribe against Western women peace activists with the words:

> I do not wish to ridicule feminism; I know little about it and am prepared to believe that it is far from being the invention of a few hysterics, bored housewives, or rejected mistresses. Still, I have to note that in our country, even though the position of women is incomparably worse than in the West, feminism seems simply 'dada'.[31]

It seems pertinent to quote these inflammatory remarks by Havel, since they are symptomatic of a prevalent attitude to feminism on the part of former dissidents and others in East Central Europe, which is discussed further below.

Where are the Dissident Women?

The post-socialist fall in the level of female political representation in East Central Europe is also significant for its contrast to women's widely acknowledged key role in the dissident groups whose activities helped to prepare the way for the upheavals of autumn 1989. Former Charter 77 member Jiřina Šiklová has noted that one fifth of Charter signatories and a third of its spokespersons were women. Over half of the members of the Committee for the Unjustly Prosecuted (VONS) were women, and a quarter of those imprisoned in 1981 for their activities on VONS's behalf were women. Yet it was well-known male dissidents such as Havel, Jiří Dienstbier and Jaroslav Šabata who made it electorally. Similarly in Poland, only male members of Solidarity such as Lech Wałęsa and Jacek Kuroń became members of the government.

'Only three out of the repeatedly persecuted dissident women are today members of the Federal Assembly,' Jiřina Šiklová pointed out in 1990, and 'two of them have no intention of running in the next election.' 'Why is it,' Šiklová went on to ask, 'that those women who had been doing the grey, routine, sometimes even dirty work at the duplicating machines, who translated texts, copied political essays and manuscripts which later found their way into samizdat or exile editions, are no longer active in political life?'[32]

One reason would appear to be that even in dissident organizations, women performed the more menial and less visible tasks, a hypothesis which is discussed at greater length below. A further implication is that high profile dissent played the role of a substitute career for men displaced from their professions on political grounds, but that its significance for women was, while not of lesser import, certainly not the sole focus of their activities. For women, their role within the family perhaps made up for the loss of career. And the very fact of occupational segregation mitigating against women's rise to the top of career hierarchies may well have meant that women had less invested than men, in a personal sense, in career successes.

There is a suggestion of '*plus ça change*' in all this, if one takes account of Barbara Jancar's assertion that in Poland in the past, 'in neither the official nor opposition organizations were women elected to leadership positions consonant with the size of their representation'. Jancar's view is in part based on, and echoes, the findings of Polish sociologist Renata Siemieńska. Men formed the majority of members of the Workers' Defence Committee (KOR) and the Confederation of Independent Poland. And although four demands specifically concerning women were included in the Gdańsk and Szczecin agreements signed between the Interfactory Strike Committees and the Polish authorities in 1980, Siemieńska points out that they concerned on the one hand, childcare and hence women's traditional role within the family, and on the other, a particular group of women in a female-dominated profession – nurses.

At the same time, although women accounted for half the membership of the newly formed Solidarity, the Interfactory Strike Committee included only two women, but sixteen men. Elections in spring 1981 resulted in a total of only 7 per cent female delegates being sent to the first National Solidarity Congress, and an even smaller percentage of women entering the National Commissions. The Conciliatory Commission's nineteen members included just one woman; there was one lone woman among the National Commission's 82 members, and there were three women of the total 21 members of the Auditing Commission. In a parallel process, the Polish Communist Party (PUWP) 1981 elections for its Ninth Extraordinary Congress, for the first time not including fixed quotas for women, resulted in half as many women delegates compared with previous such elections. Renata Siemieńska also reports a drop from around 20 per cent to 10–15 per cent female involvement in the early 1980s in local PUWP committees, on administrative authorities and as production managers.[33]

In an even earlier articulation of women's under-representation in prominent dissident roles, Piri Márkus commented in 1982 that in Hungary 'there is no general understanding about women being oppressed, and the subject is laughed at. There are hardly any *samizdat* books written by women, and extremely few women are involved in the decision-making bodies of the intellectual "opposition".'[34]

Márkus's, Jancar's and Siemieńska's findings tend to support the theory that at least in Poland and Hungary, it was not only after 1989 that women were pushed aside. Rather, these indicators suggest a continuum, or at most a relative disenfranchisement, not an absolute change. Women were involved, it transpires, at the grassroots or rank-and-file level in both opposition and official political organizations prior to 1989, but never at a commensurate level in leadership posts. For example, as of 1991, there were no women leaders of Solidarity trade union divisions, and the union had given its short-lived Women's Commissioner the push.[35] Certainly, it seems clear that without specific quotas for women, their role in political élites is negligible, on a par with those Western European countries which have the worst records.

In Hungary too, the lack of women government ministers stood in awkward contrast to the pivotal role played by women in the democratization process, as leading members of the Dialogue peace group and the environmental Danube Circle which had from 1984 organized ultimately successful publicity and demonstrations to dissuade the Hungarian government from going ahead with the proposed Danube Dam.[36]

And the first all-German elections almost obliterated the former opposition candidates of the UFV (Independent Women's Association), New Forum and the East German Greens. One leading female member of each made it into the Bundestag, Christina Schenk for the UFV, Ingrid Köppe for New Forum/Alliance 90 (Bündnis 90), and Vera Wollenberger for the Greens.

The German case is somewhat different, however. Partly as a result of the unification process superimposing at a stroke western-style politics on the East, the sidelining of former dissident groups occurred in the five new Federal *Länder* earlier than in other former state socialist countries. The marginalization of women preceded this more general process in the other countries, as the anti-politics of the past were transcended and institutionalized with the entry of former dissidents into the structures of mainstream politics.

In Eastern Germany, this trend towards remarginalizing the former opposition began even before unification. In a bitterly ironic scenario, former dissidents went on hunger strike during the last days of the democratically elected GDR government in September 1990. They were partially successful, not in preventing the release to the West German security services of the archives of the Stasi (the Staatssicher-heitsdienst – the state security services of the former GDR), but in insisting that the archives remain in Berlin rather than being transferred to Bonn. As early as January 1990, Bärbel Bohley, one of the hunger strikers, leading member of the Frauen für den Frieden (Women for Peace) in the early 1980s and co-founder of Neues Forum (New Forum) had stated that 'the hardest thing we have to come to terms with is the fact that we will remain in opposition'.[37]

It is of course possible that the more recently evident re-marginalization of former male dissidents (such as George Konrád in Hungary, or Jiří Dienstbier in the Czech lands after the failure of the Civic Movement to gain seats in the June 1992 elections) might create a new 'anti-politics', albeit a different one from that originally envisaged by Konrád in his book from which the term was coined. The formation of the Democratic Charter in Hungary in December 1991 would appear to be one of the first steps in this direction, signalling disillusionment with mainstream politics and the sidelining even of male former dissidents.[38] In Poland too, many former Solidarity activists were ousted in the 1992 elections.

Why No Women? Break or Continuity?

The crucial question to be addressed here is to what extent the present absence of women from mainstream political structures represents a break, or alternatively a continuity, with women's political behaviour in the past. Answers to this question may enlarge our understanding of women's role within the political structures of state socialism. They may also enable us to look forward to possible future developments in relation to issues of women's citizenship. The centrality of this enquiry is clear from the issues of economic, social and reproductive rights dealt with elsewhere in this book. The current transformations in all former state socialist societies have thrown up myriad questions which beg intervention. They cry out for women to speak up on their own behalf, to defend or to demand economic, political, reproductive or social (welfare) rights.

There is of course an issue of perspective and interpretation here, as in so much of what is occurring in East Central Europe. If women experienced their working lives as a state-imposed obligation, then the right to work is not necessarily one they will wish to defend. Similarly, if they equate political participation with the travesty of democracy perpetrated by the state socialists, then they are not likely to take to the streets in the name of increased political representation. And finally, if women collude with men, as they appear to be doing in several of these countries, in definitions of femininity and masculinity and the separate activities appropriate to each, then a notion of citizenship rights which have to be won in struggle is not likely to be at the forefront of their minds. The one rights issue which appears to have potential mobilizing power is that of reproductive freedom. Yet even there, Polish activists report that the trauma and resignation born of economic 'shock treatment', together with passivity carried over from the past, are contributing to ever lower levels of women prepared to act on their own behalf.

Women's citizenship rights are certainly not simply co-terminous with increased representation in the formal political institutions of the state. Nevertheless, the current low levels of female representation in the parliaments and governments of East Central Europe make their defence, or indeed the articulation of alternatives, objectively difficult. The most frequent response to this problem is that with the enormous economic difficulties of unemployment and inflation associated with marketization (currently interpreted in several of these countries as being synonymous with privatization), women's rights are a luxury that these governments cannot afford to indulge.

This response is perhaps understandable within the ethic of a well-functioning market economy, which at least in the nineteenth-century capitalist version adopted in most of East Central Europe, precludes, in the short term, the issue of social justice. The fact that it is questions of social policy, social justice, and social welfare generally and not just women's citizenship rights which are being sidelined serves to illuminate one of the central contentions of this book. The issue of women's rights, far from being peripheral, can be regarded as central, a prism through which to observe and illuminate the development of these societies in terms of human rights, citizenship rights, social justice and the well-being of society as a whole.

The crucial question of break or continuity in women's political behaviour will inform several further questions. Were women more politically active under state socialism, and if so why? Do women inherently prefer to become more involved in politics at the regional, local or grassroots level than in centralized mainstream political structures? Did women fail to take advantage of the new openings created by the democratization process and the formation of new political parties? Or did they, as Jiřina Šiklová suggests, get pushed aside by men in the rush to political power? Have they rejected politics as 'dirty', tainted by the over-politicization of state socialism, or do they agree with the many male politicians who assert that the public sphere of politics is really a male precinct? Have they been paralysed by the shock of a lost identity and anxiety for the future, the overwhelming material worries and economic pressures of the current transition process? Or is their political inaction akin to their apolitical cynicism and passivity under the stifling constraints of state socialism?

First, there is the sometimes overplayed claim that state socialist women politicians represented no more than a sham gesture towards gender equality. In her analysis of the democratization process, Sharon Wolchik claims that the absolute decline in women's representation is in fact less disastrous than it may seem, since the social and educational background of female representatives under state socialism was such that they remained passive. Now, finally, 'the concentration of women deputies among those who were ordinary workers or agricultural workers that prevailed during the communist period has ended'. In contrast, she asserts that women politicians in the current period can equal their male counterparts in terms of qualifications and the ability to participate actively. It seems to me, however, that what this view reflects is more the general shift in these countries away from egalitarianism to a new belief in the efficacy of elitism. In somewhat contradictory fashion, Wolchik simultaneously concedes that what the small numbers of women deputies in the current legislatures signal is a rethinking of what constitute 'proper roles for women', a rethink which has major implications for women's citizenship rights.[39]

The question of tokenism aside, there is no doubt that women were more politically active under state socialism. First, it was an integral part of official discourse that women were citizens with equal rights in all spheres of life, and indeed that they had an obligation as well as a right to involve themselves at the political and decision-making level of society.

This involvement was more often evident at the regional and local level in terms of formal politics. And if at all, then it was at the local level that women felt able to influence decisions about their environment. Hence in the former GDR, for example, 38 per cent of district council members in 1989 were women, a higher percentage than the 32 per cent female representation at central government level. As of 1986, 25 per cent of local mayors were women. In Hungary, 17 per cent of mayors were women in 1991, but only 3 per cent of mayors of cities (i.e. with more than 10,000 inhabitants).

There was also a high degree of female involvement in trade union activity, even though here too women's representation in the leadership structures was not commensurate with membership levels. In 1986, women made up 53 per cent of total union membership in the GDR compared with only 23 per cent in West Germany. Yet despite accounting for 45 per cent of the executive of the national federation of trade unions (the FDGB), women held only 20 per cent of the seats on the FDGB's ruling council. Women were also prominent in school governing bodies, as they are in Western Europe. And in a structure for which there was no parallel in Western Europe, women were active in the neighbourhood committees which were said to resolve many domestic disputes, to the extent that cases of violence against women rarely reached the courts. Women also comprised 47 per cent of the membership of residential area arbitration commissions.[40]

The relatively high figures for women's involvement at the decentralized level, where politics appears more accessible, more able to be combined with domestic and childcare responsibilities, may well provide a structure which future women activists could follow. It also parallels research findings in the West. Some political studies suggest that women find the committee mode of mainstream party politics inimical to their way of operating. Its procedural formality makes it harder for women to relate to the issues under discussion, and hence difficult for them not to feel alienated and marginalized. In addition, party political meetings are often held at anti-social hours, so do not lend themselves to being meshed with family life. This is why, for many Western women interested in mainstream political participation, the old question of a forced choice between career and family often still holds.

Recent research by Pippa Norris underscores earlier radical critiques of the notion that women are politically passive, or less interested and active than men in conventional or mainstream politics. She suggests that in the course of the 1980s, what little gender difference there may have been earlier has disappeared. The radical critique had asserted that conventional studies 'frequently neglected not only the *locus* but also the *modus operandi* of women's participation'. This bears out the view that women are more likely to be involved at the local rather than national level, in 'ad hoc participation in a range of local voluntary organizations, community action groups, neighbourhood and civic groups, residents' associations and parent-teacher associations'.[41]

Vicky Randall has documented women's involvement in Britain since the 1970s in urban-based community action groups, and highlights particularly the significant impact of the Greenham Common Women's peace camp. Joni Lovenduski emphasizes the 'importance of the organizational infrastructures created by women's groups, especially voluntary organizations'.[42]

Norris sees this type of political participation as more inherently difficult to document, since both ad hoc and protest politics tend to involve unstructured and transitory involvement. In addition, she argues 'that traditional studies of participation have assumed male norms of citizenship, described by such activities as voting, campaigning or lobbying, then sought to explain why women have failed to act like men, rather than exploring female-oriented modes of political behaviour.'

Given the lack of space for the articulation of alternative viewpoints or ways of organizing under state socialism, what dissidents longed for was the possibility of creating precisely such ad hoc, informal associations and networks. What does seem from the British case to have clear potential implications for the future in Eastern and Central Europe, is the wide-ranging involvement of women in informal or community politics.

Hungarian sociologist Júlia Szalai has documented the extent to which during the pre-1989 process of liberalization in Hungary, women were instrumental in establishing the informal networks crucial to the functioning of the 'second' economy. Through this experience, women have developed flexibility and entrepreneurial skills which will stand them in good stead, both in the process of marketization and in the re-creation of civil society. Women were more highly represented at the local government level where, for example, decisions about childcare are made. And their involvement was always higher in civil society-type organizations than in formal political institutions.

Szalai foresees that women will be key players in the establishment of the myriad non-governmental organizations that comprise the infra-structure of civil society, including consumer interest groups.[43] Since the market tends to debase the concept of citizenship to a level at which citizen is synonymous with consumer, and citizenship rights embody no more than individual rights of redress in the consumer context, it is debatable whether consumer associations can be regarded as a high point of informal political activity in civil society. Nevertheless, her point remains that women have the ingenuity and skills to develop the necessary structures. Other examples of grassroots involvement in the past are difficult to document and were anyway on a small scale, given that the socialist state did not tolerate alternative political groupings. The role of peace, environmental, and women's groups prior to 1989 and their putative future role will be examined in Chapter 6 below.

Did They Jump or Were They Pushed?

If there is discontinuity between women's involvement in the past and their relative invisibility in present political processes, then this would suggest that there is some truth in the idea that women have failed to take advantage of the openings offered by the process of democratization. This may be because of the token nature of political experience and consciousness for those women involved in the past in both state and anti-state structures. It may also be that dissident women found it less easy to adapt to the structures and modes of formal politics than their ex-dissident male counterparts who went on to form the government in Czechoslovakia, Poland and to an extent in Hungary and the 'interim' GDR.

There are structural reasons why women are less flexible and agile at crossing the boundaries between state socialist and democratic political systems, or between the informal and formal spheres of politics. Women have less free time at their disposal.[44] Their role as mother and unshared domestic duties make it much more difficult to take advantage of political openings. Many women tell of their involvement at the level of street demonstrations in the turbulent days of autumn 1989. But although their husbands may have pushed the pram through the streets, it was they who went home from the demo to feed and put to bed the children. Meanwhile their menfolk ingested revolutionary fervour. Flushed with the romance of talking through the smoke-filled night and far from the mundane reality of menial domestic drudgery, they became intoxicated by the power of planning the future in the Magic Lantern theatre in Prague. Hana Entlerová of the Czechoslovak National Women's Union, the former official women's organization, underlines the fact that 'it was a phenomenon of the revolution that women did come out on to the street, but from the start they were not on the coordinating committees'.[45]

Women's relatively high level of political involvement in the past itself helps to explain their current lack of activism. This can be interpreted as their rejection of state socialist pressure to take on positions of social or political responsibility in addition to their full-time jobs and domestic chores, the 'triple burden' under state socialism.[46] Klára Ungár, a candidate in 1990 for FIDESZ, the Federation of Young Democrats, a party which some predict may win the 1994 Hungarian elections, describes the difficulties for women in politics, asserting that socialist 'equality' in fact added burdens to women's lives. In Hungary, she pointed out 'the woman has to work, we don't have the possibility to choose. In every family we need two or more incomes to live . . . And women can't argue for more rights at home, because the men are doing two jobs, maybe working twelve hours a day'.[47]

Not surprisingly, the easiest of their burdens to shed, and the first to go in rejecting what women perceived as the over-politicized past is that of political participation. In conversation, Jiřina Šiklová voices the feeling of many former dissidents when she says that for her, 1989 represented a moment to savour the renewed possibility of 'ordinary life', and to take up afresh the profession denied to her as a Chartist by the state socialists. She also feels that women had less of a need than men to seek exposure and profile, or to experience the adrenalin rush and affirmation of political prominence.

There is also an element of truth, however, in the interpretation that women have been pushed aside in the post-1989 rush to power. Miťa Castle-Kaněrová raises this possibility for Czechoslovakia when she writes: 'One might conclude that though some women have re-established "normality" by returning to a more passive form of coping with new economic circumstances, others have been forced under-ground by "male apartheid".'[48] All but one of Civic Forum's leaders during 1990 and 1991 were men, and Civic Forum had no specific policy dealing with women's rights or needs during the transformation process. The only Polish party to include a women's platform in 1990 was the PSP-DR, a tiny and electorally insignificant splinter group from the Socialist Party.

In early 1992, pressure was being exerted on the Czech Social Democratic Party by their North American sponsors to put women candidates higher on electoral lists. This pressure seems not to have borne much fruit, since no women were elected to represent the Social Democrats at Federal Assembly level in the June 1992 elections (which put ten Social Democrats in the Chamber of the People and six in the Chamber of the Nations), and only two women out of sixteen Social Democrats were elected to the Czech National Council.

An 'Allergy' to Feminism

Women politicians are not necessarily conscious of the need to articulate women's needs as distinct from those of men. Czech politician Dr Jaroslava Moserová is a surgeon specializing in burns, who treated Jan Palach, the young martyr who immolated himself in protest at Soviet occupation in January 1969. She represented an area she described as a 'moonscape' brown coal mining area in Northern Bohemia, in the Czech National Assembly. She felt that women politicians and especially the official women's organizations had in the past been figureheads without profile, accounting for the currently anti-feminist sentiments of most intellectuals. Feminism was, she maintained, erroneously equated with previous state policy on behalf of women. As Sharon Wolchik puts it, 'faced with the state's appropriation of the goal of equality ... many citizens in these countries appear to have rejected the goal of women's equality itself'.[49]

Denying that women in her constituency, with its high level unemployment and dire environmental problems, might have particular problems of their own, Dr Moserová was generally hostile to this viewpoint. Indeed she spoke of an 'allergy' to feminism, a view she herself described as shortsighted. She expressed the opinion that women and men were not equal in terms of the qualities they possess. Women were less ambitious and therefore more objective, which meant they carried responsibility 'with misgivings'. She herself, although eminently eligible, would never accept a ministerial post for this reason. By contrast, men were much more decisive, with a capacity as 'do-ers' which made political life easier for them.

While Moserová conceded it was necessary to have the female viewpoint represented in parliament, she felt that women 'didn't mind' not being adequately represented politically. In this interview in September 1990, Dr Moserová predicted, incorrectly as it turned out, that in two years' time, by the 1992 elections, women's issues would emerge as a topic for political discussion. It had 'just happened', she felt, that after 1990 there were no women ministers in the Slovak National Council, and only one each in the Czech National Council and the Federal Assembly.[50]

Moserová's views on female 'difference' seem to echo those expressed earlier by a prominent dissident writer, Eva Kanturková. In her book of interviews, *Douze femmes à Prague*, Kanturková argued that 'feminism has been eradicated in our society by having been brutally transformed into a new form of women's slavery: obligatory work. Thus, if in Czechoslovakia there is one thing that a woman wishes to obtain for herself, it is to recover her undistorted feminine essence rather than to promote herself.' The misleading equation of feminism with state socialist policies for women has already been mentioned, as has the reaction against it taking the form of an idealized femininity. While the desire to cultivate the femininity denied by women's hard labour in the past is understandable, it obscures the issue of how women's interests and indeed their citizenship rights may best be represented.[51]

The widespread view that women as leading political actors represent a political handicap appears to echo the anti-feminist 'allergy'. In line with the general knee-jerk reaction against all left-of-centre political parties as too close to state socialism, the Social Democrats were from the outset in a poor position in Hungary. But the Hungarian media made clear that the electoral fortunes of the Social Democrats were not helped by their being the only Hungarian political party to have a woman leader.[52] The relatively liberal, ex-dissident based Free Democrats (SZDSZ) did have a short-lived women's group in 1990 and a last-minute pre-election statement on women. But a young spokeswoman for the student-based Federation of Young Democrats (FIDESZ) was at a loss to know what to say on the subject of women – that was something they 'really hadn't thought about'.

In Poland a positive initiative to overcome such prejudice has been taken by a cross-party group of women politicians. Defying resistance from male politicians, they set up in spring 1991 the first ever Parliamentary Club of Women Deputies under the chair of Barbara Labuda. Forty of the total 62 women deputies in the Sejm and seven female senators joined. They saw the function of this Women's Caucus as monitoring women's interests in relation to legislative changes under consideration by the Polish Sejm.[53]

The view frequently expressed, and not just by male politicians, in all of these countries is that alongside the grave and pressing problems of economic restructuring, unemployment, and inflation, any talk of women's rights is at best of secondary importance, at worst a frivolous 'extra'. The fact that the economic transformation process will have specific consequences for women's employment, for example, for which it might be important to formulate policies before rather than after the event, is an argument which scarcely impinges on their consciousness. Nor do they see the connection with broader issues of citizenship rights.

At the level of official discourse then, there is a lacuna with regard to the question of gender equality. This is as true of party political rhetoric as of government policy, and is reflected in the radical drop in the formal

169

political representation of women. On all these levels, there is evidently a strong element of discontinuity with state socialism's *overt* commitment to women's emancipation.

Present invisibility may not necessarily imply a lack of activism. Indeed it was demonstrably the case that the activities of women in dissident movements also remained for the most part invisible. Women's work was crucial to the survival of these movements. Among many other things, they provided safe houses for dissidents on the run from the authorities and for the transmission of information in and out of the country; they acted as couriers, and produced and distributed samizdat publications.

In Poland, this level and type of activity during the 1980s era of martial law echoed earlier activities during the Nazi occupation and the Second World War. At that time too women carried messages, worked as stretcher bearers, as printers and distributors for clandestine presses, and even fought in the Warsaw Uprising. Even then, 'save for a few exceptions, women did not, however, occupy prominent positions in organizational structures'.[54] Nor did these essential functions give women the sort of high profile enjoyed by many male dissidents during the 1980s. Indispensable though their activities were, women played practical and supporting roles. It was men who occupied centre stage, who were known in the Western media and revered as the ideologues of intellectual resistance.

As early as 1985, in her study of women in opposition in Poland and Czechoslovakia, Barbara Jancar argued that 'women in opposition appear more marginal to the organizational structure of opposition movements, with visibility in leadership positions depending on male endorsement'. Expanding this argument, Jancar appeared to liken women in opposition to Western feminist movements or women's peace movements in their choice of non-hierarchical structures and spontaneous tactics. In this context, she asserts: 'Where structures and organization are not primary issues, as in Charter 77 or in the Polish strikes, women have demonstrated their ability both individually and on a mass basis to profit from an unstructured situation and in the case of Poland, to force the government to accede to their demands.'[55]

Once again, women play the chorus and work as stagehands in the theatre of dissidence, leaving centre stage and stardom to the male figureheads. This substantiates the proposition that women are happiest at the grassroots activist level, either not needing or not wanting to take on roles that might catapult them into the limelight. This argument in turn reinforces the rationale for women's invisibility in the current political scene as the result of their easier involvement in ad hoc social movements rather than in the formal structures of mainstream politics. In the past, reflects Polish ex-dissident Krysia Lityńska, the choice for women was made easier. Things were black and white – one felt one had to do something. Now, by contrast, the political scene is more complex, and involvement in it requires ambition and self-presentation, both of which women are relatively less good at or inclined towards.[56]

Referring to the current situation in East Central Europe, Sharon Wolchik argues that 'the continuation of such a politics of social movements ... might have been beneficial to women', but that the current 'trend ... away from non-partisan groupings towards more traditional party organizations ... may further decrease women's participation in the future'. We see such a situation reflected elsewhere. In her documentation of the experience of women's movements in Latin America, central in the movements to overthrow repressive régimes, but marginalized in the transition from authoritarian to democratic rule, Jane Jaquette writes that in Uruguay, 'despite a long history of women's activism and women's political role in the transition, not one woman was elected to the Uruguayan parliament when democracy was restored. This forced feminists to ... conclude that their political visibility during the transition did not necessarily translate into political power at the polls'.[57]

There is a widespread view in all of the former state socialist countries that politics itself is 'dirty', a sphere of activity which in state socialist practice was both corrupted and over-intrusive. The retreat into the private sphere is justified by many as a reaction to the over-politicization of daily life in the past, intensified by insecurity and material pressures in the present. In the summer of 1992, Hanna Jankowska of the Pro Femina movement reported on the very small numbers of both pro-choice and pro-Life demonstrators outside the Sejm on the day in July when the anti-abortion bill received its first reading. She said that in Poland, the numbers of 'people engaged in any kind of voluntary activity are fewer and fewer'. 'I think,' she added, 'it is due to the general fatigue of society, the feeling of hopelessness and lack of influence on political decisions, the disgust with political quarrels.'[58] A state of shock, despair and fatigue combines here with the notion that politics is somehow at once inaccessible and despicable.

The search for new, morally and ethically untainted values which could replace 'dirty' politics, centres on the family and woman's role within it as upholder of national cultural traditions. Men see politics as 'no place for women', and women themselves see the world of political infighting as 'unfeminine'. This in turn reinforces the traditional notion that politics and the public sphere are male domains, separate and distinct from the sanctity and moral superiority of the private sphere, where women predominate.[59] The newly articulated restatement of the private/public dichotomy is very influential in the current transformation. It links the economy's need to shed labour with the search for a new identity untainted by association with state socialism. In this, it imbues women with a rhetorically central role in the 'ethical purification of the nation', thus masking an actual loss of economic, social and political citizenship rights. Sociologist Maja Korać asserts that the newly (re-) emerging nationalisms of East Central Europe in effect 'delete' all human rights 'except the "right" to identify oneself with the nation'. The current conflict in the former Yugoslavia, she argues, has:

> left women with mainly two 'possibilities' to overcome the burden and uncertainty of their passivity and to become 'active' in this madness of war. First as heroic mothers, who devoted the lives of their sons for the great historic goal of their nation, appearing in public and the media, celebrated as shining examples of national pride. Second, by becoming one of them and taking up weapons and killing. Although it is not very common, these women become 'media stars', presented as one more proof of 'our tragic destiny'. For women with a certain degree of personal and political awareness, who couldn't accept these pre-defined roles, there was the third 'opportunity' left: to become even more invisible than before.[60]

A further explanation for women's apparent lack of participation in the public sphere, at least in that of formal political structures, may lie in the very trauma and upheaval of the transformation. It could be argued that because women did not identify as much as men with the past political system, its overthrow does not affect them in the same fundamental way. Nor, since they were both legislatively and in practical terms assigned the roles of worker and mother, does unemployment strike so centrally at their identity – they did not hold high-level and therefore the most heavily compromised posts under state socialism, and whatever happens, they still have their maternal role to fall back on.

Yet this is not the full story – as always, women's role is characterized by paradox. For in other ways the trauma of transition is borne and mediated precisely by women, which in turn could explain their unwillingness or inability to become political actors. It could be said that the 'short, sharp, shock treatment' of economic transition to the market affects women particularly acutely, in that it is they who must struggle to make ends meet. And while the availability of goods has eliminated the queueing and running from one shop to another of their daily existence under state socialism, the loss of family income through unemployment and rampant inflation means that they are 'priced out' of shopping. If anything, therefore, providing food for the family is more stressful now than it was then – a shortage of commodities has been replaced by a shortage of cash, representing a dramatic inversion of the situation in state socialist days when there was a money overhang – people had considerable private savings but nothing to spend them on.

The Role of Patriarchy: State Socialist and Nationalist

Women's antipathy to participation in mainstream political structures may also mark a continuum in attitudes of cynicism and withdrawal, masks which became the person in the adverse political climate of state socialism. Irene Dölling has argued persuasively that present political passivity is the result of what she calls the 'patriarchal-paternalist' principle operating at state level under state socialism, with, as Dorothy Rosenberg elaborates, 'non- or even anti-emancipatory effects'. Writing about a similar phenomenon of political passivity in Poland, Elżbieta Tarkowska and Jacek Tarkowski argue more broadly that: 'Tradition, culture, religion, economic factors, and history in general seem to constitute a definite "amoral familism". Until it becomes possible to go beyond this – no small task – the vibrant public life which civil society and social movement analysts have projected will remain a mere abstraction floating above the reality of a political culture of apathy and resignation.'[61]

State socialism as patriarchy constructs 'Father' state as assuming the right to speak in the name of all. Dölling suggests that 'the Party' (so closely related as to be indistinguishable from the state) behaves like a kind of pre-bourgeois pater familias. A common complaint of people living in state socialist countries concerned the way in which what they read, and even what they thought, was prescribed by a state which did not trust them to act as mature and responsible citizens with their own powers of discernment and political judgement. Thus the state disempowered and infantilized would-be citizens, while simultaneously acting as 'benevolent' and all-providing 'father' in terms of social welfare.

In their remarkably similar analysis of Poland, Tarkowska and Tarkowski speak of a 'paternalistic welfare state':

The welfare states which emerged in socialist countries after Stalin's death were based on an unwritten social contract which traded submission to the state for patrimonial protection and social security. The state protected citizens from competition by providing full employment, health services, and free education, even if at low quality. The result was low productivity, a decline in the work ethic, low morale, and a general ethos summed up in the popular saying 'We pretend to work; they pretend to pay us'.[62]

As one would expect, this authoritarian 'father' figure brooked no disobedience from his 'children', who were given no space nor granted permission to articulate alternative political discourses. The emergence of an apolitical stance of passivity and cynicism is understandable in this context.

As Polish sociologist Mira Marody writes: 'Here is a vision of politics which leaves no room for the active participation of individuals in the shaping of political decisions.' In this paradigm, 'the "authorities vs. society" dichotomy is merely a logical crowning of the division into the world of authorities identified with politics and the world of ordinary people who are the object of political decisions'. This sense of politics under state socialism as 'not only separate from the world of the ordinary people but alien as well', has enormous ramifications for the present. Marody contends that its incapacitating effects made even 'oppositional activity appear to be a different lifestyle rather than an activity pursuing accomplishment of concrete political goals'. In the present, she sees a 'paucity of political thinking – not to be confused with think- ing *about* politics ... which is not favourable to the process of democratization'.[63]

Lena Kolarska-Bobinska speaks of the 'anomy' pervading Polish society in the 1980s as an inhibitor in the re-creation of a vibrant civil society. And for Czechoslovakia, Miľa Castle-Kaněrová cites the resignation arising from the fact that 'Communism acted on women's behalf – they were never active participants'.[64] It is scarcely surprising if out of the apathy, resignation, or anomy caused by 'patriarchal- paternalist' state socialism, a culture of autonomous, active and democratically inclined political subjects has not appeared overnight.

This contradiction is particularly applicable to women's rights. Women were 'emancipated' from above. Social (welfare) and economic rights were handed to women on a plate, so that there is no tradition of political agitation in favour of reproductive rights, the right to work, to maternity leave or to a childcare place. Rather, there is a kind of passivity born of taking these rights for granted – it has even been argued that there was no consciousness that these realities of women's lives embodied rights, until they were taken away. Dorothy Rosenberg emphasizes 'GDR women's failure to appreciate their relative privileging within East German society', and points out 'how nearly invisible the extensive system of transfer payments, subsidized day care, family and parental leave, free health care, free abortion and affirmative action programs was to most women'. Regine Hildebrandt, Minister for Women, Labour and Health in the East German state of Brandenburg, says that East German women in the past enjoyed 'a system of favourable conditions which they accepted as normal. "Now we are experiencing for the first time that we have to battle for our rights".'[65]

Some Western political scientists have contended that women are more conservative in their voting behaviour than men. Such a contention appears to be confirmed by the March 1990 GDR elections. Whilst the UFV (Independent Women's Association) together with the Greens received only 2.7 per cent of the vote, 46 per cent of all GDR women voters supported the CDU-led conservative Alliance. This led Irene Dölling to conclude that 'the vast majority of women in the GDR have no interest in emancipatory or feminist ideas and practices and, in fact, reject them'. Dorothy Rosenberg, however, counters the suggestion that these GDR women were either politically passive, or voting against their own interests. Rather, like most politicians in East Central Europe at that time, they were placing what they saw as 'economic interests – perceived immediate and significant economic gain – ahead of what they saw as a narrower one, "women's interests"'. Rosenberg hypothesizes that GDR women voters' 'failure to perceive this as a conflicted choice was due, at least partly, to ignorance of the real contradiction between these categories in the West'.[66]

Certainly it did not take long for the voters to rue the day they fell for the ruse of 'voting for bananas' and the Deutsch Mark. This awakening is visible in the relative strength of the East German women's movement, local consumer groups, and shopping chains which favour retaining GDR products. In July 1992, a non-aligned pressure group called the Committee for Justice was formed with the aim of forcing government attention onto problems specific to the new (or 'young' as they are paternalistically termed by some West German politicians) Federal states.[67] The (by spring 1993) still unresolved wrangle over abortion rights has brought home to East German women very clearly the pitfall, voiced by many in Eastern Europe, that the present transformation may mean nothing more than the substitution of one absolute patriarch, the state, by another, embodied in the laws of the market.

Democracy and Citizenship Rights

It may be that state socialist patriarchy reared passive citizens and that the shock of the transformation has numbed people. However, once women realize that what they have lost constitutes citizenship rights, it is likely that they will be moved to defend them. The Czech politician Dr Jaroslava Moserová saw the main issue for women as economic, in that they would like to have choice about staying at home or going out to work. Choice is a key word for many women, something they felt they lacked under state socialism. However, as Dr Moserová added, this choice is unlikely to be granted, since most men do not earn enough to be the sole breadwinner, so women's wages will continue to be necessary for family survival. In addition, other preconditions for such a choice, in terms of reproductive rights and childcare facilities, are clearly under threat in several East Central European countries.

A defence of women's citizenship rights may well focus first on reproductive choice, hence on the disputed right to abortion, and on childcare facilities threatened with closure. Surveys suggesting that the majority of women in many countries would want to work, even without the pressures of economic necessity, suggest that a subsequent focus may be the right to work. The feminization of poverty will highlight issues of gender-based discrimination. And it is only a matter of time before women recognize that the right to a voice in terms of political participation is necessary in order to press for and to monitor relevant legislation and its implementation.

When studying developments in East Central Europe, it is important for feminist analysts not to succumb to the temptations of the 'colonialist gaze' adopted by Western businessmen and politicians, and so bitterly resented by East Germans and others in East Central Europe.[68] This necessitates a constant awareness of and sensitivity to the enormous differences in life experience. It is likely that Eastern European women's responses to their present situation will differ as a result of their national culture and their more recent state socialist history from the past twenty years of feminism in the West. Former Chartist and gender studies pioneer Jiřina Šiklová suggests that women *will* get involved politically, but in a creative and new fashion which differs from that envisaged by Western feminists: 'Probably our women will not stress so much the importance of politics and will not consider a complete equality quota representation in all leading executive positions as the maximum point of their emancipation. ... I believe that our women who have had the experience of living under totalitarian régimes will not merely mimic men but that they will discover a new way of political participation and leadership with enough space for solidarity to uphold our "traditional" female qualities.'[69]

Notes

1. Rut Kolínská of Prague Mothers, described in 1990 by Civic Forum (OF) as 'the new women's movement', made a powerful case here against women's triple burden under state socialism. She was quoted in the *Guardian*, 7.6.90.

2. Jiřina Šiklová is quoted by Ruth Rosen, 'Male Democracies, Female Dissidents', in: *Tikkun*, vol. 5, no. 6, 1990, p. 101.

3. Programme of the Women's Rights Section in the Democratic Union (UD), cited in: Jacqueline Heinen, '"Polish Democracy is a Male Democracy"', in: *Women's Studies International Forum*, vol. 15, no. 1, 1992, p. 135.

4. Opinion survey quoted in *Gazeta Wyborcza*, 17 July 1992; cited by pro-choice activist and spokesperson for Pro Femina, Hanna Jankowska in a letter to Barbara Einhorn of 10 August 1992. The attitudes it documents were verified by, or perhaps reflect the fact, that Poland in June 1992 installed Hanna Suchocka as its first female prime minister.

5. This phenomenon is documented in: Vicky Randall, *Women and Politics: An International Perspective*, 2nd edn, Macmillan, Basingstoke, 1987, pp. 58–64; and Jane S. Jaquette, ed., *The Women's Movement in Latin America: Feminism and the Transition to Democracy*, Unwin Hyman, Boston, 1989.

6. Jiřina Šiklová, 'Women in Leadership: Women in Politics', conference paper, Harvard, 1992, p. 7.

7. Jaquette, *The Women's Movement in Latin America*, 1989, p. 206.

8. The *Guardian*, 7.6.90.

9. For an East–West comparison of the dates when women were granted the vote, see Table 10 in the Appendix.

10. Mira Janova and Mariette Sineau, 'Women's Participation in Political Power in Europe: An Essay in East–West Comparison', in: *Women's Studies International Forum*, vol. 15, no. 1, 1992, p. 123.

11. Women comprised 15.7% of the deputies to the new Congress of People's Deputies elected in 1989, and the smaller Supreme Soviet chosen from this Congress included 18.5% women, compared with 32.8% in 1984. Levels of female representation in the Supreme Soviets of individual republics fell from an average 35% to just under 15% in Uzbekistan, 11% in Turkmenia, 7% in Ukraine and Belorus, 5.4% in Russia, and just 4.8% in Moldova. On local soviets, the past average of 50% women fell to 35% in Latvia, 34% in Lithuania, 30% in Kazakhstan, 29% in Moldova, 25% in Turkmenia, and 23% in Estonia. Source: Mary Buckley, 'Political Reform', in: Buckley, ed., *Perestroika and Soviet Women*, Cambridge University Press, Cambridge, 1992, pp. 57–58.

12. Gail Lapidus, 'Gender and Restructuring: The Impact of Perestroika on Soviet Women', in: Valentine Moghadam, ed., *Democratic Reform and the Position of Women in Transitional Economies*, OUP, Oxford, 1993.

13. The Anna Petrasovits story was reported by the *Guardian*, 7.6.90; see also Rosen, 'Male Democracies, Female Dissidents', 1990, p. 11.

14. The 1975 average figures for the Soviet Union and Eastern Europe are taken from Sharon Wolchik, 'Eastern Europe' in: Joni Lovenduski, ed., *The Politics of the Second Electorate: Women and Public Participation*, Routledge, London, 1981, p. 257. In the GDR

in the mid-1970s women made up about one third of the SED's membership of around 2 million, but held only 13% of Central Committee seats (Source: Barbara Einhorn, 'Socialist Emancipation: The Women's Movement in the GDR', in: Sonia Kruks, Rayna Rapp, Marilyn Young, eds, *Promissory Notes: Women in the Transition to Socialism*, Monthly Review Press, New York, 1989, p. 287). In 1982, women constituted 26.8% of the Polish Communist Party (PUWP), 25.6% of the United Peasant Party and 32.5% of the Democratic Party in Poland (Source: Renata Siemieńska, 'Women and Social Movements in Poland', in: *Women and Politics*, vol. 6, no. 4, Winter 1986, table 3, p. 23). In 1989, women made up 53% of the population of the Soviet Union, but only 29% of CPSU members (Source: Buckley, 'Political Reform', 1992, p. 60).

15. Only 3.3% of Central Committee members in the Soviet Union, 8% in Poland, 12% in Hungary, 13% in the former GDR and 15% in Czechoslovakia were women (Sources: Wolchik, 'Eastern Europe', 1981, p. 260; Harry G. Shaffer, *Women in the Two Germanies: A Comparative Study of a Socialist and a Non-Socialist Society*, Pergamon, New York, 1981, p. 89; Randall, *Women and Politics*, 1987, pp. 97–101). Between 1981 and 1991, the percentage of women on the Central Committee of the CPSU hovered between 3.8 and 4.6 (Source: Buckley, 'Political Reform', 1992, p. 60).

16. Sources: Renata Siemieńska, 'Women in Leadership Positions in Public Administration in Poland', Paper prepared for conference organized by the Friedrich Ebert Stiftung and the Federal German UNESCO Committee, 1–4 July 1987; Einhorn, 'Socialist Emancipation', 1989, p. 287; Janova and Sineau, 'Women's Participation in Political Power in Europe', 1992, table 5, p. 122; Buckley, 'Political Reform', 1992, ibid.

17. Janova and Sineau, ibid., 1992, pp. 116–17.

18. Sources: Zofia Kuratowska, 'Present Situation of Women in Poland', in: *The Impact of Economic and Political Reform on the Status of Women in Eastern Europe and the USSR*, Proceedings of United Nations Regional Seminar, Vienna, 8–12 April 1991, ST-CSDHA-l9-UN, New York, 1992. For the further drop in the 1992 Polish elections, see Jacqueline Heinen and Anna Matuchniak-Krasuska, *L'avortement en Pologne: La croix et la bannière*, l'Armattan, Paris, 1992.

19. For 1990 Czechoslovak election results, see Miťa Castle-Kanerová, 'A Culture of Strong Women in the Making?' in: Chris Corrin, ed., *Superwomen and the Double Burden: Women's Experience of Change in Central and Eastern Europe and the Former Soviet Union*, Scarlet Press, London, 1992, pp. 116–117. For the 1992 results, Zdeněk Kavan, personal electoral analysis, August 1992. In Slovenia too, there has been a double drop. In the parliament of the Republic of Slovenia after the first democratic elections of April 1990, the proportion of women was 11.3% as compared with 25% under state socialism. In the elections of December 1992, 248 or 12% of the total 2,070 candidates were women. But many of them were entered on the lists of parties which were not expected to enter parliament. The prediction for the proportion of women in parliament after the elections was 4–8% (Source: Milica Antić, 'Women's Rights in Post-Socialist Slovenia', paper presented to the conference on 'Mary Wollstonecraft and 200 Years of Feminism', Sussex University, 5–6 December 1992).

20. Source: Kavan, ibid.

21. The proposition that left-leaning and (former) Communist parties elect more women than other parties was confirmed during the 1989/90 elections in other East Central European countries. The Bulgarian Socialist Party (former Communists) had 11.4% women representatives in parliament after the June 1990 election, as compared with only 6.3% women amongst opposition Union of Democratic Forces (UDF) representatives. The Hungarian Socialist Party (former Communists) had 15% women representatives compared with 4.8% for Hungarian Democratic Forum (MDF) and 9% for the Alliance of Free Democrats (SZDSZ). In Poland there were 20.9% female representatives for the former Communists compared with 11% for Solidarity. Czechoslovakia constituted something of an exception in June 1990, with the Communists and Civic Forum almost pegging level at 9% and 7.3% respectively, but the Christian

Democrats got no women candidates elected, and the National Slovakian Party (HZDS) representatives were 50% female! (Source: Janova and Sineau, 'Women's Participation in Political Power in Europe', 1992, Table 6, pp. 124–25.)

22. Janova and Sineau, ibid., 1992, p. 125. For the information on the GDR, see Dorothy Rosenberg, 'Shock Therapy: GDR Women in Transition from a Socialist Welfare State to a Social Market Economy', in: *Signs*, vol. 17, no. 1, autumn 1991, pp. 141–42.

23. Sources: (for Hungary) Katalin Koncz, 'The Position of Women in the Decision-Making Processes in Hungary', paper prepared for East–West Conference: 'Building a Europe without Frontiers: The Role of Women', Athens, 27–30 November 1991; (for Czechoslovakia) Barbara Einhorn, Interview with Dr Kosínková, Auditor General of the Federal government, Prague, September 1990; Castle-Kanerová, 'A Culture of Strong Women in the Making?', 1992, p. 117; Kavan, personal electoral analysis, 1992.

24. Krysia Lityńska, former dissident, in conversation with Barbara Einhorn, Warsaw, 17.6.91.

25. Anna Popowicz in interview with Barbara Einhorn, Warsaw, June 1991.

26. Interview with Anna Popowicz in: *Le Monde*, 8.6.91, cited by Janova and Sineau, 'Women's Participation in Political Power in Europe', 1992, pp. 126–27. Further information in: Heinen, '"Polish Democracy is a Male Democracy"', 1992, p. 134. For the equation of abortion with the Holocaust by the Pope and other Catholic Church dignitaries, see Chapter 3 above.

27. Report on Hanna Suchocka's instatement as prime minister from the *Guardian*, 9 July 1992.

28. Hanna Jankowska, spokesperson for Pro Femina, the Polish pro-choice orgaization, letter to Barbara Einhorn, 10.8.92.

29. Šiklová, 'Women in Leadership, Women in Power', 1992, p. 1.

30. Rosenberg, 'Shock Therapy', 1991, p. 141.

31. Sources: Interview with Magda Kučerová by Barbara Einhorn, Prague, September 1990; Rosen, 'Male Democracies, Female Dissidents', 1990, p. 12; Václav Havel, 'An Anatomy of Reticence', in: *Václav Havel or Living in Truth*, ed. by Jan Vladislav, and translated by E. Kohak, Faber and Faber, London and Boston, 1986, p. 180. The context of Havel's remarks is elaborated in the Introduction above.

32. Šiklová, 'Women in Leadership: Women in Power', 1992, p. 2.

33. Barbara W. Jancar, 'Women in the Opposition in Poland and Czechoslovakia in the 1970s', in: Sharon Wolchik and Alfred G. Meyer, eds, *Women, State and Party in Eastern Europe*, 1985, p. 170; Siemieńska, 'Women in Social Movements in Poland', 1986, pp. 28–32.

34. Piri Márkus's views are taken from an article written in 1982 and cited by Chris Corrin in: Bob Deacon and Júlia Szalai, eds, *Social Policy in the New Eastern Europe*, 1990, pp. 190–91.

35. For accounts of the 'resignation' of Małgorzata Tarasiewicz as Solidarity Commissioner, see Jolanta Plakwicz, 'Between Church and State: Polish Women's Experience', in: Corrin, ed., *Superwoman and the Double Burden*, 1992, p. 88; Małgorzata Tarasiewicz, 'Women in Poland: Choices to be Made', in: *Shifting Territories: Feminism in Europe*, special issue no. 39 of *Feminist Review*, winter 1991, p. 185; for a more detailed account in this study, see Chapter 6.

36. The role of women in the Danube Circle has been documented by Zsuzsa Béres, 'Hungary in Transition: The Ecological Issue' in: Sara Parkin, ed., *Green Light on Europe*, Heretic Books, London, 1991; Chris Corrin, 'Magyar Women's Lives: Complexities and Contradictions', in: Corrin, ed., *Superwomen and the Double Burden*, 1992, pp. 58–59, 65.

37. Bärbel Bohley's speech to a Nottingham University conference on the GDR in January 1990 was cited in Barbara Einhorn, 'East Germany: Behind the Wall . . .', in: *Peace News*, no. 2325, 12 January 1990, p. 5.

38. The text of the Democratic Charter 91 is reproduced, and discussed by George Konrád in: *East European Reporter*, vol. 5, no. 1, Jan–Feb. 1992, pp. 36–37.

39. Sharon Wolchik, 'Women and the Politics of Transition in Central and Eastern Europe', in: Moghadam ed., *Democratic Reform and the Position of Women*, 1993.

40. Rosenberg, 'Shock Therapy', 1991, p. 141; Einhorn, 'Socialist Emancipation', 1989, p. 287. For the Hungarian figures, see Koncz, 'The Position of Women in the Decision-Making Processes in Hungary', 1991.

41. Pippa Norris, 'Gender Differences in Political Participation in Britain: Traditional, Radical and Revisionist Models', in: *Government and Opposition*, vol. 26, no. 1, winter 1991, pp. 60–61.

42. Vicky Randall, *Women and Politics*, 1987, p. 64; Joni Lovenduski, *Women and European Politics: Contemporary Feminism and Public Policy*, Wheatsheaf, Brighton, 1986, pp. 126–27.

43. Júlia Szalai, presentation to EC workshop on 'The Impact of Economic and Social Changes on the Position of Women in Eastern and Central Europe', Brussels, 24–25 January 1991.

44. See Table A2 in the Appendix.

45. For descriptions of the gendered intoxication of revolutionary fervour, see Corrin, ed., Introduction to *Superwomen and the Double Burden*, 1992, Barbara Einhorn, 'New Enemy Images for Old: The "Boys' Debate" around Timothy Garton Ash's *We The People*', in: Mary Kaldor, ed., *Europe from Below: An East–West Dialogue*, Verso, London, 1991, pp. 130–35; Hana Entlerová was quoted in the *Guardian*, 7.6.90.

46. For early usage of the term 'triple burden', see Barbara Einhorn, 'Socialist Emancipation: The Women's Movement in the GDR', in: *Women's Studies International Quarterly*, 1981; Maxine Molyneux, 'Women in Socialist Societies: Problems in Theory and Practice', in: Kate Young, Carol Wolkowitz, and Roslyn McCullagh, eds, *Of Marriage and the Market: Women's Subordination in International Perspective*, CSE Books, London, 1981; Hilda Scott, *Women and Socialism: Experiences from Eastern Europe*, Allison and Busby, London, 1976; Christine White, 'Women and Socialist Development: Reflections on the Case of Vietnam', mimeo, 1980.

47. Klára Ungár was quoted in the *Guardian*, 7.6.90. For a report on Fidesz's electoral prospects, see the *Guardian*, 21.8.92.

48. Castle-Kaněrová, 'A Culture of Strong Women in the Making?', 1992, pp. 121–2.

49. Wolchik, 'Women and the Politics of Transition', 1993.

50. Dr Jaroslava Moserová, interview with Barbara Einhorn, Prague, September 1990.

51. Eva Kanturková is cited by Jancar, 'Women in the Opposition in Poland and Czechoslovakia in the 1970s', 1985, p. 178.

52. Chris Corrin, 'Women in Eastern Europe', in: *Labour Focus on Eastern Europe*, no. 1, 1992, pp. 45–48.

53. For an account of the formation of the women's parliamentary caucus, see Heinen, '"Polish Democracy is a Male Democracy"', 1992, p. 135.

54. The descriptions of women's role in oppositional activity and in the Warsaw Uprising are based on key informant interviews by Barbara Einhorn with women involved in both, in Czechoslovakia and Poland during 1990 and 1991, with Jiřina Šiklová, Zofia Dobrska, Krysia Lityńska, Marta Woydt. For documentation, see also Ruth Rosen, 'Women and Democracy in Czechoslovakia', in: *Peace and Democracy News*, fall 1990, pp. 3–4, 35; and Siemieńska, 'Women in Social Movements in Poland', 1986, p. 15.

55. Jancar, 'Women in the Opposition in Poland and Czechoslovakia in the 1970s', 1985, pp. 176–77.

56. Krysia Lityńska, in conversation with Barbara Einhorn, Warsaw, June 1991.

57. Wolchik, 'Women and the Politics of Transition', 1993; Jaquette, *The Women's Movement in Latin America*, 1989, pp. 190–91.

58. Hanna Jankowska, letter to Barbara Einhorn, 10.8.92.

59. It is interesting to note that people participating in the mass demonstrations in

Poland during the 1980s saw their participation as 'something that belongs to . . . the realm of *morals* rather than politics' and thus as legitimized in a negative sense, because it was thus 'stripped of the odium of being "political"' (Mira Marody, 'Perception of Politics in Polish Society', in: *Social Research*, vol. 57, no.2, summer 1990, p. 266).

60. Maja Korać, 'Nationalism and War in the Balkans: The Place and Role of Women', paper presented at the conference on 'Mary Wollstonecraft and 200 Years of Feminism', 5–6 December 1992.

61. On state socialism as patriarchal, see Irene Dölling, 'Between Hope and Helplessness: Women in the GDR After the "Turning Point"', in: *Shifting Territories*, 1991, p. 10; whose ideas are taken up by Rosenberg, 'Shock Therapy', 1991, p. 147. On political passivity in Poland, see Elżbieta Tarkowska and Jacek Tarkowski, 'Social Disintegration in Poland: Civil Society or Amoral Familism?', in: *Telos*, no. 89, fall 1991, pp. 103–09.

62. Tarkowska and Tarkowski, ibid., p. 106.

63. Marody, 'Perception of Politics in Polish Society', 1990, pp. 257–74.

64. Lena Kolarska-Bobinska, 'Civil Society and Social Anomy', in: Bob Deacon, ed., *Social Policy, Social Justice and Citizenship in Eastern Europe*, 1992, pp. 56–71; Castle-Kaněrová, 'A Culture of Strong Women in the Making?', 1992, p. 105.

65. Rosenberg, 'Shock Therapy', 1991, p. 148; Regine Hildebrandt is cited in the *Guardian*, 6.5.92. Just as women in the GDR did not perceive the rights they did enjoy as worth defending, nor conversely were they aware of their relative disadvantaging. This paradoxical state is typical of women's consciousness in all the former state socialist countries.

66. Dölling, 'Between Hope and Helplessness', 1991, p. 4; Rosenberg, 'Shock Therapy', 1991, pp. 148–49.

67. For reports on the formation of the Committee for Justice, see the *Guardian*, 18.7.92, and Christina Schenk, member of the Bundestag for the East German UFV (Independent Women's Association), writing in: *Weibblick*, no. 7, 1992, pp. 10–11. An opinion poll conducted in the new Federal states in August 1992 revealed a massive decline in support for the CDU in all five of them. The number of votes for the CDU if state-level elections were to be held in 1992, would have fallen by an average 15% from the levels recorded in the Federal elections of October 1990. As a result, the CDU would lose outright to the SPD in all but one of the new Federal states, and even there it would be defeated by a putative SPD-FDP coalition (reported in *Stern* magazine no. 36, 27.8.92, pp. 150–54).

68. Susan Bassnett, 'Crossing Cultural Boundaries or How I Became an Expert on East European Women Overnight', in: *Women's Studies International Forum*, vol. 15, no. 1, 1992, pp. 11–15.

69. Šiklová, 'Women in Leadership, Women in Power', 1992, p. 17.

6

An Allergy to Feminism: Women's Movements Before and After 1989

We were isolated from each other for the past forty years. The iron curtain has been broken. Now we often use common terms and words with different meanings, to signify different things and problems. ... We have a lot of experience with a 'directive emancipation', reduced very often only to the duty and necessity of mandatory employment, and we tend to transfer this experience to the feminist movement. ... We are sceptical of every form of messianism, and this scepticism is directed to feminism as well. Slogans like 'sisterhood is global' ring bells of marxist slogans like 'proletarians of the world, unite!' – and they are simply suspicious to us.

Jiřina Šiklová[1]

Poland is a country which has a woman prime minister. A woman is president of the National Bank. A woman leads the biggest trade union federation. A woman is chief of the Polish television. A woman was the first Polish ombudsman and became one of the most respected politicians. A woman runs the Business Club. Millions of Polish Catholics worship the Black Madonna of Częstochowa, 'the Queen of Poland', who can be considered our national goddess.

And yet the word 'feminist' sounds in this country like an insult. Almost every outstanding Polish woman, when interviewed, speaks in a rather typically feminist way, but she always adds: 'For God's sake, don't think I'm a feminist!'

Hanna Jankowska of the pro-choice Pro Femina
group in Poland[2]

In the past was the monolithic official women's movement, allegedly independent but in fact a semi-official, bureaucratic, centralized and top heavy mass organization which acted as the state's agent on issues of women's 'emancipation'. In the present are a plethora of tiny, fragmented and disparate, often single-issue and almost always explicitly non-feminist groups, existing alongside the purportedly reformed and democratically intentioned old women's unions and councils. What happened in between? Why did the democratically created space for the articulation of political alternatives, so sorely missed by those few women's groups that did exist in some form before 1989, not result in the emergence of a mass grassroots women's movement akin to those in Western Europe? And why does one encounter such an antipathy to feminism?

It may well be wrong to impose an expectation of feminist activism, derived from the West European experience of the 1970s and 1980s, on a situation which is socially, politically, and culturally different. What is more, the Western women's movement too has diversified, shrunk, is fragmented and relatively inactive. Nevertheless, there are many issues crying out for women to raise their voices in defence of their own interests. In the upheaval of transition in East Central Europe, as we have seen, women stand to lose those social (welfare) and employment rights which they did enjoy under state socialism, without in the short run appearing to gain much in exchange. This makes the non-emergence of a mass women's movement appear as yet another paradox.

What the present transformation period does make clear is that it is impossible to make assumptions about anything. In the absolute rejection of the past, the pendulum has swung to the opposite end of the political spectrum from state socialism. This has led to an ever-increasing fragmentation and splintering of political parties, particularly in Poland and Czechoslovakia. It has meant the total rejection of state socialist policies on 'emancipation' and of feminism too, in a faulty equation of the two. What it has not brought, ironically, is either a total obliteration of the former official women's organizations, or a painstaking re-evaluation of state socialism's record on behalf of women. Rather, as in many other spheres, it has left a hole where state socialism was, without there being new initiatives, theoretical perspectives or policies to fill the silent void around issues of women's rights, women's status, women's citizenship.

Both for the historical record, and to assess future potential, it is important to analyse the role of the official women's movement in the past and to try to gauge the range and motivation of women's groups emerging in the present transition. And does the relative lack of women's voices, women's pressure groups, represent a continuity, in terms of political passivity, or the lack of time at women's disposal under state socialism? Or have their voices been silenced by a male-dominated set of political priorities, by moral agencies such as the church, or by market forces, as suggested in the discussion of women's magazines in Chapter 7?

The Official Women's Movement

The history of the official women's movement is chequered, in much the same way as the history of reproductive rights. In the Soviet Union and several other state socialist countries there was an ambivalence on the part of leading comrades as to the necessity of a separate group to monitor women's interests. Was this to be viewed as a form of deviationist separatism, diverting from the collective striving towards a unitary goal? Or did women, as a result of their double exploitation by men and by capitalism, have needs that were not identical to those of men, and hence need an agency specific to their interests?

During the Stalinist period, this question was answered in the negative. The *zhenotdel* (women's department of the Party) in the Soviet Union was closed down in 1930, and the 'woman question' declared resolved. When state socialism established itself in other East Central European countries after the Second World War, there was almost universal consensus that women's organizations were superfluous. Only the former GDR differed. It was not until the post-Stalinist thaw that an official women's movement was created in other East Central European countries. And despite the apparent nod in the direction of pluralism indicated by their establishment, these organizations had become by 1989 totally hidebound, insensitive and unresponsive towards the very many real needs of women.

The *zhensovety* (local women's councils) in the Soviet Union date from the Krushchev era's attempt to transform state socialism into something more closely resembling participatory democracy. Genia Browning explains that 'despite their "ad hoc" appearance, the growth of the *zhensovety* arose primarily not from women's demands but as a result of CPSU policy'. Nonetheless, their formation from 1959 onwards (although some had come into existence even earlier) represented an about-turn of policy with regard to the existence of women-only organizations.

The *zhenotdel* women's section of the party which had existed in the early post-revolutionary years had been dismantled in 1930 on the grounds that 'women had already acquired equality, therefore no longer represented a distinct social category with separate needs'. The dominant discourse had argued that the abolition of private property had obliterated class (and presumably, it was assumed, also gender) conflict. This discourse was to influence the policies of the other state socialist countries. It provided the rationale for failing to foster organizations devoted to women's needs.

In the Soviet Union, the later *zhensovety* did represent an element of autonomy, in that they operated locally, independently of one another, with the aim of providing mutual support and raising women's political consciousness. In this latter sense, Browning argues that they resembled to some extent the concept of the early feminist consciousness-raising groups in the West. Certainly they differed markedly in both structure and substance from the centralized Soviet Women's Committee, an appointed body existing at national level only.[3]

The other state socialist countries deemed that women's equality under the law made a separate organization specifically designed to protect their interests unnecessary; Sharon Wolchik interprets as a sign of 'reformist tendencies' in the mid- to late 1960s in Czechoslovakia, the fact that members of the National Women's Committee, 'refuting the official notion that women were equal [. . .] drew attention to unresolved issues in women's lives'. In 1967, a mass women's organization was re-created, based on the view that conflict between various social groups persisted even under socialism, and that it was therefore legitimate 'for particular social groups to have organizations to defend their interests'.[4]

In the GDR it was determined from the outset that women's organizations were necessary. Those anti-fascists and communists who returned from exile in Moscow with the aim of building socialism in Germany were of the opinion that attitudes did not change spontaneously. Undoubtedly influenced by their own recent experiences and mindful of fascism's grip on people's minds, they felt that it was necessary to educate people for democracy. They therefore rejected the view that all that was necessary to relieve women of their double oppression was the elimination of private property.

In October 1945 they set up anti-fascist women's committees, dedicated to mobilizing women for the laborious task of clearing the débris of ruined cities. The so-called 'rubble-women' (*'Trümmerfrauen'*) have become legendary for their brick by brick sorting and reconstruction, representing a heroic version of 'women's work' by picking up the pieces left by the man-made devastation of war. In March 1947, the DFD (*Demokratischer Frauenbund Deutschlands* – Democratic Women's Union of Germany) was founded as a successor to these anti-fascist committees.

185

From the outset, the DFD saw its task as twofold. On the one hand it intended to raise women's political consciousness, overcoming the legacy of fascism and educating women for democracy. Simultaneously, it was dedicated to galvanizing women to burst out of the domesticating fetters of Nazi ideology and become involved in the public sphere of paid labour. The latter aim could be interpreted as sheer expediency in view of the acute shortage of male labour in the immediate post-war era. Yet it was couched in Marxist terms whereby labour force participation was defined as the essential precondition for emancipation, both in terms of economic independence from men, and for the unfolding of individual potential.

The DFD was subsequently responsible for initiating early and progressive legislation on behalf of women. The 1950 Act for the Protection of Mother and Child and the Rights of Women laid the basis for all later GDR legislation on women's rights. It is clear from the title that this law already contained the seeds of women's juridically promulgated dual role. Yet it should not be forgotten that it predates all relevant United Nations conventions. But the DFD's early activist characteristics were later lost in an increasingly rigidified and bureaucratized organizational structure. Inflexibility rendered the organization apparently unable to adapt to changing conditions. Hence by the demise of the GDR in 1989, over 90 per cent of women of working age were either employed or in vocational training. Yet the DFD's activities were still geared to activating full-time housewives, by then a tiny and dwindling constituency. By the late 1980s, its membership was also ageing. Only 25 per cent of DFD members were under 35 as opposed to 45 per cent of the GDR's total female population. Its educational courses focusing on preparation for marriage or on household management could be said to have lost touch with the needs of GDR women. In retrospect it was derided as an organization comprising 'knitting and crochet circles'.[5]

Independently and in advance of the 1989 'revolutions', then, the official women's councils and unions of state socialism had become anachronistic and top-heavy party-dominated organizations, regarded as both irrelevant and oblivious to the needs of women in their countries. As Hungarian sociologist Mária Adamik ironically notes, the 'official – or rather artificial – voice' of the Hungarian Women's Council had been 'largely discredited, despite an attempt to reform itself by changing its name in 1988'. After 1989, the DFD avowed a change of heart, distancing itself from past practices, yet in language and style its representatives and documents betrayed unreconstructed old-style

186

bureaucratic jargon. And although its statute professed commitment to cooperating with all manner of autonomous women's groups, its domineering stance deterred independent GDR women's groups in March 1990 from nominating a joint electoral list with the DFD.

Czechoslovakia provides an illustration of the feeling that these organizations were not just out of touch, but actively corrupt. The Federal Women's Union was disbanded in 1990, but the Czech Women's Union has inherited the accusation that considerable resources were misallocated in restoring to its former glory one wing of a former Renaissance palace in Prague, while women's needs went unheeded. The Union disposed over massive assets from its affiliated publishing company Mona and perpetuated old-style élitist, closed-shop forms of politics. In Poland, Izabela Nowacka, newly elected president of the Polish Women's League, declared frankly in 1990 that her organization had 'no experience of defending or fighting for women's rights' and hence wished to learn from the experience of the Western women's movement.[6]

In most of these countries barring Poland, there has been either a refusal to countenance, or failed attempts to institute, cooperation between new autonomous women's groupings and these old-style women's organizations. The latter appear unable, on the whole, to operate democratically rather than autocratically. A broadly-based coalition of women's groups would have had access to the old organizations' countrywide network of groups and financial resources. Yet the inability of the old orthodox groups to adapt to operating as equals with autonomous grassroots groups presents a severe hindrance in the context of the 'very strident anti-feminist movement', particularly in Hungary.[7]

New Women's Groups

The small and diverse women's groups on the scene at present offer a vivid contrast to the congealed structures and inflexible working methods of the old-style mass women's organizations. One can differentiate between those groups which have maintained a precarious and tenuous existence since the early 1980s, most of them self-avowedly feminist, and those groups which appeared in the run-up to or the aftermath of the events of 1989.

When interviewing former dissidents in general, it is clear that they felt a solidarity of 'us' in opposition to 'them', the institutions of the state. This explains why women involved in former dissident movements such as the Dialogue peace group and the Danube Circle environmental group in Hungary, Charter 77 in Czechoslovakia, or Solidarity in Poland, did not perceive themselves as having interests distinct from those of their male counterparts.

The small feminist groups of the 1980s, where they did not arise out of previous dissident or peace group involvement, began as academic study groups reading Western feminist texts. The Polish Feminist Association is a case in point; as were a number of groups of students and female professors who met regularly but informally, in private flats, during the 1980s in the GDR. Other groups in the GDR used the umbrella of the church in a more explicitly activist orientation. This was true not only of the Women for Peace, but also of numerous lesbian groups. In a state which defined all grassroots activity and even alternative lifestyles as dissidence or political opposition, 'coming out' became a doubly political act.

Czechoslovakia

Looking at the present, the case of Czechoslovakia is particularly striking. Jiřina Šiklová, a vivacious personality, respected sociologist and eminent former Charter 77 member, spent a year in prison during 1981–82 and another seven as a cleaning woman for smuggling literature in and out of Czechoslovakia. Now she is back in post at the Charles University in Prague. In August 1991 she founded the country's first Gender Studies Centre. It has no premises, but operates out of her central Prague flat, with one part-time librarian. With financial and practical support from the North American Network of East-West Women, the Centre has established a library and resource centre. During the winter of 1991 and the spring of 1992, they organized a lecture series at Charles University, as well as working to get women's voices heard and gender issues aired in the media. Yet support for the Centre is thin, and Šiklová feels there is a great need for education so that women overcome their misgivings about feminism and begin to understand some of the issues at stake. Jana Hradilková, the Centre's librarian, speaks of the need for a 'subtle approach' to 'circumvent the ingrained resistance to feminism', a resistance which is understandable, Hradilková maintains, because 'feminism smells like an ideology and people have had their fill of ideology here'.[8]

Outside Šiklová's flat the spectrum of women's groups is very broad. By the end of 1990, there were thirty-seven registered women's groups in Czechoslovakia. Yet with the exception of the old Women's Union, these groups were all tiny. As Czech writer Eva Hauserová points out, the very 'term "women's movement" is terribly discredited by the Communist Women's Union'.[9] The spectrum ranges from groups representing the particular interests of minorities such as Gypsy women or Jewish women, through Social Democratic and Christian Women's Unions, Women in Science and Technology, or Women in Management, to the old Women's Union. This last claimed a newly democratic will to work together with all new groups while still possessing, as of 1990, a membership of half a million, a strong and intact country-wide network, financial resources and organizational experience in the face of which none of the tiny new groups were able to assert themselves. By the spring of 1992, the new women's groups felt that it was impossible to cooperate with the Women's Union, who simply wished to dominate. Prague Mothers, an autonomous environmental organization whose self-definition rests on their identity as mothers, contrasts with the Movement for Women's Equal Rights in Bohemia and Moravia, which claims independent status but sounds in its centralized and bureaucratic structure and the language of its programme reminiscent of old times and the Women's Union.

Most of the new groups focus particularly on women's maternal function. Ironically, this includes even the Political Party of Women and Mothers, founded in January 1990, which defines itself as feminist and political. Alena Valterová, its founder, states: 'We will not organize knitting or cooking classes', unlike the old Women's Union, 'a social club' which she likens to 'a club of stamp collectors'. Rather, 'our aim . . . is the defence and representation of the socially weak and disadvantaged'. In particular, the Party intends to take on the plight of lone mothers. Eva Hauserová expresses her doubts about this Party, since 'it again associates women with family and children, which is, as I see it, backward . . . [and] it doesn't create any new social and family model'.[10] As of summer 1992, the Political Party of Women and Mothers seemed to be vanishing into oblivion.

New Humanity, registered on 4 July 1991, also used the term feminism in their group statement. Yet they too combine support for parity in female political representation, state responsibility for childcare, and 'equal professional opportunities' for women, with an idealization of the family and the quality of women's mothering in achieving the 'harmonious society' to which they are dedicated. Miroslava Holubová, a spokesperson for the group of academic and professional women (some of whom helped draft the 1992 election programme for the ODS, the Civic Democratic Party), for her own part vehemently rejects any association with feminism. In an interview in late March 1992, not long before the elections in Czechoslovakia, she spoke of the post-'velvet revolution' opportunity for men to become more assertive in their entrepreneurial male role which had been emasculated by state socialism, and for women to allow their caring maternal talents to flower, thus enhancing masculinity and femininity.[11] Perhaps paradoxically, Holubová sees New Humanity as carrying forward the tradition of the interwar Czech feminist movement. One of the group's aims is to reclaim the magnificent premises in central Prague which were originally built for those earlier feminists.

The Club for Modern Women includes some dissatisfied members of the old official Women's Union and aims to create a national network of groups, with a rather conventional set of goals, 'dedicated to providing domestic help, language lessons, babysitting, psychotherapy, and legal advice for women at home with their children'.[12] Even the old-style Movement for Women's Equal Rights in Bohemia and Moravia aims to train women for increased political representation, while supporting the formation of 'hobby clubs' for women, and of educating young girls 'in consideration of their future motherhood, housekeeping, and developing their abilities in cooking, sewing and handiwork'.

Prague Mothers, formed in 1988, is one of the most active and well-known of the new groups. It is based on a campaign to publicize and oppose extreme environmental pollution in Prague which resulted in a massive increase between 1965 and 1985 in the incidence of respiratory and skin disorders among children. They resist strenuously any association with feminist goals or aspirations, stressing first and foremost their commitment to motherhood. Many of them are Catholics, with large families. Rut Kolínská, a spokesperson for the group, maintains: 'We want to return to the base, dividing men's and women's roles to allow women to care about the family. According to the ideas of Masaryk [the president of the interwar democratic republic, whose ideas are being enthusiastically rediscovered], the base of a happy society is the family, and the woman is the leader of this ideal.'[13]

Poland

The Polish Feminist Association based in Warsaw and the Poznań Women's Club are both tiny groups, but with a long history of discussion and activism, operating as autonomous organizations within state socialism. Both were formed in 1980, and both see themselves as feminist. The Poznań Club initially had a peace and ecology focus, and became re-established in 1985 as an eco-feminist group. Sociologist Ewa Gontarczyk-Wesoła of the Poznań Club had by 1991 also managed to set up a feminist library and to obtain permission from her university to begin a Women's Studies course.

In the case of the Polish Feminist Association, their considerable international reputation far outweighs their numerical strength of only 15–20 active members. According to spokeswomen Bożena Umińska and Jolanta Plakwicz, the Feminist Association was founded in opposition to the male-dominated structures of Solidarity. Indirectly instrumental in their emergence was the first feminist seminar at Warsaw University initiated in the early 1980s by the sociologist Renata Siemieńska. One of the first issues to claim their energies in the post-socialist period has been the attempt to undermine abortion rights epitomized by the first Catholic Church-sponsored draft law submitted to the Sejm in 1989. Together with the many groups that sprang up specifically to resist this draconian curtailment of women's right to reproductive choice, they organized a demonstration in the summer of 1989. The ongoing saga of the pro-choice movement and the Church-based campaign for an outright abortion ban is documented in detail in Chapter 3.

The threat to abortion rights led to a mushrooming of new women's groups, not all of them feminist, but most of them single-issue, united in their defence of women's right to reproductive choice. One of these, formed in June 1989, was Pro Femina. Uniting men and women, it describes itself as working 'to protect reproductive rights, the right to privacy, the right to choice'. On the opposite side of the spectrum are various Catholic women's associations, with their strong emphasis on women as mothers.

Pro Femina galvanized the pro-choice campaign, by gathering signatures for petitions and organizing demonstrations, and were successful in delaying a decision on the draft anti-abortion bill and in forcing the government to consult women's groups on the issue. However, after 18 months the sheer fatigue of this uphill struggle, and the fact of being thrown so immediately into political activism, was taking its toll on the small number of women involved. Whereas in spring 1990, Pro Femina had 60 names on its contact list and could count on getting 10–15 people to meetings, the burden of their considerable organizational efforts was always carried by three to four key activists. By spring 1991, the group was struggling to survive. When the new anti-abortion bill was debated in the Sejm on 24 July 1992, there were fewer demonstrators than ever before – both supporters and opponents of choice – in front of the Sejm.

This 'burn-out' phenomenon was not restricted to Pro Femina, nor was it helped by the inter-group fragmentation and mutual political suspicion left as the legacy of state socialism. The tiny Polish feminist organizations are 'usually an object of jokes' according to Polish sociologist Mira Marody. Marody alludes to the emphasis placed by female representatives of the so-called 'élite' on 'a return to traditionally conceived' gender roles and in this context cites an interview with Maria Nurowska, a well-known Polish author, entitled 'To Restore Manhood to Men'. Further, she refers to a paper by Melanie Tatur which underlines the notion of a rediscovered femininity and masculinity, stating that the '"new" women's movement is no longer based on the assumption of equal rights for equal individuals, but demands the right and "social space" to articulate and realize female identity and life world'.[14]

However, on the positive side, it is also true that the Church-sponsored anti-abortion campaign helped cement diverse women's groups. Early 1990 saw the first meeting of 14–15 women's groups brought together by the then Head of the Women's Office within the Ministry for Labour and Welfare, Dr Góralska. This tradition was revived in 1991 by the then Under-Secretary of State for Women and Family Affairs, Anna Popowicz. A second example of an outside catalyst was another meeting of women's groups, also organized in spring 1991, in connection with a French-initiated campaign to promote sex education and contraceptive availability in Poland. This campaign united church women with the formerly communist Women's League. The League and the Democratic Union of Women (DUK), which was founded in 1990 and is linked with the Social Democrats, are the only organizations to have a nation-wide network of women's groups.

The Polish Women's League, founded in 1945, was in the past financed by the Polish Communist Party (PUWP) and played a contradictory role, initially mobilizing women to participate in the labour force, but in times of economic stagnation reassuring women of the importance of their role as mothers. By the late 1980s, it was running beautician, hairdressing, cosmetic and cooking classes. Its 1990 version of its own history describes it as an 'independent social organization' set up as early as 1913 with the purpose of involving women in the struggle for an independent Polish nation. As in so many current recastings of identity, the League's immediate state socialist past has dropped into the black hole of history in favour of its earlier nationalist credentials. Now it struggles to be self-financing, relying on membership fees plus the income from various economic ventures. It has managed to maintain 100,000 of its past membership of 600,000. Izabela Nowacka, the League's first elected rather than appointed president, says that the Countrywomen's Circles active in the Peasant Party may be larger. Clearly, however, there is a marked contrast in terms of numbers, structures and resources between the League, and Pro Femina or the Feminist Association.

As of 1991, the League seemed to be genuinely eager to cooperate with other women's groups, especially in the abortion and family planning campaigns. They had managed to get a plan for vocational schools for girls and retraining programmes for women accepted by the Ministry of Education. However, initially at least the courses were to be limited to training as waitresses and seamstresses, strictly feminized occupations for which existing vocational schools lacked sufficient opportunities. 'I know, I know, I'm not very happy about it,' said Nowacka, adding that she would like to be more ambitious and offer computer courses.

Both short-term retraining and longer-term perspectives were geared to helping women adapt to economic restructuring. The League's programme attempts to persuade women to be flexible, by accepting the reality that women's employment prospects lie in the service sector, and also in revaluing the 'underestimated position of housewife. ... We would like to show the value of work at home. Our organization wants to stimulate and educate women to be "enlightened housewives."'

In terms of political involvement, the League wishes to mobilize both economically active women and housewives in order to 'reconstruct the links in the local community'. This, however, appears to be reactive rather than initiatory, its purpose damage limitation, 'to counteract the negative phenomena of social life'. Privatized services, part-time jobs in the informal sector, and social welfare which is locally funded and provided, form the context. The League wishes to see women using 'their knowledge and experience' to provide an 'efficient system of social care. We want to organize local markets of various products and services such as: babysitting, handicapped person-care, services in house-keeping, etc. On the one hand it will be helpful to many people, and on the other hand it will give a possibility of earning money, particularly to unemployed people and housewives.'[15]

Danuta Waniek of the DUK (Democratic Union of Women), formed in 1990 and loosely linked with the Social Democratic Party, states that the Union has 3,000 members. She emphasizes the stark contrast to other women's groups which she describes as small and exclusively university- or intelligentsia-based (although DUK is itself, she adds, in large part composed of women with tertiary education). DUK works closely together with Pro Femina, both of them on the left of the political spectrum and therefore, maintains Waniek, subject to mistrust and job discrimination.

Unlike the Women's League, DUK's views on the politics of the family remain strongly social democratic and explicitly feminist in orientation. They hold society and the state responsible for the material well-being of families and support 'the maintenance of the necessary elements of the welfare state'. Within the family, they oppose traditional gender relationships characterized by dominance and subordination. 'We consider that paternalistic relations in a family and the society do not respond to the requirements of a modern family, in which a woman and a man bear equal responsibility for each other and for bringing up children.'

DUK plans to resist women being made redundant on gender grounds, and to ensure observation of the ILO Convention providing for equal pay for work of equal value. They wish to see the introduction of part-time and flexi-time working hours, and of retraining courses geared to facilitating women's adaptation to the economic reform process. They also demand that women's work in the household be recognized as creating 'both the material conditions of a family and some 30 per cent of gross national income'.

DUK proposes to prepare women candidates for political participation at both national and local level. They strongly oppose the traditional role models currently in vogue as both ahistorical and inappropriate to the current era. Their programme states in no uncertain terms that 'unfriendly myths and stereotypes, recently brought to life by conservative forces, originate from the times when the majority of women were not economically active and the majority of the society lived in rural areas'. They propose to 'defend the rights acquired by women in previous years [and to] fight for their systematic increase'.

On the issue of abortion rights, DUK, together with the Polish Feminist Association, Pro Femina, the Women's Council of the Trade Unions, and two other organizations, launched an 'Appeal to European Public Opinion' on 20 March 1991. The Appeal argues for a woman's right to decide in a context of sex education and freely available contraception. DUK argues that 'compulsion in the matter of procreation would deeply infringe and violate our personal freedom'. In both their programme and this Appeal, DUK argue against what they call the 'confessionalization' of social life, warning of the danger of a return to medieval practices of Church-led witch-hunts. Putting the issue squarely in focus as one involving fundamental citizenship rights, the Appeal ends by saying: 'We do not agree that our civil rights and personal freedom should be offered as a "gift" to Church authorities (as it has been suggested). There is no agreement among us to make such a sacrifice.'[16]

Despite the element of burn-out already discussed, sociologist Małgorzata Fuszara argues that the anti-abortion bill accelerated the growth of new women's organizations, which are now expanding their agendas beyond reproductive rights. She suggests, therefore, that in the longer term, the anti-abortion campaign may have shot itself in the foot: 'Mobilization of the Polish women's movement seems to me to be the outstanding achievement of the parliamentary campaign to ban abortion.'[17] Nevertheless, these developments took place in a context in which the dominant discourse was that 'there is no place for feminism in Poland'.[18]

Women's issues were given a boost in Poland by the publication of a Helsinki Watch report in early 1992,[19] which showed the extent to which women were discriminated against in terms of being the first to be made redundant, and furthermore that this was occurring via a disregard for laws officially still in force. The report states that 'though all people in Eastern Europe stand to benefit from their governments' increased respect for human rights, women in Poland and elsewhere find themselves at increasing risk of discrimination. ... In this transition period, past abuses and present political, social and economic pressures are combining with serious consequences for the equal rights of women.'

The report appeared at a time when the government Plenipotentiary for Women, Anna Popowicz, had been dismissed and her post discontinued, as detailed in Chapter 5. The abolition of this post came on top of the resignation of Solidarity's short-lived Women's Commissioner. The Women's Section had 10,000 members, with active groups in 17 out of 38 regions. Unlike the situation in UK trade unions, female Solidarity members did not automatically become Women's Section members, and there was some confusion about the basis for membership.

Małgorzata Tarasiewicz, the Women's Commissioner, had begun to organize leadership training courses for women unionists, with the cooperation of women unionists from the UK and Canada, under a two-year scheme agreed by the Solidarity leadership in 1989. Shortly after the creation of the Women's Section, Marian Krzaklewski was appointed to work with local Solidarity branches. He attempted to prevent the Section's formal registration within the union, claiming that the wording of their statute was unclear.

Krzaklewski represented an influential group of union leaders for whom loyalty to the Catholic church meant more than keeping Solidarity's Western union affiliates happy by creating the Women's Section. The crunch came over abortion. Krzaklewski declared himself pro-life, and proceeded to block the activities of the Women's Section at every step. For example he prevented women delegates from representing Solidarity at international trade union meetings in Canada and Britain on the grounds that they lacked a satisfactory moral stance, by which he meant the pro-choice attitudes of some members of the Women's Section.

Tarasiewicz eventually resigned in spring 1991, feeling that her position had become untenable. Two weeks later her assistant was sacked. On 16 June 1991, Krzaklewski asserted on television that the Women's Section had not been liquidated, since in fact it had 'never existed', being a 'temporary' provision.[20]

Hungary

In Hungary, a strident anti-feminist lobby exacerbates the difficulties faced by feminists. In an exchange in the literary-political bi-weekly *Hitel* during the summer of 1989, Gyula Fekete, a prominent male politician, had written that feminists are 'murderers of mothers', involved in the 'abuse and devaluation of motherhood'. In her reply, Professor Enikö Bollobás wrote that feminists 'work for the benefit of women *and* men, for the autonomous human being', and that 'feminists are gravely concerned for overworked, over-driven and exhausted Hungarian women, who are exploited by both family and society'. Her draft statement for Hungarian Feminists, a short-lived group formed in September 1989, asserted that 'the goal of feminism in Hungary, as well as elsewhere, is the spiritual liberation of women and men from oppressive hierarchical relationships'.[21]

Another hindrance is the false equation of feminism with state socialist policies for women's 'emancipation'. Feminist and sociologist Mária Adamik writes that 'the last forty years of so-called socialist women's emancipation is associated with the previous régime and therefore discredited and rejected – while it itself provided an excuse not to let even the thought of feminism into the country. In spite of growing impoverishment, words like solidarity and equality are still not really acceptable'. As Klára Ungár, an economist who stood for FIDESZ, the Alliance of Young Democrats, in the 1990 Hungarian elections put it: 'Socialist "equality" in fact added burdens to women's lives.' As a result, she maintains: 'Western feminists think our desire to return home is terrible. . . . But feminism is similar to the Green parties: of course we need their ideology, but they will be of more practical value in five years' time.'[22]

A third set of obstacles impeding the growth of a mass women's movement is formed by a combination of material hardship and ideological straitjackets. Zsuzsa Béres, one of the founders of Hungary's Feminist Network, says bluntly: 'Feminism is a word of ill-repute in this country. . . . Here in Eastern Europe, feminism is starting out in the face of enormous odds: economic recession, galloping inflation, rapidly growing poverty, a return to Christian conservatism.' In the face of these odds, Béres writes that:

> Fed up with unsatisfying, low-paid jobs, repulsed by an extremely aggressive political scenario and overawed by the prospect of being branded feminists (i.e. anti-male, anti-child, anti-family, lesbian), the majority of Hungary's women are not fighting back. For most, the name of the game is survival.[23]

In this atmosphere it is hardly surprising that it took a long time and much discussion to settle on a name for the Hungarian Feminist Network (Magyar Feminista Hálózat). In the end, it was perhaps not so much a commitment to feminism per se which decided the choice as the feeling that here was one word not yet tainted by association with or cooption by state socialism. Even such seemingly innocent words as 'Association' or 'Organization' failed the test. Since they gave themselves the name at their official founding meeting in June 1990, the Hungarian Feminists have been rethinking it. Does the term 'feminist' alienate and therefore exclude a wider group of potential supporters than it unites? Following the example of some Western groups, there was some thought of changing the name to 'Hungarian Women's Network'.

Even before the name was chosen, however, the group's very existence raised hackles in the intensely anti-feminist atmosphere which prevails in Hungary. 'I know those women' was a view expressed by women as well as men: 'they're neurotic, and besides, there's something unhealthy about a meeting in which only women take part'. By mid-1992, the 'Network', which is based solely in Budapest and is without countrywide links, consisted of approximately fifty women. Campaigns included collecting 7,000 signatures in summer 1990 to oppose government attempts to restrict access to abortion, a demonstration in support of Polish women's abortion rights, and a demonstration against the Gulf War in January 1991. The anti-Gulf War statement condemned all wars as 'crude, extreme manifestations of patriarchal society', adding: 'Women are placed on a pedestal for their capacity to give life, yet no one mentions the controversiality of sending these lives out to war, where they die as the tiny nameless wheels in an inconceivable machinery of power.' In conclusion, the statement maintained: 'We feminists advocate cooperation and solidarity instead of power struggle and competition, and the non-violent solution of all conflicts and disagreements, as the only behaviour worthy of human beings.'

In January 1992, the Feminist Network was successful in securing a grant of $10,000 from the Global Fund for Women, and $2,000 from Planned Parenthood, to support its pro-choice campaign against government plans to enact prohibitive legislation. The international recognition of their efforts embodied in these grants gave the Hungarian feminists great affirmation and new impetus. They hoped to use the money to launch a media campaign, thereby reaching a wider spectrum of women. Their original membership had come from two directions: on the one hand academic women trying to establish Women's Studies programmes in Hungary's universities, and on the other, women activists from environmental and peace groups.

Before 1989, many of the Network's members had been active in the activities of the Dialogue peace group or the environmental Danube Circle, a participation which 'remains largely unrecorded and unrecognized'. When oppositional groups were being formed during the 1980s, the first Hungarian feminist group had been set up within TDDSZ, the Democratic Union of Scientific and Research Workers. Subsequently, a seminar series on 'Women and Society' was held at Szeged University by Professor Enikö Bollobás who became, for a period after 1989, First Secretary at the Hungarian Embassy in the USA. Out of this seminar grew a group calling itself Hungarian Feminists, which published statements and analyses in 1989–90, but does not seem to have survived the departure of its founder.[24]

In Szeged, a local branch of the Alba Club was set up in 1991 by Rita Szilágyi and her husband Zsólt Kopniczky, one of Hungary's first conscientious objectors. The Alba Club is a nation-wide organization, originally formed to unite conscientious objectors, but currently a more broadly-oriented 'non-violent organization for peace', including green activists and feminists. In 1992, an Alba Women's Workshop was mooted, but as of August 1992, this had not got off the ground. The reasons advanced by Rita Szilágyi for this were the overwhelming problems of survival during economic transformation, and a lack of programme, resources and time for 'self-education'.

The Szeged Alba Club was very active in its first year, organizing a peace education conference, an international peace camp, and a 'conscientious objection' event on the central square of Szeged. Three of the women behind the projected Alba Women's Workshop have become entrepreneurs, and one of their projects for the future is to set up a women's refuge with SOS phone line and temporary accommodation, which Rita Szilágyi describes as 'like a lunatic dream in Hungary, for so far there is no organization which would sponsor the smallest women's initiative'.[25]

Former Soviet Union

In Russia, a group of women knowing virtually nothing about Western feminism, in December 1979 circulated ten copies of the first feminist samizdat entitled *Women and Russia: An Almanach to Women about Women*. This led to the involuntary exile of four of the 'ringleaders'. In a foreword to the 1984 Western edition of this text, Robin Morgan describes the book as the first in which 'Russian women speak for themselves' and describes these women as 'not anti-socialist but anti-totalitarian. They expose the patriarchal structure of the Left as well as the Right, of their Politburo as well as their husbands, bosses, fathers.'[26]

In her introduction to the 1984 English edition, one of the group, Tatyana Mamonova, describes the people behind the publication as opposed to all forms of violence and war 'in keeping with the nature of women'. She describes feminism as 'the strongest emergence of humanitarianism', advocating 'an understanding of the value of life and of the value of women in sustaining and contributing to the quality of life through their full and equal participation in both the burdens and benefits of an egalitarian society'. Mamonova reports that dissident men in the Soviet Union responded in an unsympathetic and sexist manner to the publication. In retrospect, however, she feels that despite the expulsions, the *Almanach* was successful in forcing discussion of women's issues into official discourse.

Nevertheless, it took some years and the proclamation of *glasnost* before feminist discourse and analysis again surfaced in the public domain. The March 1989 issue of *Kommunist*, the theoretical journal of the Communist Party, published an analysis of gender roles by three women researchers of the Academy of Sciences.[27] This event was a landmark. The article supported the principles of autonomy and choice for women and argued for men's active participation to lessen women's overburdening. Child and family benefits should be available to either parent in order to facilitate such sharing of parental responsibilities.

In the same year, Natalia Zakharova, Anastasia Posadskaya and Natalia Rimachevskaya, the authors of the *Kommunist* article, established the Centre for Gender Studies within the Academy of Sciences in Moscow. Anastasia Posadskaya is the Centre's current Director. Following publication of the article, she and her co-authors were invited to submit a position paper for policy on women to the Congress of People's Deputies, and subsequently granted advisory status to the Committee for the Protection of Maternity, Childhood and the Family. Members of the Centre have been instrumental in the formation of autonomous women's organizations such as LOTOS, the Independent Women's Democratic Initiative (NEZHDI – the acronym meaning Do Not Wait!) and the First Independent Women's Forum.[28] Other feminist groups also came into existence in 1989–90. In Moscow, Natasha Filippova was involved in facilitating a network of small groups called SAFO. In Leningrad, Olga Lipovskaya was publishing *Women's Reading*, a samizdat journal circulated in an edition of thirty typed copies.

Meanwhile, the Soviet Women's Committee, renamed as the more neutral Union of Women, 'is clearly changing ... but women in independent groups criticize it as a conservative organization, as a product of the communist past, and as attempting to maintain its monolithic grip over fresh women's groups'. Anastasia Posadskaya stressed as early as September 1990 that 'they are not elected by anybody ... they should acknowledge that they represent only themselves, not all Soviet women'.[29]

The First Independent Women's Forum, entitled: 'Democracy Without Women is No Democracy' was held in Dubna near Moscow from 28–31 March 1991. It provided the first opportunity for autonomous women's groups to get together. About 200 women came, from 25 cities. The final document challenged the patriarchal structure of society and acknowledged the existence of discrimination on grounds of sex in the former Soviet Union. It attacked 'the myth of "women's natural functions", that women have a purely biological, predestined role.' The accusation levelled at women 'of being to blame for many social problems, such as the increase in the divorce rate, juvenile delinquency, prostitution' was energetically opposed. The report pilloried 'the practice of representing women purely as sex objects'. Political representation should be proportional 'without gender bias'. Disproportionately high female unemployment should be countered by training courses for women entrepreneurs as well as other re-employment possibilities. And the family should treat all its members as 'individuals with equal rights'. The Forum established a Women's Information Network. 'From Problems to Strategy' was the title of a Second Women's Forum held in Dubna from 27–29 November 1992.

Women-only political parties formed in the republics of the former Soviet Union ranged across a wide spectrum, from the United Women's Party of Leningrad, which aims to 'unite all grains of female intellect' in one powerful political party, to the Party of Women of Sovereign Russia, founded in Tomsk in Siberia, which is wary of male-dominated political organizations and proposes to create an autonomous feminist movement. The Christian Democratic League of Women of Moldova argues that 'society would benefit from greater recognition of differences between men and women', while the self-help group Women for Social Renewal, officially registered in September 1989, is an entrepreneurial group.

In her account of new women's organizations, Olga Lipovskaya also mentions new women's magazines, which 'are still searching for their identity, confusing patriarchal material with more or less "emancipated" ideas'. The Committee of Soldiers' Mothers was initially formed in Moscow and Leningrad in 1989 by mothers of Afghanistan veterans; it has now become prominent in protesting against the maltreatment of soldiers doing their military service.[30]

According to Olga Lipovskaya, there are also powerful anti-feminist or conservative organizations such as Caritas in Lithuania which is pro-life and pro-family, or Russia (Rossiya) in Moscow which is part of a nationalistic movement called the Movement for the Spiritual Rebirth of Russia. The programme of the latter states that, 'a woman is first of all a mother and a wife and she is responsible for the spiritual education of children and men'. Her femininity is enlisted in the cause of '"restoration of the Russian Home", which means some kind of traditional community'. Lipovskaya opposes such views, and in a 1991 interview she expressed disappointment with the new democratic political organizations which have emerged over the past few years: 'I don't know one with women's issues in its platform.' She felt there was 'no civil society, no concept of individual rights, no political culture'. Feminism was hampered on the one hand by press reports accusing women of all the system's faults and of having lost their femininity, and on the other by the fact that 'our level of understanding is so low, women don't see the discrimination against them'.[31]

There are also organizations defending the interests of particular groups such as Only Mothers which has plans for charity shops to improve the plight of poverty-stricken lone mothers. However, 'Moscow mothers aren't flocking to join' this group. As Elena Prokoryeva, a lone parent, says: 'You need time to the organize that kind of cooperation. After working, queueing, cooking and cleaning, women just don't have the energy.'[32]

The Ukrainian Women's Union was formed in 1990, but sees its antecedent in an organization of the same name founded in L'vov in 1917 and dissolved in 1939 when the Soviet Union took over the Ukraine. By 1991, the Union of Ukrainian Women claimed to have over 6,000 members, and affiliates in most regions of the republic. Their aims thus far appear to be dominated by national, rather than women's liberation. In the introductory paragraph of its statute, the Union declares:

> For centuries a Ukrainian woman was the guardian of the home hearth, took care of the customs of the ancestors, national language, morality, ethos, education, culture, participated in the struggle for the high ideals of Ukrainian statehood.

According to Salomea Pavlychko, 'the main goal of the Ukrainian Women's Union is to take care of the formation of national consciousness, to engage women in public activities and to elevate the spirituality of Ukrainian women'.[33]

Elena Suskova, chairwoman, reported in spring 1992 that despite the fact that less than 3 per cent of politicians in Ukraine after the ending of the quota system were women, the Union of Ukrainian Women did not see itself as a political organization. Rather, its goal was to foster the mother tongue and disseminate knowledge of the long national tradition. She saw Ukraine as multi-ethnic, and conceded the right of other ethnic groups to publish newspapers and journals in their own language. However, Ukrainian must be the official language of instruction. The Union saw language as the basis of nationality, and nationalism as a struggle for ethnic survival.

One of the Union's prime aims was to encourage Ukrainian women to preserve the ethnically Ukrainian population 'from extinction as a nation'. A document produced by the Union on 'Ukrainian Women and Reproductive Function' subsumes reproductive rights to this goal. In an analysis of the root causes of the low birthrate among Ukrainians, the paper allocates responsibility to 'the destruction of the economy, the spectre of unemployment, the impoverishment of families, fear of the future, of the after-effects of the Chernobyl catastrophe, and of giving birth to weak and sickly children'.

One section of the paper goes further, attributing the 'androgynization' of women to their status as workers. Hard labour and the wearing of male clothing at work is held to alter female behaviour and physical movements to the extent that male hormones are stimulated, which makes women unwilling and ultimately also unable to become mothers(!).[34]

A report from Estonia also stresses 'the importance of women's reproductive capacity for the country' as 'vital to protect Estonia's unique culture', but nevertheless disputes the view that 'real women are mothers'. The Estonian Women's Union, founded in 1989, also sees itself as legal successor to the organization of the same name which existed between 1920 and 1940.[35]

Former German Democratic Republic (GDR)

In the GDR on 3 December 1989, over 1,200 women from more than 60 different women's organizations met in the Volksbühne, a Berlin theatre. They resolved to set up the UFV (Independent Women's Association – Unabhängiger Frauenverband) in a spirit of euphoria and optimism shortly after the Wall was opened. The UFV was to act as an umbrella organization for the multiplicity of women's groups which existed country-wide and across a very wide political spectrum, from the radical feminist Lila Offensive or Lilo (Purple Attack) to socialist feminist groups like Sozialistische Frauen Initiative or SOFI (Socialist Women's Initiative), and from groups committed to working nationally within the political structures, to grassroots groups dedicated to working at the local level, setting up crisis telephones, Women's Centres, cafés, feminist libraries and women's refuges.

As early as the summer of 1989, women academics at the Humboldt University in Berlin had decided to set up the ZiF (Zentrum für interdisziplinäre Frauenforschung), the first ever inter-disciplinary centre for Women's Studies in the then GDR. They were surprised at how easy it was to gain approval from the Dean of Social Sciences, and support from the university, which allocated them three research and technical posts. And they were gratified that over 100 women attended the opening ceremony in December 1989, 60 of them colleagues from the Humboldt University who expressed interest in working together with the ZiF.[36]

A first major project undertaken by Professor Irene Dölling, co-founder of the ZiF, was the commissioning and analysis of diaries kept by women during a three-month period in autumn 1990. The purpose of this was to document and monitor the impact of changes in everyday life resulting from currency union and German unification, with a particular focus on the subjective perception of change.[37] The ZiF also organized the so-called ring-lectures between the Humboldt University (HU) in East Berlin and the Technical University (TU) in West Berlin.

Eva Schäfer, a researcher from East Berlin, gave the first of these in March 1990, speaking on the women's movement in East and West. The discussion revealed unexpected dissent and the dumbfounded realization on both sides that although they lived within what was now once again one city, the women were divided. A deep chasm formed by very different life experience, different discourse, different concepts and consciousness separated them, a divide which has been dubbed 'the Wall in our heads'. This discovery stunned women in the two parts of Germany and began what has proved to be a long and tortuous process of mutual acquaintance beset by severe problems of communication. Bärbel Bohley, founder member of the Women for Peace, described the feeling of former GDR citizens after the fall of the Wall: 'We still speak German ... but we are unable to make ourselves understood.'[38]

Initially, it had seemed as if the UFV would become a mass movement, with considerable influence and a large presence in the mainstream political process. There was a feeling of exhilaration and the hope that, inadequate as the GDR's approach to 'emancipation' had been, it nevertheless provided a basis upon which demands for measures which they saw as guaranteeing real equality of opportunity for women could build.

The UFV demanded equal pay for work of equal value, quotas to ensure parity of representation in political structures, freedom from exploitation as sex objects in pornography, an end to sexual harassment at work and domestic violence, reproductive choice, equality of rights for lesbians, and a fundamental reorientation of society in order to facilitate greater gender equality at work and at home. The preamble to the UFV's 1990 programme offered an analysis of women's situation which reads remarkably like those of Western feminist documents. It pilloried state socialism as patriarchal, stating that:

> Women's disadvantaging, discrimination and oppression has continued over the centuries. Caught in the bind of a gendered division of labour which allocates to women the main burden in the family and the household and makes them economically dependent on men, women are reduced to a mother-centred role expectation, marketed as sex objects, and largely excluded from economic and political decision-making bodies. ... Socialism as we know it has also failed to transcend male-dominated structures, patriarchal power-based gender relations.[39]

In the first roundtables and the first democratic GDR government, the UFV's hopes and expectations appeared to be on the verge of fulfilment. A Women's Roundtable was established and Representatives for Gender Equity were appointed at local and regional level in all localities with a population of more than 100,000. In an ironically satisfying turn of the tables, almost every local council was persuaded to let women's groups take over former Stasi buildings. They established Women's Centres, some of them doubling up as women's refuges, and provided crèches, cafés, counselling for unemployed women and a wide variety of educational courses.

In September 1990 the UFV called the first ever all-Berlin mass demonstration. Under the motto: '*Keine Einverleibung der DDR*' ('No Incorporation of the GDR'), this protest focused not only on the 'takeover' terms of impending unification, but on the notorious paragraph 218 which kept abortion illegal in the Federal Republic. Yet despite these early successes, support for the UFV had already dwindled significantly by early 1991. And at their national meeting in March 1991, faction fighting within the organization massively undermined its ability to act politically. Many groups specifically rejected a political role for the UFV, geared to defending rights previously enjoyed by women in the GDR. Their preference was for it to be lifestyle-oriented and focused on more practical projects at the local level.

In 1992, the UFV began to set its sights on a long haul. In September 1991 it had decided after much deliberation against becoming a political party and in favour of remaining an independent movement. UFV parliamentarian Christina Schenk noted that unification (or 'annexation' – '*Anschluß*', as many citizens in the 'new' Federal states call it) had necessitated a change of strategy. The political agenda of the UFV could no longer focus on the feminist construction of an alternative GDR, but was forced into a rearguard, damage limitation exercise on behalf of former GDR women thrown into the wilderness of united Germany's capitalist market economy.[40] To this end, the organization aimed to publicize issues concerning women, and to bring to the attention of politicians the fact that half the electorate are women. In April 1992 the UFV organized a conference on the feminization of poverty in Eastern Germany, and followed it up with a public 'hearing' to which they invited reporters and politicians.[41]

The former GDR was exceptional in that it was the only country, prior to 1989, where specifically women's peace groups emerged. The case of the Frauen für den Frieden (Women for Peace) in the former GDR provides an interesting example of a transition in attitude towards women's groups on the part of the women themselves. A loose-knit group of friends, they came together originally to support the families of conscientious objectors.[42] It did not take long, however, for them to become involved on their own behalf.

In March 1982 the state provoked them into action with the promulgation of a revised Law on Conscription containing fundamental changes which had not, as provided for in the Constitution, been the subject of prior public debate. The revised law required, for the first time in the GDR's history, the conscription of women in times of emergency. The Women for Peace submitted a written objection, to which they had a legal right under the GDR Constitution, in which more than one hundred and fifty women formally distanced themselves from 'violence as a mode of conflict resolution'. They stated that:

> We do not regard military service for women as an expression of our equality, but as standing in contradiction to our existence as women. We regard our equality as consisting not in standing together with those men who take up arms, but in solidarity with those men who have, like us, recognized that the abstract term 'enemy', in practice means exterminating human beings, and this we reject.[43]

At this stage, the state's response to this 'provocation' was distinctly paternalistic. The women received no reply to their petition, despite a regulation specifying the citizen's right to a response within thirty days. Several women were questioned as to which man was behind the idea or had 'put them up to it'.

The group participated regularly in the Protestant church-led Peace Weeks held every November during the 1980s, and ran a Peace Fair on church property every June. They organized study groups on various aspects of peace politics and campaigned against the sale of war toys and compulsory pre-military training in secondary schools. They also ran an informal self-help play group/nursery school, one of whose aims was to make children aware of peaceful means of conflict resolution.

What most embarrassed the GDR's state security (the Staatssicher-heitsdienst or Stasi) was the ability of the Women for Peace to stage public actions, and the difficulty of isolating its 'ringleaders'. This demonstrated grassroots organizational potential which was inevitably perceived as a significant political threat. Moreover, in addressing to *both* superpowers their objection to nuclear weapons and the arms race at various small public demonstrations, the Women for Peace came inexorably into conflict with official GDR 'peace politics'.

Government policy insisted that the United States was the imperialist aggressor who had initiated each escalation of the arms race, and that 'brotherly' Soviet warheads were 'peaceful' or somehow benign, offering protection in their commitment to the defence of socialism. For their non-partisan opposition to *all* nuclear weapons, the Women for Peace were stigmatized as opponents of the state, driven into the dissident corner, and hauled in for frequent bouts of questioning by the Stasi.

During November 1983, in the wake of the Bundestag decision to deploy Pershing II and Cruise in the Federal Republic, the GDR had responded with a somewhat reluctant welcome to the first nuclear weapons, Soviet SS22s and 23s, ever to be stationed on GDR territory. In the wake of this unpopular decision, in early December 1983, four of the Women for Peace were arrested, at the same time as myself. Two of them, Bärbel Bohley (later a founder member of New Forum) and Ulrike Poppe (a founder member of Democracy Now) were held for six weeks on charges of the treasonable 'hypothetically possible' passing and misuse of information, which carried a 2–12 year sentence. The alleged grounds for their arrest was a dialogue across the Cold War divide. In meetings with this author on behalf of the Women's Committee of END (the Campaign for European Nuclear Disarmament), they had been involved in the preparation of a planned publication in Britain on official and unofficial women's peace activities in the GDR.

In terms of self-identification, the Women for Peace and visiting British and other West European peace women, including Petra Kelly of the West German Greens, held lively debates during 1982 around the issue of women-only peace groups, for which the GDR Women for Peace could see no reason. They felt that they were acting in solidarity with those men who supported their anti-war stance, and had organized as women primarily in opposition to the new clause in the Law on Conscription. However, by the end of 1983, a subtle transformation had taken place in their views and they had become clearer in their identity as a women's peace group. On the one hand they felt inspired by the example of the Greenham women in Britain, and felt too that in mixed groups their voices tended not to be heard. On the other, they enjoyed the Stasi's evident confusion and inability to deal with their non-hierarchical mode of organization.

The women began to see links between patriarchal structures of domination and subordination and the military madness which had brought humanity to the brink of the nuclear abyss. Whilst, in the West, many women already active in the women's movement were among the initiators of women's peace groups, the converse transition was true in the GDR. There, the experiences of the Women for Peace in the pursuit of what they called 'inner' as well as international peace, had led them to a form of feminist awareness.

Despite intensive Stasi surveillance, the Women for Peace had succeeded in autumn 1983 in arranging a demonstration of thirty women dressed in black on the Alexanderplatz, the central square of East Berlin. The women collectively and demonstratively posted their individual refusals to be called up for medical examinations. This action was successful in having call-up procedures for women halted. 'How do they do it?' asked 'my' puzzled Stasi officer in the course of endless prison interrogations. 'I don't understand it either,' I replied, 'they are quite amazing – fantastic organizers really, given that they have neither access to photocopiers nor a "telephone tree" of the kind we use in the British peace movement when we want to mount an action rapidly.'

In the short term, however, one could assert that the Stasi was successful, at least in the sense that the group disintegrated in the wake of the mistrust sown by these imprisonments. Many core members went on to co-found the mixed group Initiative Frieden und Menschenrechte (IFM – Initiative for Peace and Human Rights) which was formed in 1984, was instrumental in the events of 1989 and after, and still remains active today. In the long run, however, the Women for Peace continued as activists, kept their commitment to grassroots solidarity, and remained true to the principles of peaceful conflict resolution.

Monika H., the Stasi 'plant' who had ingratiated herself as friend and confidante of several Women for Peace members, was at least in part responsible for the arrests. She, too, subsequently moved on to the group Initiative for Peace and Human Rights. That Monika was one of more than 100,000 IMs (*informelle Mitarbeiter* – 'informal' colleagues) of the Stasi (with the cover name: Karin Lenz) became clear to the other Women for Peace at the beginning of 1989. They confronted her, but it was not until June 1989 that she finally admitted her role.

Long before the opening of the Stasi files in January 1992, a letter from Monika initiated a series of meetings, which resulted in a book published in 1990. It was far from the minds of her 'friends' from the group to take revenge, in what would have been understandable bitterness at the persecution she had facilitated or the suffering and hurt she had caused them. On the contrary, two of them, Katja Havemann and Irena Kukutz, conducted the series of conversations with her in an exemplary attempt, not to forgive, but to fathom the mechanisms of state socialist oppression.

They wanted to try to comprehend how it was possible for the Stasi to play on the psychology of someone with Monika's deprived history, using her weaknesses, her fears, her need for warmth and a sense of 'belonging', to make her a tool of persecution, poisoning the lives of those she befriended. For them the process of naming the demons of the past, of documenting past misdeeds and their effects on both victims and perpetrators, was necessary in order to prevent a repetition in the future. Too many people wish to forget, to suppress the memories. Only by bringing into the light of day the way people were misused can the horrors of the past be dealt with. Their jointly fashioned testimony provides a constructive attempt to come to terms with the past which has since rarely been emulated.

The kind of repression and psychological manipulation used by the socialist state against those it defined as oppositional, disappeared with the demise of the system which supported such institutions as the Stasi. The very fact that such in-built structures and mechanisms of oppression no longer exist has to be seen as an enormous liberation. Only now is there the space, in both literal, legal-political *and* psychic terms, to think about reconstructing civil society formations and legally validated oppositional activities.[44]

Former Yugoslavia

Even though the new groups are small, there are hopeful signs that women are beginning to resist current efforts to relegate them to the role of passive national icons. By reviving civil society initiatives to oppose ethnically-based fighting in the former Yugoslavia, women there are asserting active citizenship rights. On 2 July 1991, a parliamentary session in Belgrade was interrupted by several hundred parents, mostly conscripts' mothers, who stated: 'Men are the controllers of the war and of our sons. We do not give them permission to push our sons forward to kill one another.' Staša Zajović concludes from this that 'the very role – reproduction – which marginalizes women in their private lives has had the effect of converting them into active participants in the political life of the nation'.[45]

In a sequel to the Parliamentary action, women's direct action continued through the autumn of 1991. In September 1991, an international Peace Caravan initiated by the Europe-wide Helsinki Citizens' Assembly, had toured the former Yugoslavia. Inspired by the example of some Italian women from Perugia, the Women in Black began their demonstrations. Every Wednesday at peak traffic times, about fifty 'Women in Black' gathered in silent protest on a central Belgrade square. They unfurled a banner on which stood: 'Women in Black – Against the War' and distributed leaflets, which read: 'Women wear black when close family members die. We are wearing black in memory of all victims of this senseless war. We protest against irresponsible nationalist leaders who understand nothing but brutal military might.' Women are also active in the Belgrade-based Centre for Anti-War Action which transcends the mothers' actions in terms of a political agenda demanding peace through negotiated settlement.[46]

As we have seen, there are considerable intra-country differences. Tradition, religion, recent history and current concerns give the situation and potential of women's movements varying nuances in each case. In the former GDR, proximity to West Germany meant more familiarity with the concepts and arguments of Western feminism than was possible in most of the other countries bar Yugoslavia. Nor was the environment quite so inimical to the growth of feminist ideas – indeed in the 1980s the Protestant church in the GDR offered physical as well as ideological space for feminist groups. Furthermore, an unbroken tradition of social democratic and socialist feminism, symbolized in the person of Clara Zetkin, offered the advantage of continuity. Such opposition to feminism as there was, based itself upon Marxist orthodoxy rather than religious doctrine or national tradition.[47] In the present, the five new Federal states have perhaps the most politically effective as well as most explicitly feminist movement of any. Yet it seems that unification has had a hand in slowing, if only temporarily, the initial enormous impetus of the UFV.

Czechoslovakia may boast a plethora of women's groups, many of whom identify with the thriving pre-Second World War bourgeois feminist movement. Yet these groups are individually tiny and together disparate, united only by a commitment to the family as the basis for social stability and to the centrality of women's maternal role within it. Jiřina Šiklová's Centre for Gender Studies, indeed the project of gender studies itself, is very much a minority voice in a hostile or at least unreceptive environment.

In Hungary, the weight of semi-feudal peasant tradition and Catholicism together help fuel the virulent anti-feminism against which the Hungarian Feminist Network struggles almost alone, except for small groups of professional and businesswomen. Yet the Network's energy, together with their success in gaining international support, are cause for optimism in estimating their chances of survival. And perhaps in the mid- to long-term, speculates Hungarian sociologist Júlia Szalai,[48] women's experience in the informal networks of the past, their adept ability to juggle and improvise using scarce resources, will stand them in good stead for creating the autonomous grassroots organizations of a future civil society.

In Poland, conversely, sociologist Renata Siemieńska has pointed to a primary identification with the family and the nation as a factor, alongside state socialist oppression, which mitigates against the emergence of intermediate social movements.[49] And at least in the short term, while women are fully occupied mediating for the family the shock waves of the transition, their organizational efforts will tend to be minimal and to remain invisible, ironically not unlike their domestic labour under state socialism. In the former Soviet Union, dire material conditions affecting food availability and health care, combine with patriarchal and nationalist ideology to discourage the mass of women from organizing themselves.

The conservative and powerful influence of the Catholic Church in Poland has had the ironic effect of uniting disparate and mutually suspicious women's groups in the struggle to defend women's reproductive rights, whereas the outward catalyst activating women in the case of the former Yugoslavia has been the brutality and mindlessness of militarism. Whatever the form of women's movements, whether feminist or single-issue, environmental or conservative, only the future will tell whether they are successful in achieving equal citizenship status and choice for women.

Finally, it is clear that there is no way that Western feminists can or should assume that their experience of struggling for greater gender equality can be projected onto the very different life experiences and

211

environment of East Central European women. The prospect of East-West dialogue opened up by the end of the Cold War is exciting. For it to bear fruit as part of a joint adventure to reformulate the feminist project necessitates a process of listening in a spirit of openness and mutual tolerance. The difficulties in communication experienced by feminists in East and West Germany, coming from similar ethnic backgrounds and cultural traditions and speaking the same language, may be illuminating for the wider project of East-West dialogue on gender issues.

Regine Hildebrandt, Social Democrat Minister for Women, Labour and Health in the East German state of Brandenburg, highlights some of the differences underlying problems of communication with Western feminists: 'We are not interested in slogans but in tackling the problems that exist. It will be a long time before we understand each other. ... In the old West Germany, women gained emancipation through discussion; we had it in practice. However, that practice is now collapsing beneath us.'[50] Ulrike Helwerth, a West German feminist writing in *Weibblick* (*Women's View*), the monthly newsletter of the East German UFV, states:

> Communication between women in East and West is faulty. Two years after the fall of the Wall and one year after unification the German sisters, like the rest of the two German halves, seem more mutually alien than ever. At every opportunity we confirm on both sides that we can't get along together. We constantly renew our prejudices about each other. Western women are arrogant, know-alls, anti-men and anti-children, dogmatic and intolerant. Eastern women are conformist, good mummies, obsessed with men and not a bit radical. In each case we take the other 'from over there' to be less emancipated and independent than we are.

Helwerth pleads for a new start in which both sides get off their high horse and finally subject 'our respective "feminist paradises" to critical scrutiny'. Such an analysis could provide the basis for a new understanding crucial to the establishment of a new women's movement, which, she concludes, 'we have bitter need of in this "fatherland"'.[51]

Notes

1. Jiřina Šiklová, former Charter 88 activist, sociologist at the Charles University and founder of the Gender Studies Centre in Prague.
2. Hanna Jankowska, 'The Reproductive Rights Campaign in Poland', Paper

presented to the conference on 'Mary Wollstonecraft and 200 Years of Feminism', University of Sussex, 5–6 December 1992.

3. For a detailed analysis of the history and role of the *zhensovety*, see Genia Browning, *Women and Politics in the USSR: Consciousness Raising and Soviet Women's Groups*, Wheatsheaf Books, Brighton, 1987. For the founding of the *zhensovety*, see ibid., pp. 52–61.

4. Sharon Wolchik, 'Women and the Politics of Transition in Central and Eastern Europe', in: Valentine Moghadam, ed., *Democratic Reform and the Position of Women in Transitional Economies*, OUP Clarendon Series, Oxford, 1993.

5. For a fuller description of the history and analysis of the role of the DFD, see Barbara Einhorn, 'Socialist Emancipation: The Women's Movement in the GDR', in: Sonia Kruks, Rayna Rapp, Marilyn B. Young, eds, *Promissory Notes: Women in the Transition to Socialism*, Monthly Review Press, New York, 1989, pp. 283–86.

6. Sources: Mária Adamik, 'Hungary: A Loss of Rights?', in: *Shifting Territories: Feminism in Europe*, special issue no. 39 of *Feminist Review*, winter 1991, p. 166; Barbara Einhorn, 'Where Have All the Women Gone?, in: ibid., pp. 24–25.

7. Adamik, ibid., 1991, p. 169.

8. Jana Hradilková, in: *Prague Post*, 22–30 March 1992.

9. Eva Hauserová, 'The Cult of Motherhood', in: *Everywoman*, July/August 1991, p. 20.

10. Hauserová, ibid.; Mila Castle-Kaněrová, Interview with Alena Valterová, in: *Shifting Territories*, 1991, pp. 161–5.

11. Miroslava Holubová, Interview with Barbara Einhorn, Prague, March 1992.

12. Source: Ruth Rosen, 'Women and Democracy in Czechoslovakia: An Interview with Jiřina Šiklová', in: *Peace and Democracy News*, Fall 1990, p. 38.

13. Rut Kolínská was quoted in the *Guardian*, 7.6.90.

14. Mira Marody, 'Why I am Not a Feminist? Some Remarks on the Problem of Gender Identity in the USA and Poland', ms., 1992.

15. Sources: Programme document of the Polish Women's League; Barbara Einhorn, interviews with Izabela Nowacka, Prague, October 1990 and Warsaw, June 1991.

16. Sources: Documents of DUK; Barbara Einhorn interview with Danuta Waniek, Warsaw, June 1991.

17. Małgorzata Fuszara, 'Legal Regulation of Abortion in Poland', in: *Signs*, vol. 17, no. 1, autumn 1991, p. 128.

18. Księżopolski and Fracziewick-Wronka, in Bob Deacon and Julia Szalai, eds., *Social Policy in the New Eastern Europe: What Future for Socialist Welfare?*, Aldershot, Avebury, 1990, p. 47.

19. Helsinki Watch, 'Hidden Victims: Women in Post Communist Poland', in: *News from Helsinki Watch*, vol. IV, issue 5, 12 March 1992.

20. Sources: Małgorzata Tarasiewicz, 'Women in Poland: Choices to be Made' in: *Shifting Territories*, 1991, pp. 182–87; Barbara Einhorn interview with and letter from Małgorzata Tarasiewicz, Warsaw, June 1991, July 1992.

21. Enikö Bollobás, 'Feminist Thorns for a Hungarian Sexist', in: *Hitel*, vol. 2, no. 13, 21 June 1989.

22. Mária Adamik, 'Hungary: A Loss of Rights?', in: *Shifting Territories*, 1991, p. 166; Klára Ungár was quoted in the *Guardian*, 7.6.90.

23. Zsuzsa Béres, 'A Thousand Words on Hungarian Women', published in: *Budapest Week*, March 1991, and reprinted in: *Trouble and Strife*, issue 23, 1991.

24. Sources: Chris Corrin, 'Women in Eastern Europe', in: *Labour Focus on Eastern Europe*, no. 41, 1992 , p. 45; Ottilie Solt, writing in the intellectual weekly *Beszélö*, excerpted in: *East European Reporter*, vol. 4, no. 4, spring/summer 1991; Zsuzsa Béres, founder-member of the Network, 'The Feminist Network', manuscript, July 1992; 'Hungarian Feminists' Statement', published in: *Peace and Democracy News*, Fall, 1990; other analyses by this group in manuscript form.

25. Rita Szilágyi, letter to Barbara Einhorn, July 1992.

26. Robin Morgan, Foreword to Tatyana Mamonova, ed., *Women and Russia: Feminist Writings from the Soviet Union*, Blackwell, Oxford, 1984. An earlier translation of the *Almanach* was published by Sheba Feminist publishers in England in 1980.

27. Natalia Zakharova, Anastasia Posadskaya, Natalia Rimachevskaya, 'How We Are Resolving the Woman Question', in: *Kommunist*, no. 4, March 1989; excerpted and discussed by Cynthia Cockburn, 'Second Among Equals', in: *Marxism Today*, July 1989.

28. For an interview with Anastasia Posadskaya by Maxine Molyneux, plus reports and documents on NEZHDI and the First Independent Women's Forum, see: *Shifting Territories*, 1991.

29. Ibid., pp. 136, 141–8; Mary Buckley, 'Political Reform', in: Buckley, ed., *Perestroika and Soviet Women*, Cambridge University Press, Cambridge, 1992, p. 67.

30. Olga Lipovskaya, 'New Women's Organizations', in: Buckley, ed., *Perestroika and Soviet Women*, 1992, pp. 72–81.

31. Jonathan Steele, Interview with Olga Lipovskaya in: the *Guardian*, 4.4.91.

32. Susan Poizner, 'The Sorrows of Mother Russia', in: the *Guardian*, 30.6.92.

33. Sources: I. Havrylyuk, 'Ukrainian Feminists Preach Pre-War Domestic Doctrines', in: *Soviet Weekly*, 4.10.90; Salomea Pavlychko, 'Between Feminism and Nationalism: New Women's Groups in the Ukraine', in: Buckley, ed., *Perestroika and Soviet Women*, 1992, p. 91.

34. Elena Suskova, 'Nationalism in Ukraine', speech delivered to the Women's Commission of the Helsinki Citizens' Assembly, Bratislava, March 1992; and Union of Ukrainian Women document on reproductive function circulated at the meeting by her.

35. A. Laas, 'The future for Estonian Women: "Real Women are Mothers"', published by the European Network for Women's Studies (ENWS), Brussels, 1991.

36. For an account of the history of the ZiF and feminist research in East Germany, see Irene Dölling, 'Frauenforschung mit Fragezeichen? Perspektiven feministischer Wissenschaft' ('Women's Studies with a Question Mark? Prospects for Feminist Scholarship'), in: Gislinde Schwarz and Christine Zenner, eds, *Wir wollen mehr als ein 'Vaterland'*, Verlag Rowohlt, Hamburg, 1990, pp. 35–56.

37. This project was itself the outcome of East-West dialogue between researchers. An attempt in 1990 to get British research support for an East-West project using diaries to document popular perceptions of the massive upheavals post-1989 had failed. However, joint discussions of this project followed up by a Foreign Office-funded visit of Dorothy Sheridan, archivist of the Mass Observation Archive at Sussex University, inspired the ZiF project in Eastern Germany. A selection of the diaries has appeared as Irene Dölling et al., eds, *Unsere Haut: Tagebücher von Frauen aus dem Herbst 1990* (*Our Skin: Women's Diaries from Autumn 1990*), Dietz Verlag, Berlin, 1992. For an analysis of the diaries, see Irene Dölling, '"Man lebt jetzt regelrecht von Tag zu Tag, weil nichts mehr sicher ist" – Tagebücher als Dokumente eines gesellschaftlichen Umbruchs' ('"You really live from day to day now, because nothing is certain any longer" – Diaries as Documents of a Social Transformation'), in: *Berliner Journal für Soziologie*, Heft 1, 1992, pp. 103–11.

38. Bärbel Bohley, 'Vierzig Jahre Warten' ('Forty Years of Waiting'), in: Bohley et al., eds, *40 Jahre DDR ... und die Bürger melden sich zu Wort* (*Forty Years of the GDR ... and the Citizens Speak Up*), Büchergilde Gutenberg and Carl Hanser Verlag, Frankfurt, 1989, p. 6 [my translation, BE].

39. UFV Programme, 1990. A substantial extract, translated by Barbara Einhorn, was published in: *East European Reporter*, vol. 4, no. 2, spring/summer 1990, pp. 53–54; the programme is also discussed in: Barbara Einhorn, 'Where Have All the Women Gone? Women and the Women's Movement in East Central Europe', in: *Shifting Territories*, 1991, p. 27.

40. Christina Schenk, 'The Opportunity of Policy Making', a report in a series entitled: 'Feminism in Parliament' in which she defends her role against the view of some former dissidents and some feminists, that participating in the structures of formal politics

inevitably coopts and corrupts movement politics. The report was published in the May 1992 issue of the UFV's monthly journal, *Weibblick* (*Woman's View*, a play on the word Weitblick, meaning 'farsightedness', or 'vision').

41. Interview with Marinka Körzendörfer in the New Forum-sponsored newspaper *Die Andere* (*The Other*), no. 12, 1992; Barbara Einhorn, Interview with Christiane Schindler, Berlin, March 1992.

42. The GDR was unusual amongst state socialist countries in offering the option of non-weapon-carrying military service in 'construction brigades'; nevertheless, some men chose total conscientious objection, which carried a mandatory prison sentence.

43. The full text of the petition to GDR Head of State Erich Honecker was published in *END Journal*, issue 2, February/March 1983, pp. 10–11 (trans. Barbara Einhorn). In the light of the myriad armed conflicts which have broken out since the end of state socialism, their position on peaceful conflict resolution reads like an utopian one; ironically it was a view commonly held by peace movements during the Cold War period. For a fuller account of the activities of the group, see Einhorn, 'Sisters across the Curtain: Women Speak Out in East and West Europe', in: *END Journal*, issue 8, February/March 1984, pp. 26–28; and Einhorn, 'Socialist Emancipation: The Women's Movement in the GDR', 1989, pp. 297–300. Reference is also made to the activities of the group, and this author's relationship with them, in the Introduction above.

44. For a record of these conversations, see Irena Kukutz and Katja Havemann, *Geschützte Quelle: Gespräche mit Monika H. alias Karin Lenz* (*Protected Source: Conversations with Monika H. alias Karin Lenz*), Basisdruck Verlag, Berlin, 1990.

45. Staša Zajović, 'The War and Women in Serbia: Patriarchy, Language and National Myth', in: *Peace News*, March 1992.

46. Source: Branko Milinković, 'Yugoslavia: Women at the Forefront of the Peace Movement', in: *Lutherische Welt-Information*, no. 34, 14 November 1991.

47. Western feminist texts tended to be handed round circles of friends in brown paper wrappers. What little discussion of the Western women's movement there was in academic publications during the mid- to late 1970s dismissed it as reformist and self-indulgent. Western feminists were caricatured as 'man-hating late bourgeois bluestockings' who substitute gender warfare for class struggle. For a fuller discussion of these critiques, see Barbara Einhorn, 'Socialist Emancipation: The Women's Movement in the GDR', in: *Women's Studies International Quarterly*, vol. 4, no. 4, 1981, p. 437.

48. Júlia Szalai, 'Some Changes', 1992.

49. Renata Siemieńska, Interview with Barbara Einhorn, Warsaw, 31 March 1990.

50. Regine Hildebrandt, quoted in the *Guardian*, 6.3.92.

51. Ulrike Helwerth, 'Farewell to the Feminist Paradise', in: *Weibblick*, 2/92, pp. 8–10 [my translation, BE].

7

Imagining Women:
Literature and the Media

There was once an old man who had three daughters. The two older daughters thought of nothing but dressing themselves up in fancy clothes, but the youngest liked to keep house, was nimble and quick and did whatever she set out to do better than anyone else. She was beautiful too, more beautiful than tongue could tell or pen could write, with eyes as bright and blue as the sky and a plait of golden hair that reached below her waist.

Fenist the Falcon, a Russian fairy tale[1]

The image of the female tractor driver is out, as is Superwoman wearing a hard-hat on a building site. Cinderella of fairy-tale fantasy and dreams is back – whether to stay is not yet clear. She works, yes, but only in the household, so that her feminine qualities are not marred by the fatigue and premature ageing incurred by the hardships of the double burden. This picture may be pretty, but it signals a nineteenth-century model of domesticated women with no claim to citizenship rights in society. Yet it is precisely to the literature of the nineteenth century and to earlier mythical typologies that the countries of East Central Europe are turning in their search for new role models following what they see as the failure of state socialism's egalitarian model for women.

This chapter will look at the issues of gender and citizenship through the construction of women's roles in literature. The stereotypical dichotomy between virgin and whore which characterizes much nineteenth-century literature as well as earlier myths, was supplanted during the socialist era by the worker-mother duality. Since the late 1970s, women have begun speaking for themselves, rejecting both types of prescriptive roles and focusing on the real problems and contradictions faced by individualized and rounded female characters.

Why literature? State socialist occlusion of the space for articulating alternative views in public discourse meant that literature attained the status of political statement and sociological evidence. If one wanted to understand everyday life in the state socialist era, and particularly the texture of gender relations in reality, then it was to literature that one turned. Official cultural policy had designated an important role for literature as agitation or propaganda designed to raise consciousness in terms of commitment to the socialist project. Writers were exhorted to communicate directly with their readers, in an accessible literary style. Literature became a more widely read media form than the often turgid daily newspapers. This made it especially sensitive, and subject to the eagle eye of censorship, which in turn, some have speculated, rendered literature particularly subtle.[2] Authors and the reading public became adept at 'reading between the lines', complicit in an elaborate game designed to quench people's thirst for a discourse which bore some relation to the reality they lived.

One of the strongest initial reactions against state socialism was a rejection of its didacticism, its normative and prescriptive stance on issues of individual behaviour. Citizens as newspaper readers were infantilized, being told not only what to read, but what to think. Democracy's main virtue and attraction, in the popular understanding prior to 1989, was that it would confer on the individual the right to freedom and self-determination. There is in East Central Europe a strong wish to attain adult status as political subject, as autonomous citizen capable of moulding one's individual destiny rather than remaining passive object-beneficiary of public policy. Socialist theory promised the full development of individual potential within a society which harmonized individual and collective needs as its ultimate aim; but in practice state socialism had subordinated this aim to the interests of social welfare, economic growth and demographic survival.

At the same time, however, the shock of transition is currently muting this aspiration, reducing it for many to the 'fear of freedom'. There is a desire to escape into compensatory models and images which might assuage the pain of the present. Literature has always expressed the passions, sensitivities, dreams and longings of men and women. And as always in times of material hardship, romanticized literature is now enjoying a revival. It offers a vision of what the Germans call a 'heile Welt', a world of bygone concord in which interpersonal relationships are intact, a world which is not subject to the ravages of economic transition or the stresses of international market dynamics.

It is perhaps not so curious, then, that the current search for identity involves a retreat from unaccustomed complexity, a reaching

217

out for the presumed simplicity of a past agrarian idyll. National difference, suppressed by the imposed homogeneity of Soviet-type socialist societies, is re-asserted by recourse to nineteenth-century literature, seen as epitomizing the culture of nationalist striving for independence.[3] The emancipatory thrust of this literature is its resistance to foreign domination, its assertion of national sovereignty and cultural specificity. It is important to the nationalist project to shape new notions of the individual. Literature has been historically relevant to this project in giving voice to national as well as to individual aspirations.

These nineteenth-century literary models constructed woman as synonymous with national virtue betrayed, as morality incarnate, both victim and actor on the stage of history, suffering and strong, weeping and offering resistance. In the current period of chaos and complexity, there is resort to the 'feminine principle' as the solution to the nation's ills. What is not acknowledged so overtly is the patriarchal character of the largely agrarian past culture, nor its clearly prescribed hierarchy of gendered separate spheres related through a system of domination and subordination. In the immediate past, socialist realist dogma privileged the sphere of production over social reproduction and personal and sexual social relations. In the literature of the 1950s at least, the 'heroine-worker', in conflict with reactionary forces hindering socialist construction, eclipsed the emotional conflicts and psychological splits experienced by individual women in the invisible realm of gender relations. Today too, the renewed iconization of woman as national symbol obfuscates the problems encountered by real women.

Currently fashionable discourse idealizes the 'feminine' while circumscribing women's roles and curtailing their freedom of movement, relegating them to primary responsibility for the family and custodianship of the moral and ethical values of the wider ethnic or national group. In searching to establish sources for this return to the eternal female, it is illuminating to look at the construction of women's roles in the literature of earlier periods. This is not to suggest that literature can be read as a simple or direct reflection of social reality, still less, as was once required by socialist realism, of reality in its optimistic or 'revolutionary' perspective. Nevertheless, as feminist literary criticism in North America and Western Europe has established, an analysis of literary representations of women does reveal certain patterns in terms of the normative role models of the society of the time and the limited range of possibilities and choices for female characters.

This chapter does not attempt an exhaustive literary analysis. Instead,

218

examples drawn from various national literatures will point to the strength of female symbols and stereotypes which inform those cultural traditions and which explain in part the resurgence of a much more traditional range of role models, after more than forty years of state socialism. If, in the current search for national identity, there is a return to the nineteenth century, when Polish or Czech nationhood was in its formative stage, so too it is evident that current idealizations of the family and the rewriting of female roles owe much to the literature of the nineteenth century.

I shall begin by examining some of the associations between nineteenth-century literature and nationalist aspirations in Poland and Czechoslovakia, and then go on to look at representations of the nation as a woman. Myth and fairy tale are often used to illustrate 'eternal' female attributes, drawn on in constructing ideal types. Depictions of female characters in nineteenth-century Russian, Polish and Czech literature reflect a fundamental ambivalence which derives from earlier myths, reinforced or remoulded by Christianity. Such a duality in images of women is common to many cultures but takes on a specific form in connection with portrayal of the nation's fate.

Next, I shall look at the portrayal of women in the literature of Stalinist state socialist Europe. The doctrine of Socialist Realism ostensibly subverted what it saw as reactionary nationalism and traditional, gendered, role models. Yet the incorporation of women worker-heroines into the text without questioning imputed, 'naturally' feminine, behavioural traits or traditionally structured gender relations, made for unconvincing cardboard characters. Thus there is a sense in which early socialist realist texts failed to break the mould of earlier role models. It was not until the 1970s that women began to speak for themselves, naming the real contradictions and the high cost of their supposed 'emancipation' under state socialism.

The final section of this chapter examines the impact of market forces on women's ability to speak for themselves, through a study of two women's magazines. It raises the question, do the pressures of the market impose a new uniformity of female role models, silencing independent women's voices?

Yearning for the Past: The Idealized Literary Nation

Nationalist aspirations are central to the literatures of both the Czechs and the Poles; indeed 'the emergence of modern Polish literature coincides roughly with the time when Poland, partitioned by Russia,

Prussia and Austria in 1795, ceased to exist as an independent state'. And 'in the case of the Czechs, literary creation has time and again been part of a larger struggle against oppression and foreign domination, for the preservation (or resurrection) of the language, for the very existence of the nation'.[4] National identity was most fiercely celebrated in literature precisely in periods of its historical fragility. The theory that nationalist sentiment surges in periods of instability, upheaval or perceived external threat to the nation goes some way towards explaining its current revival. Rejection of the compromised identity imposed by state socialism, and loss of social cohesion, has left a sense of insecurity and dislocation.

There appears to be an almost equally strong sense in both Poland and Czechoslovakia that their territory, once the site of powerful nations whose past glory is mourned, has been, for much of history, simply a staging post in other nations' campaigns and policies of domination. 'History has cast the Czech and Slovak in the role of victim and it is in this role that the characters in most ... stories appear. The Czech and Slovak nations have been the victims of war and foreign domination which almost obliterated their languages. Their country has been the battlefield of half a dozen major wars and, against their will, the bivouac of myriad foreign armies.'[5]

The second half of the nineteenth century saw the beginnings of an autonomous Czech culture. Jeanne Němcová speaks of this national revival as 'the work of a large and versatile band of men and women who accepted the patriotic mission of awakening their countrymen to a new appreciation of their heritage, to a pride in their land and language'. The list included musicians like Dvořák and Smetana, and writers like Božena Němcová and Jan Neruda for whom the arts 'were to be the expression of the spirit of the nation'.[6] Exiled from Poland during partition (by Russia, Prussia and Austria, from 1795 until 1918), 'the three great "bards" of the Polish Romantic era', Adam Mickiewicz (1798–1855), Juliusz Słowacki (1809–49) and Zygmunt Krasiński (1812–59), 'inspired, for a generation and more, the enslaved nation'.[7]

In the nineteenth century, semi-feudal hierarchical social relations still held sway. As Celina Wieniewska makes clear, the lack of industrial revolution in Poland meant that there was 'no gradual emergence of the middle class to a position of power – at most a drifting of the impoverished landed gentry into the towns and cities and into badly paid civil service posts; no social movement which would break down the sharp division between the traditional classes of the arms-carrying and land-owning nobility and the landless, largely illiterate, peasantry.'[8]

Both aristocratic and peasant households in the largely agrarian society of nineteenth-century Poland suggest role models for women which denied them the right to autonomy and self-determination (according to Steven Lukes, two of the essential ingredients for liberty). Instead, these models preached female self-denial in the interests of both individual and national family (thereby isolating and prioritizing privacy, in Lukes's view the third pre-requisite for liberty).[9]

Gendered Symbolism: The Nation as a Woman

Tatyana Tolstaya points to the reproduction of 'mythological models', in part taken from Russian folklore, when she sets out to define 'what is Russia?'[10] In these recreated myths, or 'invented traditions',[11] the ceremonial trappings of national imagery frequently cast the nation symbolically as a woman. Examples are *Mat' Rossiya* (Mother Russia), Britannia, Germania, Polonia and Marianne. Wendy Bracewell points to the use of monumental female figures, usually mothers, as iconographic symbols of virtue personified, construed as synonymous with the nation.[12]

In both Polish and Russian literary and cultural tradition, the links between woman and nation are strong. Barbara Heldt has recently pointed to a paradox here. On the one hand 'the patriarchal myth of the pure nature and abstract goodness of Woman has endured to this day, not least because it is also a symbol of nationhood ... the icon of Woman as Motherland unites where the myth of Revolution has failed to do so'. But on the other hand, 'no "feminine" principle has ever determined the social order. Yet persistently, the more powerless women have been in actuality, the more powerful the myth that has arisen of their redemptive, caregiving, nation-identified essence.'[13]

The symbol of woman as personification of the nation is linked in many East Central European countries with organized religion through the medium of the Virgin Mary. In Russia, the icon of the Virgin Mary 'remained the national totem: it was hung in a corner of every Russian home, preceded all armies into battle; before it all oaths were sworn and conflicts resolved'.[14] From this, Francine Du Plessix Gray infers that 'Russian culture has been equally marked by men's ambivalent awe and resentment of forceful females, and by a singularly intense worship of the Virgin Mother'.[15]

In Poland, Polonia is a martyred victim who embodies Poland's fate as a nation continually carved up during its history and mourning its lost independence. The Holy Mother was in the seventeenth century also crowned Queen of Poland. Polish literature makes this linkage of nationalism with religion explicit in identifying the nation, Polonia, with the Virgin Mary / Holy Mother, patron saint and simultaneously Queen of Poland. Of this national icon and Polish nationalist aspirations Andrzej Szczypiorski writes in his novel *The Beautiful Mrs. Seidenmann*:

> Where is the Virgin Mary of Jasna Góra, Ostra Brama, Piekary, Kobryń – cities near and far – if in the course of one man's life, on the corner of Zygmuntowska and Targowa streets in the capital of the nation that at one time stretched from sea to sea, ruled over Gdańsk and Kudak, Glogow and Smoleńsk; if ... before the eyes of only one man, during his lifetime, in the course of thirty years, a mounted Cossack from the steppes, a Prussian officer, a Nazi and a Red Army man, were changing the guard here, then where was the Virgin Mary of those cities near and far, the queen of this nation? ... Was this country merely the territory for foreign armies to march across, the land between the front lines, the strip of ground between them? ... the outpost of the free world, squeezed in between tyrannies ... Only a strip of land, a piece of ground, an outpost? And nothing more?

Yet in the same novel, Pawel, through whose eyes much of the action is reflected, comes to deplore the myth of sacred Polish nationalism in view of events like the Warsaw Ghetto and Stalinism, in which Poles themselves were complicit:

> At long last the myth of our uniqueness, of this Polish suffering that was always pure, righteous and noble, has bitten the dust ... Sacred Poland, suffering and brave. Holy Polishness, drunken, whoring, venal, its mouth stuffed with claptrap, anti-Semitic, anti-German, anti-Russian, antihuman. Under the picture of the Holy Virgin ... holy blasphemous Polishness ... dared to call Poland the Christ of Nations and was rearing informers and denouncers, careerists and dimwits, torturers and bribetakers; who elevated xenophobia to the rank of patriotism.[16]

These extracts illustrate the fact that Polish nationalism, whether affirmed or rejected, is seen as having religious significance, personified in the suffering figure of the Virgin Mary degraded by 'whoring' human weakness. The critique of nationalism too is couched in terms of the gendered dualism of good and evil, the virgin and the whore, a duality which will be explored further below.

Marina Warner's book *Monuments and Maidens* includes a reproduction of the colossus 'The Motherland', which commemorates the Soviet victory over Germany in the Second World War and dominates

Volgograd. In it, according to Warner, 'the sculptor Evgenii Vuchetich combined the scale of Bartholdi's matron with the dynamism of Delacroix's freedom-fighter'.[17]

Vuchetich's 'Motherland' provides an apt illustration of the duality whereby images of suffering or protective maternity and Amazonian warriors are combined in the iconography of a nation. Elizabeth Waters refers to the 'convention within Western art of representing liberty and the nation (in times of war as well as peace) as a woman [and to] the practice, dating back to the eighteenth century, of deploying the female figure as an allegory of revolutionary struggle and revolutionary government'.[18] The image of 'the weak, vulnerable woman fighting can be peculiarly powerful', according to Wendy Bracewell, 'harnessing the struggle of good against evil and the weak against the powerful, to the struggle of the nation against its enemies'.[19] In this incarnation, the feminized national icon is portrayed as a vengeful warrior, protecting the nation's cultural heritage, fending off attackers in defence of 'hearth' and (national) home.

This duality in symbolic representations of the nation also characterizes literary portrayals of women, in a manner found in various European cultures. Both female types depicted in the gendered symbolism of nationhood are often united in the figure of the mother: at once passive and active, protected and protecting, victim and avenger, subdued domestic creature defended in hearth and home by male warriors, and avenging fury in the name of the nation wronged. One of the dominant literary models, for example in Russian and Polish literature, is that of the strong but suffering 'mother of the nation'. Joanna Hubbs writes that: 'Russia as motherland has been the source and object of much art, literature, and speculative thought. But as the Russia who calls for self-sacrificing champions, she also represents suffering and constraint. Her dual nature as the fount of creativity and its limit assumes metaphysical as well as social and psychological dimensions, raising the question of the proper relationship of the individual to the whole.' An object personifying Mother Russia is the *Matrioshka* doll whose 'iconographic presence continues, unobserved, to express a mythology of maternity'.[20]

Yet women's sexuality upsets this vision of the powerful and protective, revered but asexual mother.[21] Representations of external attack are often masculinized as rape of the 'female' nation. Here woman becomes a symbol of fecundity and source of the nation's strength, or of victimization, this duality giving expression to a further ambivalence. Female sexuality is either sanctified in motherhood or else a powerful force which is feared and rampant, needing to be tamed or destroyed. This is a literary trope common to many cultures: the representation of woman as virgin/mother or alternatively as whore.

The Virgin and The Witch: Passivity and Potency

The duality of female figures is forcefully expressed in Russian mythology and literature. Russian Orthodox Christianity includes an intense cult around the Virgin Mary as Mother of God, saviour and protector of the nation, a figure who is strong, but suffers, yet does not articulate or act upon her suffering. On the more powerful side of the equation, Tatyana Mamonova points out that in pre-Christian epic myths, giant male *bogatyrs* were matched by mighty female *palenitsas*. She asserts that from the tenth century, patriarchy in Russia 'either destroyed the mythical heroines, or made them over to fit their image of the subservient, prone-to-sin woman'. Hence she views it as significant that 'strong females in Russian folk tales are almost always represented by negative characters'.[22]

Joanna Hubbs has linked the 'powerful maternal archetypes' of Russian cultural tradition with 'the misogyny of its Orthodox church'. Orthodox theology regarded women as 'the source of all spiritual danger', emphasizing their 'mental inferiority and their powers of witchcraft'.[23] The magically endowed and feared strong woman of Russian mythology is embodied most powerfully in Baba Yaga, the witch grandmother, who lives deep in the dark forest surrounded by a fence topped with skulls. Nevertheless, Tatyana Mamonova questions the purely negative signifiers associated with this figure, given that she is also a wise woman knowledgeable in herbal remedies. She points out that Baba Yaga is also known for her good advice, most particularly in assisting 'clever young girls' or 'wise maidens' to throw off patriarchal repression. In both *The Frog Princess* and *Vassilisa the Wise*, Vassilisa is punished by her father for being born wiser than him. She needs all her wits, and the assistance of Baba Yaga, to throw off her father's evil spell which transforms her into a frog and a stream in the respective stories.[24]

The youngest, domesticated, dutiful, clever and beautiful – though nameless – sister in *Fenist the Falcon*, described in the epigraph to this chapter, represents, like Vassilisa, a Russian version of Cinderella. Vassilisa's 'stepmother and stepsisters envied her her good looks and forced her to work very hard so that she might grow thin and that her face might turn dark in the wind and sun. Vassilisa bore everything meekly and with every day that passed became more

224

beautiful, while the stepmother and her daughters, though they sat around and did nothing, were eaten up by spite and grew gaunt and ugly'. Eventually, 'wanting to be rid of Vassilisa', they send her into the deep dark forest to fetch a light from Baba Yaga the Witch, 'who gobbled up people in the wink of an eye'.

Yet contrary to expectation, Baba Yaga helps both Vassilisa, and the nameless maid in *Fenist the Falcon*, to despatch the wicked stepsisters and to accomplish all the tasks they have been set, thereby overcoming all obstacles which stand between them and happiness in the form of being wedded to the tsar. The tsar wishes to reward Vassilisa for her cleverness in spinning, weaving and sewing shirts 'fit for none but a tsar to wear'. But when he sets eyes on her, it is her beauty which causes him to fall 'madly in love with her'. Fenist the Falcon ditches the princess who 'betrayed' him, 'who loved me so little that she was ready to trade me for a few trinkets', for the faithful devotion of the nameless maid, 'who passed through dense forests and crossed sandy deserts' for his sake and 'who loved him so well that she asked for nothing but to see him'. The assembled 'boyars and princes and the rest of the folk' concur with his judgement. 'So Fenist the Falcon sent away his false wife and he wed his true wife, and they lived happily ever after.'[25]

Vassilisa and the nameless maid unite the duality. They embody enterprise and courage on the one hand, beauty, the virtuous industriousness and submissive devotion of domesticated and selfless womanhood on the other: as the extract cited at the beginning of this chapter illustrates, they are 'meek' and hardworking, yet beautiful and skilful. What more could any prince desire?

Baba Yaga the witch, however, is the dreaded dark side of female sexuality. Yet things are not so simple. To the beautiful maid who is Fenist the Falcon's 'true love', Baba Yaga is the wise woman of the woods, her accomplice in applying intelligence as opposed to devotion to the tasks she is set. Baba Yaga 'the grandmother' may be rejected, feared and alone in the forest, but she is also a source of knowledge and strength. In short, then, the duality is clearly not a simple distinction between the wifely virtue of the beautiful and true princess on the one hand and the wicked witch on the other. Indeed Baba Yaga appears in various guises in different fairy tales. And in another paradox, 'Marya Morevna the lovely Tsarevna' in the tale of that name is herself strong enough to vanquish a 'mighty host' before being turned into a maiden in distress by her own beloved prince who disregards her instructions and thereby sets free the monster.

Clearly there is duality within each of the female roles as well as between them, as the story of *Marya Morevna* illustrates. What is most fascinating is the way present role models for women appear to be reviving the typology of fairy tales by conjuring up a somewhat simplistic model of domesticated wifely virtue as a magic circle of protection against the harm that might lurk in the dark depths of the world outside. An intact family presided over by a wife-mother is presumed to inure men against cut-throat individualism in the marketplace. By contrast the market is rife with secret spells and dangerous sexuality ensnaring men, luring them off the well-trodden path of traditional family mores. The relationships of (male) domination and (female) subordination within the family appear as safer territory than the relations of competition and amorality in the jungle of the marketplace. It is in nineteenth-century literature that this world of safe, because known, patriarchal patterns may be found, together with nationalist aspirations for independence.

Literary Antecedents: The Cinderella Split

In the nineteenth century, the image of women in Russian literature remained polarized between the redemptive spiritual strength of the Virgin and the seductive but dangerous beauty of the flesh. It is significant that in the Russian case at least, the dominant literary discourse of the nineteenth-century novel (unlike the English novel) was largely male in its authorship. 'There is no lack of general pronouncements about how women act or feel or think in Russian literature,' but, as Barbara Heldt points out, 'these have been overwhelmingly made by men.' She writes of 'a central metaphor of male writing about women: the visual trope of woman objectivized and named by man, who is doing the fictive viewing and narrative commentary.'[26]

Francine Du Plessix Gray speaks of the duality expressed in nineteenth-century Russian novels between 'an idealization of women's moral virtues which led to the creation of heroines considerably more powerful than their male counterparts', and 'a paradoxically negative, ascetic attitude towards women's sensuality and intellect'. Their sexuality is regarded as 'only safe when their energies are totally sublimated in that holiest of duties which is motherhood'.[27] Barbara Heldt describes 'the Russian heroine' as very often not a person in her own right, despite her near perfection, so much as a 'mere foil for the male and his larger preoccupations'. While male characters are typified by Turgenev as 'superfluous men', their female counterparts remain in a sense faceless embodiments of virtue. 'All the works are structured so that the hero is centre-stage; the heroine approaches for a falling-in-love section, followed by a dramatic confrontation in which the hero will bolt, defeated by her moral superiority.'[28]

In a parody of the concerns of nineteenth-century Russian literature Abram Tertz writes that it 'contains a great multitude of love stories in which a defective man and a lovely woman meet and separate without any result'. Thus not only the witch or the wise woman, but also the literary paragon of virtue, remains at the end of the story, like so many modern Russian women in reality, alone.[29]

The fact that these heroines are simultaneously portrayed as beautiful and desirable, yet deeply frightening, illustrates a deeply ambivalent attitude towards women and female sexuality. This derives from a puritanical streak not unique to socialist realist literary figures, but very deeply rooted in Russian culture and tradition, which portrays 'women in love, even within marriage', as 'a force that must in some way be neutralized'.[30]

Baba Yaga's fairy tale fence of human skulls suggests further that female sexuality has magical powers which are all-consuming and fatal. Indeed in an embodiment of deep psychic fear, the dark implication is that Baba Yaga eats men, a trope present in the mythology of diverse cultures. 'The day passed, and the night, and it was only toward evening of the next day that Vassilisa reached Baba Yaga's hut. The fence round it was made of human bones and crowned with human skulls, the gate was no gate but the bones of men's legs, the bolts, no bolts but the bones of men's arms, and the lock, no lock but a set of sharp teeth. Vassilisa was horrified and stood stock-still.'[31]

The stark duality between moral virtue as strength, indeed 'terrible perfection' (Heldt), and subordinated docility in ascribed female roles, is unified in the mother figure. In much male-authored nineteenth-century fiction, women's options are severely circumscribed: they can choose maternity or solitude. Barbara Heldt speaks of the 'great cost' for female characters of trying to mould 'an independent existence' and suggests their fate may be even worse. She names examples of several female figures in whom can be observed 'a progression in disregard for and defiance of the observing males'. They end up 'distant, preoccupied, unconscious or dead. ... A heroine's insistence on self-definition is usually violently punished, for whether as objects of desire or as objects of male self-definition, their striving toward self-naming has dire implications for the men who do the naming.' Heldt summarizes this ambivalence using the concept of a double burden: 'Socially limited, but morally superior – women have a double burden within a tradition of fiction which focused on self-definition but excluded women from the self to be defined. Women were predefined by most male writers whether liberal or conservative. . . . Deviation from superiority resulted in woman fallen or stridently attempting self-definition in a context of futility. The expectation of perfection, when disappointed, led inevitably to a terrible opposite.'[32]

Larissa Lissjutkina postulates an extraordinary unification of this duality in the archetype of the prostitute in Russian culture.[33] She points out that both Tolstoy and Dostoevsky portrayed the prostitute as men's saviour, in that through her body she relieves men of their sin, carrying their cross for them. More recently, family life has been colloquially called a 'cross' which it is the fate of Soviet women to bear. Motherhood is constructed as woman's holiest duty. The solution for this ambivalence proposed by Lissjutkina allows her to interpret the post-*perestroika* boom in pornography and prostitution as liberation from the desexualization of life under state socialism. She carries this through to the extreme of characterizing the prostitute as a 'pioneer of the market economy, an independent entrepreneur, bravely breaking taboos'.

This somewhat unorthodox hypothesis has the prostitute not as victim but as heroine of the transition period, a pathbreaker who utilizes the transformation process to the hilt, symbolically knocking both the asexual transcendental mother figure of religion or literature, and the de-sexed worker-mother of state socialism into a cocked hat. Whilst the image of the prostitute may appear to embody the neo-liberal notion of the individual in the marketplace – rebellious, unprotected, exposed to danger, but liberated – it dodges the issue of relational bonds. It is clear that the split implied in this duality between 'damned whores and god's police'[34] does not offer much in terms of role models for the mass of today's Russian women. And whilst there is a need to re-establish the bonds of family and community, and to overcome the sense of an atomized society, so long as men define the nature of these institutions, they will continue to produce such splits which stereotype women.

The strong, suffering, asexual female archetype is also typical of Polish literature and cultural history. Here the duality of the Virgin Mother/Mother Russia as opposed to the whore gives way to a trinity of roles embedded in the Catholic church, the nation, and the family. Polonia, the personification of the nation, is also, in the figure of the Black Madonna of Częstochowa, known as the Queen of Poland. Poland was seen as the victim of repeated rape in partition and occupation by other powers. This is the basis in nineteenth-century Polish Romantic literature for constructing the Patria as a female suffering victim, and for the notion of suffering and even masochism as central to the sense of national identity. Bożena Umińska speaks of the metaphorical 'duty of unhappiness' and of women steeped in self-sacrifice for the honour of the lost Patria. She emphasizes the power and persistence of the Polish mother image which remains central, dominating Polish literature 'unfortunately to this very day'.[35]

Popular tradition construes the protective mother as suffering *and* strong. She protects the hearth and works to provide for her family while her husband is fighting in insurrections to reclaim the nation, or exiled to Siberia, during the 150 years of partition. The poem *The Polish Mother* by Adam Mickiewicz,[36] the most influential Polish poet of the nineteenth century, describes this 'strong, supportive, self-sacrificing woman' who brings up her son in the name of the Patria. In the bitter realization that his heroism can not succeed (in the context of partition), she must be prepared to accept his being wounded, exiled or killed.

Umińska points out that men 'ceased to be fathers, they were just warriors in the patriotic cause', that symbolically therefore, one can speak of the 'death of the father' in this literary tradition. In the face of absent menfolk, the female figure carried a great burden of responsibility, and had to labour without reward, acting as 'deputy-father' as well as mother. As a result of this variant of the double burden, she was often portrayed as hysterical, temperamental or carping. She was also ultimately alone, like the strong heroines of nineteenth-century Russian novels. Yet 'the more she suffered, the more noble and elevated she was'. Popular imagery shows this Polish woman as sad and solemn of visage, clad in mourning black with a cross prominently displayed upon her breast.

The second female trope of Polish Romanticism is the 'hero-virgin', also created by Mickiewicz. This originated with the title of another poem, about a real-life woman called Emilia Plater who commanded a fighting squad during the 1831 war with Russia. In the poem, Emilia becomes 'a living monument' who displays extreme spiritual and physical chastity, 'a real skyscraper of virtue and heroism'. Other poems by Mickiewicz and Słowacki feature pale background women, 'chosen' by the hero. In preferring someone richer they prove unworthy of the hero's love, and he, disillusioned, plunges into a substitute love for the Patria and the national cause.[37]

Mother love was linked in nineteenth-century Czech literature with the rural family idyll as a symbol of nationalist aspirations. Even in the writings of several well-known women authors from this period, women characters tend to practise self-denial in the name of the family, property or the good of the community. Božena Němcová's (1820–62) classic novel *Babická* (*Grandmother*) attempts to delineate Czech national character through its depiction of village life, in the process idealizing both 'simple Czech village women' and the 'relationship between two social classes – the grandmother and the local countess'. Rural social milieux also dominate the work of Karolína Světlá (1830–99). Her main characters cover the contradiction-laden spectrum of female role models. A first embodiment in the story 'Black Peter' (1871) of a woman who 'freely decides over her own destiny' and 'gives up her social standing in order to have control over her own life' is countered by the norm whereby 'the female characters of her novels and stories usually give up their happiness in the name of higher ideals' often within a 'marriage without love'.[38]

The twentieth-century inter-war period was a 'time of expansiveness in Czech culture and art'. Alongside female characters 'who were misunderstood and suffering', the novels of Marie Majerová (1882–1967) 'precipitate a shift of characteristic female protagonists from village women to women workers', thus starting 'a trend towards what later became called socialist realism'. Nevertheless, Majerová's works are concerned with 'the struggle against an unjust social order', to which women's status is subordinated. Hudcovská, a country woman in the novel *The Siren* (1935) is beaten by her husband – the patriarchal family is alive and well in Majerová's works. In *Martyrs* (1921), a character expresses Majerová's insight into the social standing of Czech women when she says: 'We women are indeed impoverished as far as our general interests and relationships to others are concerned. We have been curtailed like the trees on a French avenue, trees that can spread their branches so far, to a given line, and no further.'

The writer Marie Pujmanová (1893–1958) moves from a 'celebration of family life' as the ideal harmonious environment in her first novel, to post-First World War portrayals of disrupted inter-personal relationships. In *Dr. Hegel's Patient* (1931), the central character Karla rebels against the social conventions dictated by false middle-class values and 'battles for her right to become a single mother'. However, Pujmanová's famous novella *Foreboding* (1942) returns to the notion that the only route to coping with uncertainties and anxieties (in this case provoked by the Nazi occupation) lies 'through family togetherness'. The family as the cure for all social ills is being prescribed again, as a placebo for the pain of material insecurity and psychic trauma in the present period of social upheaval.

The Worker-Mother: Was Cinderella a Socialist Realist Heroine?

Elizabeth Waters draws attention to the fact that Soviet political iconography in the first fifteen years after the Revolution tended to favour the male form. The common use of female allegory to represent Revolution was short-lived in the new Soviet Union, and the female figure to emerge in the 1920s was the *proletarka*, the red-kerchiefed woman worker. The *proletarka* continued to dominate during the period of the first five year plan (1928–32), in ironic opposition to the fact that 'despite the talk of female emancipation, the party gave the woman question an even lower priority than before: the *Zhenotdel* was closed down in 1930 (on the grounds, ostensibly, that women had become the equals of men and hence were in no further need of a special organization), and public discussion of women's rights ceased.'[39]

A later example of political iconography which 'over the years became one of the most familiar of Soviet images', argues Waters, was the statue by Vera Mukhina depicting 'The Industrial Worker and the Collective-Farm Worker'. Ostensibly affirming the equality of the sexes, the individual figures in this male-female pair were in fact merely ciphers, the statue's purpose being 'a celebration of the alliance of the working class and the peasantry. The female image is undoubtedly a strong one, but the couple in one important sense undermines rather than affirms sexual equality because a secondary role is assigned to the woman, not by the arrangement of the figures, but by the allocation of symbols – the sickle to the woman, the hammer to the man. Though peasants still constituted the vast majority of the population, they took second place according to Soviet ideology in the struggle to build communism.'[40]

Nor did early socialist realism offer more positive depictions of women's sexuality or autonomy than had been present in nineteenth-century literature. Rather, the scenario 'girl meets tractor' subordinated sexual relations in their entirety to the collective enterprise. Early Soviet or East German '*Aufbau*' ('production') novels like Fjodor Gladkov's *Cement* (1956) were dedicated to socialist 'construction'. Women as workers and wives subordinated both career and individual aspirations to their men who struggled against sabotage in heavy industry. Katrin in Eduard Claudius's *Menschen an unserer Seite* (*People by Our Side*, 1954)[41] has a factory job, not a career. Her husband's fiery struggle to set a huge brick-making kiln in motion dominates the narrative. And an important sub-plot concerns his opposition to her going out to work at all, rather than caring for him and their child.

Katrin is described in the clichéd gender terms of the '*Heimat*' novel (nationalist novels depicting idealized rural life in the 'Fatherland') as a 'strapping' woman whose 'good, broad peasant's face' displayed 'plump, healthy apple cheeks one felt like biting into'. Her decision to go out to work is explicitly motivated by official rhetoric: 'How can you believe I could be satisfied with life in the kitchen? I am not just a woman you sleep with and who keeps the nest clean. The Party says our construction needs all hands. And what about me, should I stay home in response to that?' His reply is: 'Oh, well, you are hardworking ... you could achieve something. Go on then! Me and the child, we're not important. Go on then, whether or not we survive is irrelevant!'

Despite the wooden phrases and hollow sloganizing, there is ambivalence in the portrayal of Katrin Aehre, which matches precisely the ambivalence in official policy towards women's emancipation. Her prime responsibility for the family is not questioned: her husband's 'reactionary' resistance must be broken down, but not by reallocating gender-divided domestic responsibilities. Her decision to go out to work is motivated by the economic needs of the moment, translated into party discourse, yet at the same time she explains it as a need to express herself, to prove herself, to gain affirmation in her own right, for 'You have to understand,' she tells Hans, an 'activist of the first hour', 'that I'm not first and foremost a woman, but a person'.[42]

The didactic function of this *Aufbau* literature was to persuade reluctant husbands and women themselves that women should be mobilized into the workforce. If the huge print-runs of such novels was any indication, then one might infer that the didactic approach was efficacious.[43] But its effect on traditional gender relations can be assumed to have been non-existent. Domestic tasks were portrayed as exclusively the woman's responsibility, and sexuality did not make an appearance.

'Schematic portrayals of women' in Czech socialist realist literature 'were as transparent as the stories themselves'. In the novels of the 1950s, 'the woman became a satellite of "socialist man", whether it be in the working or social environment. She was everywhere, and everywhere she was devalued.' Meanwhile, real life women, alienated by such cardboard characters, read pre-war romantic novelettes or 'serialized fairy tales in ten volumes'. Marie Čermáková and Hana Navarová state that 'these books were borrowed, not published, they were laughed at, but read ... a drug of the 50s, a secret narcotic for which women reached when they are alone, during those rare moments they stole for themselves.' In the 1960s too, literature was dominated by male authors and male characters. 'The woman's position was given by the status of her man.'[44]

Bożena Umińska depicts the post-1945 period of Polish literature as a 'silence' with regard to female literary figures with profile. The 'production' novels of the 1950s produced no convincing characters of either sex. For women, there were two varieties of schematic existence, as 'wife-comrade supporting her husband at work, or wife in an old bourgeois style, who did not understand the importance and appeal of the historical moment'. She adds that there were also 'women-workers, like a faceless mob', and that this 'blind alley' in literature lasted for over a decade. In the 1960s, she asserts, far from greater psychological depth, there was merely the reverse side of the schematic Stalinist coin, with cynical, idle male characters supplanting the selfless idealists of the 1950s and, instead of women-workers, women from the social margins who wanted only to marry a rich man. Umińska sees this as 'another incarnation of the "unhappy woman, lover of unhappy hero"' trope, with the lover as a modern version of the Romantic hero. In general, literature of this period boasted 'not one portrait of woman-as-individual'. Female figures 'were reduced to serving as part of the background, a decor, or "landscape" for the male hero'.

Matka Królów (*The Mother of Kings*) by Kasimierz Brandys featured a widowed cleaning woman who brings up her three sons alone. Umińska calls her 'a proletarian version of the Polish Mother' and remarks upon the fact that when the novel was subsequently filmed to great acclaim in 1988, no one noticed that 'while she is so heroic, she is also very passive, that she has no influence on her sons' minds or behaviour, that she never tries to understand the world she lives in, and that she has no impulse to rebel, to free herself – she merely – as the idea of the Polish Mother requires – "carries her cross"'.[45]

By the mid-1960s in the literature of the GDR, although the scene was still the factory or construction site, fictional roles for women had been enhanced. A shift in the political line at the beginning of the 1960s emphasized women's education and training. As a result, female heroines were no longer manual workers, but skilled workers or professionals such as architects, teachers or journalists. The central conflict concerned not so much the production process in heavy industry as commitment to socialism and to the GDR itself. In a shift of focus, this conflict centred on and was symbolized by an individual love relationship. Thus in Christa Wolf's *Der geteilte Himmel* (*Divided Heavens*, 1963)[46] the Berlin Wall, built in 1961, divides the lovers. Rita, the central figure from whose perspective the story is related, decides for socialism and the GDR and against joining her disenchanted lover in West Berlin. But for the first time in GDR literature, the high personal emotional cost of this decision is evident. The story is told by Rita retrospectively, from the psychiatric ward where she lies turned to the wall, after an 'accident' at the locomotive works which was probably a suicide attempt.

Socialist realism had required of literature that it provide a 'verisimilitudinous reflection of reality', with an optimistic perspective; 'reality in its revolutionary potential'.[47] Individual concerns were to be effaced in selfless dedication to the common goal of building socialism. In the latter part of the state socialist era, literature became the vehicle for alternative viewpoints for which there was no other forum. Already by the late 1960s, a less 'black and white' and programmatic, a more complex and contradictory, version of reality was being allowed to creep in, with more individually delineated main characters who problematized their relationship with the state and the collective project.[48]

Nachdenken über Christa T. (*The Quest for Christa T.*, 1968) by Christa Wolf[49] was one of the first – and most enduring – of these. It addressed the discrepancy, indeed the painful mismatch, between the prescriptive picture of 'objective reality' socialist realist-style, and the subjective reality of one interesting and introspective individual who has difficulty fitting into the mould, who is definitely *not* the 'positive hero' demanded by cultural policy. 'Just for once,' writes the female narrator, 'I want to discover how it is and to tell it like it is: the unexemplary life, a life that can't be used as a model.'[50]

The narrator engages in an attempt to recreate the reality which was Christa T. Her friend from student days, Christa T. has died young, probably from leukaemia. In depicting the self-doubts, insecurities, and ambivalence of the isolated Christa T., her sensitivity and vulnerability, but also her marvellous, self-contained autonomy, Christa Wolf defied the demand for literary characters whose development leads them towards integration into and affirmation of state socialist norms. Moreover, Christa T.'s untimely death obliterated any possible 'optimistic perspective' concerning 'reality in its revolutionary potential'. Rather, her constitutional inability to conform to the sloganizing and false optimism of the state socialist society of the 1950s stands as a critique of the dominant discourse's version of the collective future.

Even more fundamentally, 'reality', which the narrator attempts to piece together, the reality which was the person Christa T., remains elusive. Moreover, the very attempt to evoke the substance of one individual life ends up by questioning the tenets of socialist realist cultural policy. For 'memory puts a deceptive colour on things'.[51] How then to recreate a past reality in a manner at all objective or 'true to life'? Nor can the other sources the narrator consults, such as the letters, diaries and fragments of writing *by* Christa T., not to speak of other people's feelings *for* her, be held to constitute 'documentary' evidence. Rather, they represent reality as filtered through individual subjective perceptions.

Paradoxically, therefore, and daringly, the narrator speaks of 'what it is that one has to invent, for the truth's sake'. An ex-pupil of Christa T.'s reminds her of a phrase she had quoted from Maxim Gorky about 'the half-real and half-imaginary existence of human beings'. What has become important is the quest for truth itself: 'A word came up, as if newly invented: truth. We kept repeating it, truth, truth, and believed the word was more closely than ever our concern.'[52] This multi-layered novel constructs through the narrative quest a case for individual subjectivity, imagination and creative fantasy. More than that, in validating the experiences of an apparent 'social misfit', Christa Wolf posits the realization of individual potential as fundamental to a truly humane society of the future.

Christa T. had ostensibly withdrawn from the socialist project into an individualist, escapist dream. But perhaps it was she who was closer to self-discovery, to self-realization. 'The most important thing about her,' writes the narrator, 'is this: Christa T. had a vision of herself.' She also had a vision of the world they idealistically believed in and intensely desired. She wrote: 'We must do something to make life worth living for all people.' Crucial to this ideal society, in Christa T.'s view, was 'originality'. She wrote too of the quest 'to become oneself, with all one's strength', the 'long and never-ending journey toward oneself.' The narrator reflects on the 'difficulty of saying "I"' from which Christa T. suffered, and which was in part induced by state socialism's dismissal of the subjective. She concludes: 'Nothing could be more inappropriate than pity or regret. She did live. She was all there. ... If I were to have to invent her, I wouldn't change her. I'd let her live. ... If I'd been allowed to invent us, I'd have given us time to stay.'[53]

Misunderstandings or a failure in communication, and a stereotyping of women into roles exploited but disdained by men, were the hallmarks of gender relations in Czech literature of this period. Čermáková and Navarová point to the dominance of the male perspective in Czech literature of the 'normalization period' from 1969 on, whether in 'official', dissident, or emigré versions. They describe Milan Kundera's heroines as living in 'lost history', 'be it at home, in emigration, or en route between the two. They are lost, especially to themselves.' Umińska has spoken of an 'uncritical attitude towards traditional patterns of women's role', and the misogyny of male writers, in Polish literature of this period. Čermáková and Navarová illustrate a similar attitude in the evocation of notions of 'the so-called masculine and feminine principle'. They cite Ludvík Vaculík's *Czech Dream Book*: 'Men have become feminized, even in everyday life, similarly women have lost their femininity.'

Misogyny was also evident in the reduction of women to, and their humiliation through, sexuality, for example in *The Unbearable Lightness of Being* or the much earlier story 'The Hitchhiking Game', by Milan Kundera. In the latter, two lovers play at being casual acquaintances, she a hitchhiker picked up by him. In a horrible twist, their assumed masks become fixed and the acted relationship between kerb-crawler and whore, one the lovers can no longer choose to shed. In the bedroom scene, the girl's despair at the turn of events leaves the young man unmoved; the stereotype annihilates her individuality. The narrative perspective invites the reader to share the man's disgust and rejection of her:

> The impression that certain outlines delineated her as an individual was only a delusion to which the other person, the one who was looking, was subject – namely himself. It seemed to him that the girl he loved was a creation of his desire, his thoughts, and his faith, and that the real girl now standing in front of him was hopelessly alien, hopelessly *ambiguous*. He hated her.... He longed to humiliate her. Not the hitchhiker, but his own girl. The game merged with life.[54]

Cinderella Speaks for Herself: Female Voices Seek a Hearing

'So far, little change' might serve as a summary of progress in expanding literary role models for women in East Central Europe. Neither individual female characters nor gender relations would appear to have diverged very far from the dualities of mother and/or other female appendage to the male character. Socialist realism, even in its more individualistic later incarnations, does not seem to have offered much of an emancipatory advance on nineteenth-century literature in these respects. What was new, however, at least in the former GDR from the mid-1970s on, was the quality of women's voices in a body of writing by female authors. Two genres predominated: documentary, 'oral history' testaments to women's lives and experiences, and short stories. The former preferred the real to the rhetoric of official discourse; the latter served, in the words of East German author Brigitte Martin, as fiction short enough for overworked women to read in the snatches of time available to them on the way to work, or under the drier at the hairdresser's.[55] Like Natalya Baranskaya's novella *A Week Like Any Other* (1969) in Russia, these works depicted real-life struggles and the contradictions with which women were faced in their daily lives.

It is noteworthy that many women writers, both in the nineteenth century and today, have chosen not to subvert the established discourse of the novel, but to express themselves in another genre. Anna Akhmatova and Marina Tsvetaeva chose poetry or autobiographical writing as their vehicle to project a more emotive, and perhaps more personal voice in the search for what Christa Wolf has called 'subjective authenticity'. The Russian authors Natalya Baranskaya, Julia Voznesenskaya and Tatyana Tolstaya, like many women writers in the GDR, chose short prose forms, often marked by an ironic wit. Barbara Heldt speaks of the 'self-creating form of autobiography', and maintains that 'the woman's world created in these autobiographies ... is permeated with a different view of self and of family and society from that ascribed to women by men. Men are not the central preoccupations of [these] women, whose chief concern is to lead independent lives as people.' Heldt maintains that autobiography and poetry are the two genres preferred by women authors to give expression to the distinctive timbre of female voices.[56]

The search for an authentic female voice articulating itself in new literary forms which integrate the author's voice with the subject matter arose, perhaps, from the feeling that the identity ascribed to women in the dominant literary tradition did not fit their experience of reality. The most radical element in the new female voices of the mid- to late 1970s was their assertion that subjectivity – long frowned upon in socialist realist literature – together with imagination and fantasy created a truth more authentic than any 'realistic' representation of 'objective reality' which socialist realism purported to offer. As Christa Wolf had already put it in *The Quest for Christa T.*: 'We aren't capable of saying things exactly as they are,' and moreover, 'one cannot, unfortunately, cling to the facts, which are too mixed up with chance and don't tell much. ... The years that re-ascend are no longer the years they were.'[57]

The official discourse claim that women's emancipation was a goal already achieved was exploded in Maxie Wander's *Guten Morgen, Du Schöne* (*Good Morning, Beautiful*, 1978).[58] This collection of interviews documented real women's feelings about their lives, their work, their relationships. The impact of these authentic voices was enduring. The book immediately became a bestseller, was later dramatized as a stage performance and a radio play, and has since been reprinted many times in both East and West Germany. Many of the women expressed dissatisfaction in the areas of sexuality and self-determination, but perhaps most shocking of all was their propensity for frank and fearless self-expression. This was attributed by many critics including Christa Wolf to an enhanced self-esteem acquired as a result of their altered life experience under state socialism. In a reflective essay on Wander's collection, Christa Wolf asserted that their legally guaranteed equality and the affirmation gained through their working lives enabled women to begin to ask new and fundamental questions about the nature of social relations. Indeed 'what they have achieved and take for granted', she maintained, 'is no longer enough. Their first concern is no longer what they have, but who they are' in a search for identity which questioned alienating and hierarchical structures.[59]

Ruth, aged twenty-two, a waitress living alone with her five-year-old son, is dissatisfied with her lot. On the one hand she dreams of a personal solution, a lover who will really understand and care for her; on the other, what she fantasizes about is a whole society characterized by such caring relationships:

> I think this is my conflict: I live in an age where lots of things are possible for a woman, but I'm a coward. ... This insane conflict between what's possible and what I'm afraid of is killing me. ... You always have to put on an act for men, otherwise you scare them away. I never met one guy who was interested in finding out what I'm really like, and why I'm that way. They all had one thing in mind with me. ... And still I'm waiting for a miracle. ... Sometimes I ask myself: What society are we building, anyway? A person has dreams, you know. People are born and have a dream. I dream that people will treat each other like people, and there won't be any more selfishness, no more envy, no suspicion. A community of close friends. So. Someone'll be around to say yes to me then.[60]

Christa Wolf asserted that the volume provided 'authentic verification' of the way women's private life and personal emotions had been altered as a result of participation in the public sphere. 'It's too late now to say "That's not what we meant". It's becoming clear: unrestrained subjectivity can become a criterion for what we call (inaccurately, I believe) "objective reality".' Wolf interpreted the seventeen essays as expressing 'the spirit of a concretely existing utopia. ... Collectively ...

they give an intimation of a community where the rules would be sympathy, self-respect, trust and friendship. Marks of sisterliness, which, it seems to me, appears more frequently than brotherliness'.[61] As Sara Lennox put it, 'what the women in this book envision, however indistinctly, is a socialist order which, repudiating production-oriented goals ... sets as its first priority the humanization of human beings, the self-fulfilment of specific, concrete individuals'.[62]

A more fundamental questioning of traditionally ascribed gender roles had come earlier with the experimental stories in the volume *Blitz aus heiterm Himmel* (*A Bolt from the Blue*, 1975).[63] Male and female authors were asked by the editor, Edith Anderson, to imagine waking up one fine morning transformed, not, like Franz Kafka's Gregor Samsa in *The Metamorphosis*, into an insect, but (and perhaps even more fear-inspiring?) into the opposite sex. Anderson had trouble finding enough male authors to collaborate in the project, and their stories are relatively weak, with the exception of one by Günter de Bruyn which shows considerable insight into the career hindrances and subtle dis-criminatory attitudes with which women are confronted at work, and another by Rolf Schneider which depicts the dystopia of a female-dominated world of bees.

Christa Wolf's contribution to this volume, entitled 'Selbstversuch' ('Self-Experiment'),[64] points to the disastrous potential of gender-segregated life experience. A female scientist agrees to undergo a sex change in order to investigate the world of male emotions. She breaks off the experiment when she discovers that male dominance based on cool rationality hides emptiness and, worst of all, an inability to love. This counterposing of the (male-dominated) emotionally crippling world of exalted rational discourse and career hierarchies with the multi-dimensional world of (female-denoted) subjectivity, insight and emotions has become central to much of Christa Wolf's subsequent writing. The ultimate expression of the Enlightenment view of man as a rational being is, in Wolf's view, the nuclear abyss.

In Wolf's novel *Störfall* (*Accident*, 1987),[65] the narrator struggles to find ways of uniting the two halves of the brain, seeking a more 'whole person' approach. Only thus can we face up to the 'blind spot' in our culture and in each of us which has led us to revere the icons of rationalism and scientific progress to the exclusion of other more emotion-based and life-conserving endeavours. A more integrated approach represents the only hope, Wolf suggests, of overcoming humanity's death wish, of averting nuclear and ecological disaster. On the perfect spring day of the Chernobyl disaster, the narrator observes that the invisible clouds of radioactive doom have 'knocked the white cloud of poetry into the archives'. They have rendered withdrawal into any kind of *heile Welt* 'no longer an option', as Dorothy Rosenberg notes. Rosenberg sees Wolf as attacking 'the concept that while cooperation and mutual respect are appropriate standards of behaviour in the private sphere, the public sphere can only be managed through aggressive competition and force; they [Wolf and Irmtraud Morgner, whose story 'The Tightrope' is cited in Chapter 2] reject this social schizophrenia as lethal in the political arena and inhuman in both public and private life.'[66]

A younger generation of women writers publishing mainly short stories in the late 1970s expanded on this new feminist perspective. Their main characters were principally women, their subject matter the yawning gap between state socialist rhetoric on emancipation, and women's everyday lived reality. One of the striking features of these stories is their wry humour and self-irony, elements notoriously lacking in earlier socialist realist literature. A commonly shared butt for their satirical wit is the personification of the double or triple burden, the stereotypical Superwoman whose virtues were trumpeted by the state socialist media and in particular by women's magazines.

Such a Superwoman might be, for example, chief engineer on a building site, profiled on the front cover of the magazine in a hard hat and portrayed in a feature-length article inside the magazine as an eminently feminine wife and exemplary mother, immaculately dressed, in her orderly flat, flanked by handsome husband and charming children. No cinders, no frayed edges, no weariness etched into her face. Indeed the photos and the articles implied that Superwoman achieved the integration of all these roles with her little finger, and to add insult to injury, she was still smiling, with makeup intact!

Indeed, it is indicative of state socialism's failure to address issues of individual autonomy and sexuality that its 'emancipatory' project never questioned traditional feminine stereotypes. This was particularly paradoxical in countries where fashionable clothes could often be obtained only by making them oneself, where physically demanding jobs, and a lack of fitness classes or leisure opportunities meant that maintaining one's health and looks was a tall order. Furthermore, it simply multiplied the pressures on women, adding yet another unattainable ideal, 'fashion plate', to aspire to, on top of the 'heroine-worker' and 'heroine-mother' role models. For the harassed worker-mothers of the real world, struggling to get through their paid work, to pick up children and shopping on the way home, cook, clean, mend, wash, help with homework, and put children to bed before collapsing in a heap in front of the TV news, the notes for tomorrow's work meeting, or homework for their further education course, Superwoman was not so much a joke as an insult, deeply resented.

Charlotte Worgitzky's witty 'Karriere abgesagt' ('Farewell to a Career', 1978)[67] involves a – for state socialism shocking – secret revelation. It is one of several stories published in the GDR around this time which knocked the Superwoman role model. Superwoman status can be achieved, these stories divulged, only by means totally incompatible with 'scientific socialism', namely magic, the supernatural or divine intervention! The female narrator of 'Farewell to a Career' unburdens herself at the outset of her need to confess, so that all other women may know how she came to achieve Superwoman status. As a student, she meets and is wooed by Oswald, whom she later marries. He is two years ahead of her and therefore under less pressure to deliver essays on time, or to be sitting on a hard wooden lecture hall bench by eight in the morning. She, however, suffers acute weariness, ultimately even falling asleep one night while he is kissing the soles of her feet. Predictably, he accuses her of not loving him as much as he loves her.

One night, an angel (probably female, she deduces from the blue stockings the angel wears) appears to her and grants her one wish. She wishes never to need sleep. The angel grants her wish, adding that unfortunately, at the present level of social development, she is obliged to impose one condition. The condition is that the narrator remain faithful to her Oswald. Unconcerned with petty details, the narrator eagerly accepts. The result is that her career goes from strength to strength – she finishes essays on time and becomes secretary of the student group. Once graduated, she quickly rises in the teaching profession to become principal of a school, she has four children, *and* she becomes a city councillor. The narrator reports that her diligence and achievements became the subject of admiration: 'People used me as an example and as a model case of gender equality; I received bonuses and medals'.[68] There are tensions, however. Oswald's career is overshadowed – he feels resentful. He remains a mere teacher, which she concedes must be difficult, for a man, to be married to a school principal. He feels the need to assert his manliness with a series of pretty young things. And why should he do his own ironing or mending when she has the whole night to complete all those domestic chores?

Sitting awaiting her turn to go on stage at a televised ceremony in honour of 'our best people', the narrator speculates idly as to whether the other recipients of this honour might also have made a 'midnight pact'. Suddenly, the penny drops. They are all men. They will have wives, she reflects, who do for them all the chores for which she needs the additional 8–12 hour night shift. Deeply disillusioned, she has a disappointing fling with a young dramaturge. Thenceforth the spell is broken. She is overcome by deep and unshakeable fatigue. Only when she falls asleep during a staff meeting does the school agree to let her give up her post as principal. Alarmed, they send her to the doctor. When she attempts to tell him the truth about the angel, he insists that she seek psychiatric help.

As I have indicated, there was no lack of women's voices articulating a reality very different from that proclaimed in the posters and slogans of state socialism. The double burden was successfully reconciled, they maintained, only at great cost. Only magic could possibly produce Superwomen. For women to affirm their subjective reality and to attain individual autonomy on an equal footing with men, public participation was not enough. A fundamental restructuring of the private sphere was also required. These insights, however, are scarcely heeded today. The current search for an identity uncompromised by past associations in East Central Europe, privileges the majority voice of patriarchal family models. Hence the significance of nineteenth-century literature. Yet again, the more unfamiliar, recent or lesser known, questioning female voices remain unheard.

The Market Rules OK? Cinderella Voiceless in the Echo Chamber

The duality or trinity of roles ascribed to women in the cultural traditions and epitomized in the literary heritage does not offer much elasticity in terms of role models for today. State socialism's failure to address gender issues such as sexuality and autonomy was also reflected in socialist realism's individual self-denial in terms of the paternalistically defined collective goal. Women's reality *was* voiced in documentary literature and in the minority genres of autobiography and poetry. But sceptical short stories never found the resonance of the favoured novel form.

It is no surprise that in more patriarchal and agrarian societies like Poland and Russia, where organized religion with its female icons remained influential throughout the state socialist era, the dominant role models in the current era's search for new modes of behaviour and social relations should now be those of the strong but suffering and chaste mother. This role is extremely expressive of present reality where women are not only made redundant and relegated back to the home, but also carry the brunt of hardships caused by the transition to the market as they try to feed the family. For them, the difficulty of acquiring food for the family, through hyper-inflation or the removal of subsidies, or because one or both partners have become unemployed, differs only in kind from the past when the problem was dictated by scarcity and faulty distribution networks rather than price.

A striking example of duality in the images of women in the current transition period can be seen in the split between the imagery of maternity and that of pornography. In a strong reaction to the muzzling of the media under state socialism, one of the first visible effects of a free press in East Central Europe was a boom in pornography. Protests from women whom this offended, for example from the UFV in the former GDR, were met with the argument by respected liberal journalists and editors that soft porn symbolized not only the right to freedom of expression, but also liberation from the prudish and puritanical nature of state socialism. 'The erotic self-expressiveness of the younger generation' is championed by many as the ultimate expression of media freedom. Even beauty contests are eulogized for their 'mortal wound' to the Soviet model of womanhood, exposing instead an image of 'eroticism, physical beauty, the spirit of entrepreneurship, common sense and elegance'.[69]

Pornography's boom is also alleged to be a healthy example of the operation of market forces, namely of consumer-led demand. In so far as the Catholic Church in Poland opposes pornography, it does so exclusively in moral terms, not in terms of the exploitation of women involved. Certainly state socialism's neglect of sexuality and gender relations has come home to roost in dual form – as pornography, that is utilizing women's bodies as an object for consumption on the one hand, and on the other, in the sanctity of marriage and motherhood as the reincarnation of a patriarchal model of gender relations.

If pornography is questioned exclusively in terms of morality, this, like the problem of reproductive rights, raises questions about women's rights as citizens. Women may have gained political freedom with the introduction of formal democratic rights, but this freedom may remain abstract if at the same time their 'freedom' to have their sexuality exploited in the name of market forces remains unchallenged. The boom in pornography appears to lend credence to the suggestion that women as citizens are muzzled, in that their objections to exploitation by pornography go unheard.

If women's ability to be heard in the media was limited in the past by the ideology of state socialism, it appears that their voices are now muffled by the constraints of a new profit-led market ideology which constructs them as ideal consumers, or as objects of consumption. Women's magazines are a form of mass media which are crucially concerned with the shaping and marketing of female identity. A combination of market forces and new/old stereotypes can be seen to have influenced the style and content of women's magazines in the former state socialist countries. Examples from Poland and the former GDR, illuminate how market forces both reflect and amplify the new traditionalism about women's roles and opportunities. In East Germany, the market has swallowed up the earlier mass-circulation women's magazine. In Poland, paradox allows the image of career woman to coexist with the glamour and gossip aspects of new glossy mags.

New Recipes Cause Indigestion and Sudden Death

In East Germany, the pressures of market forces were brutally direct. After the Berliner Verlag, in which *Für Dich* (*For You*) was located, was taken over in 1990 by Robert Maxwell and the Hamburg firm of Gruner & Jahr, a new deputy editor was installed, bringing with her a new 'recipe' for the magazine. *Für Dich* had earlier been, if not the official journal of the Women's Federation, then close to being its mouthpiece. However, in the short spell between autumn 1989 and German unification in autumn 1990 it had maintained its market following of 500,000. Indeed it could have increased its circulation greatly had it not been restricted by paper allocation problems.

The reason for its new-found popularity was that it had allied itself with the emerging women's movement in the then GDR. Journalists from the magazine had been among the first to make demands that women's interests should be furthered in any 'alternative', independent GDR, with the slogan: 'No state without us.' They were also instrumental in setting up, together with actresses and sociologists, the first meeting, in a Berlin theatre, of the UFV.

In the magazine they set up an emergency helpline and ran features on violence against women, the problems of foreigners in the GDR, and advice for the newly unemployed. Their fashion pages were geared to creating wardrobes for actual, individual, but non-celebrity working women. In contrast, under the new régime, the magazine featured exotic holiday destinations. It had double page spreads on cookery and diets, house plants and home care, beauty tips and fashion, and an agony aunt in place of features on women's health and sexual and marital problems.

Journalists at *Für Dich* were informed that the magazine now had to be profitable, which it could only achieve with a market share of 600,000. This was a tall order: the new management had to cope with old ingredients – poor quality GDR-produced paper, GDR technology producing indifferent colour photo reproduction, and journalists committed to defending women's economic, political and social rights. The result was doomed to failure in competition with its much glossier West German rivals. The only possible way for *Für Dich* to survive in the marketplace would have been precisely in offering their 'different', GDR-oriented product. The magazine was finally closed down in September 1991 due to 'unprofitability', or 'uncompetitiveness'.

A glance at the change in cover headlines shortly 'before' unification but 'after' the takeover epitomizes the change – from 'Emancipated Woman or Mother?' already an equivocation, illustrating the conflicts inherent in the dual role, and applying the pejorative West German term '*Emanze*' to liberated women, to a simplistic stereotype of the feminine: 'A Woman as Beautiful as Springtime', with tropical holiday paradise illustrated above – fantasy and idealization meshed. The 'before'-takeover cover, for no. 33 1990, also features an article attacking porn, headlined 'Who Likes Porn? Not Us!'. The 'after' cover, from no. 12 1991, previews from the magazine's content new hairstyles, the marine look in fashion, a column entitled 'fate' featuring someone who was mugged and robbed with the title: 'I went through hell', an advice column, the Philippines as 'exotic' holiday destination, and 'Sister Monika's Patient Who Had AIDS'. In one of the two pages allotted the journalists to carry on with 'their' previous format, is an article on work and careers, profiled as: 'Professionally competent, yet still turned down for the job. What rights do women have?'

'Women and Life' Transformed: 'Your Style' Corners the Market

Krystyna Kaszuba used to be deputy editor of *Kobieta i Życie* (*Women and Life*), one of the two women's magazines with the highest circulation in socialist Poland. The magazine was connected with the publishing house of the Communist Party, but was able to resist becoming the official mouthpiece of the Polish Women's Union. The Women's Union ran its own magazine entitled *Zwierciadło* (*Looking Glass*), with a circulation of 800,000 compared with *Kobieta i Życie*'s 150,000. By early

1990, these positions had been reversed, with *Kobieta i Życie*, now a cooperative venture, publishing 450,000 copies compared with *Zwierciadło*'s 40,000. Despite its relative independence from state socialism, however, *Kobieta i Życie* had in fact tended in the past to be relatively conformist in content.

In the new media freedom of 1990, *Kobieta i Życie* introduced advertising and ran a readers' forum to gauge what readers would like the magazine to include. In late 1992, its editor Anna Brozowska said that 'Polish women have had a gutful of politics. They don't want to be preached at any longer; what they want is to be entertained'.[70] Many of its articles were, as a result, rather more traditional than one might have expected in a post-state socialist country. Regular features included cooking and gardening hints, fashion, and a medical advice column. One new feature, very popular with readers, was the 'gossip column'.

However, more controversial articles in 1990 had included one on the discriminatory treatment of teenage expectant mothers who were often forced to leave school and attend adult education classes. Another, written by a man, reported teacher reactions to the question of whether they taught sex education. In the context where a booklet on contraception developed by the Family Planning Association had just been pulped as a result of Church-led criticism, this was a controversial subject. One school librarian responded that books on pregnancy were 'not needed', citing the fact that the medical bookshelves in the library were dust-covered. Krystyna Kaszuba pointed out that at that time *Kobieta i Życie* was the only women's magazine that fought for women in politics and management. It was also the only women's magazine to report continuously on the abortion debate.

Once a month the magazine published articles on female-dominated professions such as teachers, or women in light industry. It ran a campaign to support ten female candidates in the 1989 Polish elections, of whom only one, the journal's then editor Anna Szymańska, was elected.[71] Earlier emphasis on getting women into management positions had by 1990 changed to a focus on unemployment.

However, in the face of uncertainty over continued funding and the opprobrium associated with the Communist publishing house, Krystyna Kaszuba sought an alternative. She found a male publisher who acted as financial backer to help her establish a new magazine, closely modelled on Western European publications such as *Cosmopolitan* and *Elle*. By June 1991, *Twój Styl* (*Your Style*) had grown in a year from a circulation of 100,000 to 300,000. A sister magazine for younger women, *To Ty* (*That's You*), was launched in May 1991.

Kaszuba's concept was to create a Poland-specific magazine, addressing the high level of women's education in Poland but also the strong Polish family traditions, interpreted in line with the demands of the market and what Kaszuba read as the mood of the transition period. In fact, in a curious way, the product appeared to follow an older-style role model, closer to, say, *Woman's Own* than the career-woman oriented *Cosmo*. Popular figures spoke of their first love. There were fashion and beauty tips as well as sewing and knitting, cookery and health features. 'Alice in Banking Land' gave financial advice about coping with the new market situation. There were stories of celebrity women such as Wanda Rutkiewicz, the internationally famous Polish climber, Ewa Fibak, the wife of a tennis star, who herself runs an art gallery, or General Jaruzelski's daughter Monika. Kaszuba was subsequently proud to recruit Monika Jaruzelska to write for *To Ty*, the magazine for younger women. Jaruzelska made her début with a feature based on interviews with psychologists, pop singers and actors, who spoke about their attitude to love.

Such celebrity stories not only represent a departure from describing the lives of more average professional or working women. Portraying women who are famous, in most cases not in their own right, but in patriarchal manner reflecting the glory of their husband's or father's position, devalues women as autonomous individuals. The articles on the rich, glamorous and famous are part of a conscious reaction against what Kaszuba saw as state socialism's refusal to profile 'personalities'. She made no response to the concern that such unattainable role models are potentially damaging, especially in the present economic crisis, insisting instead that this kind of 'politics of envy' provided just the escape from the drudgery of their everyday lives which Polish women wanted. What they emphatically did not want, what they have had a surfeit of, she maintained, were stories of the difficulties and contradictions faced by real women in their everyday lives.

While socialist didacticism is rejected, the implicit ideology of *Twój Styl* is not acknowledged. Negativity or even problems are out – success stories are in. Kaszuba claims that an article about women with violent husbands produced a flood of letters complaining about these 'stupid women' and expressing a preference for information on 'coping women'. Hence the magazine does not deal with current issues. As pro-choice activist Hanna Jankowska remarked: 'The most popular glossy women's magazines prefer to avoid the embarrassing abortion question.'[72]

The lack of current affairs coverage does not mean, however, that

Twój Styl focuses on women as homemakers to the exclusion of career women. Kaszuba emphasized that her aim was to reflect positive attitudes in the face of unemployment and the upheavals of economic transformation. She told me in June 1991 that retraining for women was woefully inadequate, a 'drop in the ocean', and often very expensive. Nevertheless, she did want to use *To Ty* to encourage younger women to have the courage to change profession, to learn new skills. Further she noted that women were having difficulty in getting loans to establish new businesses, and that high interest rates and repayment conditions were unfavourable. However, *Twój Styl* regularly featured 'enterprising women' who have changed their lives by going into business. It ran a series that focused on women such as a nurse, who became an entrepreneur producing the equipment for handicapped children designed by her doctor husband; or the four women interpreters who had set up a consultancy, producing an EFL textbook and setting up an Italian language school.

Kaszuba further maintained that *Twój Styl*'s readers have rejected the strong Polish mother image. Hence, although there was a series on famous mother/daughter pairs, and interviews with psychologists about the mother/daughter relationship, there were no articles about children.[73] The setbacks of real life crept in only in the monthly series on 'How I overcame personal adversity/health problems/trauma'. It is clear, however, that such stories of personal fate in *Twój Styl* reflect the duality to be found in literature between strong and suffering female role models.

This dual imagery was forcefully replicated and expanded to include the strong or enterprising woman imaged as whore in an article in the business journal *Gazeta Bankowa* (11 June 1991). It featured six women who formed a joint venture to try to save Coopexport Cepelia, a collapsing state export firm dealing in Polish folk art. The article was headed by the first half of a Polish proverb: 'If the devil can't do anything, send in the women.' Next to the article was a cartoon vamp – exaggerated breasts, legs, curls, cigarette holder – with the caption 'Businesswoman' in English.

The fear of women's creative power and sexuality which is evident in much mythology and in the Baba Yaga witch of Russian fairy tales also has its contemporary parallel in popular culture. Pop songs current in Bulgaria after 1989 not only denigrated women in a patriarchal sense, but went further, blaming women for the disillusionment with the state socialist ideal. Flying in the face of linguistic logic, according to which 'communism' is masculine and 'democracy' feminine in German and many Slavic languages, woman was equated with communism, the betrayer of men's democratic ideals.

A hit song popularized by the Bulgarian UDF (Union of Democratic Forces) was entitled 'The Farewell Dance'. The video featured a beautiful woman dressed in red, with red tiara and red mask – Communism personified – who in certain moments appeared diabolical, or as a vampire. She was dancing with state security men, with Communist functionaries, and with naïve but disillusioned young men who sang the text: 'Farewell, my darling, when you were young and beautiful, I believed in you – but now you are a hundred years old, and I realize that you have deceived me all along.' This song was used by the UDF as an electoral vote-catcher in October 1991, symbolizing, as Dimitrina Petrova writes, that: 'The Big Lie, the Evil, the Past (female) is pushed aside by the Truth, the Good, the Future (male).'[74]

This chapter has examined old and new images of women in East Central Europe. At present, it seems that the political iconography of state socialism, that is of the woman worker who is also a mother, has temporarily been rejected in favour of a notion that 'real' women are exclusively mothers. Making over the utopian state socialist female ideal in essentialist terms which stress women's 'true' nature and prescribe a newly feminine image, is exemplified in an article by the Bulgarian journalist Silva Rakneva. In April 1991 she wrote in *Zhenata Dnes* (*Woman Today*):

> It has taken us too long to realize that we have irretrievably confused our ideas of equal rights. ... We looked around and saw that we had turned nature upside down. ... Despite all our efforts, we shall never reach men's self-confidence. The likeness we seek, the endeavour to prove by both appearance and brains our real qualities and independence *are doomed to failure*. ...
>
> And if our shoulders are bent with exhaustion, if our eyes never smile, if our lips are tightly set – it is because we lack recognition. It is because behind our backs we are reproached – for the emancipation that we ourselves fabricated. And which we cherished. To the point of being today less feminine, less admired, less appreciated. Just the opposite of what we once wanted.
>
> It will take some time until we suppress protest in ourselves. We shall scatter, each of us taking her own path. Different. Filled with children's laughter. Inspired by men's love. Enjoying many professional victories. To each according to what suits her. The world cannot do without us. But the world has certainly had enough of seeing us in jeans and shirts, dragging kids along to the kindergarten, running to catch trams and

trolleys, loaded down with shopping bags, rushing into the workplace at the last minute, choked with embarrassment: what to do first?

We don't like ourselves this way. *At last*, we can admit it.[75]

The new, reductionist ideological construction of women's feminine-maternal role has been crafted by social, political, religious and market forces which do not necessarily reflect the current aspirations of women themselves. Women may appear to be colluding in the short term with their relegation to primary responsibility for hearth and home. And the case of *Für Dich* could be taken to indicate that independent women's voices have a difficult time being heard in the clamour of the marketplace. Notwithstanding its attempt to conform to market pressures, however, *Twój Styl* has not abandoned the career woman entirely in favour of the mother and homemaker. And it is questionable whether in the long run women themselves will wear the exclusively maternal self-image.

Notes

1. *Fenist the Falcon*, a Russian fairy tale, retold in English by Irina Zheleznova, Goznak, Moscow, 1977.

2. Zdzisław Najder, a Polish literary scholar of Joseph Conrad, said of the East European state socialist context: 'All political discussions happened in novels and poems. There were no politics, but there were writers.' Borges wrote of literature under totalitarian-style régimes in Central America: 'Censorship is the mother of metaphor.' Both voices are cited by A. Alvarez in his introduction to *The Faber Book of Modern European Poetry* (Faber, London, 1992), which was extracted in: the *Guardian*, 21.11.92.

3. In the Czech case, Jaroslav Hašek's *The Good Soldier Schweik* is still one of the most widely read texts. In his essay 'The Tragedy of Central Europe', Czech novelist Milan Kundera (in: *The New York Review of Books*, 26 April 1984) interprets Schweik as a symbol of Czech attempts to preserve national identity under the Austro-Hungarian Empire with his strategy of 'pretending to be an idiot ... [as] the last possible method for preserving one's freedom'. The subsequent first republic between 1918 and 1938 is revered as *the* success story of Czech nationhood.

4. Celina Wieniewska, ed., Introduction to *Polish Writing Today*, Penguin, 1967, p. 9; George Theiner, ed., Introduction to *New Writing in Czechoslovakia*, Penguin, 1969, pp. 21–2. The latter collection coincidentally features not a single woman writer.

5. Jeanne W. Němcová, Introduction to *Czech and Slovak Stories*, Oxford University Press, Oxford, 1967, p. vii.

6. Marie Čermáková and Hana Navarová, 'The Woman in Czech Literature', ms. 1991; Němcová, *Czech and Slovak Stories*, 1967, p. ix.

7. Wieniewska, *Polish Writing Today*, 1967, p. 9.

8. Ibid., p. 9.

9. Steven Lukes, *On Individualism*, Blackwell, Oxford, 1973, p. 125.

10. Tatyana Tolstaya, decrying Solzhenitsyn's reactionary nationalism, 'Tsar of All the Answers', in: the *Guardian*, 25.6.92.

11. Eric Hobsbawm cites the 'personification of "the nation" in symbol or image, ... as with Marianne or Germania' as part of a process of 'inventing traditions' which accompanies national movements, and which 'we should expect ... to occur more

frequently when a rapid transformation of society weakens or destroys the social patterns for which "old" traditions had been designed'. (Hobsbawm, introduction to Eric Hobsbawm and Terence Ranger, eds, *The Invention of Tradition*, Cambridge University Press, Cambridge, 1983, pp. 4, 7).

12. Wendy Bracewell, 'Problems of Gender and Nationalism', ms., 1992.

13. Barbara Heldt, 'Gynoglasnost: Writing the Feminine', in: Mary Buckley, ed., *Perestroika and Soviet Women*, Cambridge University Press, Cambridge, 1992, pp. 61, 73. Writing about new women's groups in the Ukraine, Salomea Pavlychko gives another example of mother-worship in the equation of woman and nation. She points to the centrality of the term *Berehynia*, signifying an ancient cult whose revival the Ukrainian Peasant-Democratic Party posits as the main goal of independent Ukraine. *Berehynia* combines 'the main goddess of home cosiness, the cult of the mother (keeper of the family and the nation) and the cult of the child'. *Berehynia* is also addressed in the statute of the Ukrainian Women's Union as 'the main symbol of this rural culture, the home hearth itself, the peasant house with all its attributes', in which 'a woman singing folk songs, sewing a folk blouse, teaching the same to her daughter and granddaughter is the centre of this idyllic world of the lost and adored past'. Pavlychko points to the paradox whereby such a notion of the salvation of rural culture, equated with national culture, in fact implies restoration of 'peasant patriarchal structures'. (Salomea Pavlychko, 'Between Feminism and Nationalism: New Women's Groups in the Ukraine', in: Buckley, ed., *Perestroika and Soviet Women*, 1992, pp. 87–91).

14. Francine Du Plessix Gray, *Soviet Women Walking the Tightrope*, Virago, London, 1991, p. 117.

15. Shared religion is one constitutive element of national community. Another 'standard criterion today of what constitutes a nation with a claim to self-determination, meaning to set up an independent territorial nation-state, is ethnic-linguistic', writes Eric Hobsbawm, 'since language is taken, wherever possible, to express and symbolize ethnicity'. Benedict Anderson too has stressed the importance of language and a shared cultural heritage in constituting the 'imagined communities' underlying nationalism. Many of the newly independent states of Eastern and Central Europe have made language the passport to citizenship. The importance of language in defining national identity also provides some explanation for the focus on nineteenth-century national literature as part of the search for untainted values following the demise of state socialism with its emphasis on class conflict rather than on national difference. (Sources: Eric Hobsbawm, 'Whose Fault-Line is it Anyway?', in *New Statesman and Society*, 24 April 1992; Benedict Anderson, *Imagined Communities*, Verso, London, 1983, reprinted 1991).

16. Andrzej Szczypiorski, *The Beautiful Mrs. Seidenmann*, trans. Klara Glowazewska, Macdonald, London, 1991, pp. 129–39, 159.

17. Marina Warner, *Monuments and Maidens: The Allegory of the Female Form*, Weidenfeld and Nicolson, London, 1985, plate 1.

18. Elizabeth Waters, 'The Female Form in Soviet Political Iconography', in: Barbara Evans Clements, Barbara Alpern Engel, Christine D. Worobec, eds, *Russia's Women: Accommodation, Resistance, Transformation*, University of California Press, Berkeley, 1991, p. 228.

19. Bracewell, 'Problems of Gender and Nationalism', 1992.

20. Joanna Hubbs, *Mother Russia: The Feminine Myth in Russian Culture*, Indiana University Press, Bloomington, 1988, pp. xv, 237.

21. Mother Russia of peasant culture is the fount of creativity, but remains virginal like the Holy Mother of Orthodox religion. Hubbs points out that she is equated with 'Mother Earth' who 'seems to need no mate. She is self-moistened, self-inseminated'. Hubbs, ibid., 1988, p. xiv.

22. Tatyana Mamonova, *Russian Women's Studies: Essays on Sexism in Soviet Culture*, Pergamon Press, Oxford, 1989, p. 3. Mamonova explains that the *bogatyrs* were heroic figures in Russian folk tales. They were fortune seekers, literally larger than life, and

possessed of Herculean strength, famed for their warlike exploits. According to Mamonova, pre-Christian epics 'were equally peopled with folk heroines – the *palenitsas* – mighty women *bogatyrkas*' [i.e. female *bogatyrs*].

23. Joanna Hubbs was cited by Du Plessix Gray, *Soviet Women Walking the Tightrope*, 1991, p. 116.

24. Mamonova, *Russian Women's Studies*, 1989, p. 5.

25. *Vassilisa the Beautiful, Fenist the Falcon, Marya Morevna*, retold in English by Irina Zheleznova, Goznak, Moscow, 1976 and 1977.

26. Barbara Heldt, *Terrible Perfection: Women and Russian Literature*, Indiana University Press, Bloomington, 1987, pp. 2, 9.

27. Du Plessix Gray, *Soviet Women Walking the Tightrope*, 1991, p. 118.

28. Heldt, *Terrible Perfection*, 1987, pp. 12–15. Nevertheless, this is not to say that there are no strong female characters drawn, in particular, by Tolstoy, who was indebted for them to his wife's diaries, and Chekhov.

29. In an allusion to the same duality, as it affects contemporary reality, historian and self-professed feminist Elvira Novikova accuses the Soviet media of promoting marriage by counterposing 'two basic images of women in our folklore – the Cinderella sweetie pie who sacrifices her life to her family, and Baba Yaga, the wise independent witch who lives alone in the forest and is doomed to solitude'. Elvira Novikova is quoted by du Plessix Gray, *Soviet Women Walking the Tightrope*, 1991, pp. 88–9.

Abram Tertz, 'What is Socialist Realism?', is cited by Heldt, *Terrible Perfection*, 1987, pp. 15–16. Tertz goes on to describe the way woman is a cipher: 'The woman in this literature was the touchstone for the man. Through his relations with her he exposed his weakness . . . compromized by her strength and beauty. . . . For indeed . . . woman is a sort of vague, pure and lovely thing. There's no need for her to be more concrete and more defined, it is enough for her (does one ask much of women?) to be pure and lovely to save man.'

30. Du Plessix Gray, *Soviet Women Walking the Tightrope*, p. 120.

31. *Vassilisa the Beautiful*, 1976.

32. Heldt, *Terrible Perfection*, 1987, pp. 61–2.

33. Larissa Lissjutkina, 'Lieber Hure als Feministin' ('Rather a Prostitute Than a Feminist'), in: *Deutsches Allgemeines Sonntagsblatt*, 8 May 1992 [my translation, BE].

34. *Damned Whores and God's Police: The Colonization of Women in Australia* is the title of a book by Anne Summers, Penguin, Harmondsworth, 1975.

35. Bożena Umińska, 'The Portrayal of Women in Polish Literature', ms., Warsaw, 1991. The following section on Polish literature is indebted to, and the citations are from, this work.

36. Umińska, ibid. The novel emerged as a literary genre late in Poland, after the 1850s. This explains the dominant role of Romantic poetry, which functioned as the only available forum for the enunciation of political consciousness. Hence the poet was 'supposed to assume the role of prophet' and poetry expressed 'national and patriotic feelings' about Poland 'as it was or as it should be, not as it is'. In this latter sense there is a certain continuity to be observed in the current re-casting of myth.

37. Cyprian Kamil Norwid (1821–83), a later Polish Romantic poet, analyses Romantic patriotism in remarkably modern, almost psychoanalytic terms: 'Oft have I been struck by a curious thing, that the younger a nation is, the more immoderately and almost, dare I say, indecently, it falls in love with its Mother, the Patria!' (Sources: Umińska, ibid.; Bolesław Klimaszewski, ed., *An Outline History of Polish Culture*, Interpress, Warsaw, 1984, p. 173).

38. The following discussion is based on 'The Woman in Czech Literature' by Marie Čermáková and Hana Navarová, ms., Prague, 1992. I am indebted to the authors.

39. Waters, 'The Female Form in Soviet Political Iconography', 1991, p. 238.

40. Ibid., p. 240.

41. Eduard Claudius, *Menschen an unserer Seite* (*People By Our Side*), Verlag Volk und Welt, Berlin, 1951, pp. 10, 52–3, 228–9, 274–5 [my translations, BE].

42. Elfriede Brüning's *Regine Haberkorn* (1955) exhibits a similar motif in that the husband only reluctantly assents to Regine's decision to accept work at the factory where he works, on condition that the job is a temporary one and will not interfere with her housework. For a more detailed analysis of the latter novel and the portrayal of women in East German literature, see Dorothy Rosenberg, 'The Emancipation of Women in Fact and Fiction: Changing Roles in GDR Society and Literature', in: Sharon L. Wolchik and Alfred G. Meyer, eds, *Women, State and Party in Eastern Europe*, Duke University Press, Durham, 1985, pp. 344–61.

43. Rosenberg, ibid., points out that *Regine Haberkorn* went through 16 printings between 1955 and 1974, with a total of 123,000 copies.

44. Čermáková and Navarová, 'The Woman in Czech Literature', 1992. The dominance of male authors is reflected in a Penguin collection of *New Writing in Czechoslovakia* (1969) which features not a single female author.

45. Umińska, 'The Portrayal of Women in Polish Literature', 1991.

46. Christa Wolf, *Der geteilte Himmel*, Mitteldeutscher Verlag, Halle, 1963. An English version entitled *Divided Heavens* was published in East Berlin by Seven Seas Publishers, 1964.

47. The official definition of socialist realism was formulated by Andrej Zhdanov at the First Congress of Soviet Writers in Moscow in 1934. It reads: 'Socialist realism demands of the artist a depiction of reality which is historically concrete, corresponds to the truth, and gives a revolutionary perspective.' Definition quoted from Barbara Einhorn, *Der Roman in der DDR 1949–1969: Die Gestaltung des Verhältnisses von Individuum und Gesellschaft – Eine Analyse der Erzählstruktur* (*The Novel in the GDR 1949–1969: The Portrayal of the Relationship between Individual and Society – An Analysis of Narrative Structure*), Scriptor Verlag, Kronberg, T., 1978, pp. vi, x. For a more recent definition of the terms 'Socialist Realism', 'positive hero' and others characterizing the cultural policy of state socialism, see Eric W. Herd and August Obermayer, eds., *A Glossary of German Literary Terms*, 2nd edn, University of Otago, New Zealand, 1992.

48. On this transition, covering the period 1949–69, see Barbara Einhorn, 'The Structural Development of the Novel in the GDR: 1949–69', in: *GDR Monitor*, no. 1, summer 1979, pp. 13–29.

49 Christa Wolf, *Nachdenken über Christa T.* (1968), translated by Christopher Middleton, as: *The Quest for Christa T.*, Virago, London, 1982.

50. Ibid., p. 45.

51. Ibid., p. 3.

52. Ibid., pp. 23, 111, 133.

53. Ibid., pp. 51, 117, 144, 149, 174–75.

54. Milan Kundera, 'The Hitchhiking Game' in: *Laughable Loves* (1969), John Murray, London, 1978, pp. 21–22; see also Kundera, *The Unbearable Lightness of Being*, transl. Michael Henry Heim, Faber, London, 1984/1985.

55. Brigitte Martin, Interview with Barbara Einhorn, Berlin, October 1978.

56. Christa Wolf, 'Subjective Authenticity: A Conversation with Hans Kaufmann', in: Christa Wolf, *The Fourth Dimension: Interviews with Christa Wolf*, Verso, London, 1988, pp. 17–39; Natalya Baranskaya, *A Week Like Any Other* (1969), cited in Chapter 2 above; Julia Voznesenskaya, *The Women's Decameron* (1985), transl. W. B. Linton, Quartet Books, London, 1986; Tatyana Tolstaya, *On the Golden Porch* (1987), transl. Antonina W. Bouis, Penguin, Harmondsworth, 1989.

On the use of different genres to express the distinctive timbre of women's voices, see Heldt, *Terrible Perfection*, 1987. This phenomenon can also be observed in Croatian writing by women. In *Marina, or About Biography*, the poet Irena Vrkljan has written a piece which interrogates the biographical form by interpolating the author's voice and autobiographical material in a way reminiscent of Christa Wolf's *In Search of Christa T.*

Dubravka Ugrešić too plays ironic games with the conventions of writing, in which, 'as author, she is an integral part of her writing'. Common to many women writers appears to be a blurring of the distinction between genres, between literary subject and the authorial voice. This has led Celia Hawkesworth to speak of 'an alternative genre, a new form capable of expressing new perceptions and characterized by a search for authenticity', features which distinguish, as Hawkesworth sees it, feminist writing. Sources: Celia Hawkesworth, 'Dubravka Ugrešić: The Insider's Story', in: *The Slavonic and East European Review*, vol. 68, no. 3, July 1990, pp. 436–46, here p. 438; Hawkesworth, 'Irena Vrkljan: *Marina, or About Biography*', in: ibid., vol. 69, no. 2, April 1991, pp. 221–31, here p. 230; Ugrešić's novel *Fording the Stream of Consciousness* was published in English in 1991 (Virago, London). For an interview with her and Croatian journalist/writer Slavenka Drakulić, see the *Guardian*, 23.1.92.

57. Wolf, *The Quest for Christa T.*, 1982, pp. 23, 33; for a discussion of the relationship of fantasy and creativity in *The Quest for Christa T.* to reality as prescribed by Socialist Realism, and also of Wolf's earlier *Divided Heavens*, cf. Einhorn, 'The Structural Development of the Novel in the GDR: 1949–69', 1979, pp. 21–26.

58. Maxie Wander, *Guten Morgen, Du Schöne* (*Good Morning, Beautiful*), Verlag Der Morgen, Berlin, 1978.

59. Christa Wolf, 'Berührung' ('In Touch'), was first published in: *neue deutsche literatur*, no. 2, 1978, pp. 53–62, and later appeared as the foreword to the West German edition of Maxie Wander's book, *Guten Morgen, Du Schöne: Frauen in der DDR* (*Good Morning, Beautiful: Women in the GDR*), Luchterhand, Darmstadt and Neuwied, 1978, pp. 9–20. An English translation by Jeanette Clausen appeared in: Edith H. Altbach et al., eds, *German Feminism: Readings in Politics and Literature*, State University of New York Press, Albany, 1984, pp. 161–70; here p. 166.

60. Wander, *Guten Morgen, Du Schöne*, 1978, pp. 51–63. This interview with Ruth B., a 22-year-old waitress, unmarried with one child, is entitled 'Waiting for a Miracle'. These excerpts were taken from the translation by Naomi Stephan, in: Altbach et al., eds, *German Feminism*, 1984, pp. 170–78.

61. Wolf, 'In Touch', transl. Clausen, 1984, pp. 161, 163.

62. Sara Lennox, 'Maxie Wander's *Guten Morgen, Du Schöne*: Women in the GDR', conference paper, 1979.

63. Edith Anderson, ed., *Blitz aus heiterm Himmel* (*A Bolt from the Blue*), VEB Hinstorff Verlag, Rostock, 1975. For a discussion of this volume, see Einhorn, 'Socialist Emancipation: The Women's Movement in the GDR', in: Sonia Kruks, Rayna Rapp, Marilyn Young, eds, *Promissory Notes: Women in the Transition to Socialism*, Monthly Review Press, New York, 1989, pp. 293–94.

64. Christa Wolf, 'Self-Experiment: Appendix to a Report' ('Selbstversuch'), translated by Jeanette Clausen, in: *New German Critique*, no. 13, winter 1978, pp. 109–31.

65. Christa Wolf, *Störfall*, Aufbau-Verlag, Berlin and Weimar, 1987. English translation by Heike Schwarzbauer and Rick Takvorian, published as *Accident: A Day's News*, Virago Press, London, 1989.

66. Wolf, *Accident*, 1989, p. 55. Dorothy Rosenberg, 'Redefining the Public and the Private: Women Writers in the GDR', in: Mona Knapp and Gerd Labroisse, eds, *Frauen-Fragen in der deutschsprachigen Literatur seit 1945* (*Women's Issues in German-Language Literature Since 1945*), Atlanta, Amsterdam, 1989, pp. 131–59.

67. Charlotte Worgitzky, 'Karriere abgesagt' ('Farewell to a Career'), in: Worgitzky, *Vieräugig oder blind* (*With Two Pairs of Eyes or Blind*), Buchverlag Der Morgen, Berlin, 1978, pp. 77–92.

68. Ibid., p. 80 [my translation, BE].

69. Viktor Erofeev, 'Sex and Perestroika', in: *Liber*, no. 1, 1989, p. 17; reprinted in: *Constructiv*, no. 12, December 1991, pp. 19–21; and commented upon by Heldt, 'Gynoglasnost', 1992, p. 165.

70. Information on *Kobieta i Życie* is taken in part from various numbers of the

magazine itself, and from an interview with the then deputy editor Krystyna Kaszuba in March 1990. Subsequent editor Anna Brozowska made her remarks at an international conference of women journalists in Germany in late 1992. They were cited in the German feminist magazine *Emma*, no. 12, December 1992, p. 26 [translation mine, BE].

71. Anna Szymańska, formerly editor of *Kobieta i Życie*, had been elected to the Polish Sejm for the PUWP, the Polish Communist Party, in 1989, but she did not stand again in the second democratic elections. Instead, she became editor of a new magazine, also run as a cooperative, entitled *Kobieta i Styl*, whose title suggested that it wished to compete not only with the older *Kobieta i Życie* but also with the newer *Twój Styl*.

Kobieta i Styl's September 1992 issue had Princess Stephanie of Monaco on the front cover and featured a Mills and Boon-type romance, and an article about Katherine Hepburn and Spencer Tracy. Regular series included fashion, makeup, interior design, health, diet, exercise, cooking, and knitting patterns. Two double-page spreads gave practical advice on pre-menstrual syndrome and cervical smears, there were articles on homosexuality, children, and a psychological advice column. Five pages were devoted to a gossip column featuring famous film stars and other personalities and another three pages on horoscopes complemented a two-page article on astrology.

72. Hanna Jankowska, 'The Reproductive Rights Campaign in Poland', Paper presented to the Conference on 'Mary Wollstonecraft and 200 Years of Feminism', Sussex University, 5–6 December 1992.

73. By contrast, the older magazine *Przyjaciółka* (*Female Friend*) still focused very heavily on motherhood and the family. With an edition of 1,300,000 in 1992, *Przyjaciółka* had survived the transition to the market with by far the largest circulation, despite being a slim weekly magazine with paper quality and colour reproduction reminiscent of state socialist days. Its readership was largely composed of rural women. Its 3 December 1992 edition featured family problems, children in hospital, holidays for mums, toys for kids, the TV programme for the week, cooking, sewing, knitting, horoscope and Lonely Hearts columns, but also unemployment rights, a feature on UNICEF, and a piece on sexology.

74. For this analysis see Dimitrina Petrova, 'The Farewell Dance: Women in the Bulgarian Transition', Paper presented to the Conference on 'Mary Wollstonecraft and 200 Years of Feminism', Sussex University, 5–6 December 1992.

75. Silva Rakhneva, 'Nai-Posle' ('At Last'), in: *Zhenata Dnes* (*Woman Today*), special issue, April 1991, quoted by Petrova, 1992, ibid.

Can Cinderella Become
a Citizen?

On the whole, women will probably come off losers in many respects:
the 'revolution' of 1989 left the patriarchal system of power intact,
transforming its more superficial manifestations from bad to worse.

What could be done? At least some of us, women who have been part of
the Great Experiment, understand something which could be passed
down to our daughters: that capitalist society is not the only option; that
beyond it there can be another, more mutually concerned way of living. It
may be very far away, especially now when the failure of 'Communism' is
taken to mean the failure of each and every effort to transcend capitalism.
So we can only try to keep the flame burning – the small flame of
sympathy, of simple concern for the other. Sisterhood may play a
powerful part in this commitment.

Dimitrina Petrova, Bulgaria[1]

Active citizenship and the revival of civil society was what the upheavals
of 1989 seemed to promise for the former state socialist countries of
East Central Europe. Yet since then, women's rights appear to have
been eroded. Women have been made redundant on a mass scale, and
currently constitute the majority of the unemployed in most of these
countries. The levels of female political representation have fallen
drastically. Laws guaranteeing the right to have one's job held open
during maternity and extended childcare leave are being ignored.
Reproductive rights are massively under attack, with moves in several
countries to rescind the laws providing the right to free and legal
abortions.

Gender issues are at the hub of potentially explosive processes of
historical and social transformation. The family and the nation are being
posited as central in the search for identity and for new ethical and moral
values. Yet while market-oriented democratic theories stress individual

autonomy, nationalist pressures subordinate women yet again to a collectivity which denies them participatory citizenship and democratic control. Nationalism appears, as for much of its history, to be constructing a definition of autonomy and citizenship which is male. Woman, even when represented as the Nation, is in fact the quintessential Other of nationalist discourse. This construes women as passive beings who are not viewed as mature political subjects, yet are in their reproductive role simultaneously the crucible of the nation, for whose protection (male) citizens are prepared to lay down their lives. Indeed one might argue that in this too, there is more continuity with the state socialist period than at first meets the eye. The fact that the 'Woman Question' was posited by the socialist states of East Central Europe as a discrete issue, with gender relations a woman's problem rather than a subject of concern for society as a whole, suggests a similar inscription of woman as different, as Other.

Nationalism in the nineteenth century confined citizenship and suffrage to property-owning adult males. Women, confined to the private sphere, were excluded on the basis of gender. State socialism catapulted women into the public sphere of work and politics. But the fundamental contradiction for women in East Central Europe was that 'they did not get emancipation as citizens but as a right to work, together with certain advantages as members of the labour force (which can be manipulated to meet the demands of the economy), and as mothers (who can be made responsible for the nation's demographic situation)'.[2] Now, market pressures are retrenching women, sending them back to hearth and home, where nationalist ideology tells them that their primary responsibility is to 'produce babies for the nation'. This book contends that currently resurgent nationalist ideologies are building a concept of citizenship in East Central Europe which is both gendered and more generally exclusionary. Exclusion on grounds of sex, ethnic group, or language defines a national identity which is profoundly undemocratic, and inherently dangerous.

The reality of women's current and changing situation in East Central Europe remains paradoxical and contradictory. Neither state socialism nor the newly democratic societies seem able to provide the environment in which women could develop their full potential as equal citizens. In the past rights were given, from above, now they are taken away by market and 'new' ideological pressures.

The patriarchal socialist state expanded workplace rights at the expense of 'citizen rights'.[3] But there was no miraculous transformation after autumn 1989. Rather, there seems at one level to have been a simple reversal. Women now 'find themselves in the peculiar position of having gained a significant expansion of their civil rights at the expense of vital economic ones'.[4] Socialist patriarchy cramped and confined the exercise of individual initiative and autonomy; unemployment and the traumas of social upheaval and economic insecurity do not empower women to become active, participatory citizens.

Nor is the elevation of the market to an absolute good favourable to the flowering of a socially just society. T. H. Marshall's earlier prioritizing of 'the social rights of citizenship' has renewed relevance in the face of the growing social inequalities and poverty in East Central Europe. Yet it is also true, as Ursula Vogel and Michael Moran note, that Marshall's 'focus on class . . . was bound . . . to conceal or marginalize the continued existence of other divides, notably gender'.[5]

Theorists of nationalism and the nation-state have emphasized its conferral, at least in theory, of a unitary and egalitarian status as citizen. Citizenship was defined in terms of membership of the nation-state. In practice, as William Rogers Brubaker argues, in the model of the French Revolution 'the principle of unitary citizenship ... far outstripped revolutionary practice, to which distinctions of class and gender were crucial'.[6] English history too provides ample illustration for the fact that women were excluded from citizenship status on the basis of their lack of majority in the eyes of the law, based on their inability to own property. Flora Anthias and Nira Yuval-Davis emphasize that in conceptualizing the more recent relationship between women and the state, it must be remembered that 'the very project of the welfare state itself has constructed the "state subject" in a gendered way'.[7]

Hence gender, while rarely encountered in works on nationalism and the nation-state, has in practice operated as an exclusionary mechanism, hindering female entitlement to citizenship rights, and to the duties of citizenship. Reviewing historical concepts of citizenship and past social practice, Vogel and Moran conclude: 'It is not merely that citizenship is gender-specific, but that the very formulations of this concept in past and present have been *predicated* upon gender division.'[8] They also point out that concepts of citizenship and the nation-state are currently disputed and problematic, and that 'under pressure of economic and political crises, the frontiers of membership may contract'. Tendencies in East Central as well as some of Western Europe to confine citizenship status to the members of one ethnic or linguistic community at the expense of another are examples of such a contraction. Relegating women to the private sphere in the name of the national interest, depriving them of the right to autonomy and self-determination through active participation as citizens in the public sphere, is another.

A culture of active citizenship necessitates both state legislation and social infrastructure, *and* for people to have the political space for articulating demands and exerting pressure. An independent women's movement *and* a political climate responsive to women's needs are crucial ingredients in implementing the kind of gender equality essential to democratic societies. Vogel emphasizes that both grassroots activism and the involvement of women at the level of state institutions are necessary to the implementation of gender equity and women's autonomy. And participatory citizenship needs to be non-gender-specific, she suggests, to be meaningful and effective for both men and women in a democratic society.[9]

One of the current problems with realizing such a conception of citizenship is the general distaste felt across East Central Europe for any form of state intervention whatsoever. Hungarian sociologist Júlia Szalai writes: 'There is a strong and broad opposition in our countries to everything that has the slightest flavour of "statism". It is a long process to get rid of the idea and practice of the totalitarian state and to define a state that is "ours", that is created and controlled by the democratic processes of the civil society. . . . We shouldn't throw away, however, all the concepts of solidarity, public responsibility, less inequality and so on, those values that have been long associated with the concept and practice of the state.'[10]

Indeed the reaction against state intervention is so violent as to render almost impossible any careful examination of the state socialist record on women's behalf. Nor is it easy, in the aftermath of state socialism, to hypothesize alternatives. As Slavenka Drakulić wrote in 1991: 'We may have survived communism, but we have not yet outlived it . . . [because] what communism instilled in us was precisely this immobility, this absence of a future, the absence of a dream, of the possibility of imagining our lives differently. There was hardly a way to say to yourself: This is just temporary, it will pass, it must. On the contrary, we learned to think: This will go on forever, no matter what we do. We can't change it.'[11] Such a failure of imagination, overlaid with women's physical exhaustion, opens the way for an idealized vision which unites woman, family and nation.

It will be interesting to see how far, in the future, the loss of economic and social rights encourages the emergence of a women's movement devoted to the goal of gender equality. Of equal importance will be recognition by the new democratic states of the advantages to be gained in terms of social cohesion from fostering forms of active citizenship which encompass both women and men. Given the strength of exclusionary nationalist forms of self-definition, the prospects are not rosy. Current nationalist ideologies too often assert themselves, not in positive terms, expressing pride in the national traditions or cultural heritage, but rather in defensive or aggressive terms *against* the Other. Such self-identification in terms of what one is *not* make women the next to be excluded after ethnically different Others. Only time, the revival of civil society networks, and women's activism may change this.

One could conclude that the story has no happy ending. If socialism subordinated women to the macro needs of the economy and demographic demands, as some maintain, so now nationalism is instrumentalizing women by reducing them to their reproductive role. State socialism's commitment to women's 'emancipation' could be read as having become debased to a matter of form and externality rather than genuine concern. Nationalism is overtly dismissive of the notion that women have needs other than maternal ones which should be addressed during the transition period. Against the difficulties and short-term setbacks, however, must be set the positive potential. This emanates from women themselves, resourceful through years of 'improvisation'[12] and making do, buoyant despite the pressures of the past and uncertainties of the present.

Validating women's subjective experiences of contradiction, of continuity and change, may make a substantive contribution to addressing the problems of the environment, of intolerance, and of conflict in East Central Europe today. The very notions of participatory democracy, or of politics from below, reject the privileging of male-dominated institutionalized forms of experience gained in the public sphere and of politics as exclusively concerned with electoral questions or the affairs of government.

It is thus in the organizations of a revived civil society like the emerging women's movement that hope for future transformation lies. Transcending the difficulties in East-West communication and avoiding the 'colonialist gaze' of many Western institutions, East-West networking can contribute to the process of renewed understanding. The non-hierarchical and egalitarian approach of the women's, environmental and peace movements in Western and East Central Europe informs productive dialogue taking place between scholars and activists. Through such dialogue may come a mutual redefinition of the concept of citizenship itself, as a non-exclusionary category informed by the need for social justice as well as gender equity.

Nothing like a tendency toward the emancipation of women is observable in Bulgaria. We cannot even define the process as aimed at improving women's situation or promoting rights.

In this context, I have to rely on the increasing role of what some day is going to be widely viewed as civil society vis à vis the state. The next generation of women will probably try to change the very mechanisms of social change, through building the living tissue of civil society. I do not mean that East European women will strictly walk in the footsteps of their Western sisters. I think that our East European experience has not been a trivial one, and that we must learn from each other.

Dimitrina Petrova, Bulgaria[13]

Notes

1. Dimitrina Petrova, 'The Farewell Dance: Women in the Bulgarian Transition', Paper presented to the Conference on 'Mary Wollstonecraft and 200 Years of Feminism', Sussex University, 5–6 December 1992.

2. Mária Adamik, 'Hungary: A Loss of Rights?', in: *Shifting Territories: Feminism in Europe*, Special issue no. 39 of *Feminist Review*, winter 1991, p. 169.

3. Prue Chamberlayne, 'Neighbourhood and Tenant Participation in the GDR', in: Bob Deacon and Júlia Szalai, eds, *Social Policy in the New Eastern Europe: What Future for Socialist Welfare?*, Aldershot, Avebury, 1990, pp. 155–56.

4. Dorothy Rosenberg, 'Shock Therapy: GDR Women in Transition from a Socialist Welfare State to a Social Market Economy', in: *Signs*, vol. 17, no. 1, autumn 1991, p. 129.

5. Ursula Vogel and Michael Moran, eds, *The Frontiers of Citizenship*, Macmillan, Basingstoke, 1991, p. xi. In the introduction to this volume, Vogel and Moran refer to Marshall's 'seminal essay on "Citizenship and Class" ', which was originally prepared as a lecture in 1949 and appeared in T. H. Marshall, *Class, Citizenship and Social Development*, Greenwood Press, Westport, 1973, pp. 65–122.

6. William Rogers Brubaker, 'Immigration, Citizenship and the Nation-State in France and Germany: A Comparative Historical Analysis', in: *International Sociology*, vol. 5, no. 4, 1990, pp. 379–407.

7. Flora Anthias and Nira Yuval-Davis, eds, *Woman-Nation-State*, Macmillan, Basingstoke, 1989, p. 6.

8. Vogel and Moran, *The Frontiers of Citizenship*, 1991, pp. xii and xvi.

9. Ursula Vogel, 'Is Citizenship Gender-Specific?', in: Vogel and Moran, eds, *The Frontiers of Citizenship*, 1991, p. 82.

10. Júlia Szalai et al, 'Social Policy and Socialism: Citizenship, the Working Class, Women and Welfare', in: Deacon and Szalai, eds, *Social Policy in the New Eastern Europe: What Future for Socialist Welfare?*, 1990, pp. 34–5.

11. Slavenka Drakulić, *How We Survived Communism and Even Laughed*, Hutchinson, London, 1992, pp. xvii, 7.

12. Similar terms are used both by Hana Navarová to describe family life in Czechoslovakia, and by Júlia Szalai in reference to the experience gained by women in Hungary's second economy – see Chapter 2 above.

13. An example of such dialogue is to be found in the Women's Commission of the Helsinki Citizens' Assembly, an organization dedicated to the peaceful overcoming of intolerance and xenophobia, to an international politics from below whose purpose is the celebration of difference between women as a basis for solidarity. Dimitrina Petrova, 'On Women in Eastern Europe', Speech in Aalborg, August 1991.

Appendix: Tables

Table A1.1 Children with crèche (nursery) places in the relevant* age group 1970–89 (%)

Country	1970	1980	1985	1989
Hungary[1]	7.4	10.1	12.3	8.6
Poland[2]	4.7	5.2	5.1	4.4
Germany Former German Democratic Republic (GDR)[3]	29.1	61.2	72.7	80.2
Germany Federal Republic of Germany (FRG)[4]	–	–	–	3.0 (1987)
Netherlands[4]	–	–	–	2.0
UK[4]	–	–	–	2.0 (1988)

Table A1.2 Children with kindergarten places in the relevant* age group 1970–88 (%)

Country	1970	1980	1985	1988
Czechoslovakia[5]	–	82.8	96.4	97.0
Hungary[1]	51.1	77.9	87.2	85.7
Germany Former German Democratic Republic (GDR)[3]	64.5	92.2	94.0	95.1
Germany Federal Republic of Germany (FRG)[4]	–	–	–	67.5 (1987)
Netherlands[4]	–	–	–	52.5
UK[4]	–	–	–	37.5 (1988)

* *Relevant crèche age: 0–3 years. Relevant kindergarten age: 3–5/6 years.*

Sources:

[1]Júlia Szalai, 'Some Aspects of the Changing Situation of Women in Hungary', in: *Signs*, vol. 17, No. 1, autumn 1991, Table 4, p. 164. The drop in the use of childcare facilities after 1987 is due to extended child care leave.

[2] Renata Siemieńska, Data compiled from *Polish Statistical Yearbooks*.

[3] Gunnar Winkler, ed., *Frauenreport 90*, Verlag Die Wirtschaft, Berlin, 1990, Tables 4.27, p. 142, 4.28, p. 143.

[4] European Commission Childcare Network, 'Childcare in the European Community 1985–1990', Report coordinated by Peter Moss, Commission of the European Communities, *Women of Europe* Supplement no. 31, Brussels, 199.

[5] Ludmila Venerová, 'Brief Survey of the Situation of Czechoslovakian Women at the Beginning of the Transitional Period from Centrally-Planned to Market Economy', in: *The Impact of Economic and Policical Reform on the Status of Women in Eastern Europe and the USSR*, Proceedings of United Nations Regional Seminar, Vienna, 8–12 April 1991, ST-CSDHA-19-UN, New York, 1992, Table 10.

Table A2 Time use of women and men in selected activities (hours per week)

Country	Year	Economic activity		Unpaid housework						Personal care and free time	
				household chores		childcare		total			
		F	M	F	M	F	M	F	M	F	M
Bulgaria	1965	42.6	52.9	25.6	11.1	2.9	1.4	28.6	12.5	97	103
	1988	37.7	46.9	29.3	14.3	4.3	1.1	33.7	15.3	97	106
Czechoslovakia	1965	29.8	44.4	36.0	12.7	4.7	2.5	40.7	15.1	97	109
Hungary	1965	34.0	56.6	36.3	5.5	4.7	2.5	41.0	7.9	93	103
	1976	26.7	41.5	30.2	10.9	3.0	1.4	33.3	12.3	108	114
Poland	1965	30.5	52.2	33.5	9.7	5.3	2.7	38.9	12.4	99	103
	1984	24.9	42.2	30.5	7.7	4.4	2.0	34.9	9.7	108	116
USSR	1965	43.0	53.2	32.3	14.0	3.6	1.4	35.9	15.4	89	99
	1986	38.5	49.0	25.7	14.6	4.4	1.5	30.1	16.1	99	103
France	1965	21.7	51.8	35.0	9.9	7.6	1.3	42.6	11.3	104	105
Germany (FRG)	1965	13.3	42.4	39.3	10.2	4.9	0.9	44.2	11.1	111	115
Netherlands	1975	5.8	27.3	27.1	7.1	5.3	1.6	32.4	8.7	130	132
	1980	7.1	23.9	27.9	7.4	5.5	1.5	33.4	8.8	130	135
Norway	1972	14.4	40.0	32.8	5.7	4.4	1.2	37.2	6.9	117	121
	1981	17.1	34.2	25.1	7.1	4.8	2.0	29.8	9.2	121	125
UK	1961	16.5	45.7	31.3	4.3	2.6	0.4	33.9	4.8	118	118
	1984	14.1	26.8	26.4	10.3	3.6	1.1	30.0	11.4	124	130

Source: The World's Women: Trends and Statistics 1970–1990, Social Statistics and Indicators, Series K, No. 8, UN, New York, 1991, Table 7, p. 101.

Table A3 Life expectancy at birth by sex (years)

Country	1985/90		
	F	*F minus M*	*F change, 1970 to 1990*
Czechoslovakia	75.0	7.5	1.6
Hungary	74.0	7.5	1.7
Poland	75.5	8.0	2.5
USSR	74.2	9.2	0.7

Germany
  Former German Democratic
  Republic (GDR)
	76.2	5.8	2.2

Germany
  Federal Republic of
  Germany (FRG)
	78.2	6.6	4.8

Austria	77.8	7.2	4.4
France	79.8	8.1	4.4
Italy	79.1	6.7	5.2
UK	78.1	5.7	3.5

Source: The World's Women: Trends and Statistics 1970–1990, Social Statistics and Indicators, Series K, No. 8, UN, New York, 1991, Table 5, p. 67.

Table A4.1 Female activity rate (as % of total economically active population) 1980–88

Country	1980	1988
Bulgaria	48.7	50.0 (1987)
Czechoslovakia	46.2	47.3
Hungary	44.8	45.8
Poland	43.5	45.5
USSR	51.2	50.8
Germany Former German Democratic Republic (GDR)	50.5	49.9
Germany Federal Republic of Germany (FRG)	37.9	38.5 (1987)
France	38.5	42.7 (1989)
UK	38.9 (1981)	43.3 (1990)

Sources:
Alena Kroupová, 'Women, Employment and Earnings in Central and East European Countries', Paper prepared for Tripartite Symposium on Equality of Opportunity and Treatment for Men and Women in Employment in Industrialized Countries, Prague, May 1990; *Yearbook of Labour Statistics* 1981, 1991, 1992, International Labour Office, Geneva.

Table A4.2 Working age women who are economically active 1980–88 (%)

Country	1980	1988
Hungary	–	70.1 (1990)
Poland	–	65.0
Germany Former German Democratic Republic (GDR)	80.5	83.2*
Germany Federal Republic of Germany (FRG)	52.7	55.4 (1987)
France	57.5	59.2 (1989)
UK	59.7 (1981)	67.7 (1990)

* 91% if women in higher education and training are included.

Sources:
Yearbook of Labour Statistics, 1981, 1991, 1992, International Labour Office, Geneva; Gunnar Winkler, ed., *Frauenreport 90*, Verlag Die Wirtschaft, Berlin, 1990, Table 3.1, p. 55, and Winkler, ed., *Sozialreport 90*, Verlag Die Wirtschaft, Berlin, 1990, Table 3.1, p. 78.

Note: Working age for women was 15–55 in most of Eastern Europe, 15–60 in Western Europe. The norm in Eastern Europe was for women to work full-time; the overwhelming majority of economically active women in Western Europe worked part-time.

Table A5.1 Girls entering vocational training in selected occupations in the former German Democratic Republic and Hungary, 1980–89 (%)

Occupation	GDR[1]		Hungary[2]	
	1980	1989	1981	1987
Garment industry	99.9	99.4	96.4	98.2
Textile industry	96.6	95.3	96.3	98.1
Leather industry	96.3	90.6	82.0	79.6
Chemicals industry	82.5	82.3	–	85.0
Secretary	99.8	99.8		
Salesperson	98.2	95.6		
Post Office worker	94.8	90.0		
Data processor	82.8	70.0		
Electronics	49.8	19.5		
Machine builder	8.3	5.8		
Toolmaker	11.9	5.2		

Sources:
[1] Gunnar Winkler, ed., *Frauenreport 90*, Verlag Die Wirtschaft, Berlin, 1990, Table 2.9, p. 44.
[2] Commission of the European Communities, 'Women of Hungary', Supplement no. 32 to *Women of Europe*, research by Eva Eberhardt, assisted by Júlia Szalai, EC, Brussels, 1991, Fig. II.3, p.13.

Table A5.2 Female students in higher education by subject in the former German Democratic Republic, Poland and Hungary, 1971–89 (%)

Subject	GDR[1]		Poland[2]		Hungary[3]
	1971	1989	1970/72	1985/86	1987
Teacher training	62.2	73.0	70.4	–	73.4
Economics	38.4	66.7	63.6	56.6	64.6
Medicine	70.7	55.2	65.8	62.3	54.4
Law	–	–	50.0	45.7	57.3
Maths/Sciences	33.2	46.0	59.9	61.5	–
Agriculture	35.1	46.4	42.8	45.2	31.2
Art	40.8	44.6	46.9	51.3	–
Technical subjects	15.8	25.3	25.2	19.8	15.3*
Theology	41.4	46.1	–	–	–
Humanities	63.4**	62.2**	74.5	75.5	–
Physical education	31.5***	40.3***	37.5	35.8	–

* Engineering   ** Literature and language   *** Includes cultural and art history

Sources:
[1] Gunnar Winkler, ed., *Frauenreport 90*, Verlag Die Wirtschaft, Berlin, 1990, Table 2.12, p. 47.
[2] Renata Siemieńska, *Płeć, Zawód, Polityka: Kobiety w Życiu Publicznym w Polsce (Gender, Profession, Politics: Women in Public Life in Poland)*, Warsaw University: Institute of Sociology, 1990, Table 6, p. 65.
[3] World Bank, Europe and Central Asia Region, Population and Human Resources Division, Report No. 8213, Monica S. Fong and Gillian Paul, 'The Changing Role of Women in Employment in Eastern Europe', 1992, Table 17, p. 50.

Table A6.1   Female average earnings as % of male average earnings by
employment status in Hungary

	1972	1977
Managers	77.4	82.9
Managerial personnel	72.7	76.3
Top-level specialists	80.0	82.9
Medium-level specialists	75.6	80.9
Low-level specialists	76.8	77.1
Secretarial personnel	70.7	82.1
All non-manuals	62.1	65.8
Skilled workers	72.0	72.5
Semiskilled workers	72.3	74.3
Unskilled workers	68.7	75.0
All nonagricultural workers	67.5	68.4
Agricultural manual workers	70.8	83.5
Total	69.1	71.2

Sources:
Rózsa Kulcsár, 'The Socio-Economic Conditions of Women in Hungary', in: Sharon L.
Wolchik and Alfred G. Meyer, *Women, State and Party in Eastern Europe*, Duke University
Press, Durham, 1985, Table 11.7, p. 203; Mária Ladó, 'Women in the Transition to a
Market Economy: The Case of Hungary', in: *The Impact of Economic and Political Reform on
the Status of Women in Eastern Europe and the USSR*, Proceedings of United Nations
Regional Seminar, Vienna, 8–12 April 1991, ST-CSDHA-19-UN, New York, 1992.

Table A6.2   Female average earnings as % of male average earnings by sector

	Czechoslovakia	Hungary (blue-collar)	(white-collar)	Poland
Industry	65	65	52	–
Construction	71	65	56	82
Mining	–	–	–	56
Agriculture	83	68	55	87
Science & research	73	–	–	80
Trade	76	76	67	83
Transport	–	70	57	84
Services	–	76	64	–
Education	72	–	–	81
Health Services	66	–	–	80
Culture & arts	–	–	–	90
Finance & insurance	–	–	–	92

Figures are for average earnings for Czechoslovakia; monthly wage in the non-private
sector for Hungary, 1989; and monthly compensation for Poland, 1990.

Source: World Bank, Europe and Central Asia Region, Population and Human Resources
Division, Report No. 8213, Monica S. Fong and Gillian Paul, 'The Changing Role of
Women in Employment in Eastern Europe', 1992, Table 13, p. 47.

Table A7 Distribution of active wage-earners by skill level,
staff group and gender in Hungary 1970–88 (%)

	1970		1980		1988	
	Men	*Women*	*Men*	*Women*	*Men*	*Women*
Total manual workers	76.6	64.6	75.7	57.5	78.2	58.3
Skilled workers	34.1	8.9	43.5	11.1	46.0	14.4
Semi-skilled	22.8	27.1	22.4	33.3	23.1	29.8
Unskilled workers	19.5	24.1	9.7	10.8	9.1	14.1
Family agricultural cooperatives	0.2	4.5	0.1	2.3		
Total non-manual workers	20.3	31.9	26.1	39.4	21.8	41.7
Self employed and helping family members	3.1	3.5	2.7	3.1		
Total	100.0	100.0	100.0	100.0	100.0	100.0

Sources: Rózsa Kulcsár, 'The Socio-Economic Conditions of Women in Hungary', in: Sharon L. Wolchik and Alfred G. Meyer, *Women, State and Party in Eastern Europe,* Duke University Press, Durham, 1985, Table 11.2, p. 197; Mária Ladó, 'Women in the Transition to a Market Economy: The Case of Hungary', Table 8, in: *The Impact of Economic and Political Reform on the Status of Women in Eastern Europe and the USSR,* Proceedings of the UN Regional Seminar, Vienna, 8–12 April 1991, ST-CSDHA-19-UN, New York, 1992.

Table A8.1 Female employees as % of all employees, by sector (1985–90)

Sector of Economy	Bulgaria (1985)[1]	Czechoslovakia (1986/1989)[2]	Former German Democratic Republic (1989)[3]	Hungary (1988)[4] (1985)	Poland (1989)[5]	Former USSR (1989)[6]	Romania (1989)[7]
Agriculture, forestry, fishing	49.1	32.4	37.4	39.9	23.2	39.0	21.8
Mining	}46.6	17.6	}41.0				
Manufacturing		40.6		43.2	37.2		43.1
of which, female-dominated sectors:							
Textiles		74.4	66.9		63.3	83.0	72.7
Clothing		89.3			74.0	93.0	88.1
Chemical industry						58.0	
Leather industry		67.5			48.2		
Food industry		52.4	47.1			74.0	
Construction	19.3	13.6	17.2	19.0	20.0	21.0	14.0
Transport	}25.4	23.0	26.4	}28.2	24.4		12.9
Post and telecommunications		66.7	69.0		58.7	84.0	53.4
Retail and Trade, incl. hotels and restaurants	69.4	76.2	71.9	65.4	69.7	73.0	62.5
Finance and insurance	78.6	75.2			84.5	87.0	
Services		60.0	55.9	62.7	70.1	89.0	
of which, female-dominated sectors:							
Education		74.9	77.0		76.5	73.0	68.2
Health		85.9	83.0		}81.4	86.0	75.4
Social Welfare		90.1	91.8				

Sources:

[1] Sabine Hübner, Friederike Maier, Hedwig Rudolph, 'Women's Employment in Central and Eastern Europe: Status and Prospects', Paper prepared for ILO: OECD-CCEET Conference on 'Labour Market and Social Policy Implications of Structural Change in Central and Eastern Europe' Paris, 11–13 September, 1991, OCDE/ILO/DG(91)143, Table 5;

[2] Hübner et al., ibid., 1991, Tables 5,6; Alena Kroupová, 'Women, Employment and Earnings in Central and East European Countries', Paper prepared for Tripartite Symposium on Equality of Opportunity and Treatment for Men and Women in Employment in Industrialized Countries, Prague, May 1990; Liba Paukert, 'The Changing Economic Status of Women in the Period of Transition to a Market Economy System: The Case of Czechoslovakia after 1989', in: Valentine Moghadam, ed., *Democratic Reform and the Position of Women in Transitional Economies*, OUP Clarendon Series, Oxford, 1993;

[3] Gunnar Winkler, ed., *Frauenreport 90*, Verlag Die Wirtschaft, Berlin, 1990, Table 3.12, p. 67; Hildegard Maria Nickel, 'Ein perfektes Drehbuch: Geschlechtertrennung durch Arbeit und Sozialisation' ('A Perfect Script: Gender Divisions Through Work and Socialization'), in: Gislinde Schwarz and Christine Zenner, eds., *Wir Wollen mehr als ein Vaterland' (We Want More Than a 'Fatherland')*, Rowohlt, Hamburg, 1990, pp. 73–90;

[4] Mária Ladó, 'Situation and Perspectives of Women in the Labour Market: The Case of Hungary', Paper prepared for ILO: OECD-CCEET Conference on 'Labour Market and Social Policy Implications of Structural Change in Central and Eastern Europe' Paris, September 1991, Table 11;

[5] Renata Siemieńska, *Płeć, Zawód, Polityka: Kobiety w Życiu Publicznym w Polsce (Gender, Profession, Politics: Women in Public Life in Poland)*, Warsaw University: Institute of Sociology, 1990, Table 4, p. 92; Training and Education Office, International Confederation of Free Trade Unions, Brussels, Appendix 61/W/3(b) of Paper prepared for 5th World Women's Conference, Ottawa, 21–25 April 1991; Zofia Kuratowska, 'Present Situation of Women in Poland' in: *The Impact of Economic and Political Reform on the Status of Women in Eastern Europe and the USSR*, Proceedings of United Nations Regional Seminar, Vienna, 8–12 April 1991, ST-CSDHA-19-UN, New York, 1992.

[6] Judith Shapiro, 'The Industrial Labour Force', in: Mary Buckley, ed., *Perestroika and Soviet Women*, Cambridge University Press, Cambridge, 1992, Tables 2.1, 2.3, pp. 16, 18; Hübner et al., 'Women's Employment in Central and Eastern Europe', 1991, Table 6;

[7] Mariana Celac, 'Romania', and Dumitra Popescu, 'Present Situation and Trends Affecting Women in Romania', both in: *The Impact of Economic and Political Reform on the Status of Women in Eastern Europe and the USSR*, Proceedings of United Nations Regional Seminar, Vienna, 8–12 April 1991, ST-CSDHA-19-UN, New York, 1992.

Table A8.2   Female employees as % of all employees, by occupation (1970–85)

Occupation	Bulgaria (1985)	Czechoslovakia (1970)	Hungary (1970)	Poland (1970)
Agriculture	49.9	52.8	45.8	57.5
Professional/ Technical	51.0	41.6	47.2	49.8
Administrative/ Managerial	27.6	13.8	15.3	27.1
Clerical/Sales/ Services	77.5	75.5	67.0	68.6
Production & Transport Workers	34.5	29.0	28.2	24.7

Source: UN Compendium of Statistics and Indicators on the Situation of Women for 1986, UN, New York, 1989, Table 12.

Table A9.1   Women in leading positions* in Hungary, 1960–80 (%)

Occupation	1960	1970	1980
Managers of enterprises, directors of institutes	7.4	6.4	12.1
Directors of agricultural cooperatives	2.4	2.9	5.6
Leaders in public administration	8.1	11.8	19.6
Leaders in municipal administration	12.5	15.3	29.1
Technical managers, chief engineers, works managers	1.7	4.2	3.1
Financial managers, business executives	21.0	33.8	40.9

Source: Rózsa Kulcsár, 'The Socio-Economic Conditions of Women in Hungary', in: Sharon L. Wolchik and Alfred G. Meyer, *Women, State and Party in Eastern Europe*, Duke University Press, Durham, 1985, Table 11.3, p. 199.

Table A9.2   Women in leading positions by sector in the former German Democratic Republic (GDR), 1988 (%)

Sector	Women's share of leading positions
Industrial total	21.0
Coal & energy	13.2
Electronics	15.9
Chemicals	17.3
Machine building	14.2
Light industry	44.0
Construction	11.2
Transport	21.5
Post & telecomm	41.7
Retail	62.0
Total (in the Economy as a whole)	31.5

Source: Gunnar Winkler, ed., *Frauenreport 90*, Verlag Die Wirtshaft, Berlin, 1990, Table 3.33, p. 95.

* The term 'leading positions' is used rather than 'management', since the sources do not distinguish between lower level managerial or supervisory positions, and top management.

Table A10   Women in Parliament (lower house), East–West comparison (%)

Country	Parliamentary seats occupied by women			Year of women's right to vote
	1975	*1987*	*1990*	
Austria	7.7	11.5	10.9	1918
Denmark	15.6	29.1	30.7	1915
France	1.6	6.4	5.7	1944
Italy	3.8	12.9	12.8	1945
UK	4.3	6.3	6.3	1918
Germany Federal Republic of Germany (FRG)	5.8	15.4	20.5[a]	1919
Germany Former German Democratic Republic (GDR)	31.8	32.2	20.5[b]	1919
Bulgaria	18.8	21.0	8.5	1944
Czechoslovakia	26.0	29.5	8.6	1920
Hungary	28.7	21.0	7.2	1945
Poland	15.9	20.2	13.5	1918
USSR	32.1	34.5	20.3	1917

[a] *All-German elections December 1990; after unification.*
[b] *GDR elections March 1990; before unification.*

Source: Mira Janova and Mariette Sineau, 'Women's Participation in Political Power in Europe: An Essay in East-West Comparison', in: *Women's Studies International Forum*, Vol. 15, No. 1, 1992, Table 1, p. 117; *The World's Women: Trends and Statistics 1970–1990*, Social Statistics and Indicators, Series K, No. 8, UN, New York, 1991, Table 3, p. 39.

Index